D0064676

Liberalism

Liberalism

The Genius of American Ideals

Marcus G. Raskin

ROWMAN & LITTLEFIELD PUBLISHERS, INC.
Lanham • Boulder • New York • Toronto •Oxford

ROWMAN & LITTLEFIELD PUBLISHERS, INC.

Published in the United States of America
by Rowman & Littlefield Publishers, Inc.
A wholly owned subsidiary of The Rowman & Littlefield Publishing Group
4501 Forbes Boulevard, Suite 200, Lanham, Maryland 20706
www.rowmanlittlefield.com

PO Box 317, Oxford OX2 9RU, United Kingdom

British Library Cataloguing in Publication Information Available

Library of Congress Cataloging-in-Publication Data
Raskin, Marcus G.
  Liberalism : the genius of American ideals / Marcus G. Raskin.
    p. cm.
  Includes bibliographical references and index.
  ISBN 0-7425-1590-7 (cloth : alk. paper)
  1. Liberalism—United States. 2. Liberalism. I. Title.
  JC574.2 .U6R37 2004
  320.51'3'0973—dc21

                                                            2003008682

Printed in the United States of America

♾ ™ The paper used in this publication meets the minimum requirements of
American National Standard for Information Sciences—Permanence of Paper
for Printed Library Materials, ANSI/NISO Z39.48-1992.

For Mel Raskin on His 80th Birthday

Contents

Note to the Reader

There is a profoundly mistaken belief that there is an exhaustion of possibilities for liberal democracy, and that American civilization has no choice but to play out the fate of being the greatest imperialist power since Rome, as one commentator put it. This in effect means wars without end in a period of nuclearism wherein humanity itself is at stake. It means telling the citizenry and its knowledge workers to shut up, don't question, and go along, even if it means dropping off the ledge. It means accepting economic oligarchy of a very greedy type. Obviously, this is a deep crisis that touches many aspects of modern life—economic, social, political, medical, psychological, even aesthetic—and will take many working together over the course of this generation to comprehend, offer and link alternatives, and aid social movements that understand and act on these purposes.

The first stage of liberalism is called the Adam Smith–John Locke and Thomas Jefferson period, in which laissez-faire and the conception of removing fetters from the people, invariably white men, would result in greater freedom. Further, if given the chance to conduct their own affairs without having to carry the burden of a parasitical palace court, aristocrats, and silly appurtenances of power, the middle classes would do so responsibly and in ways that would be of maximum benefit to themselves and others. People could choose their representatives with the option of changing governments, according to Jefferson and Locke, by violent revolution if necessary. Perhaps the most farseeing and radical of the early liberals was Tom Paine, who understood government as an oppressive machine when it was not controlled by the people. Except for Paine (who remained a member of the working class and was very sensitive to class issues), first-stage liberalism was burdened with flaws from the start. Many of its adherents believed in slavery and the use of slaves as fungible commodities. In other words, not only was slavery countenanced; it ended up proving indispensable to the operations of the laissez-faire system. Because the South needed to grow more cotton and had the land and cotton gin, slavery expanded.

Although slavery was of concern to Adam Smith, who implied as much in *Wealth of Nations,* John Locke had fewer problems in adjusting to its existence. His concern was breaking the European serf system. Thomas Jefferson believed in political equality but did not extend it to slaves in his practical decisions, whether public or private. Even the most farseeing, the most humane are also men of their times and consequently cannot be expected to transcend them too often without being marginalized. Ambitious men never want to be too far ahead of their peers and where political and economic power lie.

Twenty years after the Civil War the nation of limited democracy that Jefferson praised would not have been easily recognized, although Jefferson set the framework for the American future. He doubled the size of the United States with the Louisiana Purchase and set the terms for the massive displacement of Indian natives. For commercial reasons slavery was expanded, and Indian wars became a way of life for the American state.

European and Asian immigration and the emergence of an urban industrial working class supplanted independent yeomen and farmers, and as a result liberalism took on a new purpose. Its stance slowly changed so that its adherents, who sometimes paraded under the name progressive—even radical—became more than the nation's Whiggish mediators and reasonable men. Liberals came to be identified with the underprivileged and the poor, and the adherents of liberalism brought forward ideas of justice and political equality. Through law and force the oligarchic claim of priority for property rights over all others was extended to the protection and strengthening of the modern corporation. Capitalism had changed, and so had the state. Indeed, together they became what Smith despised: overbearing, monopolistic, and selfish. First-stage liberalism, without liberal tenets, was transformed into conservatism and defense of oligarchic reaction.

It was clear at the beginning of the twentieth century that capitalism had to change radically if it was to withstand the onslaught of movements that seemed to be shaking the foundations of the republic but had their own parochial battles. An increasingly conscious black working class was played off against whites; immigrants who fought for economic and political power were pitched against other immigrants and women. Violent struggles between labor and management were often initiated by strike breakers and the police. Women who sought identification with those who would help in their liberation found that deep class divisions inhibited the possibility of solidarity with women and men of different social classes. But the relative weakness of those on the Left who sought radical or incremental changes could still affect adversely the power of the propertied class. Irritations from noisy reformers and professors could get out of hand, and they needed to be contained. Slowly it became clear that the arguments of the liberals and the Left had to be answered through partial co-option, a trick that Otto von Bismarck played on Social Democrats when he adopted some of their social welfare schemes. Like Bismarck, who sought unification at home and a world role for the "new" Germany, the United States was also ready to be a world player, but it needed a modicum of calm internally. For these conditions to exist there had to be a change in the operations of capitalism itself. And thus began the era of progressivism, an early period of second-stage liberalism that was thought to be a way of saving first-stage liberal capitalism. It had four objectives:

1. Introducing rules of the game of capitalism so that the players controlled their wolfish and predatory practices, staying within the bounds of monitored capitalist competition.
2. Strengthening the regulatory power of the federal government.
3. Legitimating one segment of the working class while delegitimating another.
4. Expanding American military and economic power throughout the world.

The changes that would contain stage one liberalism and stage two liberalism provided a Hegelian synthesis with a Hobbesian view of executive power. Thus, government intervention, the rise of economic liberalism, and second-stage liberalism are discussed as linked conceptions that came to fruition during the New Deal and Fair Deal periods. The federal government was thought to be the best place for the unrepresented and the poor to be heard and to have some benefits beyond sending their sons to foreign wars and paying taxes. However, there was another, more successful beneficiary.

The stubborn fact was that throughout the period of second-stage liberalism the national and international corporation used the power of the state to grow. But the international corporation was also an instrument of the national security state, which sought stability and American military expansion.

The question raised in the second stage of liberalism was whether in humane terms this brand of liberalism succeeded or failed. In a number of respects it succeeded as a result of struggle by social movements pressing their cases throughout the society and in the government. These movements opened the door to democratic inclusivity, none more successfully than those of the 1960s, which caused a profound change in the character of what was publicly permissible culturally and to some extent politically and economically.

Throughout the twentieth century left liberals sought a humane leader who would see far and act as the door opener to the excluded. He was in one sense to be a strong sovereign, one Hobbes might have respected. Were Presidents Theodore Roosevelt, Woodrow Wilson, Franklin Roosevelt, and Lyndon Johnson liberals at all, or during their times were there people and social movements that might better fit the ideal of liberalism? And did their failure leave open the door for the return of first-stage liberalism, now perverted into selfishness, greed, and mass manipulation of the public? It is devastating but true that in the twenty-first century first-stage liberalism has emerged as the new capitalism, claiming for itself efficiency and unconcern about the wretched except in the most vague and rhetorical ways.

Stage two liberalism, understood as government intervention in the domestic economy to set a standard for decency, surrendered itself to the global corporation as the mark of efficiency and promoted the national security state as the means of ensuring American dominance. As a consequence, second-stage liberalism failed at balancing the different classes in democracy in securing political equality and economic justice. In this sense these presidents also failed. Yet the New Deal and the Fair Deal sought to keep disparities in income within a psychologically acceptable range, one in which the disparities were less egregious than they are at the beginning of the twenty-first century.

At the beginning of the twenty-first century thousands of groups have formed that begin from a framework of liberal reconstruction, each group with its own issue, each beginning to find that its respective concern is related to other issues and groups, and each with an intuitive understanding of the debilitating effects such disparity has on people's lives and on the nature of democracy. New thought and broader movements are likely, although political organizers believe that the most efficient way to organize is around a specific issue.

This leaves us with stage three liberalism and its possibilities. The experience of the last fifty years in American life, and indeed in other nations, is that to separate moral and political thought from social practice leads to disaster. And to assert that what is—in terms of the distribution of power, knowledge, information, and talent—has to be, will yield failure for liberals and in turn failure for society. The framework of third-stage liberalism necessitates inquiries into questions thought to be far apart from one another. To not replicate false divisions of knowledge, problems, and movements, serious critical and reconstructive work demands emphasis on the synoptic and the crossover. In a period during which the seemingly unrelated are tied to one another through communications and the limits of specialization, and where shibboleths demand cross-examination and demystification, stage two liberalism has proved to be unsuccessful in finding a set of value guides for organizing knowledge and inquiry as a moral project. The task of stage three liberalism is to articulate reconstructive values that point to specific policies and reject others.

During the Clinton period a certain style of thought and practice found itself in politics and the university; it flew under the flag of "newness" and "new progressivism." Here I do not refer to deconstruction but rather to what was called the "Third Way." Its adherents thought that in politics and knowledge two plus one equals three, and they were adding first- and second-stage liberalism together. But the third way was really an exercise in subtraction. It surrendered control of governments to international markets and corporate leaders; it surrendered ideas of general disarmament to militarism. It added to greater mystification and separated further social movements from democracy and ways of organizing knowledge for the common good while trumpeting a "communitarianism" that sought to skirt the major structural issues of war and the economy.

President William Clinton also floated ideas about communitarianism and the third way based on the idea that the energy and vitality of the global corporation would save the world. Of course, as a tactical matter some attention was to be paid to "human rights." Clinton and the Democratic Party did not rise to the level of even being corporate liberals. In the wake of the assault on civil liberties, the corruption of the economic and political system, the need for a new stage of liberalism is obvious.

Third-stage liberalism begins from the premise that no society, no set of relationships that is not pathological, can exist without affections. And within each person there is the capacity for affections (caring, empathy, love, and cooperation) that can be either fulfilled or degraded by institutional structures. This premise, so necessary for the perpetuation of humanity, is avoided or degraded by other impulses such as greed, hypocrisy, arrogance, and the unquenchable quest for power.[1] The power of democracy is that it does not snuff out the capacity for affection, and its adherents are aware that the struggles of democracy are meant to strengthen this capacity and gain strength from it.

Thus, third-stage liberalism does not accept power as synonymous with politics.[2] Nor does it assume that certain institutions such as family or community are without serious problems. In third-stage liberalism new knowledge, accompanied by an active and expanded moral consciousness, must include standing with the unseen other, those who were once described as the wretched of the earth. Each age seeks this possibility on the basis of new knowledge and consciousness of the Other in different ways.

A common framework of agreement and dialogue can be found for the reconstruction of institutions and democracy itself in order to fulfill the aspirations of humanity.

Preface

Political struggles throughout the twentieth century centered on liberal democracy and its adversaries. Whether it was the Bolshevik Revolution, whose champions looked at liberal democracy as a bourgeois affectation that offered an exceedingly limited meaning of freedom based on individualism enjoyed by one class; the fascists and Nazis, who believed that liberal democracy personified the very meaning of weakness, flaccidity, and the racially mediocre as opposed to the racially, physically, and intellectually superior; those who claimed that modernism and liberal democracy were godless, destroying family life while seducing people with promises of material well-being; or those who believed in the Book, whatever the book was, as the alpha and omega of Truth, of how to live, of what was proper gender conduct and the revealed word of God—all agreed that liberal democracy was enemy Number One.

And so this is a defense of liberal democracy. It is not the kind offered by Isaiah Berlin in 1949, which emphasized negative freedoms against the state and the collective.[1] It is more in line with a pragmatist's conception of reconstruction, that critical mode of practice and analysis that is meant to keep liberalism vital by explaining its centrality in American life. This task requires me to review the rationalizing of the modern state and imperial expansion. As I suggest, liberalism was transformed and defeated by war preparations and corporations that often operated as private governments outside public accountability. The ideas of liberalism were battered by reality but always accepting of the seventeenth-century views of those, like Lord Shaftsbury, who believed that within humanity exists a moral sense that can help to guide human action.

Because this is also a book about reconstruction of institutions that impede liberal democracy and this moral sense, it considers certain root assumptions about social character, the shibboleth of family values, community, and the economy, as well as the political aspects of science and technology. Finally, I discuss possible ways of transforming the bankrupt system of oligopoly, capitalism, and the war system by introducing certain ideas of "is" and "ought" that, when linked to practices for economic, social, and political justice and equality, will reclaim the relevance and value of liberalism as the animating force behind a world civilization that builds on and recognizes a universal moral sense (capacity) that could begin to define the actions of institutions and governments.

From time to time I advert to my own experience, for the opportunity to present one's political and philosophic biography without being thrown in prison is one of the great strengths of liberal democracy. There have been exceptions to this generalization, and I of course mention them in due course. (In fact, this author was once in mortal danger of ending up in prison for antiwar beliefs.) Not surprisingly, the abridgment of speech comes during war, and to the shame of the liberal-minded such as Woodrow Wilson, who surrendered civil liberties to the Dog of War, as did Franklin Roosevelt. But to look to the second Bush administration for protection of civil liberties would be quite mistaken. An objective historian in 2050 will not be kind to the second Bush administration because it commits itself to war without end, the hubris of unilateralism, and wolfish capitalism in the midst of economic suffering within the United States and much of the world.

Acknowledgments

I have been extremely fortunate in having a wonderful family, colleagues, associates, and friends. "No man is an island," certainly not this author, and so I have been nurtured by many people. To coin a phrase, "It takes more than a village to write a book." My appreciation is boundless. I owe very special thanks to Sarah Williams, Diana Alonzo, Alix Howard, Brian Lutz, Christi Fanelli, Clint Fenning, Mark di Giacomo, and Matt Priselac for footnoting, copyediting, and critiques. No one should ever forget thanking his doctors. Charles Faselis, Richard Katz, Jerry Shields, and Mark Adkins outdo any fantasy doctor on TV for their competence and empathy.

I have been privileged to be part of the Institute for Policy Studies (IPS), which I cofounded with Richard Barnet and have directed at various times since 1963. The Institute is the place of creative thought, rational analysis, and practice "for the rest of us." The public scholars of the IPS community have had a profound and lasting effect on the consciousness of the last two generations. I have in mind Richard Barnet, Saul Landau, Barbara Ehrenreich, Norman Birnbaum, Noam Chomsky, Gar Alperovitz, Isabel Letelier and Orlando Letelier, Christopher Jencks, Bob Borosage, Rabbi Arthur Waskow, Roger Wilkins, Susan Buck-Morss, Seymour Melman, John Conyers, Herb Bernstein, Ethelbert Miller, Peter Weiss and Cora Weiss, and scores of others who continue to contribute to the betterment of humankind by using rationality as their moral instrument.

The Institute is in a period of renaissance. Sarah Anderson, Phyllis Bennis, Sanho Tree, Ralph Estes, Dorian Lipscombe, Amy Quinn, Martha Honey, Eric Leaver, Scott Williams, Nefta Freeman, Tammy Williams, Robin Weiss Castro, Joy Zarembka, Joia Nuri, Daphne Wysham, Miriam Pemberton, and Bob Alvarez are doing important work in foreign affairs, nuclear policy, national security and disarmament, adult education, economic policy, globalization, war–peace issues, and structural questions concerning democracy and politics. There are scores of professors linked to IPS in terms of these issues who contribute to IPS publications and media outlets.

IPS is fortunate in its donors. Their commitment and vision deserve special recognition. They are the MacArthur Foundation, HKH Foundation, Boehm Foundation, Rubin Foundation, Bernard and Audre Rapoport Foundation, Alan Sagne, the late Carol Ferry, the Ford Foundation, and thousands of smaller contributors.

The commitment, intelligence, and integrity of the Board of Trustees chaired by James Early have played an important role in sustaining IPS and offering wise counsel at a time that Dickens would have described as the best of times and the worst of times. No one has played a more important role in the successful renaissance of IPS than its director, the gifted John Cavanagh, whom we all admire for his leadership, organizing skill, scholarly brilliance, and optimism.

I am also pleased to be associated as a professor with George Washington University and give special thanks to its faculty in political science and public policy, as well as its undergraduate and graduate students. Professors Joe Cordes, Robert Stoker, and Hal Wolman are exemplary colleagues. GW's vice president, Don Lehman, and its president, Steve Trachtenberg, have turned the university into a world-class institution of higher learning.

I am very fortunate to have Jennifer Knerr as my editor at Rowman & Littlefield. Her wise counsel, publishing savvy, and calming demeanor I am sure work wonders with her authors as they have with me. I salute the patience and expertise of my copyeditor, production editor April Leo, the book designer, and sales and marketing people, as well as the publisher.

It is my good fortune to have four astonishingly gifted children (Erika, Jamie, Noah, and Eden). Their wisdom, good judgment, brilliance, loving natures, and slashing wit leave me speechless at times.

No father-in-law could be as delighted and thankful as I am for the spouses of my children, Keith Littlewood, Sarah Raskin, and Mina Raskin. Together they have made me a grandfather eight times over. The grandchildren are Emily, Zach, Maggie, Hannah, Thomas, Tabitha, Mariah, and Bo. Each of them represents the potential of a better future in which they can make their own mistakes and not relive the mistakes of the past. Even as an uncle there are obligations, and I thank Keith Raskin, Patty Levenson, and their spouses Sally and Barry.

And to my wife, Lynn, who has seen me through hard times with her Scottish analytical mind encased in her extraordinary beauty and loving nature: How thankful I am!

Introduction

Since I began my political and intellectual life as a liberal, I have often reflected on the meaning of liberalism. Growing up in Milwaukee, Wisconsin, the home of "sewer socialism," with a history of socialist city governments and impeccable service to the community (if you were white), the idea that "liberal" and "socialist" were dirty words seemed absurd. Other cities "reformed" themselves by bringing in nonelected, "scientific" city administrators who were ultimately responsible to the city "fathers" rather than elected officials and the voters. The "technicizing" of government by administrative managers became a tool that rationalized the power of the middle and upper classes. Liberalism's problem was that such rationalizing of bureaucracy was thought to be progressive, liberal, and linked to the fundaments of liberalism.

Some two generations later, in the United States liberalism was pilloried by all and sundry, including the Right, the Left, and the Center, and even among liberals, who became self-hating. "Socialism" had become a word that was banned from polite society, and in time so was "liberalism."[1] Not crediting the importance of liberalism to the Left, indeed its integral position as corrective and creative partner, too many on the Left attacked liberals during the Cold War period as pawns of capitalism. Liberals became increasingly vulnerable to political attack from the Right on the grounds that they wanted only to "throw money at problems" or were for "big government," favoring planning and indoctrination that would lead to an authoritarian state. Liberals were held responsible for the "loss" of China and Russia. They were pinkos, subversives, the politically correct. They stopped the United States from winning in Indochina and attempted to destroy our

1

intelligence services. And they supported a dumbing down of our educational institutions, otherwise so pristine and committed to "excellence." In the chaotic process many esteemed liberals attacked communists and the Left, fearing that they would be swallowed in the purge frenzy unleashed during the early stages of the Cold War. Together liberalism and the Left seemed to shut down. Liberals no longer called themselves liberals. They had become pragmatic, incrementalists, realists, moderates, and realistic progressives. The contested political space was surrendered to the Right, which had learned the Orwellian trick of calling things by their wrong names. Fear of freedom became freedom, fear of democracy became democracy, democratic inclusivity became exclusivity, peace became war, and propaganda became the verities of education as the universities sold themselves to the highest bidders. So if the Right and conservatives were successful politically and culturally, what did they fear?

Surely it couldn't be the Left and liberals (call their combination democratic reconstruction), who seemed to be in political and philosophic disarray—to use that wonderful phrase, even self-hating. But the Right and conservatives knew their enemy better than the Left and liberals knew themselves.

Liberals and the Left had caused a sea change in American life that could not be denied or easily repealed. Indeed, "bleeding heart" impulses that manifested themselves in political action helped to reflect and energize movements that changed the cultural character of the nation and defined the empathetic sense for the Other. It was also the case that the bleeding hearts supported the dignity and equality of people. Whether it was equal rights for women, an end to legal segregation, or attempts, often successful, to further racial justice; whether it was a caring awareness for the environment, or attempts to end poverty and gender discrimination, or commitments for elections that would go beyond the few—these changes toward liberal democracy represented the other reality struggling to survive and grow. Of course, there were different shadings to liberalism, and at certain moments they caused irreconcilable rifts among liberals and the Left. Liberalism was never a straight line to progress. Yet, every step of the way it is liberalism that is open to the human possibility, believing as it does in this invariable moral sense, turning the "ought" into the "is" for all of humanity. Human freedom and dignity can be more than a dream for the few.

SOME NECESSARY BACKGROUND

In 1959 I was an advisor to a group of young liberal congressmen.[2] Our political objective was to refocus the Democratic Party by finishing the New Deal program that had been left undone by Harry Truman's Fair Deal. We were intent on ending Dwight Eisenhower's period of Republican consolidation, which by future standards, ironically and sadly, would have been designated as to the left of President Clinton's Democratic administration. In 1960 our calling card was to be a book of two volumes called *The Liberal Papers*, which would be prepared by leading scholars of the time. The book was meant as a corrective to the turn liberalism had taken during the Cold War. The first volume concerned itself with foreign policy while the second volume was dedicated to domestic policy. When the first volume appeared in 1962, it caused a minor stir since it espoused such positions as mutual disarmament, diplomatic recognition of mainland China, and mutual military disengagement by the United States and the then Soviet Union from Eastern Europe and Western Europe. It was our view that these changes would have freed resources and people in Europe and elsewhere from the yoke of the Soviet Union and the tightening noose of nuclear war. This ensemble of ideas and policies was distinctly not the kind of propaganda language that rallied the people in favor of a cold war.

A cold war required an arms buildup that waved the devilish wand of nuclear weapons. In addition it required continued mobilization of the citizenry as well as what a distinguished Cold War theologian of the time, Reinhold Niebuhr, called accepting the reality of tragic choices that framed human responsibility in terms of the forces of light against darkness.[3] For Niebuhr the forces of light were innocence, which had to surrender their childlike ways in the face of a cold, always sober Soviet elite that knew exactly what it was doing. As has now become obvious, the Soviet leadership was confused and contradictory about its tactics, strategy, and goals and was desperate to make diplomatic deals with the United States at the expense of its "allies." Its leaders were not above drunkenness.

The Liberal Papers came up against Arthur Schlesinger Jr. and his influential book *The Vital Center*.[4] In 1948–1949 Schlesinger had offered a justification for liberals to combine with the ideological center to fight communism and Soviet imperialism. Under the theory that the Fair Deal and New Deal administrations were strong opponents of capitalist depredations, Schlesinger argued that government was not the executive committee of the bourgeoisie or a power elite, a term later invented by the sociologist C. Wright Mills. The claim of Professor Schlesinger was that such ideas badly misunderstood the character of the struggle within government and its strong knight-like qualities for liberal purposes. In terms of practical politics, some liberals stuck to ideas of social reconstruction. They did not swoon at hearing Schlesinger's song of a capitalism that would reform itself with a little nudge here and there from government. They concluded that capitalism and the national security state would be fenced off from fundamental criticism and protected by the new vital center. In fact, Schlesinger and his adherents acted as participants in the crusade of the Cold War, and in some cases far more militantly than Eisenhower.[5] It was an unwritten covenant that in this atmosphere, if social changes were to occur they would be restricted to an incremental consensus conducted within the new pillars of American life, namely, capitalism and the national security apparatus.

The problem with Schlesinger's formulation was that it narrowed the political choices and inhibited liberalism from following an independent course. It constricted political thought and narrowed itself to a pressure group with neither the power nor the interest to change the framework of the national security state or pyramidal corporate order. Schlesinger was trapped by the Democratic Party, which in its history, going back to its support of slavery, was a weak engine for liberalism unless pressed by social movements. For a generation after the end of World War II, Niebuhr's and Schlesinger's notions of tragic realism were pitted against democratic "utopian" visions that, in fact, were steeped in practical considerations, such as appreciation of the land and dignity of the people. How did Schlesinger's views achieve dominance?

No credible and conventional national political voices spoke for an alternative. Gone from the relevant political scene by 1949 was Henry Wallace, who had been raised as a Republican but found his political home in Roosevelt's New Deal. He was burlesqued for the very features that a postwar American nation needed: concern for the environment and the farmer, respect for other nations, the use and critical support of science, an end to militarism, and a global new deal that would help the poor of other nations with programs that guaranteed their economic recovery. But more important than this program, one the liberal Americans for Democratic Action (ADA) favored, was the decision taken by its leaders to assassinate Wallace's character. They claimed he was a dupe of the Soviet Union. The pyrotechnics were not all on one side; Wallace's opponents were thought of as corporate hacks and warmongers.[6]

With the incapacity of markets to answer the problem of economic depression, the lack of an international counterforce against Nazism, and fears of Soviet totalitarianism, many liberals by 1947 had lost their own sense of reality, causing them to fit into a consensus that dropped Rooseveltian ideas of domestic social reconstruction in favor of its degradation: the emerging welfare/warfare system. These new objectives accommodated new and old forces that had been unleashed through war. Schlesinger was a willing apologist for the acts and plans of American imperial responsibility, while Keynesian economists such as A. A. Berle, fearing another terrible economic depression, sought to find a soul for corporate capitalism that would justify its international power and bring forward social responsibility in the boardroom.

The subtext of *The Liberal Papers,* a title Schlesinger objected to with some vehemence, perhaps because it threatened to disturb the liberal arrangement as part of the vital center, was that U.S. Cold War foreign policy had aborted the domestic policy tasks of the New Deal. We claimed it was time to return to them.[7] In fairness, the Cold War economist Leon Keyserling, Truman's chair of the Economic Advisers, had sought to commit Truman to a policy in which workers and farmers would share in the plenitude of economic growth. The idea of economic growth that was reflective of the thought of Wallace and Harvard economist Alvin Hansen, who was viewed as second only to Keynes as an economist, also pressed the growth theory in the 1930s. It was to be (and remains) the answer to those who claimed that there must be redistribution of political and economic power. All that was needed was that the pie should grow larger, whatever its ingredients.

After the Second World War Keyserling, knowing that the New Deal had succeeded in ending unemployment through wartime spending, took a lesson. He believed that defense spending could serve as the pump for increased growth, which, with the democratic ideology of fair shares between management and labor arrived at through contract negotiations, could lead to an internally healthy economy. That is, substantial defense spending could produce higher wages and less unemployment at the cost of very moderate inflation. In this sense, the Korean War served as a godsend to an economy that suffered a 9 percent unemployment rate in the early spring of 1950.

Political leaders shied away from that type of liberalism that included détente with the Soviet Union and domestic reconstruction. Instead, the bipartisan foreign policy meant rebuilding Western Europe along pre–World War II lines, but without Nazism. European empires would relinquish their grasp on the Third World to American management. The Catholic Church, through the political leadership of Konrad Adenauer in Germany, Alcide DeGasperi in Italy, and Jean Monnet in France, created the phalanx for the North Atlantic Treaty Organization (NATO).[8]

In the United States, the tableaux of Cold War liberalism began with the acceptance of incremental adjustments in corporate capitalism yoked to the assumptions of national security laid out in such documents as National Security Council (NSC) 68. It called for increased spending with continued and unending cold war, which would simultaneously assert American paramountcy and religious stability to counteract the secular fervor of communism. But NSC 68, like so many government documents, was a justification for policies already in place or long intended.

Some civil servants concerned with domestic policy left over from their halcyon days in the New Deal kept the agenda of social reconstruction to themselves. They were intimidated by government security agents, Congress, and the media about loyalty, patriotism, and security. They knew that, through government and congressional investigations, any memorandum that they wrote could be used as an instrument to "prove" disloyalty. And by the 1950s even centrists were caught in the agonies of investigation and purge of the kind that had swept the United States after the First World War.[9]

By 1948 those in the administration who had argued for de-nazification of Germany and cooperation with the Soviet Union had lost political influence in the executive, and West Germany soon became the European centerpiece of the Western alliance.[10] Laws of internal security and secrecy, including the enshrinement of the two-party system in state laws, were passed to ensure political orthodoxy as well as social and economic shunning of liberals and radicals. These laws, regulations, and governmental attitudes spread throughout various institutions of the society and the economy, such as the media, unions, and universities. Such sentiments did not disappear with the election of John Kennedy in 1960. In fact, those politicians whose liberal credentials "were in order" did not realize how beholden they had become to the military system. This was the fate of such legislators as Senator Henry Jackson of Washington, who came to be known as the "Senator from Boeing," the giant aircraft manufacturer for the military.

Once *The Liberal Papers* appeared in 1962, the Republican leaders in Congress and the Senate, including some Democrats, insisted that I be fired from the special staff of the National Security Council, which I had joined on the day of the failed Bay of Pigs invasion. A few but not all of the original sponsors of the Congressional Liberal Project distanced themselves from the essays. Soon thereafter (during the summer of 1962) I was transferred out of national security matters into the Bureau of the Budget, where I worked on writing a draft of what came to be the Elementary and Secondary Education Act. It so happened that about the same time a book I had written with historian and theologian Arthur Waskow, called *The Limits of Defense,* was published. It questioned the confused conception of nuclear deterrence, showing how each military service had a doctrine of deterrence that contradicted the other services.[11] We adopted the Rashomon technique, which was especially useful when analyzing deterrence. Altogether nuclear deterrence was an extended work of fictive literature whose psychological plot revolved around how to frighten the antagonist in reality or illusion without frightening ourselves or damaging ourselves—foolish goals, as it turned out. Note for example damage to the environment and the human species as a result of nuclear waste and nuclear testing.

The deterrence fable has been told and retold through millions of pages of documents and over fifty years of writing and rewriting. It also resulted in transforming countless lives and the American political and social structure as nuclearism became a modern belief system in which the Bomb took on religious connotations. People were to fear it and worship it at the same time. The Bomb became the Holy Grail of great nations, none more so than the United States. But it was necessary to keep the Holy Grail out of the hands of those who were less "responsible" than those who depended on nuclear weapons for deterrence and war fighting. Whether it was Richard Wagner's Holy Grail or William Golding's legitimacy conch in *Lord of the Flies* has yet to be clarified.

Deterrence against use was first suggested in the Einstein–Szilard letter to Franklin Roosevelt as a way of countering possible German nuclear development during the Second World War. Nevertheless, the weapons were first used by the United States after the Nazi surrender. What had first caught the attention of policy planners was a report in 1939 emanating from Great Britain, the Maud report, named after the wife of Niels Bohr. The report left the impression that the nation that had nuclear weapons would rule the world.[12] Nuclear and thermonuclear preparations after the war were wildly costly and paradoxically irrelevant to political considerations of leaders once they considered the implications of using even one weapon. Yet, they were there, always talked about, planned for, with documents showing how and when they could be used in any and virtually all situations of tension and threat. And they ultimately cost the United States over $6 trillion.[13] Since having such weapons came to be thought of as the sine qua non of power, many nations sought their own nuclear weapons systems, although they were inhibited by the cost and the 1970 nonproliferation treaty. Third World nations complained that the nonproliferation treaty was discriminatory, aimed at Third World nations, for the nations that had nuclear weapons had no intention of ridding themselves of this "advantage."

During the Cold War nuclear tests by the United States and the Soviet Union were often used as warnings. They were coordinated and timed to fall immediately before important diplomatic conferences with the Soviets as a means of intimidation.[14] The Soviets also practiced this form of intimidation. The two nations were like two bulls pawing the ground, marking out territory. It was difficult, indeed virtually impossible, to give up testing and nuclear weapons even though vocal groups spoke against them and several government officials sprinkled throughout the government questioned their necessity or utility. Demonstrations, letters to congressmen, and analyses by scientists showing that the tests were poisoning the atmosphere increased the revulsion of middle America as it became clear that children holding their hands over their faces and facing down on desks would not be protected from nuclear war. As the disarmament advisor on the National Security Council staff, I interpreted my task as stopping the avalanche of nuclear and national security madness that seemed to grip the leadership from 1961 to 1963. No doubt my efforts were not universally applauded. They surely weren't very successful, if at all.

One memorandum given to President Kennedy by his national security advisor, McGeorge Bundy, referred to me as the "young menace" who, because of the attack on *The Liberal Papers* and *The Limits of Defense* in

Congress, might have to be sacrificed if the political weather got too heavy. While mildly praising me, Bundy also wanted to wait and see what would happen politically with congressional attacks before my political excommunication to the Bureau of the Budget would take place. In hindsight my excommunication should have been expected.

When I was invited onto the staff, Bundy asked what a new liberal position on disarmament would be and whether I was prepared to be the Oppenheimer of the administration. I took this as a compliment, for Oppenheimer was thought of in the upper reaches of American intellectual life as a legendary and tragic character who had been a leading scientist and administrator. It was only much later that I understood Bundy to have been asking whether I was prepared to be sacrificed for views that he must have felt were more in tune with picketers outside the White House than with those who held important positions inside. And in fact his feelings were right. I did picket the White House as a staff member during the Cuban Missile Crisis.

While in the government, my discussions with the great physicist Leo Szilard led me to conclude that I could play a more constructive role outside the government by beginning the Institute for Policy Studies, which I did with the gifted Richard Barnet. (The first full-time or resident fellows were Arthur Waskow, Gar Alperovitz, Christopher Jencks, Donald Michael, Paul Goodman, David Bazelon, Leo Szilard, and Milton Kotler, with Barnet and me serving as codirectors.) Critical thinking and government service are not very comfortable fits.

There was a fundamental question that war and cold war raised throughout much of the twentieth century: Was liberalism or democracy possible in the context either of war or cold war? Indeed, was it necessary to concern oneself with the meaning of words in an age when language was used in an Orwellian way? One could of course wonder where intellectuals fit into this story. Were they like the poets of yore who trumpeted the heroism of great statesmen, warriors, and capitalists? Were they truth tellers using their creative and intellectual powers to expose and therefore to help people see things as they are?[15]

1

★

The Liberal Purpose

LIBERAL MEANINGS

The liberal sensibility in modern time, that is, since Adam Smith, has zigzagged through a variety of stages and fashions. There is enough evidence to suggest that at first liberalism was the ideology of an emerging entrepreneurial class that wanted to protect its property from the state and accepted only those fetters that would protect its own right to be unfettered. The antiauthoritarian philosophes of France saw even more. New inventions and discoveries were changing politics, economics, and everyday life; God belonged in a box somewhere in the middle heavens, and it was past time for an end to the oppressive and the constraining, at least for the new middle classes and even for others. Liberty was the watchword. And something important happened in the tidal wave of historical change. It was not only the middle class that gained from the revolutions of the eighteenth century. Rights and equality were introduced in France and the pre- and postrevolutionary United States as a powerful incentive to outsiders, the sansculottes, and the oppressed, including so many of their heirs still waiting to receive their due.

Whatever the motivations of liberalism's originators, such as protection against the powerful who did not need rights because they had power, the concepts of rights and human rights grew.

Rights and freedom are inexorable as humanity struggles for a way out of the shadows of despair. This is not to say that, in practice, these concepts have had a free ride. It is a platitude but no less true that oligarchies and conservatives have struggled mightily against the onslaught of those liberals who tied themselves to the poor, the outsider, the pacifists, the workers, and all those who sought a seat at the table of power or who wanted to change the very nature and timber of the table. The reactions to these "subversives" have been fierce. And some liberals who called themselves "pragmatic" settled for the kind of progress that appeared to be a redefinition or extension of the status quo. Perhaps these liberals and progressives should not be judged too harshly for believing in glacial affirmative change or being caught in definitions of liberalism and progressivism that do not fit the needs of the twenty-first century.

Progress is not obvious, nor does it occur in a straight line of ascent. Progress presents itself as a rhetorical flourish, which from one generation to the next becomes the practical basis for the rearrangement of social reality. It is a rearrangement that requires being open to a new consciousness and being prepared to struggle for it in practice, never an easy matter. Post–World War II United Nations documents showed the folly of those who stood in the way of rights and universal dignity even as they were often merely the expression of aspirations for which humanity struggles. These documents came to be understood as justifications and reflections of profound change that seemed obvious and undeniable on the level of words. It is undeniable that the meanings of words and even concepts change in light of different social conditions and new discoveries. They are empty bottles, as Alfred North Whitehead put it, to be filled with new wine. Just as the worldwide depression forced a reconsideration of the role of the state in the political economy, and just as various movements of liberation, such as the labor and civil rights movements, continued their struggles for equality, it was necessary to rethink liberalism so that the tenets of political freedom and social responsibility—"who counted"—extended beyond the few and the entrepreneur. Like most ideas and actions, the ground for this social truth was understood throughout much of the nineteenth and twentieth centuries by thinkers, writers, and activists of whom Americans can be justly proud, for they represented the practical, achievable aspirations of humanity and of the individual.

By the twentieth century, it was clear that liberalism, if it were to remain relevant, was in need of profound change. Where would liberalism go for coalition and sustenance? Would it integrate with the Left, that is, with a fickle working class, the wretched outsider, professionals who were denied truthfulness in their craft because of "business" considerations, or would it stay with romantic ideas of the free market and the "self-made" man? Certainly the Clinton Democratic Party favored the latter approach, allowing it to appear liberal and act conservative. Whether conservative or Clinton liberal, both placed their faith in private property and in corporations that were to live in perpetuity allied in the United States with a dominant imperial military system. The well-off, whatever their ideology, were not going to be intimidated by wretched workers or their families within the United States or elsewhere who suffered the realities of capitalism's purpose and energy. Who would have thought that self-interest as conceived by a professor of moral philosophy, Adam Smith, would result in a pathological self-interest where it meant exploitation and the exclusion of others from the common wealth? No doubt Smith has turned over in his grave often since his death. Of course, it was not only Smith who was turning over in his grave. There were millions who thought they were encased in a living death. Farmers and laborers at the beginning of the twentieth century lived in personal turmoil. There were many who believed there was no escape from their situation, and that the words of freedom and rights were of no value in paying bills at the grocery store or changing the conditions of work; it was only through the articulation and organizing of alternatives that a wholly new situation was created.[1]

The question for any group struggling for its own rights and place is how to attain these ends. That is, what is their agency for change? Workers who formed into unions knew that such rights are not given on a platter to the deserving and certainly not to the "undeserving." Their business antagonists believed that for a well-organized and oiled "free enterprise" to work effectively, workers had to be considered part of a labor market with as few "benefits" as possible. Their status was that of a labor commodity without property rights in a job and with constant fear of unemployment. But that could no longer be the basis of modern liberalism. Blacks learned that to change liberalism and its meaning they would have to struggle for survival and inclusivity, for social and economic justice. At the very least, they had to find the means to move from the slave to the exploited class. This is an old and very difficult, but heroic, struggle in American life. And it is one that has the overlay of personal fulfillment for everyone.

Indeed, there has been no escape from ideas of equality, which are honored more often in the breach but in fact are the underlying rhythm of American life. This explains the love that millions of immigrants, even the submerged and the oppressed, whether Amerindian, Hispanic, or black, have for American society. Everyone wants equality and a little bit more.

Since the period of the Revolutionary War, this sentiment has been an underlying trope, a tendency that continues to find itself as the central purpose of civil society. Even the laws of the United States have not been averse to the sentiment of social equality when it means the equal right to become unequal. This struggle may be noted between the Declaration of Independence and the Constitution, with the latter being interpreted as primarily the protection of private property. Indeed, in the Constitution it was as if private property were synonymous with the common good itself. It does not seem to matter that the character of private property has morphed into new forms of oligarchic power through large corporations. By the beginning of the twentieth century, after brutal labor wars, exploitation of freed blacks, and completion of Indian wars, a liberal philosophic and political position was articulated in American life meant to concretize ideals for America as a civilization and curb capitalism and the growth of private property among the few, which suffocated the public space.[2]

With the end of the Civil War in 1865, American capital entered a new phase, one that highlighted astonishing contradictions as America attempted to redraft a social covenant. Being a legally oriented nation dominated in its legislatures by lawyers, the United States saw attempts to turn the Constitution into either a document of human rights aspirations or one that was constricted and meant to assert rule by oligarchy, with a claim at legalistic justification.

LIBERALISM'S EXISTENTIAL MEANING

In their identification with the oppressed and needful reconstruction, liberals sought to create the conditions for the application of reason that maximized individual freedom coupled with responsiveness and responsibility to others. This sense of responsibility was meant to create collective solidarity by securing a public framework of caring and equality beyond any constricted social, political, or economic boundaries. In practice, this meant the discovery of the self and the group as mutually reinforcing, for both set limits on each other and both were infused with the Other with attendant social and economic responsibilities.

Culturally, the liberal came to personify permissiveness with regard to the social aspects of everyday life and was prepared to be open to change, allowing structure to follow process. In the Cold War era, Dr. Benjamin Spock was thought to be the archetypal liberal who rejected, then changed his mind and accepted, and then championed, the claims of women's liberation.[3] Some conservatives saw the attitudes of men such as Dr. Spock as the very example of social decline and decay. Conservatives have dedicated their lives to rubbing out this blot on the escutcheon of Authority and Order. Like the monomaniac Captain Ahab, they will not rest easy until they catch and destroy the whale of liberalism. One such whale was George McGovern, an authentic Second World War hero, whom his opponents smeared with the preposterous notion that he was cowardly. Judge Robert Bork became the Captain Ahab in the American drama surrounding liberalism. Bork had his legal leg torn off on his way to the Supreme Court by liberals and their public interest groups. His bitterness is understandable but not commendable.

Modern liberalism, according to Bork, is the "enemy within," which is "bankrupt" of ideas. Now that the Soviets and the Nazis have disappeared from the world political scene, the nation's chief enemy, and by extension, the great enemy of Western civilization, is modern liberalism, which I take to be the liberalism of reconstruction. Its malign power did not come all at once, according to the Borkian story. It started with the Enlightenment but came to its dastardly culmination in the 1960s with the Students for a Democratic Society's Port Huron Statement. But it was really Thomas Jefferson, not the slave owner but the radical, who didn't understand the nature of man. According to Bork, Enlightenment thinkers extracted certain features from the "whole man" and turned them into the entire picture of humanity's needs, as in the case of the misplaced need for inalienable rights.[4]

Complaints against the Enlightenment were not reserved to conservatives. Left thinkers and activists from the Frankfurt school, assorted Marxists, Georg Lukacs, and any number of left scholars faulted the founding fathers and the Enlightenment's belief in the principle of inalienable rights for the person. Needless to say, both schools of thought considered the problem of alienation and societal decomposition from different vantage points. Some conservatives complained that the cause of decay was liberal emphasis on radical individualism, the pursuit of the will-o'-the-wisp phantom of happiness, which gives rise to a bottomless cornucopia of rights leading to and embracing decay of society without the promise of happiness.[5] The Left also spoke of decay and crisis. It located the problem in the character of the economic system, that is to say, in capitalism and the unbridled market system.

Modern liberals have pointed out that radical individualism is exactly what President Ronald Reagan reflected in his rhetoric, namely, unfettered individualism and selfishness, even as some of his acolytes pined for abstract Walt Disneyan ideas of community while keeping their fingers crossed. With the Reagan revolution, the devastation of local communities continued as public responsibilities were contracted out and privatized.[6] On the other hand, liberals committed to reconstruction broadened economic justice to include confrontation with the national security state because, as anti-imperialists, they did not want government to serve as the organizational lever for worldwide military economic enterprises. Those who held this brand of liberalism believed that domestically, the modern liberal state meant changing the nature of the democracy and even the republic into a system of rule *for* the many rather than rule *over* the many. These ideas and concerns were old ones in human history. They remain relevant in a personal sense.

At the beginning of the twenty-first century, most people exist in a world where they are thrown by others, by forces over which they have no control. They may be very old or very young, frail mentally and physically, too caring or too frightened. Their footsteps hardly imprint on the snow. They require care, not in some crummy colonial sense, but in the sense of understanding that there are duties and responsibilities we have for others as human beings—and that is an important function of institutions. As Willy Loman's wife put it in *Death of a Salesman,* "Attention must be paid" to the person. How do the self-reliant take care of others? First, they must surrender the idea that they are self-reliant, for that is a foolish myth that certainly adds nothing to our understanding of what we are, how we got to be where we are, or who we are. Ralph Waldo Emerson's idea of self-reliance courts the surrender of social responsibility without taking cognizance of the different stages of life that the person passes through, from utter dependence to interdependence to utter dependence. This is the human condition, and to the extent possible, modern democracy must be built on the foundation of this harsh realization.

The liberalism of reconstruction is inextricably intertwined with modern democracy, for in its conceptual basis it does not fear trusting people, which means the people are to renew their institutions and change them when they are or become repressive. In other words, modern liberals trust in the moral growth of people and their exercise of judgment in all their variability. But institutions such as family, community, and workplace are seen objectively rather than through some rose-tinted glasses.

Democracy's institutions are to be arranged in as many ways as possible to ensure the objectives of participation and deliberation. This includes the workplace. Where this condition does not exist democracy is hobbled, perhaps fatally. It is in that situation that liberals (which includes the Left) should undertake the struggle for democratization of institutions and everyday life.

Where politically the two dominant American parties are primarily corporate and national security state parties with only accidental possibility for the citizenry to exercise its reasoned understanding of what is happening, the basis is laid for not-so-friendly authoritarianism, and we see this in George W. Bush's administration, whose war without end claims pious rhetoric is the same as freedom. The citizenry, bereft of its own agencies for expression, is manipulated through the undemocratic impediments of secrecy and control. Hierarchy and authority, whether in the public or private sphere, can easily be degraded into authoritarianism, in which case liberal democracy cannot long survive. On the other hand, liberal democracy can be aggressive in its defense and in its reflection of what people want. This is why liberal democracy has "invaded" all aspects of social life and virtually all "settled" institutions, from churches, to universities, to male–female relations, to government. Its success, however, is based on having a program, a direction in which its adherents catalyze alternatives to the national security state and its economic appendage. But what binds these alternatives, and how are they to be recognized as the promotion of the common good?

IS THERE A FIRST PRINCIPLE TO LIBERALISM?

If there is a fundamental liberal principle it is the recognition of change in all things as an invariable condition of living. Pragmatists know that any first principle calls into jeopardy other closely held but fragile scientific and mystical beliefs that melt or break apart in the rocky sea of the antinomies of everyday life. In the sciences, while some have sought Truth, fame, riches, and prizes, others are prone to follow certain knowledges because of their operational predictive value, principles of aesthetic elegance, or seeming logical consistency. But we also know that such predictions are statistical and therefore depend on the context and circumstances of the particular case. We look for consistency of evidence and are satisfied that such consistency is enough to build huge structures that, over time, will wear out, although we continue to cling to them as if they are the only way of being in the world.

In what some commentators described as the golden age of anthropology, different practices in cultures were presented as a means of showing how, in our own society, relativism and deviance should not be feared. In fact, there existed—just as the French Enlightenment philosophers had argued— other cultures and "natural" styles that were instructive for one's own society. By showing variation under the guise of neutral empirical social science, an attack was mounted against racism and sexism, which these anthropologists abhorred. So modern liberalism reveled in the richness of variation and inconsistency, incoherence and probabilities, just because within self-imposed and natural boundaries that is the character of life itself. This did not mean that there is a hole in the center of one's life because the transcendent is missing, that is, the single Truth or God, an unchanging essence or Superman. It merely meant that the various transcendent attempts are incorporated in the yearnings of human beings beyond any particular culture. Politically such concepts are existential because they force onto humanity the continuing question of how to generate those social, political, and economic institutions and personal choices that give meaning to our lives.

Reconstruction offers an alternative. It holds dear human rights, social responsibility, and the Other. And it insists on creating institutions based on natural affections among people that often present themselves in moments of crisis. Perhaps natural affection and social responsibility can extend to the generation of universal community.

LIBERAL ROOTS TO REMEMBER

It did not become clear to me until later in life that my concerns about public policy, its practice and study, were meant to reconnect to much older

American traditions than those that could be teased out of the New Deal. My roots could be found in the great domestic social reform movements, which gripped so many Americans in the nineteenth and early twentieth centuries. To their antagonists, the big moneyed and propertied classes, these movements were subversive; more euphemistically stated, they were reconstructive and humanistically liberal, for their purpose was to bring the wretched, silenced, suppressed, and voiceless into the public space, thereby gaining for them relevance and dignity. Furthermore, these movements were premised on the need to find the means of changing the character of predatory capitalism without war or revolution. They were sympathetic to violence when it was used by the oppressed to escape their condition. But they condemned legitimacy and the law when they were used to mask structural violence. Most, but not all, questioned the value or the validity of religion, for often it was a cover story for human desires, some worthy, others unworthy, but hardly proof of a God. Believing too much could lead to zealotry, too often violent and oppressive in its practices.

Nineteenth-century struggles for workers, Indians, the enslaved, and women's rights, which gripped the lives of Henry David Thoreau, Frederick Douglass, Walt Whitman, Herman Melville, Mark Twain, William Garrison, Thaddeus Stevens, Charles Sumner, and Fanny Wright, stemmed from the same wellsprings that illuminated the lives of William James, John Dewey, Robert LaFollette Sr., Charles Beard, Jane Addams, Martin Luther King Jr., W. E. B. DuBois, Eugene Debs, Henry Wallace, Clarence Darrow, Linus Pauling, Emily Balch, and A. J. Muste. In their writings and political work, and within the movements of the time, they sought a different practice of human and political relationships than those who mocked the democratic ideal. They did not accept the established understandings about the irredeemable nature of man, which according to the aggressive, the wellborn, and the privileged, was consonant with social Darwinism, or of those who claimed a natural law of dominance and submission as a means of protecting their own place.

Indeed, we can conclude without much fear of contradiction that the reformist intellectual and political leaders of the nineteenth century were more strident in their condemnation than were their heirs in the twentieth century. The language used by Douglass to describe slavery and American civilization was far angrier and less diplomatic than the words of Martin Luther King Jr. Both in the nineteenth and twentieth centuries writers and intellectuals carried within themselves, as did many of the reform movements, a vision of a society that they could see but was not yet reality. Every person I have mentioned, and many more, would have favored the progressive, liberal, and radical thrust that politics took at different stages of the twentieth century. They were the other America. And they are inscribed in the work that many activists and thinkers do. They reflected what I term in this inquiry "stage three liberalism."

American thinkers, writers, artists, and activists reflected a liberal senti-ment that said that from time to time radical and exemplary action was nec-essary in practice to bring about structural changes in the social system. They carried with them a respect for the Other and the reality that head, heart, and hand would be linked as the basis of a democratic polity. For them there was an inherent dignity in human nature that social institutions had to fulfill. This was the precept of two political men, Thaddeus Stevens and Charles Sumner, who, with other radical Republicans, initiated the first period of constitutional reconstruction, which led to former slaves becom-ing citizens. It was one thing to be "free"; it was another to be a citizen with few, if any, rights after Reconstruction. Even during Reconstruction Con-gress was not prepared to break up plantations or grant "48 acres and a mule" to slaves as part of a land reform reparations program, which would have helped former slaves escape their colonized status.

Believers in American reconstruction welcomed the immigrant workers' movements of Europe, Germany, Eastern Europe, and Russia, which brought in their satchels a humanist, radical democrat, and socialist cast.[7] The establishment of Workman's circles among the Jews and cooperative societies enriched the dialogue of how to live a just and secure life (cigar makers who pooled their salaries so that one of ten would be the reader and discussion leader as the other nine made cigars). As much as the roots of the United States can be found in slavery, especially in the South, so too part of the puzzle of the American ethos can be found among the Quakers of Penn-sylvania. It can also be found in Benjamin Franklin's respect for the manner in which Indians had organized intertribal relations. In the face of tragedy and struggle, disparate individuals and groups who sought the Promised Land were often divided among themselves. Whether it was the haughty New England transcendentalists or the violent workers known as the Molly Maguires and Wobblies, a common thread could be found. It was not dif-ficult to discern the outlines of a vision of humanity that insisted on dignity and economic and social justice. And as more people sought an end to their oppression and others were sensitive to that purpose, the issues were ex-panded as we came to know more about ourselves as human beings, our needs, and our desire for universal dignity. There could be no denial of women's rights and liberation. As we come to know more about the envi-ronment, we find new meanings in the importance of nature and the need to protect it for itself and for humanity. (This vision is even more immov-able than the boulders that cover the land. And if we listen ever so slightly we can hear our own concerns in the voices of the past.)

Several of these concerns were spelled out in the platform of the Amer-ican Anti-Imperialist League, which counted among its supporters Carl Schurz, a refugee from the failed 1848 democratic revolutions in Ger-many. The words of that platform aimed at American involvement in the

Philippines could have been written—and were—by activists during the war in Indochina:

> We hold that the policy known as imperialism is hostile to liberty and tends to-
> ward imperialism, an evil from which it has been our glory to be free. We re-
> gret that it has become necessary in the land of Washington and Lincoln to
> reaffirm that all men of whatever race or color, are entitled to life, liberty, and
> the pursuit of happiness. We maintain that governments derive their just power
> from the consent of the governed. We insist that the subjugation of any people
> is "criminal aggression" and open disloyalty to the distinctive principles of our
> Government.[8]

The political and philosophic stance articulated by a founder of pragmatism, William James, made clear that the overlapping oligarchies of American life, which protected racism, sexism, imperial war, and anti-Semitism,
were wrong in every one of these endeavors. And he confronted those who
held or acted on such views at every stage of his life. But because he feared
man's instincts of aggression, which led to war, he sought creative alternatives that would channel murderous instincts. Perhaps that is why his pragmatism was never far from mysticism and socialism, which he praised.[9]

That the dominant characteristics of the twentieth century revolved
around evil, deep racism, sexism, and utopian dreams gone awry merely
meant that the "liberal subversives," more precisely the progressive liberals
in their quest for reconstruction, needed to compose a different social harmony for the complex play of modern life. People had to transcend social
roles and purposes that were less than who they were. These sounds and
feelings would be translated into suitable signs of what was reasonable and
prudent. (Obviously, what is reasonable and prudent may be open to different interpretations.) The tragedy of American politics during the twentieth century was that its leadership heard the voices of those favoring liberal
reconstruction but could listen with but half an ear. Political leaders often
contain within themselves contradictory sentiments, for they question how
they can gain power, especially in a limited democracy committed to negotiating between the various classes and interests. Politicians are faced with
the almost insurmountable task of finding the right rhetoric, the sounds and
bleatings that will seduce more than one group so that the their political
base for incremental change will be broadened.

This is the story of liberal and progressive-minded presidents in the twentieth century who sought to be brokers among competing, contradictory,
emerging claims for justice, even equality. One might say that finding the
right rhetoric is all one can expect of leaders. But this role is insufficient.
Presidents, leaders, and major political parties have not brought the
changes necessary to bring about reconstructions equal to the problems that
we face. Nor have political parties, universities, and so-called public intel-

lectuals provided a sufficient number of ideas necessary to understand and formulate solutions in more than one arena, the result being that the particular solution does not speak to a general solution. The problem is delineated too narrowly and the result is incompletion. The result is that fundamental problems such as structural racism, disparity between rich and poor, environmental questions, sexism, and American imperialism are buried in our political consciousness. Amnesia overtakes our politics. And yet healthy cells certainly remain in our body politic.

And they can guide history into a vital resurgence of freedom. We see extraordinary progress that can be made even in the face of tragedy and lost opportunities. As a result, the spirit of this age is not imperialism, it is not fascism or Stalinism, it is not racism, absolutism, sexism, or crazed religious zealotry. Quite the contrary. Its spirit may be found in the much-maligned UN resolutions, charter, and covenants, which are the proverbial eight-hundred-pound elephant of universal aspiration that won't go away. Whether the path and signposts of these documents lead to liberal reconstruction remains to be seen. Their meanings are mediated through states, and their application is up against the realpolitik and cultures of the world steeped in an oppressive past. It is important to remember that such foundational documents reflect constant struggle by movements for social justice every step of the way. Whatever the particular policies, the underlying purpose is an ever-unfolding liberal democracy based on ways of humanizing humanity. Surely that was the purpose of Adam Smith.

2

✯

The Ambiguity
of Liberal Democracy

THE JANUS-FACED STATE

Political freedom, as the process and primary objective of democracy, is fashioned by two sets of concerns. The first is the traditional concern of limits that the state cannot overstep. Such limits are traditional and are expressed negatively. They assert a zone of protection that the state cannot cross. This zone is to be so ingrained in the customs, laws, and mores of the society that when it is violated, a social revulsion occurs that cannot be overcome by corporate advertising, propaganda, or state-sanctioned violence. Citizenship, in this context, is the right to not vote, to be left alone, and not to be invaded by outsiders, assaulted by the state, or incriminated by one's own statements. But note that because government is accountable to the people, its power to stand as an enforcer of rights against racism and sexism or economic corporations is primary because, in the last analysis, government in its various facets must ensure the general welfare of all its residents. This democratic government stands in the curious dialectical paradox of being both the protector and the possible violator of the individual, especially where limits and boundaries are not ingrained in everyday practices. This is why freedom in democracy is most complete where there is the power of access, participation, deliberation, and implementation exercised by individuals within the entities in which they reside and work.

As I have said, access is integral to participatory freedom. It is the right to reach officials, to find and associate with one's fellow human beings, whether directly or indirectly, through various communications systems. It should be noted that at present in the United States there is only the appearance of access. Unless the person is part of an organization of political power, usually an interest group, or happens to be rich and so able to use that wealth in the public space, access is severely limited. This latter point was made abundantly clear by Attorney General Janet Reno in defense of President Clinton's entertaining his various wealthy contributors by having them sleep over at the White House. She put it that the "[g]overnment points to no legislative duty to provide equal access to all members of the public; and from a practical standpoint, we doubt one exists." In other words, if an elected official decides to give access only to political contributors, "no Federal violation is suggested."[1]

Since the French Revolution, the question of who or what entity best protects political freedom continues as a profound topic of debate and struggle. Conservatives have held that, according to the eminent Thomist philosopher Yves Simon, so long as men are what they always have been, "nothing will be better for the many than paternal domination by the few."[2] To conservatives in virtually all circumstances, genuine democracy is a dubious form of government, no matter how large or small the body politic or how large the territory. Behind Reno's defense of Clinton was the profoundly conservative understanding of government, although that administration's rhetoric was one of access for the excluded. Further, security is predicated on the denial of access to the public. Denied access to "intelligence," the citizenry is denied the possibility of exercising its collective intelligence, a critical aspect of democracy.

LIBERAL DEMOCRACY IN THE MODERN ERA

Yet, as I have noted, democracy has emerged as the preferred form of governing because it asserts the importance of self-rule, and while it tolerates ideas of heaven and the next life as a better place and is sympathetic to religious views that present life as a way station, there is emphasis on the here and now. It tolerates all sorts of beliefs, customs, and mores, and is by its nature relativistic. It also holds scientific and technological activities as a higher good, believing they are more verifiable and relevant to everyday life than theological concerns.[3] On the other hand, conservatives are frightened of democracy, because it is often ragged, inefficient, and without ineradicable guarantees of wealth and private property. When this sense of disorder sets in, or where a third-stage liberal democracy favors the lower classes, or where disorder from below seems to be chronic, manifesting itself as crime, those who see themselves subjectively as middle class even though they may be debtors are likely to turn to or accept military or authoritarian rule in the operation of civil institutions.[4] Democracy is a problem for those craving order. It is by no means a neutral form of government that seeks "antiseptic" rules. It is protean in its form, and therefore it is helter-skelter in its custom, ritual, and presentation.

Democracy and its liberal reconstruction recognize the political power of class distinction, which they continuously challenge and transgress. Although democracy keeps itself grounded in humankind, with its palpable needs, desires, fears, and foibles, there is an embrace of motion and movement toward equality as an underlying principle. This principle stimulates human yearning and wonder, allowing the person or group to escape or shift needs, desires, and fears.

Much to everyone's chagrin, democracy in its present form does not yield well-being in the psychological sense and is more likely to create feelings of paradox, confusion, doubt, yearning, and disappointment. As often as not, there is a spiritual "hole in the center" of democracies because people seek certainty in their lives and attachment to the transcendent. Democracy has trouble fulfilling this quest, although it allows for that possibility through toleration of religion, individual beliefs, and artistic expression. However, when it tries to provide the transcendent collectively through war or nationalist patriotic symbols, profound problems emerge that cross the boundaries of tolerance and respect for diversity. This situation is likely to occur where leaders risk the lives of the citizenry in war, especially where there is no obvious or felt threat. Leaders entrusted with imperial power find it difficult to determine what is a common good as opposed to their personal whim, expansionist interests, or dangerous steering based on misguided judgment. A constitutional democracy's political attraction is that it can act as a brake on foolhardy or mad schemes. But the constitution must encourage and then guarantee a citizenry that is participatory and deliberative. If such guarantees are not present, foolish or corrupt leaders have the power to reduce the citizenry to a passive instrument. (It is not accidental that the political root of mobilization is *mob*.)

Constitutional democracy is meant to provide protections of physical security for the individual, both against the state and against other states. These protections may appear to be the same for all states; with constitutional democracy there is a wrinkle. Although democracy's definition is never quite articulated, the phrase, "It's a free country" has as much communicative meaning to the speaker and to the listener when they share the same context as those who say, "Please pass the coffee." At a minimum, the citizenry believes democracy to be a mode of governing in which the absence of external physical constraint is joined to the principle of consent of the governed with economic sharing through whatever economic system is used.

Like other eighteenth-century Enlightenment sentiments, democracy built itself on a promise that could never escape its transcendent overtones—happiness or at least the search for it. Radicals believed that democracy, as a governing form, would release human dignity and creativity in the social, political, and economic spheres. It was believed these hopes for democracy would not leave people feeling insecure and unrequited as they moved away from the settled and the feudal. It was taken for granted by revolutionaries, however, that such hopes had to be channeled along "correct" lines because people had lived too long as virtual serfs.[5] In revolutionary France, channeling was to be accomplished through the process of science and a new reason. Virtue would be derived from them.[6]

It is hardly surprising that a clash of meaning regarding democracy occurred in the twentieth century. As some of its advocates sought to remake human nature, others believed and accepted human variability, and still others claimed minimums and maximums in the economic sphere, for individuals and groups. Some understood democracy as a limited form, while others claimed it to be cumulative in its purpose and open-ended in its method for improving humankind. Those who pursued its limited meaning sought rules and procedures that often held back popular will in exchange for longer or more studied deliberation. Those who held to the deliberative were thought by their adversaries to be sort of conservative proponents who calcified law into the defense of oligarchic power. On the other hand, there were those who believed that democracy could be easily degraded and manipulated by the corrupt if there were no rule of law and limits championing protections of the person and using the wisdom of deliberative delay. Democracy could be used by the tyrant and then discarded, or its rhetoric could lead to its own degradation.

LOCATING THE PUBLIC SPACE, RIGHTS, AND DEMOCRACY

Democratic government is the guardian of the public space. In the public space, we create a general will through dialogue and accountability about economic and social policy. We civilize ourselves, while socializing and distinguishing our wants from needs. Through this process of dialogue, understanding, social coordination, law, and custom, a framework is constructed in which all of us accept responsibility for one another. In the public space, our individuality is fused with our social selves. We recognize our egalitarian interdependence with one another, and we define our civic duties. We make real the common good through the general will, best defined as reasoned participation in the solution of immediate and long-range public problems. It is the individual's exercise and then extension of the empathic sensibility to the self beyond the selfish self, where the individual realizes joint benefit and the importance of caring responsibility.[7] (In disastrous events this sense of responsibility is manifest in the outpouring of aid given to the fallen by communities, as in the case of the New York and

Washington tragedies of September 11, 2001. Although this sentiment can catalyze a sense of community, it often passes quickly.)

In personal terms, our acceptance of the public space means that we are willing to pay the costs of sending other people's children to school, helping other people have decent housing, providing aid in accidents and natural catastrophes, and reinforcing community through unrewarded acts. It is in the public space that we learn about each other's needs, from health care to barn raising, and we work together to meet these needs. It is through the public space that we are able to transform ourselves from a lonely crowd of competing, alienated individuals into a healthy, interdependent society. Linkages between people, as well as facts, values, and context, are learned through our social involvement. In the public space, we learn about transcending class exploitation and find ways not to poison our waterways or pollute our factory workers for profit. The individual knows and continues to discover the interlinked relationship that people and nature have. Where there is dialogue with a purpose, as for example in the jury system, the general will is suffused into the common good.

A central purpose of the laws of modern democracy is to attend to the public space, where common understandings and a common good are forged inside and out of the public sphere. This is why a democratic Constitution recognizes the permeable wall between the public and the private, ensuring the primacy of political, economic, and social rights in both the public and private spheres. Individual rights, therefore, are no longer a privilege granted by the few as a method of self-protection against the many. Instead, these rights are the very meaning of social responsibility to one another.

Notwithstanding the problems of degradation and content-neutral democracy (that is, in either a capitalist, socialist, or some hybrid form), when democracy retains the principle of expanding self-rule, it is a great achievement in human history, for people who are beyond the palace court or legislative chamber are "seen" and can "say." Democracy opened the doors of possibility to those for whom the doors were hidden. The question is whether modern communication adds to or detracts from the possibilities of self-rule.

Whereas in the past it was assumed that to govern one needed control over the church and the armed forces, it now appears that control is also exercised through the media. Control is accomplished by the amount of time the ordinary citizen and child gives over to passivity—the sine qua non of television, the emptying of thought and action from politics and the narrowing of the public space and communication. In terms of television, it does not matter what is watched so long as the person is kept from acting with others. The political Right has been able to link passivity and anger at the media to action that is even to the right of most of the media. Conservatives claim the media are "liberal" even though a far better case can be made for the claim that their programming reflects the desires of people framed by capitalist realism peppered with programs of violence, whether police, criminal, or modern warrior.

SEPARATING THE REPUBLIC FROM DEMOCRACY

De Tocqueville did no service to American democracy by conflating democracy and republic. More likely this was done for his own political purposes, since he wanted to shift the views of his own class, which supported neither the French Revolution nor democracy in any form. So, to make democracy palatable, he showed that different classes, but not races, could live together in one constitutional setup. American democracy sought to go much farther than he envisioned, although he noted that the thrust for inclusivity had already begun to undercut traditional modes of domination and a rigid class system.

Since the American and French Revolutions, features of democracy have been adopted in the American experience to fit within another form, namely, the constitutional republic. As noted in the *Federalist* No. 10, the task of governing is delegated to a small number of citizens who act for the rest.[8] As the nation grew, national governmental responsibility fell to a group of guardians through election and selection. Although a republic has the advantages of stability and relative coherence as a political form, it is indirect, predicated on a mix of authoritarian, oligarchic, and popular institutions that are meant to give the appearance of counterweights to each other. It accepts the idea of elitism by social class, blood, and sometimes merit.

The republic is a conservative form with some openness on issues of technology change in the context of private ownership. Except in their willingness to ride the technological whirlwind, its managers and leaders are conservative by inclination and social character. Its education and media systems often create stories about the past and human nature intended to fit with the reinforcement of institutions and authority as they already exist.[9] The average citizen accepts such stories, believing that a public life for the average citizen is less important than the private. Although the highest appellation a person may have is that of citizen, in the republic it is privacy that a person cares most about.[10]

Modern democracy, as opposed to the republic, is based on the belief that, since the great revolutions of the eighteenth century and the technological revolutions of the nineteenth and twentieth centuries, there has been a formidable dynamic of change, creating the type of continuing turbulence that cannot rest inside a republic. Instead, the entire body politic fought its way, both violently and nonviolently, into the governing process in a real and not ornamental way. There is a double reason for this. Twenty-first-century problems are so difficult that they require the participation of as many who care to participate in their solution as possible. Note, for example, the pandemic of AIDS, which requires that virtually all modern knowledge be harnessed to change community mores to successfully confront the disease. Conversely, to the extent that people are left out of any rational process, they become objects of others and often enslaved. Given the beliefs that society's task is to promote the welfare of all its inhabitants and that decency and dignity are aspects of happiness, democracy becomes the best form for self- and group expression.

In a reciprocal sense, democracy works best through liberalism. Both are predicated on bringing forward the most creative impulses in a person through interaction, exchange of experience, public participation in a common discourse, and the arrangement of institutions to ensure that they will seek to fulfill the objective of dignity and decency for all members of society. Liberal democracy allows its citizenry to make its own mistakes, both in crafting laws and undertaking choices in personal lives. Those who craft an agenda of social reconstruction are well aware that terrible mistakes can be made, but never so great as those that issue forth from tyranny, where there is no check either on the power of command or the use of force, whether subtle or blatant.

Democratic liberals accepted second-stage liberalism, that is, the welfare state, but as Lewis Mumford put it in *The Myth of the Machine*, the welfare state brought no revolution anywhere:

> Thus the fears of the older capitalist establishment have proved unfounded: the welfare provisions, the pensions, insurance against illness, accident, unemployment, higher incomes, and a larger share of mass production—all these once-revolutionary demands have in fact stabilized the power system, not overthrown it. What is more, in the United States, no less than in Soviet Russia or China, these accommodations have only served to bind the entire population to official agencies of power.[11]

History has a way of playing tricks on what appears to be settled. The capitalist class, both the corporatist and the laissez-faire wings, merely tolerated the welfare state for strategic reasons having to do with fear of violent eruptions from those neither heard nor seen. The welfare state was a hard-won concession that legislative conservatives agreed to only where they could turn the welfare state system into one benefiting the economically striving, and where necessary, into a control system over the poor.[12] The more farseeing political leaders saw the welfare state as a necessary adjustment to keep republicanism in place.

FEARS AND DEGRADATION
OF DEMOCRACY AND THE REPUBLIC

The "contracted out state" creates a complement to the national security state, where the official state apparatus operates primarily under the guise of secrecy. The contracted out state seeks to escape liability as the agent of the state, while taking full advantage of its "private" status, shielding itself from public interference.[13] This is what is meant by the idea that government should be run as a business, where the citizenry is reduced to the status of consumer without access to the "trade secrets" of the national security apparatus or voice in the political economy. Being a consumer changes the meaning of political inclusion. Citizenship carries the idea that citizens will have some minute quantum of political power. However, being a consumer and being a citizen are quite different.

In twentieth-century America there were three levels of political engagement in the public sphere. These defined the republic and the appearance of democracy. The first level was the actual power to be part of the public play: to write, produce, and direct it. This came from wealth and blood, ambition, and, sometimes, intellectual acumen. The second was the ticket to watch the play being performed. The seats were occupied by the body politic, which from time to time may have affected the play by refusing to attend or booing those on stage so vociferously that other actors got to perform. Access to the play is what some refer to as a constitutional right. There was a third group, the associates who were acted on. They were thought of as problems, because they wanted to enter the theater and sit in the seats or even get on stage. They are the ones who might have friends in the crowded theater who yell "fire" to empty out the theater so that the seats can be filled with associates.

The chosen task of the theater owners and producers in the republic is to make politics into a form of entertainment, which gives the various classes of associates the belief that they are in attendance, participating and making choices. This is politainment. Politainment's purpose is to give circuses without bread; note President Clinton's efforts to advance civil rights and the role television plays (at its popular best) as a time waster and purveyor of "nothing." (So said the producer of *Seinfeld*.) Politainment is used to avoid a fundamental democratic purpose: changing relations among individuals and classes and narrowing differences while protecting variation and diversity. In this process, modern democracy retains its protean character.

In the actual workings of democracy, groups and interests are left out, problems not considered, self-rule contradicted, and power elites not held publicly accountable. This suggests that, like liberalism itself, the different problems the body politic faces or brings to the surface are not easily dealt with. They are not adequately dealt with through television choice making or politics constructed as entertainment, nor can they be dealt with in terms of interest group politics' horse-trading alone, or by the "enlightened" elites.

The twentieth century leaves open the question of whether the ideal sham democracies, oligarchic republics, theocracies, and authoritarian or national security states can stop humanity from committing suicide by means of war, consumerism, environmental plundering, and increasing deep economic disparities. It is also unclear whether against these problems democratic self-rule can protect political rights that were won and sanctified as part of the struggle for human rights.

There is a postmodern technological fascism that fills as many personal and social spaces as possible and permits the use of surveillance and control as defenses against the unknown and the Other. In the past these activities would have been evidence of totalitarianism to be confronted, but they are now accepted as ordinary and necessary. The rise of internal "security concerns," from controls exercised to obtain entrance into corporate and public buildings, to surveillance at banks, schools, and factories, to the massive increase of sophisticated surveillance devices and private police and security forces, is a manifestation of new and old forms of control. It should be noted that all of these features of the modern controlled state were present before September 11, 2001. Each of these features has been deepened and widened now to include elements of the military, who seem to have the power to "cross the Rubicon, the Potomac" if necessary, for security purposes. During Richard Nixon's presidency a member of his White House staff put forward a plan to handle antiwar demonstrators and restore "stability" in American life by organizing the CIA, FBI, national security apparatus, and military into a coordinating unit for information and joint undertakings, which could include break-ins, harassment, and so forth. Even J. Edgar Hoover objected.[14] But what was asked for then and thought to be excessive and an example of protofascism by a majority of the Democratic Party in Congress, as well as Republicans, is now accepted with alacrity by all officials and the vast majority of Americans. The second Bush administration proclaims the Huston Plan—and then some.

THE LIMITS OF THE CONSTITUTION
AND MODERN DEMOCRACY

Although there is nothing to suggest that the billionaires or millionaires need to be unduly concerned, buried within the fundamental meaning of democracy is the eighteenth-century French revolutionary position about democracy and self-rule. This would allow the poor to take back what had been stolen from them by the rich.[15] In the United States, it was the Federalists who feared those without property and argued that Jefferson was leading a Jacobin revolutionary movement in the United States.[16]

To the chagrin of twentieth-century conservatives, this sentiment, in attenuated form, can be found in the work of John Dewey and in the program of the third stage of liberalism, whether in the United States or elsewhere. According to John Dewey, the flowering of human beings, to use his term, "can be attained only as control of the means of production and distribution is taken out of the hands of individuals who exercise powers created socially for narrow individual interests."[17] The ends of liberalism in this sense remain valid, according to Dewey. "But the means of attaining them demand a radical change in economic institutions and the political arrangements based upon them. These changes are necessary in order that social control of forces and agencies socially created may accrue to the liberation of all individuals associated together in the great undertaking of building a life that expresses and promotes human liberty."[18] It is unlikely that these purposes can be attained through the Republican Party or centrist elements of the Democratic Party.

As is well known, major twentieth-century struggles for economic, social, and gender equality first occurred outside of the two major parties. It was only after the parties feared delegitimation in the eyes of their voting constituencies that they adjusted to the demands of movements. From the Left this required a redefinition of the Constitution in reaction to race, gender, and to some extent, class. This need for social and political readjustment led to the question of how texts are to be taken in politics, for in a society organized around written literacy and stability, ritual texts are emblems of legitimacy.

The Constitution to the conservative is not a document of inclusion. Jurisprudential conservatives such as Chief Justice William Rehnquist and Associate Justice Antonin Scalia have powerful intentions, which begin from the resurrection of the decisions of a pre–New Deal Supreme Court, for they fear the Jacobin "virus." It is not surprising that their ideas do not comport with virtually any variant of democracy, and so a harsh question needs consideration. Suppose the courts accept a passive position because of homeland defense. It is likely that constitutional guarantees will disappear or at the least be narrowed for the suspect and the different in times of crisis, a crisis that appears to have no end given the goals of the executive and Congress. (Note those held incommunicado after September 11, 2001.)

In the United States, those who profess democracy might then ask whether the purposes of modern liberal democracy can be attained within the confines of the present Constitution. We need to ask whether conservatives, who insist that the Constitution does not envisage democracy except in the most constricted sense, are correct in their analysis. Do they have sufficient legitimating support among an electorate that increasingly does not vote or is merely part of the consumer democracy where dollars are voting passports to the accumulation of opportunities? Does this mean that those committed to political and economic democracy should admit to the constricted nature of the Constitution and seek a new constitution that befits a modern democracy? Or is the Constitution, with its amending process, subject to constant revision in light of changing customs and needs? Is a different set of tactics for constitutional revision necessary, such as constitutional conventions for amendments? Furthermore, does the balance of contending forces in society obviate the radical step of "starting over" with a new constitution? There is justifiable suspicion at such a choice. The Soviet Constitution of 1935, prepared by the communist leader Nicolai Bukharin, seemed to guarantee rights and the flowering of the person. Stalin adopted it, and the horrifying purges intensified.[19]

Those engaged in political struggle and public policy know that the answer to human liberty is not found only in a document, even if that document begins with "We the People" and has a Bill of Rights. It is in the spirit of the people, but which people? Is it the people as a whole, or the poor, middle class, or rich? Is it the people at any one time, or their institutions as developed and organized over a period of time? The question of what "We the People" means in the Constitution cannot be taken for granted; if the writers of the Constitution believed that they were describing who they thought the class known as people was, this was reflected in the constitutional compromise that counted slaves as three-fifths of a person for voting purposes.

Because the anti-Federalists did not believe that the Constitution answered all questions, the amending process also included provisions for a constitutional convention. Civil war was, however, the preferred method of resolving the question of who was to be included in the phrase "We the People." The nation has used the amending process to broaden the meaning of "We the People" beyond its original historical context, through the Thirteenth (outlawing slavery), Fourteenth (granting equal rights and citizenship to persons of all races), Fifteenth (rights cannot be abridged because of race), and Nineteenth (right to vote cannot be abridged because of gender) Amendments. Yet, it appears that such constitutional agreements do not have plain meanings, for African Americans and women (who were not initially included in the amendments) seem unable to find the proper language that will change their arguably subservient status in society.[20]

Before the Right Wing ascended to the White House with Reagan, the Right and conservatives were most serious about seeking formal changes to the Constitution. They sought to restore a fundamentalist conservatism without touching the character of the capitalist system as it pertains to property and private ownership, while tolerating racism and sexism. Rightist single-issue movements called for a constitutional convention on such matters as prayer, antiabortion, and balanced budget amendments.

Liberals have not favored a new constitution.[21] They feared what the character of a constitutional convention would bring, arguing that a new convention would create a far more reactionary, authoritarian document than the republican ideas embodied in the Constitution. Liberals supported the republican, nondemocratic framework because of their fear of what the citizenry might decide in a convention. The liberal fear was linked to the concern of what majorities could do to minorities, assuming majorities are invariably unthinking mobs as opposed to deliberative fractions of a whole. Condemning Socrates to death has stood as the classic statement of how democratic majorities do very stupid things to those holding opposing opinions.[22] Since Socrates' suicide, aristocrats and their intellectual supporters have used his death as the key argument against majority rule. Barriers against the repeat of such domestic error must be constructed, according to aristocrats.

Ironically, conservatives also argue against minorities who seek to assert their will over "majorities." In this case, conservatives attack environmental and affirmative action groups for attempting to tyrannize their meaning of the majority.

The twentieth century also saw rightist grass-roots organizations claim the flag of nationalism, community, and fundamentalist values, seeking to claim faith and spirit as their political views. The thrust of their various movements appears on the surface to be Populist, anticentralist, and fearful of government to the point of secession. They remain committed to romantic ideas of individualist capitalism but which give oligopolic corporations the legitimacy they need to organize modern economic life. Rightist movements have kept the economic system of oligopoly capitalism and corporatism off the table of concern, instead restricting their discomfort to issues such as abortion, pornography, crime, and religious faith in the public space. They wish for a strong state to ensure the frayed nuclear family and the role of patriarchy domestically and in public institutions. On the other hand, they call for a weak state on issues that seek various forms of equality, reinforcing managerial corporatism as the new form of legitimacy. Their intention is to narrow the public social space where equality and equal access to resources outside their own immediate community might occur.

DISSOLUTION AND DEMOCRACY

Before the 11 September 2001 attack on the United States the undertone in American life, reflected across all ideological sectors of the population, was toward decentralization. Secessionist movements forced the breakup of the Soviet Union, which had been pasted together by war, fear of attack from the West, and imperial expansion. In the twentieth century, such movements had little support in the American context, with the exception of Puerto Rico and aborted attempts in the Southwest. Continued expansion of the American state was taken for granted, as in the case of Hawaii and Alaska, with few interested in secession. Conservatives did emphasize their rhetoric of locality and fear of the city, which presented itself as an alien world on American shores. There was a special place for an embattled Southern white culture, different from the rest of the United States. Southern values carried the residue of secession, reflected in states' insistence on flying the Confederate flag.

Since 1890 white Southerners who sought a weak central government have held extraordinary power in all three federal branches. The Civil War was merely a stage in the battle over who controlled the federal government. For example, white Southerners were able to promulgate segregation until 1964, when it was finally broken by citizen movements that changed attitudes in the federal courts and the federal government. Economically, the movement of capital from government and the private sector (in the form of defense contracts) into the South also helped to shift overt racism. On the other hand, distrust of the government retained its hold on white Southerners, as evidenced in elections using the Jeffersonian language of "States Rights," as well as the romanticization of the "Southern way of life."[23] Gentility of the "better classes" economically and socially hid the truncheon of the white sheriff. That truncheon was very much in evidence when used to defend the White Citizens Councils. But by the 1960s the truncheon and the councils politically were the club of weakness. The white Southern oligarchies knew that there was no possibility except to stay in the Union, and if possible to guide it. And in this regard the Southern oligarchies succeeded because of the seniority system in Congress, which resulted in enormous power residing in committee chairs, first through the Democratic Party and then the Republican Party, after Lyndon Johnson signed the Civil Rights Act of 1964. Conservative politicians played the strings of localism, which resonated in most geographic areas and in reinforcing a white Southern Democrat–Republican coalition.

The underlying sentiment that framed American politics was that localism and local government protected citizens against centralism and personal liberty. The juxtaposition between a weak central government, as related to economic policy, and acceptance of the structural power of great corporations found its ideological and operational home in both political parties.[24] Each party emulated the other by establishing the election system as the means to keep out interlopers.

The end of the Cold War increased the decentralist/dissolution mood. People were less concerned with the heroics of war and triumphalism. The mood of the nation was to find normalcy, but what was normalcy? For the second Bush administration the 2000 election was an attempt to find a new conservatism and a more humble nation on the world scene yet be able to overwhelm all other nations militarily. The idea was taken as gospel that all politics is local, as claimed by former Democratic Party Speaker of the House of Representatives Tip O'Neill. This sensibility dominated as regional, class, gender, and racial animosities appeared to gain the upper hand in the national body politic. Public responsibility was to be narrowed, with national identification of people coming only through commodity standardization. Racial equality and poverty were no longer national questions but instead were to be resolved on a state-by-state basis. General welfare, as determined through congressional action and authorized by the Constitution, was, through Clinton's boomerang philosophy of bipartisanship, to be determined by the fifty states. Where too many blacks were elected to Congress through redistricting, the Supreme Court would discover a means to force new elections on the spurious ground of "peculiarly shaped congressional districts."[25]

Devolution of authority is invariably a struggle in governing. The heavy hand of Jefferson and believers in town meetings claimed that democracy, in the sense of participation, can only be a local affair, where individual voices can best be heard. This was the way to answer the problem of anomie and alienation. To the extent that there was a coherent conservative position, it would appear to be one that took its cues from restricting the federal rights of due process. Speech and association could be further curbed and decided upon at the local and state levels. The political result was clear, that there could be no uniform national view on contentious social issues, such as abortion, welfare, religion in public schools, and affirmative action, whether defined qualitatively or quantitatively.[26] In practice, this meant an attempt to return those who had won or secured rights since the New Deal to associate status. To this end, the nation has revisited the principle that states should be able to impose their will against federal law, except where the Right held otherwise, as in the *Bush v. Gore* Supreme Court decision.[27]

Conservative locality is a dangerous policy. Interposition is fraught with political danger. The Balkanization of the nation into warring ethnic groups, and a new type of local sheriff and police control responsible to local oligarchies and international corporations, is already in the wings. The withering away of the democratic nation will leave the people at the mercy of a new type of technocommunications state of nature, where there is neither accountability nor responsibility. Power and accountability will have to fall somewhere. It was not accidental that Newt Gingrich, with his commitment to technofuturism and decentralization, represented a congressional district almost completely dependent on Lockheed Martin, which is in turn dependent on Pentagon high-tech defense contracts. To such conservatives the federal government's major purpose was to act as tax collector for the Department of Defense, which contracts with defense corporations such as Lockheed Martin.

Beyond this brokerage purpose, the federal government was to honor a version of John C. Calhoun's conception of states' rights. Republicans built on the 1955 Southern Manifesto, which used the Tenth Amendment to defend segregation on the ground that rights were reserved to the states and the people. In the 1996 presidential campaign, Bob Dole sought to curry favor with white Southern voters by praising the Tenth Amendment at every turn, leaving the impression that he would undo civil rights legislation and that states' rights would be paramount in his administration. These ideas were already present in Supreme Court decisions that cut back centralized authority and extended the role individual states played in controlling wages and hours for their employees.

There is a chasm between those who hold that social reconstruction through federal initiatives should act as the catalyst to extend deliberating and implementing democracy, where the federal government acts as the enabler to broaden the participatory and deliberative framework for all people at the local level, and the dissolutionists who seek to turn federal responsibilities over to local oligarchies and private corporations. This was the way of both the Clinton and the second Bush administrations, with the latter calling for a stronger federal role in education. However, the profound irony in American politics is the second Bush administration's legitimacy, which seeks a centralization of power that would have shocked the late conservative Robert Taft.

The Republican party zigzagged after September 11 in ways Lenin and Stalin would have understood. The centralization of power increased manyfold, from education to national security and internal security, even in the face of the administration's loss of the popular vote. Bush had the terrorists to thank for the change in the Republican Party's practice, if not its ideology. Patriotism took the place of reasoned deliberation. Older men told younger men that like Nathan Hale they should regret they had but one life to give to the nation. (Shades of the Allah terrorists?) In national security and defense matters, the second Bush administration took on virtually dictatorial powers.

ORIGINAL INTENT AND LOCAL CONTEXT

It was clear to the Constitution's originators that the federal government had to play a central role in the economic development of the United States. Even the doubters of the Hamiltonian position, such as Jefferson, construed the Constitution's general welfare clause to contemplate a common good through protection of the creditor commercial class. This clause was meant as a political tool to confront those very forces in society that sought to claim individual interest over the common good. This is made clear in the debates of the Constitutional Convention.[28] It was also an instrument—as Randolph Bourne, the gifted antiworld war commentator, argued in his essay on the state—to ensure that a less hierarchic form of government would be eschewed, one that held egalitarianism as the primary value.

The "back to the future" myths we carry in our heads—about how the nation of the twenty-first century is to be bound by the same Whig principles that some believed framed the political and social behavior of the fledgling American statesmen—are difficult to reconcile with present and likely future realities or needs.[29] Myths about historical realities help our minds to leap from context to universal myths. This is a seductive intellectual enterprise, fraught with danger.

A group of coastal colonial settlements inhabited by four million people, a quarter of whom were slaves, is not the same as a multiethnic nation that claims for itself single superpower status in a world its leaders hardly know or understand. In 1790 there were literally only a handful of corporations within the United States, and they were on a short leash, governed by time-limited charters. The British West India Company was not seen as a model for American economic development.

RIGHTS OF THE EXCLUDED

As the United States struggles to become a modern democracy, dropping the three-tier nature of citizenship, its racial and gender composition can only lead to changes in values and priorities that are consistent with a democratic definition of personhood, a multicultural society, and the reemergence of a democratic social character. Except under the exigency of war, not many would dare to embrace dominant nineteenth-century attitudes toward citizenship, which were, as de Tocqueville made clear, not contemplated to include blacks or Indians as citizens.[30] As we are now painfully aware, they were to be regarded as either chattel or the Enemy Other. Nor was it assumed that women would be citizens who could speak and act in the public space with or without male permission. Chinese immigrants were guest workers and were treated as half-slaves as they joined others in building the American railroad system.[31] It was only during the Reconstruction period, which lasted twelve years, that this dominant attitude was legally and socially challenged.

Overcoming these formidable political failings occurred despite the written words of the Constitution, which were interpreted in their most racist way. Even in the notorious *Plessy v. Ferguson* case, a generation after the Civil War, apartheid was written into American law, and it stayed there on the state and local levels into the 1960s. It was only then that struggles for modern democracy in the cultural realm began in earnest. The current struggles over multiculturalism can be seen as reflecting the changed character of the nation's religious beliefs and their centrality.

Although there are fundamentalist ministers who preach the gospel of virtue, acting as avenging Authority and practicing fear of the Other, there are no American ministers who are prepared to lead slaughters against Hispanics and Indians, as was the case after the Civil War.[32] The social pressures within churches were often painfully hypocritical about homosexuality, as reflected in the high incidence of homosexuality and child abuse finally acknowledged in 2000. The newly found religious and other rights and powers of women to transform the male-dominated hierarchy within institutions reached every denomination. Ironically, they were fueled by the dictates of the market, which seeks new customers for products through the stimulation of hitherto unawakened desires and needs.

The entire conception of rights has changed as well. Rights, which tend to mean political equality for and between groups, have resulted in a profoundly different sense of personhood, in reality and as a goal. Rights reflected human concern and the essence of what it meant to be human. As rights were conceived more broadly, obligations were to be met through the taxing process. Attempts were made to set limits on that type of individualism that results in the withdrawal of material resources for frivolous personal use over the demonstrated needs of the society. It is important to note, however, that by and large these attempts failed. The nation continued to genuflect to an individualism that failed to ensure a decent society for all those who were accorded rights but who did not have property as ordinarily defined in market capitalism. As a result of the "liberal-minded" population, people from different social classes had entitlements, a form of IOU from the government.

This has put the nation in a quandary, for an expansion of rights has affected the character of governing. Rights' expansion is nothing new. Much of the New Deal was given over to turning rights into entitlements. These entitlements carried cash and government-ensured aid in the category of a property right. Medicare and Medicaid became new types of property rights. Although they were rights and entitlements to the individual, they were predicated on community responsibility. In economic terms, these rights and entitlements were often subsidies to the middle class, as in the case of Medicare. It was a misnomer to speak of redistributing property when considering entitlements, for conservatives demanded to know how the nation could justify taking property (taxable income and wealth) even though subsidies increase the property of the well-off in the capitalist welfare state. (For example, metro stops near private property increase its value for home owners.)

We may think of rights as a social invention for attaining freedom in the context of democracy (in whatever stage). Just as likely, rights emerge from the biological nature and spiritual needs of humanity. That which is natural and that which is biological are melded together. Such melding may cause some concern, as in the case of the feeble-minded who may have sex drives and want to marry and procreate, or in the case of compulsive talkers who claim the right of speech as a natural right to talk all the time. Abnormalities or aberrant behavior in no way change the fundamental relationship between rights and nature for one and all. In a political sense, rights are more than individualist protections. They are the necessary social understanding to ensure that all people in the first instance are accorded that set of protections that distinguishes the human from the nonhuman.[33]

Rights, therefore, are protected through both the past and the group, and they are fulfilled with others. They emerge from their socially interdependent character, which then defines individuality. Our genetic histories are statements of our dependencies and interdependencies. It is understood that individualism begins with the person's death, not his or her birth. Then we can claim to be individualists. Otherwise we remain dependent and interdependent on one another from the beginning of life until we die. I have used this metaphor to reinforce Spinoza's notion that a free person dwells on life, not death. That which is life affirming has certain features that cannot be reflected in the sole individual but only in the group or the body politic as a whole.

The democratic political purpose is to increase the possibilities for practical and organic linkage between the pursuit of happiness, dignity, creativity, caring, wise judgment, and social justice among the people. Such objectives seem to be disconnected from public policy and are thought to be disconnected from each other. These admittedly distant objectives cannot be achieved in the present national security state, encased in a constitutional republic whose operational powers are ceded to global corporations and a warrior organization and mentality. The organic features I have mentioned are subverted by those tortuous religious beliefs that avert humanity's eyes from itself, exchanging what it can see and think about for the illusions of the hereafter. Unfortunately, many scientists also reject the here and now by claiming no responsibility for the present or their methods and social outcomes.

Modern democratic objectives are not, and cannot be, the purposes of the national security state. Nor can democratic goals be achieved in an unfettered capitalist system guided by its oligopolistic and largest financial entities. Similarly, they cannot emerge from a society that does not recognize that this is a de facto multicultural society. The question is whether the society will be one that does not guarantee covert white supremacy through clever but tortured readings of the law. While the ideals of the constitutional republic can be teased out of the preamble and the Bill of Rights, they do not go to the heart of the actual behavior of the government. It is only within the context of moving to the next stage, constitutional democracy, that structural issues of the economy and the national security apparatus can be confronted. In this context, the rule of law is a boundary setter meant to compromise the past, present, and future, with greater weight given to past understandings except where shifts in underlying social, economic, and legal struggles occur.

THE RULE OF LAW

The rule of law is the politics of the past laid on the present and future. Its hallowed nature may be no more than the product of a power grab, as for example Chief Justice John Marshall's decision that the Supreme Court had the power to declare congressional acts unconstitutional. The Supreme Court's task was to decide the boundaries Congress had to live within and to limit the power of Jefferson and the antirepublicans, much the way the conservative Rehnquist court was able to ensure its ideas by installing George W. Bush as president.

Law can never be value neutral, for neither justice nor injustice is value neutral. It is humanly constructed out of interest, purpose, consequence, and affections. It can therefore grow out of empirical judgments and "ought" considerations that are the markers for modern democracy. And because the rule of law is a conglomerate of the politics of the past, the rule of law will invariably include just and unjust principles, the venal and sometimes the noble. In other words, genuflection to the "rule of law" can be a disaster when it means following the unjust, as in the case where freedom is inhibited or destroyed just because these were the laws of the past, as for example in the Dred Scott decision.

For value neutralists, the purpose of law is to settle conflicts without bloodshed and without caring which side wins. It aims at getting the problem at hand out of the way. Concern about right and wrong is secondary. We know that law is not the same for rich and poor. Anger against the Warren court was based on its willingness to cast human rights as more important than property. The rule of law was no longer primarily the rule for the protection of property. Human rights, in a legal sense, occupied center stage. This period was short lived, as conservatives made claims that liberal judges were "result" oriented. This meant that they were building new definitions of what and who law was to defend. It seemed that the Warren court was claiming that the motto on the Supreme Court building was wrong. It should not have read "justice under law" but "law under justice." As judges who understood and were prepared to look honestly at American reconstruction, they judged well.

If democracy is the framework rather than constricted ideas of property, law, and the republic, judges will follow the Warren court and widen their focus when determining justice. Like other political, social, and legal institutions of society, they will be required to redefine property and the legally inviolate character of corporations so that they serve a common good. They will be called upon, and no doubt be pushed, to do so through communications and technology and to look internationally for wisdom. In this sense the rule of law as it relates to precedent and symmetry would be refocused and linked to clearly articulated democratic values, which would then affect and inform law. Such laws may be found in other nations as well. It has been difficult for international law to find its voice at the table of raw power as a credible instrument to trump naked power; comparative law has, in the past, found its relevance limited. However, as a result of instant communications, it may be that laws and decisions of other courts will insinuate themselves into and then change the character of municipal law.

Rules of a nation's economic responsibilities for the well-being of the person could be codified as a frame of reference from which a particular nation would judge its law. The human rights covenants would be given added weight if judges and legislatures would learn how other nations apply international law.

THE JUDICIARY: FAIRNESS FOR DEMOCRACY?

Not since Franklin Roosevelt have progressives and liberals concerned with social reconstruction taken seriously the need to revise the obvious oligarchic elements of government. It is unfortunate that liberals show little interest in changing the Supreme Court from its present oligarchic role in American life to one that derives its power directly from the citizenry. Other than fear of the electorate, there is no reason why federal judges should not be elected officials, as state judges are in a number of states. In an ironic turn, since Franklin Roosevelt's attempts to liberalize the Supreme Court by changing its number and the rules for membership, until 2000 it was the conservatives who learned the value of attacking the Supreme Court as elitist and antidemocratic—that is, until the majority of the Court delivered the 2000 election to Bush.

Even the Court's most liberal member as of 1997 decried any system of elected judges, on the grounds that they are open to the problem of financing costly campaigns and currying favor from particular groups, which would lead to tainted judicial decision making. Justice John Paul Stevens's concern does not go to the election of judges but to the problem of how to ensure that judges are not "bought," a recurring problem throughout history, and how they will recognize that in many instances property does not liberate but constricts disinterest.

During much of the twentieth century the assumption of progressives and New Dealers was that the federal judiciary comprised the financially well-off, who carried out the wishes of an ownership class implicitly or explicitly and whose most important complementary task was to resolve conflicts within the ownership class while keeping order among the unpropertied and providing protection from dissenters.[34] It was taken for granted that judges were profoundly antidemocratic by virtue of social and economic class, and more important, in the *way* they protected corporate property and ensured order. However, by 1937 not even judges wanted to be known as enemies of democracy. Once the Court was under attack, the decisions of its members changed. The character of the Court, as it related to individual rights, changed after the 1937 Court-packing fight. Against the backdrop of the civil rights movements, Warren's Supreme Court became an important teacher of the law and its relationship to democratic aspirations and human rights. If judges could escape the modern methods of campaigning and fund raising, their election could take on a deliberative function itself. The participation of the citizenry in law making and interpretation becomes an important element in democratic reconstruction and is made more so through the election of judges. Why is this eccentric idea of importance at the beginning of the twenty-first century? The Supreme Court has reverted to its conservative ways on questions of race, as the distinguished political scientist Peter Irons has pointed out. (The laws become an instrument of neglect and abuse, all under the guise of states' rights, strict scrutiny, and claims of reverse discrimination, thereby in a legal and de facto way reasserting segregated education.)[35]

DEMOCRACY VERSUS OLIGARCHY

Historians are not above reinforcing the picture of an inescapable human condition, which claims that from one generation to another, those with wealth who meld with those in power, that is, transient political leaders, will retain their command. "Is there not in short, whatever the society and whatever the period, an insidious law giving power to the few, an irritating law it must be said, since the reasons for it are not obvious. And yet this is a stubborn fact, taunting us at every turn. We cannot argue with it; all the evidence agrees."[36]

But argue and fight against this "law" we must, for not to is to surrender ourselves to immobility and servility. We would be accepting oppression as the given of human existence. Liberalism rightly abhors this view. Since the revolutions of the eighteenth century every generation has renewed this struggle by encouraging humanity to see the Other as human through confrontation, persuasion, and the organization of democratic institutions. This project defines the democratic and liberating aspects of American life. The 1960s liberation struggles were no exception.

3

★

Giving Birth to
Third-Stage Liberalism

OUR PARENTS AND GRANDPARENTS: THE NEW LEFT

T he students of the New Left had their roots in the 1950s work of the
sociologist C. Wright Mills and the 1930s League for Industrial Democracy, an organization that the fiercely anticommunist John Dewey
helped to form.[1] Mills reflected on the idea that there was a power elite in the
nation and that certain elements of liberalism had descended to "crackpot realism," meaning that politics and international affairs were reduced to sophisticated calculations based on absurd and unexamined assumptions. None
was more absurd than the one-dimensional nature of nuclear war preparation.[2] Mills was joined in this academic revision of America's understanding
of itself by William Appleman Williams, a U.S. Naval Academy graduate and
University of Wisconsin historian. Williams set out to prove that American
foreign policy was not the story of innocents abroad but of a new-style imperialism that linked democratic ideals with the political and economic business of exploitation. Students produced various documents, from the journal
Studies on the Left to the Port Huron Statement, which sought to escape the
traditional categories of the Cold War. The Port Huron Statement, a quintes-
sential liberal statement that could have been written by any left New Dealer,
seemed to reconnect to earlier reform movements that had sought social reconstruction. Yet, in its public relations stance the New Left presented itself
as not having an "agenda" of ideas that could be turned into policies and programs. This stance alarmed those who had been part of the Cold War liberal
struggle against communism and the Soviet Union. Just as so-called mainline
organizations such as the Urban League and the National Association for the

Advancement of Colored People (NAACP) feared that more militant action taken by the Congress of Racial Equality and the Student Nonviolent Coordinating Committee would create animosity with Cold War liberals, so it was that the same fears existed in organizations such as the Americans for Democratic Action, which had a tenuous hold on "respectability" during the Cold War. The New Left challenged that respectability and its value and cost as an independent liberal voice.

The New Left could not be easily pigeonholed. Before it was torn by sectarian disputes it rejected communism and war, but its members were not absolute pacifists. New leftists called for a transformation of institutions that were honed in what was thought to be a liberal time. The Old Left was influenced by pyramidal notions of hierarchy and centralized state socialism, while the New Left found comfort in Adam Smith's ideas of trade and small-scale entrepreneurial capitalism, not understanding that the Brandeis view of capitalism had become an exercise in nostalgia, much as countercultural lifestyles and economic forms were either marginalized or absorbed.

The New Left seemed to be calling for a new covenant of the kind reflected in the work of Emily Balch, the Nobel Prize-winning peace activist; Jane Addams of Hull House; Eugene Debs, the socialist labor leader; and W. E. B. DuBois, the black historian and radical activist; Supreme Court Justice Frank Murphy and Lewis Mumford. These early twentieth-century thinker–activists sought a government and a civil society that would end racism, economic disparity, the ravages of war, and callous treatment of the poor. In other words, their fundamental purpose was to change the values and attitudes of a warrior and economic corporate society.[3] But such notions on the political horizon in the 1960s appeared utopian even to those who were often praised (mistakenly) as having a "wider" view that encompassed reformist social forces.

In the 1960s the leading diplomatic historian was George Kennan. Kennan had served in the Department of State, where he was the leading exponent of containment (which he later disclaimed) and covert actions in Eastern Europe while supporting a program to settle up with Stalin over Germany. Kennan, an elitist who was adopted by liberals for his seemingly reasonable attitudes toward the Soviet Union, complained bitterly about the New Left with its counterculture aspects. Movements were not orderly, and they seemed to be turning the world upside down in the United States and other nations as well. For some in the Center and an older Left familiar with history, there was a parallel to what had happened in England from 1640 to 1660 at the time of its continuing revolution and civil war, when England created and almost sustained a republic. At that time there were Ranters, Levellers, and Dissenters, with stunning antiauthoritarian and antiauthority claims on how to live, sexual liberation and divorce, civil liberties, free press and speech, how to share, and how to confront the state. Such ideas would have resonated well with the counterculturalists of Haight-Ashbury and Woodstock.[4]

Kennan claimed that the New Left was childish and that its impact would be transient since it had no program or fixed set of points and objectives linking to people in their day-to-day lives. The New Left had not systematized any discernible purpose. Kennan's snapshot of the 1960s showed that young people exhibited a mix of existential wail and bad manners, not knowing how or what to choose with their freedom. Kennan predicted that without a program that people understood and that could be put in place by orderly governments, the New Left, that is, the new subversive liberals of social reconstruction, were doomed to failure and therefore, as a movement or ensemble of ideas, the reconstructionists could not be taken seriously. Above all, Kennan was a man of prudent orderliness who feared the unruly and mobs. At different stages in his long career, and while in the government, he had favored settling with the Soviets rather than being stuck with the Cold War and its aftermath.

His criticism of the American New Left was either ignored or laughed at by young activists. It was seen as the ravings of a foolish conservative man. They thought he did not understand that cultural and political change had nothing to do with a political program of a self-appointed group, such as a communist party, or any political party that did not understand that political action grew out of need and cultural shifts. Change erupted often out of pain or a new consciousness. It could hardly be planned for, as Hannah Arendt opined at the time. David Riesman and Michael Maccoby in *The Liberal Papers* said the same thing when they first posited that black colleges were the bastion of passivity rather than an important instrument for social change.[5] According to Arendt in *On Revolution,* all any self-appointed or even representative group could do was ride the waves of history, be prepared to exercise power, and be opportunistic at the moment significant change was under way.[6]

Kennan believed that change was anything but accidental. He was more like Napoleon the planner, and during the Cold War he said that the Department of State should be reduced to three hundred officers who would plan and implement future policies like a general staff.[7] His experience was not with American culture or bureaucracy, nor was he enamored of democracy. As a young foreign service officer, he had written an unpublished novel that called for an authoritarian system in the United States.[8] Perhaps Kennan saw the young movement organizers as modern versions of the populist Narodniki of nineteenth-century Russia, who organized among the peasants. They pointed out people's hurts but did not know what to do with their diagnosis.[9] They agitated without direction. However, throughout the world of 1968, even without a political party, the sentiment that anything was possible was thought to be the key to massive social reconstruction. What did the Paris students say? "Imagine and dare the impossible!" For them, plans and programs, attempts of an incrementalist sort that did not recognize the wholly different situation of the modern world, were impediments from the past whose outdated techniques merely exacerbated the human condition. What the words of the movements called for was a profound shift in cultural values and what was valued. But that shift during its initial stages appeared to exclude women, who were caught as the servants of men in the New Left, liberal, and civil rights movements. However, this duality could not last, for women in fact were central to the operations of the various movements, and they found that the rhetoric of these movements did not equal the reality of their everyday lives in them. They had little decision-making power and found that in meetings they were not listened to, although when men said what the women said there was respect. Women found their political existence being denied.[10] It was inevitable that a women's movement would come into being, finding its sustenance in diverse and powerful struggles with radical men, the government, established political parties, and themselves. In the latter case, from the vantage point of the twenty-first century the issues raised seem tame. Women wanted to control their own bodies, and they wanted to find love where they could irrespective of gender.

In the early stages of the New Left movement, emphasis was placed on the idea of the local and fear of the state. Paul Goodman, the gifted man of letters and my colleague at the Institute for Policy Studies for a short period, became a guru to the young for his emphasis on personal responsibility coupled with individual freedom and encyclopedic knowledge in arts, philosophy, and letters.[11] In his own life Goodman fought against Stalinism, even FDR, from his anarchist positions. And throughout the early period of the Cold War he advocated direct small solutions that could be implemented outside of government , hierarchy, the mammoth corporations, and the national security state.

Parallel to this view, but also from an anarchist perspective, is that of Noam Chomsky. His work on politics overwhelms the reader and antagonist with facts (as distinct from his work in linguistics, where facts were introduced to buttress theory). His personal courage and profound commitment stemmed from his understanding of facts as they should relate to moral beliefs and action.

Chomsky practiced a different and unconventional political science that based itself on demystification of facts, leaders, intellectuals, and their purpose. His withering critiques built on the anarchist claim that the state is little more than the organization of violence.[12] Further, it is not ordinary people who either make war or betray revolutions; it is leaders.

These ideas, which are integral to American civilization, produced a theory and practice of organizing, even a program for social reconstruction.[13]

They have had convergent paths, attacking pyramidal institutions, unaccountability, poverty, and the alienation created by failed institutions in modern life.[14] These ideas and movements changed relationships between the sexes, broke legal apartheid, and changed attitudes to war and imperialism. But where were the movements to go for protection and sustenance? It was not enough to build communes at the margins or criticize the state. In a radically revised form the state was needed.

That is to say, the democracy of inclusivity was dependent on a change in mores and customs underwritten by an activist government. In practice, the civil rights and women's movements turned to federal intervention as the means of ensuring rights of inclusivity. (Liberal Democrats and their supporters in the Kennedy administration and the foundations supported SNCC, no doubt believing that its voter registration drive in the South would result in the registration of more Democrats.) Minorities and women looked to the federal government for increased employment as well. It was in the public sector that the greatest employment gains were made by the excluded groups.[15] Not surprisingly, those committed to the limits of governmental power but who favored the authoritarianism of unaccountable corporate power fought back. They feared the spread of democracy into the social and economic structures of the society. A "new society in the shell of the old" seemed to be coming into existence through the aid of national movements, federal laws, and regulations. Opponents to these trends used God and the family while co-opting the rhetoric of individualism and self-rule against "Big Brother" incursions into local and business mores. Whether in inflicting artificial consumer desires, remaking illusions, increasing production of the unnecessary while starving the public sector, or redirecting foundation funds toward the more conventional, the struggle remains drawn in every arena of twenty-first-century American life.[16]

THE NEW LEFT CHALLENGES THE SETTLED

Through much of the intellectual and political activity of the 1960s, there was a fundamental belief in the potential of American society beyond economic growth. The civic energies of people expanded the social spaces of liberation and dignity by the actions people took in their everyday lives. Projects evolved that were intended to challenge the "settled," that is, the status quo, and point the way toward a society that was not afraid of its own ideals. The projects would be the existential acts of those who began them, for they would be risking themselves in what they had initiated. They were part of what they started, and their very being was engaged in their success. This sentiment was not far away from ideas conservatives had of the market system, in which small business entrepreneurs risked themselves economically every day and took the chance of failure as a given while retaining freedom and choice to continue failing or succeeding.

Social entrepreneurialism differed somewhat from business entrepreneurialism. The likelihood of personal gain was never high. The idea of existential political risk, resulting in the common betterment of those who needed it, was a belief and hope rather than a proof. Two consequences were to emerge from social entrepreneurialism. One was that the project, be it a freedom school, an art collective, a drama company, a people's health clinic, a community-based economic development corporation, or a rape crisis center, would challenge the dominant assumptions of the society and fling at established power a consciousness about projects that were to be defended and funded. Cumulatively, these projects would show a new web of relationships, not wholly dependent on the dominant social order, carrying within themselves the seeds of a reconstructed democracy. By the project's nature, it would directly confront an established system that was worldwide, which had learned the language of progressive liberalism but which invariably found itself as an oppressor.

In the United States and elsewhere the project starts from the principle that there are social spaces that can be filled by action, much the way there are "empty" spaces in the subatomic world that nevertheless produce "concrete" things. The project would push aside social structures that did not beat with the rhythm of a reconstructed liberal democracy. It would be the intelligent social experiment and would create new possibilities for those who participated in the project. Although these projects were to be freestanding, they would associate with one another and create the basis of a vibrant democratic culture. Projects grew and new ones emerged. In part they were stimulated by the dissonance between the way democratic society is advertised and everyday life. In the United States of the 1960s and 1970s, and even now, church basements and seminar rooms of universities are the cultural staging areas for movements of social protest, whether in the arena of identity politics, women's rights, or the environment. It is these manifestations of cultural and intellectual change that are declared to be unpatriotic.

The alliances and associations formed among these projects were based on the idea that there was ample social space to build, so long as one accepted the risks and so long as some social space to begin did exist. We know that even in Nazi Germany, fascist Italy, and communist Russia social spaces did exist for confrontation by daring projects. But to take advantage of them required a heroism often too difficult to maintain. Their sustenance required international support. It is the advantage of this period in history that there are chances for sustenance internationally through communications technology.

Not understanding sufficiently the importance of the federal government as the partner and protector of basic rights of the excluded and the marginal, the New Left did not know either how to confront big corporate capitalism or to buttress the nurturing of people against the sadistic elements of the state. The New Left, operating as it did on the basis of felt need, did not develop a fully articulated critique and alternatives to state socialism and capitalism, although there were many practical projects and some theory suggestive of the contours of the future.[17] Somehow, perhaps from the philosopher's moral sense idea and its legal articulation (the McNaughton rule), the person was to be able to distinguish right from wrong.

If the movements of the 1960s were adolescent complaints, the reality they brought into existence was a way of seeing the American experiment that Walt Whitman, William James, and Herman Melville would have seen and understood. The movements of that time sought to catalyze the formation of a new democratic social character, which seemed to challenge the dominant features of capitalism, the market social character in which relationships were reduced to commodities. But if state socialism with its attempts to construct a "new man" were farcical, and if the market character brought alienation and greed, what was left? This was the question for the New Left. Its adherents sought answers in dialogue, participation, face-to-face relationships, and romantic notions of community. No doubt William Ellery Channing, the nineteenth-century philosopher and Unitarian minister who opposed slavery and championed community free of class oppression, would have understood the New Left's impulse, as would Thoreau, who championed individual conscience, believing that the government itself was an unproductive and unnecessary instrument. These men might well have been satisfied with the New Left's attempt to protect the environment and seek local and national democracies, wide-ranging law, and new forms of education that would confront industrial oligarchies. Even the aristocrat de Tocqueville had concerns about the emerging industrial bourgeoisie, fearing that its selfish and coarse attitudes would dominate the consciousness of society. He might well have signed the Port Huron Statement. He understood that Order in the modern world was no longer a settled matter and that the common good required a democracy that would infuse the society with a spirit of "self beyond self." The questions were not abstract and went to the articulation of culture and social relationships in everyday life. What was the social character American society favored? What did the ephemeral word "community" mean? And, most important, what are the features of democracy and its transformation? Would they be in line with the unfulfilled hopes of the Declaration of Independence, or is American democracy caught in the web of the national security state and global corporations? Would it be necessary to comprehend social reality in somewhat new ways, thereby allowing us to get out of the vast cave of the shadows we find ourselves in?

4

★

Features of
Democratic Transformation

BARRIERS AND SIGNPOSTS
TO DEMOCRATIC TRANSFORMATION

What are the features of democratic transformation? To answer this question a detour is necessary as a way of explaining the direction of a preferred public policy. We need to take account of locality within an international and transnational (anarcratic) framework, within the boundaries of an evolving world civilization. Nations and individuals, even new political forms, have responsibilities to an enduring international framework that promotes the conditions of dignity and decency for all people. Responsibilities of this kind are a complex matter. In international politics such phrases are often used as rhetorical ploys to justify power moves. But suppose international law were to be taken seriously as a guide to national and personal actions. Augusto Pinochet discovered this was beginning to happen when he attempted to return from Great Britain to Chile. The general was halted because of claims that, as leader of a coup, he had caused several thousand civilian deaths. Suppose the United States finally adopted all the human rights covenants and agreed to apply them within its borders?[1] If the United States also accepted and applied the agreements reached through the International Labor Organization, the treaties proscribing the use of biological weapons, environmental agreements, and arms control agreements, such affirmation would set a framework for international relations that could then be posed against a pax Americana, that is, the tendency to impose a nationalist imperial law without concern or attention to the needs of other nations. In other words, a concern for local and national politics begins with discarding the fantastic hubris of a go-it-alone nationalism operating in the context of the new imperialism.

The September 2001 zealot attack on the United States has again given American leaders the choice of either pressing forward with a world imperial *diktat* or supporting a shared international law against crackpot geopolitical schemes that rely on military power to control natural resources throughout the world.[2]

United Nations resolutions and covenants should not be interpreted as reflecting only past ideas of national interest on the part of states. Instead, where they are supported by the large states, they are predicated on certain universal conceptions irrespective of diversity within and between cultures.[3] There are important universal features to keep in mind. They are ruled by the consent of the people. How such consent is to be expressed and what those who disagree do with their disagreement are matters of profound concern. Obviously, they are of greatest concern where there are authoritarian governments supported through corruption and superpower "need," as in the case of the U.S. relationship to Kuwait, Saudi Arabia, and other nations part of the American sphere of influence that have made no pretense at consent of the people. These egregious cases are of a different order than the struggles around consent of the governed since the American, French, and Soviet revolutions. In these latter cases the struggles have centered on where consent is necessary from the people and where participation is part of consent. In the case of the Soviet Union, where claims were made that it operated on the basis of consent of the governed (mediated through the Communist Party) but it failed to fulfill its 1935 constitution, it becomes obvious that the Soviet Union was deformed.

In the United States, perhaps the most influential political scientist of his time, Charles E. Merriam, articulated the nature of democracy; his formulation served as the intellectual underpinning to President Franklin Roosevelt's championing of a second Bill of Rights, which included economic and social rights as well as political rights.[4] These liberal, radical, and progressive ideas were the accepted aspirations of the twentieth century.[5] Hannah Arendt, who presented her amalgam of constitutional and neo-Marxist views, formulated the idea of workers' councils and Jefferson's ward republics. Regardless of whether her teacher and lover, Heidegger, exercised too great an influence on them, her ideas were also similar to those of the early twentieth-century Marxists Antonio Gramsci and Anton Pannekouk.[6] For them, workers' councils were a means of realizing democracy through culture and places of work. Marxists who retained a humanist outlook in the twentieth century claimed that workers could practice democratic procedures and embrace democracy if they engulfed, and then transformed, the state apparatus. Arendt moved the locus of power and participation, which, as in Jefferson's case, was meant to be the basic governing unit, to groups of towns. This was different from the

Marxist formula, which asserted that the human being was primarily a worker producer. This "reality" defined one's class, beliefs, actions, and even consciousness, which some Marxists thought of as independent of class. The original Marxist formula deteriorated into a commitment to the party, and then to collective leadership, or even to a single leader. What was meant to be broader based than bourgeois leadership in fact turned out to be narrower.

Left liberal New Dealers, in contrast, held that there was no contradiction between the productive and the humane, that is, being a worker and a person with rights that covered all aspects of life.

THE PROJECT OF THE THIRD-STAGE LIBERAL DEMOCRACY

The characteristics of a liberal democracy are linked to each other and make a seamless web. Future liberal democracies will proceed with due recognition of the entrepreneurial "spirit" in the economy and society but with the understanding that this "spirit" is subsumed under cooperation and empathic relationships. In this sense, those with a democratic social character will link caring, cooperation, and responsibility to one another as primary features. Such a constitutive framework yields particular policies:

- Recognition and enforcement through government action and education of the limits on wealth to ensure economic and social decency for all citizens.
- Recognition and enforcement of redistributive techniques through social, economic, and educational means to ensure political equality among people of all races, genders, and sexual orientation.
- Recognition that virtually all judgments of the state can rest in the hands of the citizenry once they take part in the participatory and deliberative process. This can be formally organized through the formation of commissions, juries over public life, and broader conceptions of election. This in no way inhibits rights to privacy.
- Realization that, depending on their size, corporations must be accountable through public participation beyond so-called consumer democracy. This requires the participation of and, where useful, control by employees, consumers, workers, and communities in the decision-making process of corporations, including investment allocation.
- Protection and enhancement of all rights of press, speech, assembly, association, and participation in the public space and in the workplace, through public subsidy when necessary. This includes means of participation for citizenry to control governments outside of elections.
- Assurances that rights should not be understood as a substitute for power of participation and decision making.

- Clear assurances that war-making powers will be limited to their constitutional use, and that special efforts will be continuously made to formulate and implement systems of international cooperation, according to purposes laid out in the Universal Declaration of Human Rights, the Covenants on Human Rights, and other documents. These champion dignity and decency and are accepted as aspirations by the international community of nations. This includes a program for general disarmament and actions to end the war system. (Note emendations in the appendixes to these two profoundly important postwar documents.)
- The use of law as an instrument to ensure that dignity and decency in all aspects of social intercourse are enforced through an elected judicial system.
- Confrontation of the undemocratic equality in the Senate between highly populated and smaller states. This change would lay the basis for the manner in which institutions need to be changed and reconstructed in terms of these ends.
- Replacement of the internal public and private policing and surveillance system, which adds to the insecurity of the citizenry, narrows basic freedoms, and reinforces preventive detention and services. The enclosure security and stockade mania, which grips gated public and private office buildings and communities, is to be ended. Public architecture and design should emphasize social openness (access) and the participatory, including public rooms.

EXPERTS IN DEMOCRATIC TRANSFORMATION

Some will raise the argument that since these issues are so complex in modern life, reasonable judgments can be made only by experts. This argument has long been an important elite position, shared in the twentieth century by Walter Lippmann and any number of scientists and professionals, who resent interference about their inquiries. They claim that their very scientific methods enforce self-policing, and that scientific issues are of such an abstruse character that the average person cannot understand the immanent nature of what is being discussed.[7] Two pillars of the political economy buttress their claim. Just as peers control "bad" science, so it is that a competitive free market will "control" foolish thoughts or inefficient products. In this framework the function of knowledge noted by Foucault and others is a means of exercising control. The specialized knowledge worker would be used as the means to decide fundamental policy questions.[8]

Nevertheless, in the twentieth century scientists and technicians had little independent political power. The saying among political elites was that the scientific priesthood was on tap, never on top. They were not thought to have proper judgment, scope, and knowledge beyond their functional concerns, granted or contracted to them by the politically and economically powerful. Few attempts were made to improve education in democracy, so that critical judgments could be made, both by specialists who were disinterested and the people as a whole. Had that been the case, popular education, in and outside of the schools, would have resulted in an improved democratic educational system, which would have addressed the question of a moral technology and moral epistemologies.[9] Scientific inquiry committed to reconstruction would have endangered those underlying activities that created metastasized technologies from nuclear and biological weapons to transportation systems.

Certain innovations and inventions have begun to erase knowledge and status barriers between specialists and the layperson.[10] Specialists are not clear on the public effects of their work even though it may have deleterious or mixed implications. The glut of information, or propaganda, controlled by and through corporations creates further mystification.

In a democratic society committed to continuous discussion, there is little reason why public juries to judge the technological and environmental implications of particular innovations could not be formed. This system would most likely have an inhibiting effect on technological innovations, resulting in a profound change in the direction of capitalism and neoliberalism.

ELITES AS INTERPRETERS FOR THE CITIZENRY

Those fearful of democracy will argue that to excite people to believe their votes count equally and to encourage them to participate in the governing process is folly, leading to disaster. Others argue that modern (postmodern) public affairs are too complex to leave to the citizen, especially in wars, be they cold wars, shooting wars, or shadow wars. Some, like Walter Lippmann, will argue that whether there is war or peace, experts and elites must act either as trustees, interpreters, or surrogates for the people. If other systems of government would show a better means to justice and equality, perhaps there would be a basis for consideration of this elitist view. But there is nothing to suggest this possibility, even though it will appear that experts in political, economic, and military matters claim their judgment about the future and future events makes them indispensable.

In democracies, public roles and goals are changing, in part because of communications technology, and because ritual and tradition are often held up to obloquy in the marketplace. Democracies are able to value a view of human nature that is premised on (and supported empirically by) the idea that "goods" are more powerful than "evils." Democracy can be so formulated as to emphasize those capacities of human nature that secure a measure of happiness and well-being.

FEATURES OF THIRD-STAGE DEMOCRACY

Four tendencies resulting from cultural and technological changes are the basis of democratic reconstruction. None of these is to be confused with mass mobilization from the top, that is, "wars on _____" (fill in the blank) or passivity.

The first tendency is representational, which may mean representing and changing the character of the needs of the represented through intense dialogue and agreed on proofs. Second is the presentational method, in which the politician or policy analyst opens the door to having the populace present its own case, as in the situation of the excluded and wretched. The third method is the packaging, where the populace has free-floating concerns without a way to organize and present them. The fourth is the creation of a project, which is meant to make an exemplary statement while taking advantage of existing social spaces to project and defend an alternative to dominant hegemonic structures.

There are several formal features to an evolving modern democracy that could bring into reality the substantive content of democracy. These features are intended to bring out the best in the society as a whole and in its leaders. They are intended to change the priorities of a body politic, which presently must endure infantilization through competing television images that are little different from the way autos or cosmetics are sold to a passive public in need of arousal. To escape this form of degraded "tutelage" requires attention to the four formal aspects of the third stage of liberal democracy: access, participation, deliberation, and implementation. It is in these four features that the possibility of bringing into reality Roosevelt and Charles Merriam's notions of rights and aspirations may come to fruition.

Access

As individuals and as a group, "ordinary" people need access to each other, the government, and those in the civil society who claim authority. In this way citizens and residents are able to make their needs and ideals known. Throughout their lives, people need access to one another to socialize themselves. In a democracy, access is the means of linking oneself within already occupied social spaces to begin projects, whether in the economic, educational, religious, social, or political spheres. Access alone is not enough;

people need to be guaranteed association. They must know they can join with others without fear. This may be as simple as the right of assembly en masse, the right of cooperation among students and professors to reach one another, or church worship. It means calling on representatives of government to complain without fear of retribution. It means access to information and documents that may be embarrassing to governments or corporations, which operate as private governments. This means ending the secrecy curtain that governments use to reinvent the past and hide their present activities. It means revising laws covering corporate documents. Presently corporations seek to escape public responsibility and liability for wrongdoing by withholding documents that should be in the public domain. For example, the tobacco industry's system of stonewalling suggests the importance of revising confidentiality rules where there is a prima facie case of corporate wrongdoing. But it also means that workers and communities using legal means shall have access to records that are concerned with economic issues. This is for the purpose of ensuring just distributions and investment decisions that result in the overall development of communities, whether in American society or abroad.

Over fifty years of war and Cold War left the body politic prone to information authoritarianism, in which the corporate or government official has virtually unlimited access to the individual, such as credit history, education, personal history, and medical information. We have created a system of secrecy for large corporations, while the individual's private life is widely known. Even in the civil society, access is becoming a one-way street. The national security state's standard of need to know access, which compartmentalizes information from different parts of the government as well as the public, is another perversion that prevents access needed for deliberation. Obviously, this problem will grow starker as people are prepared to cede their own space for reasons of security.

In the economic sphere, workers who are not owners or entrepreneurs need access to one another so that they can organize for their own interests, especially when they have no property interest in their place of employment. In the economic sphere, for access to be meaningful there must be a constitutional right of speech and association at the workplace for workers. In the workplace, where often highly skilled and articulate workers are dependent on a nonhierarchical system of communication to accomplish tasks, the struggle over speech has taken new form, namely, in regard to the use of the Internet. Once access to the Internet is granted or achieved, questions about the character of the corporation, its purpose, investment allocations, and labor policies will result. With access to corporate records, the property or "stakeholder" interest, which the worker or community has in large corporations that affect the public interest, will change the character of production. Paradoxically, surveillance and keeping records on people, so much a part of the present corporate culture, will have the dialectical effect of causing people to demand access to corporate records. This changes the character of citizenship, participation, and corporate responsibility because different interests are represented. Managers and owners are aware of the subversive character of association and speech. Their task is to narrow the boundaries of access for employees while increasing their boundaries of information about the individual through genetic testing, surveillance, drug testing, etc.

Participation

What a democracy means by participation is complex, although it assumes either that access already exists or that participation is possible because of protected social spaces—or social spaces made through participation. Participation includes rational and irrational acts, in the sense of unthinking actions in or with a group. Thus, it may mean chanting in a march or at a rally, which is nothing more than sloganeering or carrying a placard. We usually define participation in relation either to civic local activities or grievances that demand public association and action. There can be another aspect to participation in relation to civic local activities, a grievance that demands public attention and can be rectified through public association and action. But what kind of association? People may participate with others in crowds—once thought a fearful problem by the ruling classes—or in armies, which have no mind except the mind of the leaders, or so it is thought, or in lynching, which is orgiastic in nature. In the twentieth century we had ample evidence of leader dictators who were endowed with the capacity to embody in their activities the fears and unconscious feelings of a people that surrenders its capacity to think critically.

In a limited democracy we have come to believe that voting is a far superior process because it opens the possibilities for reasonable thinking about politics that may be disinterested. One must not forget that in the United States voting is a relatively new process. And of course, by no means was it extended to all. It was not until 1944 that the poll tax was declared unconstitutional. According to an MIT analysis of the 2000 presidential election, some six million people were "mistakenly" disfranchised.

In modern politics the voter is appealed to through the use of images that are to be emblematic in the voter's mind of an ensemble of issues, including the character of the candidate. The flashing image is not only the sign, but also it is thought to be the entire story. This image is meant to give the voter a sense of belonging and knowing: belonging in two senses to the system, to the individual candidate's ideas and character, and knowing that if the voter's candidate fails, there will always be another election. And of course, even if a candidate loses the vote and the opponent does a creditable job, at least the voter is represented and the extreme likelihood is that people will forget about their votes or their own allegiances. This suggests again that participation in a process that may be unsatisfactory or illegal does not stain the candidate or the process.

Voting operates as the legitimation of the system and is an expression of loyalty to it. The problem occurs for citizens who have thought deeply about the issues or are in deep need of public solution when they find that there is no escape from the institutional structures that are oppressing them. It is then that participation becomes a function of direct action and direct participation, as in the case of sit-ins, violence, or most important, finding solutions with others that do not depend on government and the formal procedure of voting. In a democratic society that values freedom, communication includes nonviolent resistance or demands—especially where modes of communication do not exist or those with the levers of power have established laws that foreclose the petitioning from being heard or taken seriously—nonviolent sit-ins, sit-downs, and other forms of civil disobedience represent the depth of feelings and need that protesters have on that issue. For workers, strikes make clear the intensity of their needs. Their demands invariably are meant to enforce economic justice, equitable distribution, and humane conditions in the workplace. The question in a democracy is how deliberation is to occur and in what way moral boundaries are to be found.

Deliberation

Deliberation moves the democratic process to its next most important level. It is in deliberation that the people exercise their prudence and reason through discourse. Here interests are weighed and exposed and a disinterested formulation for problem solving may occur within the implicit "ought" purposes of the democracy. Within deliberation, citizens decide at what level a problem may be solved, whether it is within the private or public space or at an international, national, or local level. It is in deliberation that people reach either to "their better selves" or their judicious selves, which build on empathy and the exercise of judgment beyond any specific short-term personal interest or transactions. Where the body politic does not have a decent standard of living and social services that are accepted as part of a decent society, such notions will appear as utopian unless they become part of a struggle to attain these elementary rights. These rights also include the right of access and participation. During the crisis of September 11, 2001, government officials urged people to "get on with their everyday lives" as if nothing had happened. This was another way of saying that people should not engage in critical dialogue in the public space. This notion was extended to apply to the media, which accepted guidance if not direction from the second Bush administration as to what should be discussed and shown on radio and television. Further, another means of ensuring the passivity of the citizenry is through the fashioning of antiterrorism laws, which have the intended effect of closing down uninhibited political speech and demonstrations.

In American history, are there examples of public deliberation that reflect a democratic tradition? There are still town meetings in parts of New England. When de Tocqueville wrote of them, a particular township was on average two thousand people. There was no structural differentiation between law and administration. It was taken for granted that the town's citizens would perform both functions. The system itself was prone to mistakes and inefficiency, which irritated the more "civilized" in the larger society. De Tocqueville believed that such a relationship, just because it related the various aspects of democracy, was a natural springing up "of its own accord," perhaps by God. He went on to say that "[l]ocal institutions are to liberty, what primary schools are to science; they put it within the people's reach; they teach people to appreciate its peaceful enjoyment and accustom them to make use of it. Without local institutions a nation may give itself a free government, but it has not got the spirit of liberty."[11]

We may excuse the rhapsodic quality of de Tocqueville, for in hindsight we know that class and bigotry are as likely to be found in the local institution and township as in a large one. One need only point out that the young civil rights workers James Chaney, Michael Schwerner, and Andrew Goodman were killed by a sheriff-organized posse in the township of Philadelphia, Mississippi, where force and legitimacy rested locally and had nothing to do with justice beyond a particular class and race.[12]

On the other hand, we may note three different results that coincided to reinvigorate the legitimacy of the locality. The first was the civil rights movement, which demanded the right to vote, extending dignity and power to the citizenry so that the locality, the town and village, was not an instrument of repression; the second, after considerable prodding, was the federal government, which supported the civil rights movement to change the basis upon which local governments could function.

After the Civil War, localities were no longer free agents, although many states refused to recognize the paramountcy of the federal government.[13] Eight years after Reconstruction the federal government had no choice but to again confront states' rights, that is, segregationists and local oligarchs who shaped laws to penalize and exclude black citizens. Citizens had become citizens of the United States, not merely of a particular locale or state. But in the process of federal confrontation the third result occurred. Beginning with the Reagan administration explicit anti–civil rights attitudes and legislation appeared. The national government, like the sting of the bee, lost its energy in matters of social and economic justice. States' rights again emerged as a mantra and mask for racism, although hooded. This has meant that the locale and dialogue have increased in importance, but this is a stunted deliberation because its purposes are not framed by inclusivity, economics, or social justice for all.

Deliberation, in the sense of presenting one's views and having the ego-strength to do so, comes from critical and imaginative faculties that are honed in schools. But to the extent schools are merely schools of propaganda and skill specialization, they fail at encouraging a critical and deliberative citizenry. It is not only the schools that have this social function. Ideally each institution of the society must encourage speech and deliberation in every venue. The popularity of talk radio is an example of people needing to express themselves in the public space. It is also an example of the need to link deliberation to speech on public issues.

So what does deliberation comprise? Deliberation is invariably a social activity in which the participants, at least for a moment, will drop their class and status differences. All are engaged in the framing and solution of a problem, attempting to understand each other's points of view. All are held together by a common attempt to "reason together." Judgment is a common thread, which is respected by the participants when they are in deliberation.[14] Whether the discussion is about theoretical physics, child raising, or matters of trash pickup, deliberation requires judgment. Good judgment may be found in one person or, more likely, in the group. For the group, good judgment may come from the addition of personal intuitions, specialized knowledge, and experiences. Personal interests may become secondary in the social formation of shared judgments. In the process of deliberation with others, self-interest may either cancel out or be transcended. This condition obtains where the local culture has surrendered (or is willing to surrender) prejudice based on race, gender, and religion.

We see this transformation most clearly when citizens are chosen for jury duty. With the oath and ritual inside the courtroom, as a general matter jurors take on an aura of seriousness, which comes from the feeling that their decisions matter. This seriousness of purpose is present when there are real matters to decide. However, it is not at all clear that the fundamental questions of society are presented to the public in ways that make them open for serious citizen consideration.[15] Instead, because issues are presented as flashing images or sound bites, society finds itself returning to Plato's Cave of the Shadows, with images of unreality dancing on walls and spectators concluding that the shadows are real. To escape the cave, we are required to go outside to seek others. But where outside do we go?

In our time, we are not sure how large a township should be for citizens to make good decisions. If we don't care about the quality of the decisions made, there is no reason to limit the size of the unit that deliberates. If we demand face-to-face dialogue, a very different set of concerns is raised. In the first instance, some claim the importance of the guardians, or interlocutors, who serve either the will of the people or the propertied classes. To them, deliberation could never work in a democracy, because discourse was an elitist form. This group took the position that, as a republic, deliberation was limited to guardians and their epigones.[16] In modern times, claims are made that deliberation could only be carried out by specialists and experts who have the time, skill, and inclination to assess, debate, and consider dispassionately because they have a scientific or journalistic temperament. According to this point of view, it would not help to go beyond the few who are capable of thinking, for they are the trustees of the republic.

Since all are open to bribery, flattery, and the charge of self-interest, it is necessary that deliberation occur in the society as a whole. It will become harder to bribe or flatter everyone, since rules and laws will be debated and taken more seriously, questioned, changed, reformed, or when necessary, disobeyed—all in the context of the responsibility of citizenship. This view of democracy is dependent on education that eschews narrow interest, flattery, or bribery. Education can take many forms, all of which must include debate over moral judgments and limits.

There are many venues where deliberation is practiced. They may range from cooperative apartment meetings, to neighborhood councils, to school association meetings. These deliberations are local, neighborhood, or function specific. There is presently no practical way to integrate these activities into a politics that sees deliberation in its broadest sense, using deliberation for direct democracy on fundamental questions of the economy, war, and peace, without structural changes that favor elements of direct democracy. However, deliberation in a constitutional democracy committed to social gender and political equality including economic justice cannot escape these purposes and assumptions. The question for deliberations is what ways and means are to be used to make good on the "ought" purposes of democracy.

Planning and Implementation

The deliberative process in politics leads to implementation. Without implementation, deliberation becomes an elaborate play activity. In the law, it may be a judgment for damages or prison. The key to a decision in the public space is its implementation, for it is in implementation, individually or through collective means, that citizens produce in practice the sort of society in which they not only intend to live but also want to live.

Can a democracy as a whole participate in the implementing process once decisions are made without the process being one of profound manipulation by an administrative oligarchy? In time of war, democratically oriented central governments use the small group as a means of giving the appearance of modern democracy, by including the features of access, participation, deliberation, and implementation. During World War II and half of the Cold War, the federal government found a way of combining local participation for decision making with the military's mobilizing needs.[17] Selective Service gave a quota to local draft boards for how many men were to be drafted in any particular month. Neighbors voted on how, and with whom, to fill the quota, according to administrative guidelines and military needs. This method of administrative democracy, where locales chose how and how many soldiers were to attend, was hardly bottom up. Indubitably there was political horse-trading and exceptions, as in the case of farmers who received group exemptions.

Any planning process must be democratic and continuous, in which all aspects of the problem are understood and linked to specific actions. These actions are weighted for consequential result and moral effect. Without such considerations, the moral sense disappears from the group, as does the sense of personal dignity.

In Cuba's Committees in Defense of the Revolution, neighbors were used on a block-by-block basis as a spying mechanism. Similar methods, such as civil defense and informing, were used as a mechanism of local spying and securing order during World War II. Voluntary groups such as the million-person National Security League initiated by Theodore Roosevelt during World War I or the Freicorps, precursors to the Gestapo were examples of organized systems of mass hysteria and were hardly different from mob lynchings. None of these should be understood as the basis of democracy but rather as a degradation of participation, although some would say that the defense of democracy is not a democratic proposition. Or to put this another way, for some, authoritarianism in defense of democracy is no vice.

Even provisional answers to these questions help in the fashioning of democracy so that it is more than a rhetorical flourish. As I have said, the major political features of democracy are access, participation, deliberation, and implementation. The most difficult aspect of democracy is implementation, for it is here where deliberative decisions that might be made democratically and with care are undermined; where the means and the ends too often contradict each other, because the means are not understood to be part of the ends; where administration becomes command oriented; and where democratic engagement is surrendered. There may be ways to avoid this problem through concern with democratic issues, as in the process of citizens being involved in investment allocation systems of those corporations that in fact determine markets and production and the social and economic lives of communities and cities.

Without serious matters to weigh, there is no doubt that electronic town hall meetings will become part of "politainment." These are little more than plebiscitary systems, which give the appearance of political deliberation but without the discourse necessary for people to see each other in the sense, say, that justices of the court are face to face with one another.

Third-stage liberal democracy requires new modes of political communication. These include a dedicated taxation to be applied within limits to the taxpayer's choice, including those who have earned-income tax credits, which operate as oversight committees for Congress in all districts. The purpose of these juries would be to ferret out problems and make recommendations for alternative budgets and programs, which would be linked together on a national basis as a coherent "popular way." Congress and the executive could either accept or reject these recommendations every four years.

The "popular way," as an exercise in a new level of democracy, is superior to the idea of term limits that seized the Republican Party and even independent voices during the late 1980s and 1990s. The term limit idea has the unintended effect of strengthening the bureaucracy over short-term sitting legislatures unfamiliar with the governing process. The power of lobbyists also increases against that of the elected official. Furthermore, there is an implicit question to the term limits idea: Why should the bureaucracy be protected, with seniority and rules of civil service, if Congress operates under a revolving door system? The answer seems obvious. Term limits will necessarily lead to the destruction of an indepedent civil service. Indeed, that may be the primary goal of those engaged in funding term limit lobbying.

MATERIAL CONDITIONS FOR DEMOCRACY: THE ENVIRONMENT AS PRODUCER

A more important question remains: Can third-stage liberalism create a better political program for stopping the headlong destruction of the environment than other, more authoritarian modes of government? In both stage one and stage two liberalism it is taken for granted that the environment does not produce. That is to say, production is thought of as something that nature and the environment do not do except through human intervention. But this is patently false. This conceptual error has resulted in thinking and acting on the environment as a passive thing that has no life of its own; the idea that nature can be conquered, abused, or tortured without adverse consequences is a claim of modern political ideologies. But we have found in the twentieth century that nature has within itself the power of growth and regeneration. This lesson was not learned in the Soviet Union. As bad as Western governments, including the U.S. government, have been about the environment, they have performed in a far superior manner to Eastern

Europe's former socialist states. One may point to Chernobyl and Lake Bakaal, the largest lake in the world, which is now literally dead; the work of Boris Komarov in a samizdat (*The Destruction of Nature in the Soviet Union*) and Zhores Medvedyev; and the laying waste of tens of thousands of acres of land as a result of nuclear waste.[18]

Because the ecological and environmental balance is a worldwide problem, there is every reason to find a proper means of linking production and environmental concerns on an international level. Unless significant attempts are made to gain control over international corporations; narrow the social, economic, and political disparity between rich and poor; and decrease production of harmful goods that adversely affect nature, liberalism and democracy will not be able to stop environmental devastation. They will be partners to perpetuating the grievous environmental habits of the twentieth century. An unregulated capitalism, buttressed by national security state democracy, and an open market depend on the destruction of the environment. This situation is exacerbated by the demands of war and preparation for it. As was the case with Western imperialism and state socialism, war by its nature has been (and remains) an environmental destroyer, as evidenced by the destruction in the world wars of the twentieth century, the Indochina war, and the Iraq war. The contradiction between production and environmental protection will appear in its most acute form unless there is public and continuous involvement in the production and distribution process beyond the market. Workers presently held hostage to environmentally dangerous activities for personal economic reasons will be far less likely to be economically trapped when financial security is a feature of citizenship, when a positive program of social reconstruction and maintenance is agreed to, and when environmental assets are protected. That this requires a shift in consumer desires, which are manipulated by advertisers, becomes clear. The more than $350 billion per year spent on advertising is no more than a creative corrupted form that brings together illusion and degraded information.

It is absurd to believe that employment is forever dependent on the exploitation of the environment, just as it mistaken to believe that the public must drive SUVs or the government must make nuclear missiles and cluster bombs or have a Star Wars defense. It is mistaken to believe that guarantees of annual income or of employment are predicated on the production of commodities that shouldn't be made in the first place. It is claimed that guaranteed incomes, distribution of wealth, and full employment guarantees would adversely affect the character of the people, a claim invariably made by conservatives. On the contrary, people would be liberated to undertake creative activities and modes of production that would not be dependent on the destruction of the environment. Such a program would include legislative and policy features that reconfigure the role of government in shaping the character of production in terms of stricter enforcement of health and environmental rules at the workplace. How things are made, what is made, and what is necessary for social well-being and the exercise of freedom are central concerns of liberal democracy. Such questions should be debated and determined in public discussions so that economic questions are not understood to be separate from political democracy. It is likely that questions about greed and economic and social disparity as well as environmental despoliation would be debated and linked to fairness. Fairness in the sense I am using this term is the underlying assumption of the political economy and applies to any derivative institutional arrangement such as the corporation.

Is it the top few of the great corporations who are the driving force for exploitation of nature, or workers in need of jobs, in such regions as the Pacific Northwest or Brazil? If it is the first group, several means come to mind, which could interrupt the flow of exploitation. The first is to reorganize corporate charters to include specific provisions for environmental and worker protection, backed by criminal law. The new charters would be redrawn in relation to international worker and environmental standards. The second means is the establishment of a worldwide system of international environmental courts, whose judgments could be applied by any group or nation against the offending corporation or nation. Barring such an alternative, a code of personal responsibility and penalties should be formulated that covers environmental malfeasance, such as the events at Bhopal, and which would be applied and enforced in national courts or an international environmental court. A mosaic of criminal laws and international civil penalties needs to be collected, written, and applied locally, nationally, and internationally across political boundaries. Ironically, environmental degradation and increased travel and communications enhance the principles of international human sovereignty and decrease the relevance of political sovereignty, bounded as it is by a particular geographic area. Democracies whose philosophic underpinnings have been tied to specific sovereignties are required to transcend older ideas of sovereignty for the sake of accepting the truism that the human and natural environment needs a political conception that transcends national boundaries. It is not necessary for humanity—for the United States—to assert that this is not possible and that the contradictions on specific environmental questions are too great between rich and poor nations, the technologically advanced and the humanly deficient. The rules, treaties, and awareness already organized serve as a beginning guide to the next stages of linkages between the environment and democracy.[19]

Are there rules that apply to both democracy and innovative technology? The first question to consider is where the burden should lie. Should it be with those who want to bring about change with a new product or with those who want to stop its introduction? Here it is important to note that modern liberalism, through the emergence of government regulation, began to demand a far higher standard for introducing a new product in the marketplace than did conservatism. Conservatism took to itself conceptions of progress that stem from eighteenth-century laissez-faire liberalism. As Ralph Nader and Gabriel Kolko have noted, in practice, regulatory agencies often became the champion of the regulated industry, thereby undercutting citizen or consumer concern. Weak regulatory agencies were unable to impose a standard that transcended profit and loss definitions of utility.[20] They were caught in the web of ideas of progress, unfettered capitalism, industrial lobbying, and a hard-to-define common good or public interest. There was no agreed on moral compass to guide judgments in particular cases. Furthermore, since industrialists hated intrusion and feared fettering of capitalism, they sought legal impediments against regulation and intrusion in what was thought to be management prerogatives. In the regulated drug industry, pharmaceutical companies have tolerated the appearance of regulation because it portrays them as having governmental legitimacy to a concerned public that seeks security and protection from the market.

5

★

Cultural Support
and Impediments
to Liberal Democracy

COMMUNITY IN A CULTURAL SENSE

The American system, in a cultural sense, denies the principle of Order, for social openness and empty spaces allow for and create barely contained disorder. It has not been clear how community fits with the agon, that is, conflict and competition, that undergirds American life in virtually every aspect. Nor in the United States has it been clear how the dialectic between community and competition would integrate. This unresolved problem manifested itself through the nineteenth- and twentieth-century battles among farmers, railroad titans, mine owners, ranchers, corporations, and unions and through spontaneous demonstrations that had within them the seeds of participatory democracy. American leaders sought to square the circle between Order, competition, and conflict through geographic expansion, emphasis on patriotic wars, and the creation of cooperative, "responsible" relations among management, organized labor, and public representatives. The emphasis was on "organic dialogue," which would buttress problem-solving techniques.

While such ideas were applied to the corporate–labor sector to dampen class struggle in the Cold War period, competition and winning remained the American cultural obsession. Conceptions of the adversary, of conflict and struggle, whether class or personal, had long been taken as the basis and bane of American success. Competition is there in films, sports, war, and elections; it is taught as the invariable and universal reality of life, crossing all cultures and boundaries, and used as the primal survival skill by parents. Order could be achieved only if one were, first, on top. And of course there was fear that someone would replace the nation or the person or the team or corporation on top.

By the 1970s the "corporate soul," as a means of civilizing capitalism and the corporation in previous decades, had disappeared as an ideological self-restraint. The marketing character took on a new persona, exemplified by Ronald Reagan. Selfishness and egoism came to be the new meaning of individualism. Rights to property were turned into property rights, which gave them a fetishized meaning. Property rights robbed the commons, and the sheer boldness of the Republican claims depleted the nation. The Ayn Rand objectivist school of selfishness became public policy through her leading disciple, Alan Greenspan. Some claimed that Reaganism was the continuation of policies of Herbert Hoover and Calvin Coolidge. But it is worth noting that the Reagan system was exactly the reverse of the one in which Hoover believed. Hoover had said that his system was one of "economic justice," never one of laissez-faire.

By the beginning of the twentieth century, progressives understood that unlimited conflict and competition could destroy the nation. In terms of statecraft, this realization meant that the only prudent thing to do was to dominate, manage, and prepare for conflict. In all cases, one was not to lose. Ever. Winners dictated the rules of the game, which were synonymous with the rule of law. Whether or not people wanted this cultural belief, it predominated and could be found among the upper classes and the striving middle classes that believed in "making it." This sentiment was never far from daily life in all its aspects, for there was little chance to escape the Game and its emphasis on competition. Like the lottery, there are very few winners but enough to keep the Game going.

The overwhelming and difficult task of liberalism was either to manage the conflict of interest group brokering that had been taken for granted by Marxists and capitalists alike or to transcend it through social reconstruction. The management method long ago proved to be a failure when judged in terms of democracy and the conception of self-rule. Managers managed in terms of the hierarchic top-down pyramidal organization, which made a particular product plus what they could legally or otherwise skim for themselves. Not having any other models, government was to be managed like a business, more specifically an industrial corporation. The democratic project remained stymied by a society that believed in its ideology of competition and top-down management.

Social reconstruction was no easy task to achieve. The path was continued with Martin Luther King Jr.'s understanding of the difference between the human possibility and the submissive, often masochistic, roles people were socialized and characterized into fulfilling. King made clear by his exemplary actions that reconstruction also required the application of moral intelligence and reason to public problems. He seemed to believe, as did others, that the reality of modern life is interdependent, but whether this could be manifested in an associative, nonhierarchic way seemed to be beyond the grasp of those who wielded power. Unfortunately, perhaps tragically, social reconstruction based on empathic invariance, caring, and trusting of people, as well as inchoate ideas that inform the liberalism of reconstruction, is still only a potentiality. Nevertheless, the assumptions of social reconstruction are present in everyday life. It is increasingly obvious that there are no individual choices that can be exercised without a high level of cooperation.[1] That they are not recognized does not deny their importance as the constituent aspects of survival and human dignity.

RECONSIDERING FAMILY VALUES AND CULTURES

Modern liberalism and democracy have been ruthless in subverting the stability of hierarchic family structures, patriarchy, and the nuclear family. As a result of the social movements of the 1960s, rules of patriarchy, the power of parents over children, over even property matters, as well as the older over the younger, were subverted.[2] But capitalism was the catalyst for these exchanges. Capitalism held that for the person to be truly free, emphasis must be on individual choice and markets to benefit the individual, not the family qua family.[3] The market favors the individual, not the family, except where it can add to greater consumption and gross domestic product (GDP). Socialism claimed that there were more important units than the nuclear family.[4] Even technology, that modern socializing instrument, is often more easily understood by children, thereby lessening the authority of parents.

In everyday reality, families are not hermetically sealed spaces. They must confront, without knowing, competing global forces that seek their souls, loyalty, and money. Indeed, the family often reflects these global struggles through economic purges, plants moving from North to South, workers migrating from South to North.[5] But it was not only material conditions that dictated the changes in family structures and values. Changes in consciousness, caused by social awareness, were catalyzed by feminist groups.[6] A daring sense of liberatory equality between men and women around questions of sexuality and gender shifted the mores and laws of the society, thereby threatening settled institutions. This phenomenon is not limited to Western nations but is reinforced by UN General Assembly resolutions pressed by nongovernmental organizations and globalization of capital, which is increasingly dependent on women as part of the international workforce outside the home.

Other stresses on traditional family structures are related to advertising-induced and necessary desires that cannot be fulfilled in the traditional pre-1960s nuclear family structure illusion. An adequate life requires at least two incomes in the American setting, causing power shifts and role fusing within the family. The results are clear. They can be as benign as eating prepared foods outside the communal dinner table and on the run, or as insidious as latchkey children left dreaming in front of their babysitter television, or they mean greater independence on the part of individual family members regarding the disposition of income. These changes add to the process of decentering the family structure, where a new politics of the household around sexual relations, eating, cooking, property, and child rearing now occurs.

With these changes comes greater awareness and recognition of what oppression is within the family. As a result of their own efforts, women cannot escape redefining themselves and therefore the community. Their redefinition necessarily means changing over their own social character, from one of public submissiveness to that of equality and public equality. Coincidentally, pressures on women intensify, given their need to be financially self-sufficient. Women's demands for egalitarian interdependence and equality mean the transformation of working conditions, livelihood, maintenance, production, and reproduction, both inside and outside the family. Obviously, these changes require a substantial shift in the social character of men, who are expected to change behavior and share responsibilities in the private space, sometimes as primary actors or helpmates.

Various attempts have been made to defend against these incursions and transformations of power and relationship within the family. The most recent is the rightist organizational drive to rally around "family values" as a means of finding stability against radical twentieth-century changes grounded in the earlier liberal view of individualism and personhood beyond family. The decentering process is defended against by those fearing gender equality, who seek ways of restoring traditional social roles and patriarchy. But this is hardly credible for economic reasons. When economic development and women's freedom are linked through production outside traditional "home making," international capital finds itself dependent on diverse industries, from computer chips to clothing to food processing. Furthermore, for all classes the "natural" family is a poignant and peculiar battleground, as Leo Tolstoy noted in *Anna Karenina*.

Innumerable historical descriptions, from the literature of kings and ruling families to the working classes, show the ambiguity and struggle within families. The family has never been a cozy place where the individual may repair to recover from the economic, social, psychological, and political struggles of daily life. Quite the contrary. The family either reflects these struggles in personal relations within the family, or it foists onto the public space the special problems endemic to family life, such as incest and child abuse.[7] In Western culture, generational, family, and sibling battles are the basis of our literature. Whether in *Hamlet, Oedipus, Anna Karenina,*

Ghosts, Cat on a Hot Tin Roof, Studs Lonigan, Death of a Salesman, or *The Color Purple,* the family is the microcosm of struggle. Even the Bible, used as a fundamental weapon in the creation of rightist family values, is an exercise in detailing the dysfunctionality of the family and the sometimes devastating effects on its members. One may begin by detailing the fratricide of Cain and Abel and the willingness of Abraham to sacrifice, if necessary, Isaac's life to the God he heard. Jerome Bernstein, the Jungian psychoanalyst, stated in his essay "Piercing Our Unconscious" that the biblical family conflict of treachery and patriarchal game playing could be easily translated into a modern story of psychological betrayal of explosive political proportion even as it relates to the Arab–Israeli conflict:

> If this story were told to any of us as a personal story of individuals that we knew, would we not advise both sons that they had been set up for conflict by their father who left each the same legacy and lands in two wills, excusing the conflicting mandate by saying that one brother would be more equal than the other? Would we not say to them that they should not be fighting with each other but that they together should look at the mischief done to them by their common father and the conspiracies of the mothers (Sarah and Rebecca)? Would we not point out to them that they are *both* victims of treachery—by their father, their mother(s) and even God, Himself—and that to continue fighting over that same land promised to each of them is to perpetuate the treachery and insult visited upon them by their patriarch? And, let us remind ourselves, that this story and its plot are contained in Holy Scripture and are the foundation of all three of the patriarchal religions.[8]

It is no accident that violence and murder in the direct personal sense are more liable to occur in the home and among family members than on the street, even in the most crime-ridden neighborhoods. One may speculate why parents are often willing to give their children over to be soldiers or suicide bombers. Love for a country or an abstract symbol hiding coercion trumps love for children when the state calls.

Fundamentalist religion attempts to construct a firewall of education and belief for the nuclear family as the prop of protection against the "culture of Babylon." It does not see capitalism as the foe. However, the fundamentalists undercut the most valuable aspect of capitalism, namely, the liberal choice to reject social oppression.[9] American fundamentalism may appear to be similar to, for example, Wahhabism, which asserts a strict reading of the Koran without innovations of scholars. Like American fundamentalism, Wahhabism has sought to control both the state and people in everyday life. Religion is the state's instrument for repression, just as the state is used by religious institutions and its undisciplined to encourage zealots when necessary. This is the symbiotic relationship the Wahhabi fundamentalists have with the princes of Saudi Arabia. The

Wahhab life rejects democracy and preaches otherworldliness, at least for its poor classes.

In the United States fundamentalism has a subservient relationship to the economic system. The capitalist market system is not about to surrender itself to any sort of religious fundamentalism if it means the end of a consumer market, to be replaced by family values. Instead of such a counter-revolution occurring, in American society fundamentalism is given a place in the pluralist system. It is to find a market niche for huckstering its family values, meant to fit into the reigning political and economic ideology. It can "sell" the idea that the nuclear family is more than an economic unit. But its members are not expected to believe such ideas in their highly individualized consumption patterns. Nevertheless, the family retains an economic character and is encouraged to do so through economic policies, such as inheritance laws, tax deductions, and credits. There is nothing to suggest that the Right is prepared to confront the social reality of family dynamics, which give rise to anger, violence, incest, jealousy, rivalry, television autism, economic insecurity, and sickness.

No one of these features of family life is useful in shaping democratic social character. On the other hand, the democratic social character takes into account eccentricity, difference, and individuality (one's own and that of others) without losing sight of features of the democratic community—that changing place that is inclusive and helps the person ward off isolation and loneliness. Such a possibility may or may not exist in the family. Yet, the question of love, in the empathic and caring sense, might be tentatively answered in the family. If parents are wise, this empathic and caring sense may be nurtured, helping children to develop their own capacity for caring and empathy. What may result is the emergence of a democratic social character that tamps down the violence and coercive nature of public institutions.

When we think of such matters in terms of public policy, it becomes clear that virtually every attempt to aid families takes extraordinary social, economic, and political intervention and support (what the middle classes might call "dependency" when the idea is applied to the poor and working classes). This means governmental intervention, from guaranteeing incomes and work, to passing and enforcing laws against physical abuse in families, to providing nonrepressive social services that are not used as a means to punish or humiliate the client who is denied health and environmental protections. A humane and democratic society comprehends that the person is more than a worker. This view opens the door to guarantees of rights irrespective of the person's willingness or capacity to work. Political scientists and economists are pleased to be critical of "free riders." But youngsters, the sick, and the old are already "free riders" except as they serve in a metaphorical sense as the employers of caretakers who would otherwise be unemployed.

Conservatives are fond of deriding the nanny state that provides such supports. What must surely be grating to the working poor, as I have noted, is that its members are expected to work for the well-off as nannies, caring for their children and granting to them the care and affection often missing in upper middle and upper class homes. Some will say that fulfilling this need as social policy is the creation of the welfare state in a new garb. But this is only partially true, since the American welfare state (stage two liberalism) is predicated on giving benefits without citizen participation at all levels of service.

The idea of maximum participation of the poor was raised as an important democratizing element of governing during the Great Society. According to William Cannon, a member of the Executive Office of the President under Johnson, the intended purpose of its initiation was to change welfare clients and the poor into participatory citizens. The political parties quickly ended this project in radical democratic localism. Welfarism was not to extend to the formation of a participatory democratic social character or for that matter income and wealth redistribution. Its purpose was to retain the class structure of working poor, whose supports were limited and whose political power was minimal, especially if they did not belong to unions or did not vote. If the welfare state was the instrument to tame capitalism, it succeeded in a minimal way. It was not meant to change capitalism and technology's powerful centrifugal ways, which caused communities to fly apart. The welfare state is not the primary instrument either for the creation of democracy or the nurturing of democratic social character. It is that state form that gives the unseen sufficient funds so that the middle class and above can continue to live in a world where the unseen remain unseen but clothed, housed, and fed at an adequate level. But persons and families have an even greater right in the "ought" or aspirational sense than what many nations or the international community provides. This means that practice must catch up with rational and humane ideals. United Nations resolutions and covenants call for a high level of commitment to people's dignity, shared responsibility for tasks within the family, personal responsibility as in the case of the Nuremberg principles, as well as responsibility for others, including the environment. United Nations conferences reflect the movements and needs of people throughout the world. They are a good beginning point for finding and understanding the limits, needs, and features of a modern democracy in vastly different cultural settings. Perhaps they are even more. In societies that are experiencing the changing nature of family and self, such documents legitimate different political forms, including caring and empathic capacities within people and institutions.

Throughout the world, the Right in the United States and the traditionalists of vastly different cultures struggle to kill off the UN and its conferences because they explore tendencies toward universalization and open new understandings while demystifying power. Ideas and experiences are traded, which legitimates changing social and political relationships. The foundational language of the UN, its charter, resolutions, and covenants are explored at UN conferences and become instruments for personal liberation and decolonization in the economically developed as well as poor regions.[10] It is fair to inquire whether that much-abused word *community* fits with or is antithetical to liberation.

COMMUNITY, ENCLOSURE, AND DISSOLUTION

Alienation and anomie were generated by vast population shifts from rural to urban areas—for example in Mexico, from Appalachia to Chicago, and from Puerto Rico to New York City—often enforced, and sometimes freely chosen, but invariably disruptive of romantic ideas of community. Immigrants found that cities operated as enclosure systems against outsiders. Residential zoning in the suburbs was fastened to the enclosure mentality. The "American dream" in everyday life was enclosure and stability against threats from the outside. It was not accidental that throughout the civil rights struggle, communities of whites in the South or in ethnic neighborhoods resented and fought against "outsiders," and of course that antagonistic sentiment applied to the federal government, the ultimate "outsider" acting against segregation. Similarly, trade operates against an enclosure mentality.

Expansionists at the top of the modern large corporation, including the multinational corporations, responded to ending legal apartheid well before local communities adopted such attitudes. Some corporations became allies in the struggles against apartheid. As much as any other, Andrew Young, a former mayor and ambassador as well as lieutenant to Martin Luther King Jr., understood corporate capitalism's historic role in the struggle against apartheid. Of course, Americans have lived with a different aspect of the enclosure mentality, a manifestation of the way in which the government framed the Cold War struggle within the United States. Americans have lived a contradictory duality. Since the Second World War Americans have been part of their own enclosure against the outside world, even as the government and big corporations sought every manner of engagement outside U.S. borders. This has created enormous resentments and strains on the citizenry, who have come to believe that they carry the world's burdens, and that they are being robbed by other nations because of American generosity through foreign aid.

Twenty-first-century forms of enclosure are organized within American society around internal security, whether it be internal passports to gain entrance into buildings, drug testing for employment, government identification cards to board airplanes, wiretapping or mirrors, or photographic records of customers and workers. The Rooseveltian warning that Americans have nothing to fear but fear itself is crushed to the ground by political leaders who play on insecurity and a technological system that fuels personal fears. Life becomes fearful, selfish, and dreary, in a cocoon of false security. Is this what community has come to mean in practice, little league soccer and baseball teams notwithstanding?

DECEPTIVE COMMUNITIES

The meaning of what a community is has a touch of yearning and mystery to it. Communities were shaped by inequalities upon which the free market seemed to depend. As Harold Laski put it, "The market economy made liberty a function of one's place in the hierarchy of power. It ruled out equality as incompatible with the accumulation by the investor of the ever-increasing capital necessary to exploit market possibilities. It made the real boundaries of a community no more than the limits of profitable exploitation by those who dominated the market."[11]

Since John Adams and Alexander Hamilton, conservatives have understood that markets and capitalism are far more important than community. The state had to be ready to enforce this view through repressive legislation and legislation favorable to the "better" classes. There could not be a democratic community in the sense that Henry Wallace, John Dewey, Franklin Roosevelt, and Jane Addams conceived it, that is, communities and associations of relative equals in economic terms and certainly in social and political terms.[12] Small merchants in towns and villages learned that neighborliness and community meant little or nothing when competing with giant capitalist corporations such as Wal-Mart.

Prior to World War II community was a static conception with emphasis on stability and the maintenance of the status quo. Hierarchies, customs, rituals, and resource allocation were settled, and systems of exclusion were taken for granted. However, under the pressure of internal migration and ambiguous federal commitments to civil rights after World War II (by presidential executive order blacks were to be given equal chances at getting defense contract jobs), the concept of community took on diverse and surprising meanings. Liberals who emphasized change and freedom believed that, although the idea of community was seductive, it was also dangerous, for its tenets could easily result in demeaning the powerless individual and his or her freedom. Community had been an unexamined shell, filled with segregation and apartheid by class, race, status, and occupation. The question was whether community could be influenced by a liberal project that recognized the humane capacities of caring and empathy in its universal character.

In his work, John Dewey had sought to end the dichotomy between the individual and the community, infusing the person with social responsibility. The world to him was not a bunch of solitary egos asserting their power to attain unequal status in the marketplace. The person was linked to a community made up of many loosely held associations on which the person was dependent and in turn affected. Both the wealthy and the poor could have many different associations. By inference, an individual could be a member of several different communities simultaneously. The same person could be, at least theoretically, a member of seemingly cross-cutting associations and groups, whose personal class interests were not served by any of the minicommunities to which he or she felt himself or herself to be emotionally and politically attached. For Dewey, the contradiction between the individual and the community was not tenable in modern life because it obscured the reality of human interdependence. Obviously, being a member of a minicommunity, such as a small town or subculture, was not enough. But Dewey's community was an ideal place, more a product of mind than actual situations, or an imago of a preindustrial Vermont that Dewey might have known as a child but which he surrendered once he had lived in the America of Chicago and New York.

Magazines of popular opinion, such as the *Saturday Evening Post*, sought to present the idyllic as the antidote to an urban industrial civilization that was neither simple nor civil. There are many who hold to the idea that children who lived in small towns, before the mass production of television and the bombardment of advertising, lived simpler and less dangerous lives. Perhaps they felt protected by the ever-watchful, judgment-making eyes of prying neighbors acting like American versions of fence sitters and concierges. They did not suffer the harangues of advertising bombardment and daily crises felt by the present child of whatever social class.

In terms of lived experience, community and individualism gave rise to problematic and ambiguous meanings. If individualism led to egoism and self-centeredness in the Sartrian sense—where the individual is separate from both society and history—community that passed through different stages and meanings in the twentieth century had its own explicit and implicit demeaning features around the small town face-to-face community. These were explored in popular culture and literature through novels of different value, such as Sinclair Lewis's *Babbitt*, Grace Metalious's *Peyton Place*, and James Gould Cozzens's *By Love Possessed*. Yet, underneath the turbulence there was a consistency and stability attached to the small town when viewed from the outside.

The bicycling newspaper boy on his delivery route, a popular image of countless films, brought news of the outside world to the home, which viewers (outsiders) could not get into without going to the movies. The new national community was a mass audience, the moviegoer, who communicated with others only through common symbols and lines from films. Reality, myth, and illusion were fused as never before. This cultural and political process reached its apogee with the election of Ronald Reagan, who saw the nation as a mass audience and himself as the acting president responsible for this fusion.

Other communities emerged in the second half of the twentieth century that were congruent with imperial power and a mass audience entranced by manufactured social reality. Thanks to the media, the nation saw communities everywhere, from the business community to the medical community, to the academic community, to the defense community, and even to the artistic and intelligence communities.

The complexity of the meaning of community cannot be overestimated. On the one hand, community suggests belonging but not necessarily close relations with other members. It may indicate fear of the Other for many reasons. Throughout history plagues have helped to create the idea of cleanliness against the diseased Other. Thus, one reason given for the *cordon sanitaire* against the Soviet Union was fear of the spread of influenza and other diseases. After the First World War Western Europe was in no mood to have more millions die from an "Eastern" disease. Thus, disease helped to reinforce the enemy Other. And community was narrowed to the particular group with which one feels a subjective connection, which of course was healthy, pure, and clean.

There is a universalist idea of community that begins from the premise that anything less than acknowledging the priority of a universal community with universal needs may be disastrous for humanity as a whole. This concept stands in contradiction to those who believe that universality of values is merely an instrument of the haves against the have-nots. But the reality is that it was the belief in universal values that—when attached to nonviolent movements of social justice—has enduring force, that sustains a benign conception of politics.

There is a caveat. In the past, disease was spread by religious pilgrimages outside of one's ordinary geographic boundaries, just as now disease is spread through the global market and world travel. In an earlier period risks of death were taken for God. As the great historian William McNeill has pointed out, taking a risk for God by courting disease and war proved one's holy character.[13] One might say that taking a risk for love, as Michel Foucault said, with one's probable death as a result of AIDS, is proof of transcendence of life over death. But such notions do not build community. They merely spread despair. The important political issue about the disease AIDS is that a world community of help is organized among those known and unknown for a common purpose. The world community's instrumental purpose in helping AIDs sufferers is built on human affections.

CIVIL SOCIETY

By the end of the twentieth century, community had become an elastic concept revolving around interest groups that were thought of as the spine of civil society, taken to be more important than the entire polity, the emerging democracy itself. Civil society had an ambiguous meaning. It came to mean the totality of "intermediate" institutions, such as family and schools. It comprised what the Marxist philosopher Louis Althusser called the soft institutions of social control. But there was a more important meaning, which Marxists did not adequately consider. The civil society included voluntary acts and enforceable contracts between individuals and groups, whose activities could begin without authorization from the state. Yet, this organic and laudable process, which asserts individual action and the flowering of independent action through projects and the extension of seemingly ungoverned social space, also had serious problems. When civil society is promoted as a panacea to the excesses of the market, it fails to meet the needs of the democratic polity as a whole.

Modern civil society only has meaning when it is linked to a democracy aimed at egalitarian interdependence, for which there must be a fundamental shift in power relations or in the meaning of what power is, how it is exercised, and for whom. Projects can have different features, but all must have within them a transformative power for the person and the group toward egalitarian interdependence, and thus there is no way to avoid government's engagement. Thus, a Hegelian meaning of civil society based on religion and economic corporations such as the Fortune 500 is hardly new given the power of economic corporations and religion to dominate other institutions, people, and projects.

If community as a golden lie is to evoke a warm, fuzzy feeling, how does it react to the disciplines of economic markets that dictate competition and a system of winners and losers, a condition accepted as a given? For President Clinton, the political man with a thousand guises, volunteerism was the new answer to pick up the pieces of the broken or the loser from the competitive system. He was joined in this effort by former Senator Sam Nunn, who grew up in the genteel white Southern community, and by General Colin Powell, a former chief of staff of the armed forces whose life was determined by command and following orders within the protective shell of military socialism. People are to be lent a helping finger or two to get up and run the competitive race again. But such ideas are scripts and metaphors for films. They are not the human social reality of people's lives, especially at different stages of life. Religious workers know most about the value of volunteerism and community as a safety net for capitalism.

At different times in twentieth-century history churches as the guardian of the geographic community sought to soften those aspects of the market system that led to social oppression and depression. Such feelings were real and palpable. Critics inside and outside religious circles were not engaging in some romantic attack on the discipline of the market. People feared downturns in business cycles and the whims of management, for they could be thrown on the ash heap of history as the "downsized" or "deadwood." This is why the hierarchic Catholic Church, following the various encyclicals since Leo XIII, sought to head off equality and socialism, articulating paths of economic fairness and modes of participation for workers, albeit with very limited success against market rules.[14]

For much of the twentieth century the Catholic Church was caught in its own contradictory battles about capitalism between Dorothy Day and the worker–priest movement, on one side, and on the other side the Father Feeney and Father Coughlin variety, who railed against capitalism and Jews. In the United States the Protestant churches followed the lead of Reinhold Niebuhr, and to some extent A. J. Muste, in seeking identification of the industrial working class, especially around Detroit, with religious principles. As socialists of different stripes, they sought to soften the worker's tenuous position in the framework of corporate capitalism. There was a godspell to religion that was not the rationalization of inhumane conditions, as Marx had described religion. In the twentieth century, some believers, such as the theologian Hans Kung, sought a different role for religion, which metaphorically meant that Jesus would be freed from the cross through recognition of faith and political action for and by the wretched.

As Ernst Bloch, the Jewish philosopher and religious scholar, put it, " Religious distress is at the same time the expression of real distress and also the protest against such distress. Religion is the sigh of the oppressed creature, the heart of a heartless world, just as it is the spirit of spiritless conditions."[15] This was a feeling that could extend well beyond the working class to managers and even owners. While changes in the sentiments of corporate leaders were not to be overlooked because of religious pangs they might have felt, these sentiments needed to be reinforced through the coercive instruments of the law. In American society it was no longer enough to have the promise of life after death or heaven over hell to make the affluent generous or to ensure that the poor accepted their condition as unvarying in this world, even if all were rewarded in the next world. Rewards and punishments required a different set of incentives and utilitarian payoffs, immediate and tangible, such as the accumulation of worldly goods, a job, more money, possessions, and consumer goods. Liberal theologians understood well enough the limits within which the religious impulse of sharing and generosity operated in conventional politics. Sunday morning generosity or giving away old clothes did not mean the redistribution of power toward egalitarian interdependence.

When considering fairness and justice in the economic sphere, liberals were faced with a conundrum. Voluntary agreements based on mutual affection always seem preferable to the use of force. But in a modern society this hardly seemed tenable. Even collective bargaining contracts would not exist unless there was social agreement enforced through the state and buttressed by religious participation against traditional market principles. This was the case in California in the 1960s and 1970s, when the Catholic Church had no choice but to support the grape pickers in their boycotts against the grape owners. It is doubtful, however, that MBAs would be intimidated by talk about Hell for them in the next life. Owners and their advisors would only recognize economic justice through pressure from the government and radical churches that operate through nonviolent action and existential choices that place their adherents in danger. The fashion of those who praise the voluntaristic and contractual aspects of "civil society" avoids the question of coercion that becomes necessary when the various associations of the civil society disagree over contract or culture and custom or when religious scruples fail.

It is at the edge of profound disagreement that political choices about culture are made that determine the direction and type of society being created or re-created. Disagreement in the civil society invariably results in engaging state power. Once state power is exercised, the direction of society is determined (for example, on questions of abortion). Even rituals from religion are adjusted. Here again we are back at the question of the legitimacy of state power. Not even those who wield state power want to appear merely coercive. A new rhetoric was needed to overcome the sense of powerlessness that infected virtually everyone in what Phil Green has termed a nation living in a "pseudo democracy."[16] And this rhetoric revolved around the evanescent word *community*. After all, the unwary may think that community is of a higher order of relationship between people.

THE FLAWS OF COMMUNITY

Community is praised by liberals, even fetishized by the Right—as is the family—as an unalloyed good. Both are given ideal qualities, frozen into public relations and conservative images that have no reference to the negative aspects of both. In the past, adherents of democracy understood community as the enemy of individual rights of inclusivity and progress. Indeed, in virtually all communities, equality with outsiders is never a priority and is more likely to be considered an invalid purpose, the claims of various Christian sects notwithstanding. When thought of as a geographic space, community was (and remains!) a code word for political control by local oligarchies that had marginal interest in providing opportunities, services, or enforceable rights for the less and least fortunate.

The modern, romantic view of community cannot easily escape from an unsavory past. The mythical power of community is that it represents an existential yearning that stems from an emptiness brought about by invisible market forces, revolutionary technology, capitalism, and state socialism. Exceptions might be pointed to in the early period of the kibbutz movement, when Martin Buber's attempts to present the ideal of community, a kind of communitarian socialism based on I-thou relationships, seemed to have taken root. But there was a serious flaw that has not been overcome: the problem of the kibbutz as a quasi-military outpost against Arabs. As socialism lost strength internationally and as global capitalist markets became dominant, the original idealistic notions of kibbutz communitarianism lost their appeal. By the twenty-first century capitalism and militarism were the ground upon which the kibbutz existed.[17]

Communities were predicated on exclusion and fear of the Other. Whether it is the intelligence community, the business community, the white, black, or gay community, there is the organizing assumption that a bond of identification and interest exists, giving credence and purpose to the participant's life. This sentiment may contradict universalism in the sense of human decency and respect, as well as equality, since universalism erases boundaries and opens people of different communities to equality. (This was the genius of the organizers of the early Christian Church.) Universalism recognizes similar categories of qualities in all people.

In most communities it is assumed that trust can exist only among the like-minded. And where there is a community of the partial whole, that is, the nation, there remains that form of nativism in practice that is built on exclusion of the foreign other. This meaning of community plagues all nations, none more so than the United States, where attempts by fits and starts have been made to both include and exclude immigrants when that serves economic and social purposes. Such has been the case in economic recessions and security fears of the kind that emerged after September 11, 2001.

There is a sinister meaning to community that cannot be wished away. It is unfortunate but true that ideological emphasis on community throughout much of the twentieth century found fervent supporters among those who favored the "cult of the blood." Its early twentieth-century adherents, from Alfred Rosenberg and Houston Chamberlain to Charles Murray and Richard Herrnstein, looked for community on the basis of blood and biology.[18] This is governed by the implicit understanding that those outside the community are not equal to those inside it. The dangers of such thought are obvious. The result is policies that can have devastating effects, as in the case of current welfare and criminal laws that reinforce inequality and difference to protect the "community" against "these people"—that is, the minorities and the poor. Order becomes the goal of public policy so as to protect dominant communities.[19]

Indeed, neighborhoods in the United States often organize themselves as communities to keep out halfway houses for recovering drug addicts or the mentally retarded. Tragically, many nations of the world organize themselves in terms of race and claims of cultural superiority against the Other.

As in so many other arenas of twentieth-century life, community in its life-affirming meaning rather than its romantic attack on modernism came to be linked to the ideal of wholeness and, therefore, world community. This is reflected in attempts at ecumenism, the language of UN declarations and resolutions, and ideas of transcendence, from Gandhi (who eschewed the state in favor of face-to-face communities and cottage industries) to King's universalistic purpose. The political ideal for the liberal and radical democrat of "standing with" the deprived and colonized is a central part of third-stage liberalism. It seeks to join or formulate practices of the world community while favoring and protecting small, independent communities that reflect values that, for example, were enunciated at the beginning of the twentieth century by such organizations as the Women's International League for Peace and Freedom and most recently by the gifted historian and economist Gar Alperovitz.

In the American context all politicians and most scholars and journalists appropriated certain words as if they were a mantra not to be analyzed, merely repeated. None was more successful than Ronald Reagan, who never tired of using the word "democracy" even as his political purpose was that of cementing in place oligarchy.

Unfortunately, packaging symbols, such as community and democracy, that are free of content represents an important aspect of American commercial and political genius. As an actor and salesman for General Electric, Reagan mastered the use of these symbols.

TECHNOLOGY DESTROYS AND CREATES COMMUNITY

Because the democratic liberal project stems from political revolutions, it should not be surprising that there is great fascination with and acceptance of the continuing revolutions through science and technology as they affect everyday life. Whether the automobile and truck, the airplane, or computers and semiconductors, technology has transformed communities. The management of human beings has become a technology to align human behavior in relation to the machine. A machine has boundaries structured within itself that cannot be crossed, as for example in the case of computers. The "as if" world in turn becomes an instrument for the rearrangement of social and political reality. Is there any better emblem of modern time than those who collapsed space and time into one continuum?

Whether people are sitting before a computer screen or producing information for it, modern technology changes the character and content of people's lives and the meaning of community in "real time." Every human body takes on new aspects. Like astronauts who float inside their space capsules, ordinary humans linked through internets, or described on them, appear to float or be suspended in space like a Dali painting unencumbered by a linear history or context. As political campaign managers, Disney executives, and computer experts have shown, advances in technology and communications allow the inventive to intrude, juxtaposing one event on another, linking visually *The Last Supper* with *Guernica.* A person's face can be turned into that of a tyrant as we watch. We can concoct Beethoven's *Ode to Joy* as the background music to sell the Mercedes Benz or present Siemens as a great corporation whose past is impeccable (without reference to its ties to Hitler). We can present Donald Duck as real, more real than photons, and create images of our internal thought processes and thoughts that we make believe are the way we think about life, death, parents, and shame. Words are made up to be information bytes, chock full of someone's information, sometimes accurate but always limited, that describe the contradiction of beliefs in who we are and what we think is true or false. We don't exist except as symbols in virtual reality. Some enthusiasts claim that the Internet segments audiences, thus weakening national and community ties by catering to the desires of niche audiences who have become netizens without national and geographic loyalty. There is nothing to suggest that "netizens" will develop wisdom from images and information. We are as likely to spread false information and lies as relatively truthful accounts. Rather than information "setting us free," we are increasingly puzzled and decentered by raw but manufactured images accompanied by factoids.

If everything is permitted in technology and society, why not transform linkages for people that emphasize fantasy as reality? Medical geneticists create the hope among the well-off that someday they will be able to live 150 years and genetic imperfections will be corrected. Guaranteed. In the *Purple Rose of Cairo,* Woody Allen has us watching an actor coming off the screen in a movie theater to symbolize the overwhelming power and reality of film in our lives. A computer plays chess and beats a grand master, a website sells us information and products that turn our homes into marketplaces, and university professors post courses on their websites. But what cultural meaning does such activity have? Does it enhance a world community of the kind envisioned by Gandhi, King, Buber, or Muste? Do these illusions and "advances" in medicine create community or merely emphasize disparities in lived reality?

The globalized corporate communications network creates connections on the basis of an abstract "as if" reality that requires the person to live in different worlds—bereft of relationships and feeling. Where possible, people are pleased to join the interactive dream colony where they can meld their own lives into an "as if" world that does not exist, except through the fantasy of computer images that simulate reality. Community takes on a new meaning. Slowly but surely we come to believe that the only way we can or should reach out and touch somebody is through the telephone, computer, and television. The economy that propels the technocommunity forward, against community, should not be mistaken for world community. It is merely a variant of marketeering.

While turning experiences into information bytes for exposure on a CD-ROM is a kind of progress whose value we cannot quite assess, the question still remains whether there is an "ozone" hole in the center of humanity, first noticed by Kierkegaard, that grows larger each day and cannot be salved through the microchip. Of course these are critiques. And no doubt at every stage of modernism there have been those who refused to take part or saw themselves as excluded from wondrous changes whose value was found after the invention or discovery. Holdouts such as the harmless Amish are burlesqued in music videos. Gandhi would become a postmodern image morphed into a cow that spins cloth—all to the music of Ravi Shankar. So what can third-stage liberalism address that will retain its universalistic possibility?

During the Cold War, among war planners much energy was devoted to the technology of how to manipulate time and space for war. It was thought that a president had no more than seven minutes to decide whether to send nuclear missiles against the Soviet Union if the Soviets "started it." At the beginning of the twenty-first century American war planners remain obsessed with an exquisite system of proxy war fighting through the computer, robots, high-altitude bombing, information control, and so-called high- and low-tech schemes. They are also burdened with the need to integrate military forces with each other, the economy, and propaganda. In the long-term post–September 11 period we can note that there will be a tendency on the part of the United States to attempt to erase time and space at the expense of other cultures' traditions and political needs. But technology must be understood as part of different cultures and a world civilization. When Osama bin Laden speaks to the world through television and radio, or when funds are moved from one electronic account to another, it is obvious that there is no escape of even the most antimodernist ideologies from the reality of science and technology.

DESTROYING OLD MYTHS OF COMMUNITY

Within the popular culture we can find evidence of resistance requiring its own social methodology that is not neutral, just as the social science of the status quo is not neutral.[20] The question is whether the market system, the social character necessary to survive in capitalism, and the willingness to accept illusion and the reconfiguration of culture as presented through television, the mall, and the media will be enough to keep stability and peace. Or will membership by individuals in multiple groups accommodate and choose modern markets, that is, the web and Internet, as their meeting places? Perhaps part of the answer can be found in the relationship among art, aesthetics, and technology.

This new aesthetic was created by cultural craftspeople (working with behavioral psychologists) who knew better but could not practice an art that did not justify the profitable sale of things. Soon the packaging and the sign were more important than the thing to be bought and used. The production of leisure and illusion, as well as the production of war-making goods praised in advertising campaigns, became the dominant product of the American system during the Cold War, but in this regard nothing changed at the end of the Cold War.[21]

In the twentieth century technology created an aesthetics of gigantism. Its architecture and public design, whether highways or skyscrapers, gave rise to dystopic communities. Taken together, they stood as a melding of the severe and the functional, which created its own dysfunctionality, as in the case of buildings whose windows didn't open, making each building a virus and bacterial trap from which there was no escape, or highways in cities that reinforced segregation and class separation.

An ecology of balance and "harmony" was desperately needed in the design of the city, in the products themselves, and in places of production, but none was forthcoming that would challenge the dominant styles of the market. A popular aesthetic that would present such a harmony or challenge the dominant corporate designs could be found only among marginal groups. Conservatives wanted to deny the aesthetic critique and praised the sort of art and aesthetics that hid the decadence of the perfect form that totalitarians made the standard of art and aesthetics in the twentieth century.

But what kind of present aesthetic and art accepts as settled the following conditions? According to the Brandt report of 1979:

> The North, including Eastern Europe, has a quarter of the world's population and four fifths of its income; the South including China has three billion people—three quarters of the world's population but living on one-fifth of the world's income. In the North the average person can expect to live for more than seventy years; he or she will rarely be hungry, and will be educated at least up to secondary level. In the countries of the South the great majority of people have a life expectancy of closer to fifty years; in the poorest countries one out of every four children dies before the age of five; one-fifth or more of all the people in the South suffer from hunger and malnutrition, fifty percent have no chance to become literate.[22]

Of course, nations do not accept such conditions; they have gotten much worse. It is well to keep in mind that primarily nonwhites suffer most in economic and security matters. These conditions have not improved over the last generation. This situation is relevant to attempts by American society to more than flirt with multiculturalism. The startling reality is that the assumption that the United States is a "middle class" society seems absurd at the beginning of the twenty-first century when the incomes of thirteen thousand families at the top of the income wealth scale equal those of twenty million households in the United States, according to the economist Paul Krugman.[23]

6

★

Social Character and the Liberalism of Social Reconstruction

THE FORMATION OF SOCIAL CHARACTER

There is a natural trope in people that bends toward decency and caring. It is why the human species has continued.[1] In democracy, this trope is reinforced by an emerging consciousness that calls for fairness and inclusivity for all people. In turn, this consciousness creates a continuing motion toward universalism, beginning with the person and his or her need for the Other.[2] This is the basis of an almost tectonic motion toward world civilization. In American civilization, inclusivity became congruent with egalitarian interdependence. As I have said, political equality and economic justice meant that each person had responsibility for the other. How was this responsibility to be manifested? It was through that dirty word, "government."

In the words of Abraham Lincoln, "It is the legitimate object of government to do for the people what needs to be done, but cannot be done at all, or as well, by individual effort."[3] In a highly integrated modern society, the fact that one person's function or social role differs from another's does not change the need for mutual cooperation based on recognition of the human rather than instrumental worth of the person, irrespective of his or her capacities.[4]

Throughout much of the twentieth century, democratizing movements of inclusivity in the United States and elsewhere took this view as a starting point. Their intent was to reshape social mores in the arena of most concern to their needs. These appeared to be merely changes in specific institutions where the shoe fit too tightly among those who thought themselves colonized. But in fact, as a cumulative matter the society's institutions, from churches to schools to universities, were to change through political pressure, and, as the changes occurred, they would share in the fashioning of a "rainbow" character. Formerly submerged groups, whether the disabled, gays, women, or minorities, were to benefit by the changes and gains made through direct access to resources, even democratic control such as capital, technology, and education, which guides the content of political inclusivity by seeing the Other as a person who deserves dignity. This onslaught meant that the very social character of the society was to change because consciousness had shifted.

The emerging social character would give practical life to the spirit of liberal democracy. Transformed institutions would link consciousness, the productive process, and those features of human nature that sustain dignity and decency. A preferred social character is necessary for the maintenance and expansion of democracy just as an authoritarian social character reinforces authoritarianism.[5]

The modern axial social character of democracy called for the reinterpretation and re-creation of feminine/masculine myths so that men and women would be complementary and eschew political domination of one over the other. In practical terms, this meant that the democratic social character would run counter to those myths that give rise to the social character based on that domination.

The importance of social character in the struggle for dignity and decency cannot be overestimated, for, as Erich Fromm has pointed out, social character is that "relatively permanent system of all non-instinctual strivings through which man [sic] relates himself to the human and natural world."[6] This is why there is a fierce struggle over public education, family values, patriarchy, gender, and race definition. For conservatives, including those identified with neoliberalism, social character requires control over institutions to ensure a conservative social character based on individual interests, which is translated into the politics of competitiveness that is tolerated by hierarchy and domination.[7] One sees this most clearly in imperialism, where open markets and competition are dependent on or favor domination by the powerful.

It would be easy to believe Erich Fromm's insight that the marketing social character has defined American civilization and culture.[8] Indeed, the mantra of the Clinton and Bush administrations and the Chicago School of Economics would reinforce that idea, namely, conflating the unfettered market with democracy. The marketing character gives the appearance of overwhelming all other social characters. As Fromm argues,

> For the marketing character, everything is transformed into a commodity—not only things, but the person himself [sic], his physical energy, his skills, his opin-

ions, his knowledge, his feelings, even his smiles. This character type is a historically new phenomenon because it is a product of a fully developed capitalism that is centered around the market—the commodity market, the labor market, and the personality market—and whose principle it is to make a profit by favorable exchange.[9]

But liberals understood the contradictions inherent in competition and domination. For John R. Commons, the eminent economist at the University of Wisconsin, life was a self-conscious activity, manifested through transactions. These transactions reflected power, and the power of proportion and choice. This might be thought of in modern terms as rational choice:

> It is the life of man [sic] in society, the life of expansion of the individual through opportunities and power available mainly through transactions with others, and the life of economy through proportioning these opportunities and powers. It is this scheme of proportioning, as already suggested, that reveals character, individuality, personality, and coordinates ethics with economics. For morally and ethically, this proportioning of opportunities and powers is the means of self-expression, self-development, and "self realization."[10]

However, Commons revealed a weakness in capitalism as it relates to democracy:

> Economically, it is economizing one's power over the services of others, in order to obtain the maximum result as determined by the character of the man who is thus realizing himself. The ethical aspect is the scheme of human values that centers about his personality. The economic aspect is the proportioning of all the external factors according to their instrumental value in realizing this scheme of human values.[11]

But if power—over the individual by another individual or entity—is not shared, then an unaccountable hierarchy of the powerful over the weak will naturally result. There will be a restriction of those to whom it is necessary to show justice and fairness, and indeed, of those who will make decisions. In this scenario, a democratic social character cannot be sustained in work or inside the inviolability of the corporation preached by the great moguls of the early twentieth century. Thorsten Veblen and John Dewey, among others, believed that modern capitalism had become the operational instrument to effect control over the powerless. This is why Commons placed so much faith in collective action, and then collective bargaining, as a means of balancing owner capital.

To liberals, a profound contradiction was obvious not only in the different ways that the rich and powerful lived and exercised power compared to the poor—even middle class—but also in the meaning of democracy. Democracy demanded limits to unfairness. It also asserted a very wide band of equality. For some libertarians, whether of the Left or Right, this meant attempts were to be made to return to an Edenic origin.[12] In other words, the human being, having been corrupted by institutions, could find a state of natural grace in building institutions that took advantage for social purposes.

So argued Jean-Jacques Rousseau and those Americans who developed communistic societies (often rigid and authoritarian in their social mores) on American soil that stopped and started again in a more benign form in hippie communes. For those who held to this view, it meant decoupling from the dominant mores. They wanted to escape from what they perceived to be a runaway technology, developing a "new man" who would transcend the human tragedies of history.[13] Saints could be emulated, and communities of belief and saintliness could last at least for a generation.

By the twentieth century, dictators recognized the existence of the "*volk*" and the "masses." They rejected democracy and the democratic social character as weak, flying in the face of the manlier attributes of conflict, war, and struggle. Parties and cabals stipulated that their actions were being conducted for the general welfare, whether it was Hitler in Germany or Stalin in the Soviet Union. Aggressive leaders and political groups could write their projects and adventures on the lives of others. In its most extreme form, the antidemocratic social character was thought to be an exercise of pure will. Reality would bend to the leader principle—in whatever field of endeavor.

In the political sphere this attitude was disastrous. It had already been identified as such by American revolutionaries in the eighteenth century, and by the nineteenth-century American moralist, Mark Twain. Twain lived at a time when ethics and morality were dominated by the witches' brew of race superiority, violence, and privilege. This combination showed itself in the system of slavery and its long-lived detritus, which Twain understood as an ongoing problem far more than an American dilemma. Twain understood what seventy-five years later Gunnar Myrdal did not: that racism was more than a management problem.[14] Twain saw racism as the ugly side of American narratives in which laws, policies, and custom had condoned race superiority and sought to repress the emergence of axial impulses. These were reflected in abolitionism and in Philippine independence movements that were crushed by American armed forces who claimed to be Christian civilizers. In *Huck Finn,* Twain makes clear that human rights must always trump the slavery of property "rights," whatever the consequences.

Subversive thinkers saw the American purpose on a split screen, forever triumphal and revolutionary, filled with hubris and seeking universal liberation, yet also filled with doubt and willingness to reexamine the premises of the American purpose. The writings of social reconstruction were based on an expansion of understanding and consciousness that would fit with ideas of progress and positive evolution for the individual and the group, irrespective of race. Indeed, Herman Melville, among others, sought to show in his fictional characters his own brand of what we would now call multiculturalism. There were many cultures and civilizations outside of Puritanism and Presbyterianism, as Melville pointed out. In *Moby Dick,* Queequeg says, "[W]e cannibals must help these Christians" who drive themselves and others to madness by their actions and will. The saving grace of humanity, for Melville, was the practical formation of religious and cultural relativism, a conception that is basic to democracy. The question is raised whether a democracy, which includes cultural relativism, can have a destructive effect on the world, especially where ideals and reality are in stark contradiction.

Few Western nations escaped the corrupting "civilizing mission" of triumphalism until they were forced to surrender this role to liberation struggles in Indonesia, Indochina, Latin America, and Africa. Paradoxically, as has been noted innumerable times, these struggles were given rhetorical heft by eighteenth-century Western ideals that the West contradicted in practice. Those acted upon saw that the cannibals were the civilizers. Perhaps when the "civilizers" stopped for an instant analysis of themselves, they also wondered who or what they were. This is what occurred to many during the Indochina war, as people came to recognize that their doubts and skepticism about war were not alien to the American tradition or to the formation of the American social character.

CHILDREN AND FAIRNESS

Just as organized murder in war must be learned before most young men will undertake their soldierly duties of killing, so too unfairness had to be learned to ensure that class and social stratification was maintained and reproduced. Children have a strong sense of injustice when they are confronted with a command or attitude they perceive as either unfair or against their interests. This usually means that privilege and preference are given, for no apparent reason, to one over another. While that sensibility probably reflects a growing sense of self that each child needs to mature, and while there very well might be the capacity for an innate sense or inclination for fairness, the feature of fairness is socially organized. It either receives social stimulation or it will wilt.

Children are the first boundary setters against the Other as a way to attain their own self-definition of individuality, which is not, as Dewey pointed out, the same as individualism. As a person matures, the capacity for fairness may be overcome by desires of the personal self against the Other, especially when the economics of scarcity, surfeit, or insecurity become central social and institutional goals, and selfishness is taught by parents and society as the way of negotiating life's deficits. Intentionally, unknowingly, or by default, parents internalize for their children a vision of what they want them to be, what the future may hold outside of the parent or child, even what society and the state should be like.

The present fashion among politicians is to accept the importance of the first several years of life as the person's paramount definer. The claim that children who are not helped in the first few years are lost relieves the body politic of undertaking any social welfare, economic, or educational programs on the spurious ground that there is little or nothing that can be done after the supposed formative and developmental years, except minimal maintenance and punitive "corrections." If liberals accept the premise of human development—that the traumas of childhood development in the lives of people who live seventy, eighty, and ninety years play the determining role for them individually and socially—a society mistakenly will be inclined to forfeit the idea of personal and social progress throughout a person's active life. Liberal democracy suffers grievously by asserting that a person's life is a closed book after, say, five years of age. A democracy of reconstruction asserts change and betterment, dignity and decency, as continuing purposes that people can achieve throughout their lives through a combination of individual choice and humane social organization. What must be provided are those cultural and educational possibilities as well as health aids that reinforce freedom and dignity at every stage of a person's life. It should be noted that in the United States the community college is such an instrument. The establishment of federal education trust funds is another example for personal and social dignity and betterment.

THE MIND OF VIRTUAL MAN

Some will see another social character, linked and crafted by technology, compatible with the marketing character of individualism and the play activities of children. It has been strengthened through the communications system, the military, and filmic technologies developed in war and cold war. It is the virtual man who may be emerging in rich societies as a result of the technology of communication and connection. The virtual man's experiences do not lead to social affections and identification of self with other in a loving sense. The virtual man's world is confined to a series of commands, mouse clicks, and algorithmic sentences. The machines used, such as computers, film, and television, are all instruments that complement a series of transactions in an expanded marketplace, which emphasizes the deal and knowledge as product. Implications are either secondary or tertiary concerns. The question that arises is whether these two social characters, the virtual man and the marketing character, manifested in the human, can extend themselves beyond the series of algorithmic instructions of the computer or the transaction. In other words, is there, within this emerging social character, a life-affirming sentiment?

To the extent that the virtual man and the marketing social character operate solely on the basis of functional behavior, large-scale democracy will not escape the bureaucratic and hierarchic, the efficient inefficiency within the partners of modern life: the mammoth corporation and the national security complex of surveillance, defense, police, and prison. Here we can see the tragic robotic figure of a generation past, Robert McNamara.[15] We also witness the robber baron mentality of those who have organized the existence of the virtual man through complex corporate organization, which struggles for dominance against other corporations, as in the case, say, of Microsoft.

Whereas the manufacturing barons of the twentieth century, such as Henry Ford, emphasized leaving home through the automobile, the new computer baron emphasizes staying at home and seeing the world and universe virtually. Both notions are hardly emancipatory and have their own problems of alienation and anxiety. In addition, the technology of communications fits with the mistaken idea of the disembodied, which guided so much thinking in liberal free speech. The idea of a free-floating interplay— a market of thinking, talking heads competing with one another—fits with the concept of separation of mind and body. The computer and Internet have become the triumph of René Descartes's bodiless mind and mechanical body. Yet, the twentieth century showed that there had to be an integration of mind and body for the good of humanity, of emotions and intelligence, whether in the growth of the child or the wisdom of the human being as group or societal participant. The humane and political standard would seem to require the abandonment of a free-floating market of free-floating information, just at the very moment that such a notion seems to be brought to fruition through the Internet and other such processes.

The evolutionary nature of capitalism and technology has resulted in a new symbiosis, which may become increasingly obvious during the twenty-first century and will cause a social character other than that spawned by consumer individualism. Individual workers might end up renting the means of production, namely, the Internet, as an important method of doing and creating markets for small and micro business. For workers not entrepreneurially inclined and organizers of political and social change, the Internet creates a process of reaching out to new audiences and computer pals that have common purposes and interests. This includes new markets of interest that seek to bring together "consumers and buyers." Perhaps the effects of modern communications technology may bring about a very different and surprising revolution that will turn against the hierarchic and bureaucratic. This could change the conditions of work, therefore altering one aspect of alienation in modern life. This was the intention of experimental and clinical psychologists who held to gestalt theories of mind–body integration as a means of curbing the stress of modern life.

DEMOCRATIC THERAPIES FOR THE MIDDLE CLASS: BUBER AND THE MORAL CONTOURS OF DEMOCRACY

Following the work of the psychoanalyst Alfred Adler after World War II, therapies such as problem-solving group sessions gained favor, giving the alienated person a feeling of belonging while recognizing toleration for differences. The group would make the solution of personal problems easier since most people lived in a group at work, in families, and in hierarchies. But could the group give support and provide room for confessionals and critiques of one's personal behavior? A therapy group would give the person strength to act (will) and a sense of boundaries of how to act, without being concerned about punishment, while eschewing political power in favor of personal well-being. Authority belonged in the oppositions that developed among the individual, the group, and the therapist.

Hidden behind American psychology in its various guises was a combination of optimism and will, which would encourage the person to get a fresh start and escape that which was causing personal "dysfunctionality." Beyond the hot tubs and the language of sincere insincerity, "I hear you" and "I know where you're coming from," there was an attempt to find or create social institutions that would allow the person face-to-face encounters of honesty with attributes of empathy. Were such ideas in practice foolish moments of indulgence, as conservatives would have it, and were hippies' romantic attempts to find the nonviolent in humanity and nature itself a waste of time? Indeed not, for they were reflective of yearnings and meanings that have gone unfulfilled and unexplained in modern society. That is why it is of value to look for enlightenment in twentieth-century existentialists.

Suppose we were to take Martin Buber's idea of the I-thou as a basis for democracy. It affirms egalitarian interdependence and economic and social justice, while taking account of the psychological, and even a religious and therapeutic spirit that could be found in William James.[16] Is such an idea a building block to sustain democracy? Like other existentialists, Buber did not pretend to have a complete system, a series of certitudes, an infallible method, or even unshakable beliefs. Like Melville, he realized that certainty and certitude of moral uprightness could lead to horrifying results.

Such awareness we may count as beneficial, for liberal democracy is not comfortable with a closed system, either for the individual or the group.

However, this means that a person's future puts in jeopardy what the person knows and what the person thought was his or her culture and civilization. Even with the golden noose of rationality and irrationality, science and faith, romanticism or realism, humankind stands on a very narrow and rocky ridge where there is no sureness about anything. Humankind must make judgments about much that is undisclosed, and it cannot be helped by technical information or biblical injunctions. This is the modern statement of anxiety and alienation.

But is it also democracy? This is why dialogue is so crucial among people—the dialogue of equals beyond class or social role. It is why the experiential and the traditional are important, not as controlling precedents, but as data to consider in any concrete situation. Buber's ideas of dialogue and of the I-thou leave open contradiction, inconsistency, and paradox as the modality of life. These ideas, as strong as they are, do not take us to the question of what it is that humanity, in the sense of any size group beyond two people, must necessarily take into account and accept as the ground upon which it stands. The small community can be as soulless as the large impersonal one. It is knowing the ground upon which the person stands, both in natural and political/economic terms, that liberates the person and reinforces the attributes of any size democracy. Social life in modern societies requires attention to inner feelings as a gauge to ascertain the relevance of democracy to people's inner lives. The problem with such a formulation is that totalitarians know the importance of manipulating inner feelings of boredom, alienation, loneliness, and anxiety.

THE GROUP AND MORAL LIMITS

Buber's concern is transmuted into the meaning of the boundary lines within "I-in-we" and then the small group within larger entities. Here we see different strands of the ideal community that are intended to enhance individual judgment beyond technical knowledge. There is a continuing dialogue that includes discussion about reasonable and unreasonable choices.

In the American context, small groups included families, which laid the basis for the small town. In turn, towns laid the basis for face-to-face political relationships beyond the family. According to Lewis Mumford, the township as conceived in the eighteenth century could have provided the guide for both a democratic social character and the political units in which actual face-to-face relationships could occur. Townships included a group of towns that were linked in purpose and political relationship, but were, unfortunately, according to Mumford, overlooked as political entities in the Constitution.[17]

The small group idea of politics cannot benefit anyone beyond face-to-face dialogue if the Stranger, the Other, is thought of either as an enemy or a slave. As seductive as it might appear to be, the small group face-to-face relationship does not escape the need to break down the boundary line between Otherness and its counterpart, ersatz rectitude. Groups often form on the basis of fear and disdain of the Other. They dress these fears with an ideological or religious overlay that to an objective outsider may seem petty or absurd. Differences among groups cause them to lose sight of ethical principles, which are applicable within and beyond any particular community, neighborhood, group, or nation.

The markers are premised on alterity, on alternatives, and on the continuing existence of the Other, who must be reached toward. For Buber, this is the never-ending dialogue. What happened in the small group through the dialogue of the I-thou could be translated into general terms and applied widely as a social method and beyond the immediate and present. Dialogue is key to the experimental and inquiry. However, American social science and the society mistakenly adopted measurement and categorization as a substitute for dialogue.

MEASUREMENT, SCIENTIFIC
EXPERIMENT, AND MORAL IMPLICATIONS

It is taken for granted that to survive and succeed, the person will develop a particular social character that fits with the dominant institutions and economy of the society. Obviously, any society will have different social characters, but one will always be dominant. In modern societies, examination and measurements are used by established institutions so that people will know their place. They become important instruments in deciding which social character will be favored.

Measurement became part of the means of forming American social character and determining political power. Quantitative measurement is the universal instrument in electoral, social, financial, medical, and penal settings. In people's everyday lives, measurement is reduced to a score on a piece of paper as a mode of social characterization. The chauffeur wears black, the maid a little apron, and the priest a turned around collar as a means of separation, social distance, and instant identity recognition by the Other. Similarly, a person's score became the mode of "objective" measurement of where the person "fits" into the society. For those categorized according to disease or risk of disease on the basis of statistics, it might mean hardship to obtain employment or inability to obtain insurance, although it might also mean prevention of disease. In matters of race, where statistical measurement had been used to show a pattern or practice of discrimination, courts overruled measurement with countermeasurements. In other words, statistics and measurement became a modern instrument in political rhetoric. Competing rhetorics were played on the fields of statistics and counter-statistics and scientific advocacy, from polling and marketing data to claims and counterclaims of nuclear waste and reactor damage. This is far away from the rather pristine and seemingly naïve views Dewey had of scientific inquiry.

Dewey turned to scientific inquiry as the antielitist and democratic mode, claiming that the method of twentieth-century liberalism was experimental:

> [I]t should be a generalization from the experiences of the past; a generalization which does not, however, merely repeat or restate in a literal fashion the experience of the past, but is stated in such a way that it will apply to changed conditions of the present and future; that it will serve as an intellectual instrument of survey and criticisms and will point out the direction in which efforts at change and betterment could move. It indicates that the generalization should be a hypothesis, not a dogma; something to be tried and tested, confirmed and revised in future practice; having a constant point of growth instead of being closed.[18]

But by the end of the century Dewey's form of modernism held no magic. Science and technology were recognized as limited instruments with regard to the most important questions of the "human predicament," and, as a result, science as a method rather than as an inquiry was deemed defective.[19]

The scientific experiment seemed to exclude concern for those who were the objects of the experiment under the theory that this was "good" science. On the other hand, Dewey had no intention of excluding those who were to benefit from the social experiment. They had to be full participants in the dialogue of the experiment, both in its process and outcome. Unfortunately, Dewey, as an exponent of instrumentalism, came to stand for an experimental method that seemed to fit well into the hierarchic and bureaucratic organizational structure where people became objects of the "scientific method" under the promise that their lives would improve.

The passing of the person into the "it" through the dominant ideology of "white race" perfectibility brought eugenics into Western practice. Eugenics was to be used in Nazi programs for sterilization. Northern European welfare states, including the Soviet Union, and conservatives and liberals in the United States all sought to rid the nations of slothfulness and antisocial behavior.[20] Eugenics was thought to be the corrective for mental and physical disability, aggressiveness, and anger, as well as impotence. Thus, the goal of genetic science and cloning was to move to a controlled environment where, in this Brave New World, the problems of deficit, unhappiness, alienation, and violence would disappear. Such ideas were behind the Supreme Court's acceptance of sterilization as a means of protecting the species and social order.[21] Twentieth-century governments, with scientific support, believed that human beings were blank slates awaiting any messages that the powerful, the good, or the evil wanted to write on them. Humankind was not a blank slate to be written on. Rather, conservatives held that people had certain unvarying capacities that they conflated with absolutist dogmas. But the invariable moral sense could be snuffed out by uncaring and miscare. If these capacities were left undeveloped, great damage would result to the person and the society at large. Thus, the capacity for empathy, when undeveloped, would wither, with damaging consequences for the person and society.

MODERN AXIALISM AND PROGRESSIVE DOUBTS

In the twentieth century existentialists (cosmetologists and plastic surgeons!) argued that humankind and individuals could remake and transcend themselves through choices people made. If human beings did not have this insight about their situation, they were enslaved. Science meant nothing, and education in the old verities merely reinforced the hierarchic structures that oppressed the very many for the very few, unless society would adopt the view of knowledge as power for human liberation.

Such ideas of freedom have informed all movements of the Left since the eighteenth-century revolutions. It was undeniable that nineteenth-century reform ideas resonated among the middle classes. Who, for example, could oppose clean drinking water or the separation of sewage systems from drinking water? Nineteenth-century reforms regarding clean water and sewage changed populations from a sickly mass to one of comparative health, allowing people to live longer. It did not seem onerous that taxes would have to be raised for this purpose.

Fixed principles, which defined either institutions or people as "settled," were under continuous scrutiny and attack. The fact of wanting to change the human condition, whether in a collective or individual manner, suggested that as a political matter, human natures were not fixed in stone. Transcendent essences seemed foolish in light of a materialist and pragmatist understanding of life. And the search for truth seemed to be a Sunday school purpose, or one that scientists introduced to put themselves on the side of the immutable, namely, God. Progress increased skepticism and doubt about all seemingly settled matters in science and religion.

In the American context, there was an ally of skepticism in, of all places, the Constitution. Division of power and authority among the three branches of government, a formulation of Montesquieu's *The Spirit of the Laws*, was made politically relevant in the American constitutional governing structure, based as it was on skepticism and distrust. The three branches came to check and cross-check each other. Over time this institutional brake, predicated on doubt of unilateral and unchecked power, came to be an integral part of the American social character. Doubt about the motives of others and institutions gave rise to skepticism if not outright paranoia. But the eighteenth-century notion of divided authority was related to a continuing dialogue that would attempt to reach a synthesis of the common good.

Adherents of the new man ideal were found not only among saints and the devilish. Modernism seemed to demand a different person than the type that existed before the twentieth century. Those who believed in scientism, in the escape from one's past through the cumulative discovery of nature's secrets, continued to hold to the potentiality of progress through science and technology, which would make humankind whole. However, insecurity and distrust of the Other came with emphasis on individual rights and the implications of scientific manipulations.

Mid-twentieth-century theologians, such as Reinhold Niebuhr, complained that those who held such views were attempting to replace God with Man. Humanity, to Niebuhr, could not pretend to too much, for to be too idealistic would mean the loss of the possible. But science, technology, and the Dionysian attributes in the American ethos ignited a new social character based on a universal and complementary myth of masculine and feminine. To the reconstruction liberal committed to the liberal project there was a "feedback loop." That is, by people fulfilling their capacities and abilities, a good society might result and, by attempting to achieve a good society, the citizenry's social character and individual capacities would be greatly improved, if not fulfilled.

Within this idea of perfectibility there was no reason to believe that any one period of a person's life determined his or her destiny. Modern liberals concluded that public engagement and expenditure could be profitably aimed at the objective of progress and perfectibility. It was not enough to repair or "let nature take its course." It was necessary to transcend by looking outward to the construction of the modern democratic world.

For axialists—those people who had secularized the idea of world community—each person had a trope or inclination toward an empathic and ethical willingness to do good rather than bad. Modern nations with democratic aspirations recognized this inherent attribute for all people, not only an "aristo." As Melville taught, there was a human interdependence and affection that could be denied but only at the peril of humanity. It was this problem to which Franklin Roosevelt spoke in his various addresses to the nation. He understood that there had to be restitching of the social fabric of the nation and that it could not be done without appealing to the condition of fundamental goodness in people. But this goodness was the fuel of government actions.[22] And it was not enough to restitch the fabric of society in old ways.

According to Roosevelt, the nation had to go beyond mere repair. It had to transform existing conditions and develop new institutions. It had to reach human interdependence and cooperation. But could the federal government act to empower the citizenry? Less than a generation after Roosevelt's death, the New Left both doubted and took for granted the federal government. During the Vietnam War, the New Left claimed that, within a racist and class-driven system, there was little possibility for the relativism of egalitarian interdependence, unless there was a transformation of American society's beliefs and attitudes. This transformation could not come from the federal government.

For the New Left, there was to be a kind of Jeffersonianism without racism; that is, it was to be a return to the small: the village and town accompanied by the larger society's notions of male dominance. (A condition women in the movement rebelled against.) And since many in the New Left's ancestry were centered in the East European shtetl, the Midwestern small town, and the New England town meeting, they believed that the self-reliant life inside community was the fulfilling one. The federal government had been defiled by the national security state, nuclearism, the Indochina war, and domestic programs that exacerbated cleavages in the nation. Such, for example, was the effect of the interstate highway program. These realities blinded the New Left to the federal government's positive role as the potential enabler of local community and defender against the excesses of the market and the big corporation. On the other hand, Jeffersonianism had become the shared rhetoric to hide the reality of gigantism in the economy and the decay of civil government.

EDUCATION, SOCIAL CONTROL, AND MANAGERIALISM

Through social control, expertise, and managerialism, education retained class and retrograde characteristics. School remained the extension of the factory, or for some, often blacks and other minorities, the prison. Education was not education for or through democracy, with the capacity to write and deliberate about ordinances, constitutions, and laws, but for wages, job skills, and financial profit. The liberal position, as reflected in the work of Jonathan Kozol, Dewey, Henry Giroux, and the Wisconsin School of Education, especially Michael Apple, could not overcome the great corporations, which demanded that workers be educated at public expense for particular "marketable" skills, including social skills such as employee respect, submission, and punctuality. Such conceptions fit perfectly with those who believed that the purpose of education was not to stimulate individuality, critical thought, or nonhierarchic responsibility to others. (Sports teams in some cases are the exception to the latter.) The process of education was not to question, whether it was the authority of official churches or settled institutional organizations that reinforced the class structure of society. Teachers were to ensure docility, and school principals were their foremen and forewomen. The entire educational apparatus was to have this purpose, either through standardized tests or beliefs in ideals that had nothing to do with the conduct of daily life of society or of those who proclaimed particular values as the ideal.

Throughout the twentieth century, brutal fights were waged about the content in education, what educators thought it proper to teach, analyze, and question. Hidden behind these struggles were issues of class, cultural homogenization, propaganda as knowledge, the abstract versus the concrete, and, of course, race, sex, and leisure. Because efforts at educating and democratizing are integrally linked, to discuss one is in fact to discuss the other. A struggle over the education of the young is an old story. That was Socrates' crime, according to his antagonists, who claimed, with some justification, that his students were learning the art of social and intellectual superiority against the democratic polity.

The religious and the militaristic all have their interest in educating the young. French Jesuits wanted to get children out of the house and into classrooms because of their parents' "immoral" sexual behavior and the need to protect the political authority of the faith through learning. Frederick the Great as king of Prussia believed that education could mold a model populace for fighting wars similar to that of Sparta. To modern revolutionaries, including American revolutionists, education continued to be the key to social behavior.

For modern liberals concerned with reconstruction, education has included two periods. The "great bookies," such as Scott Buchanan, Stringfellow Barr, and Robert Hutchins, claimed that discourse about "Great Books" could save democracy. Those such as John Dewey claimed that thinking was not a passive enterprise and that the task of democracy was to link theory and practice with inquiries. Dewey's project was the taming of capitalism and bringing forward to political relevance those with little or no property to shape the kind of inclusive democracy that would trump the oligarchic tendencies of capital. This would save democracy. The differences between these two schools of thought were fueled by foolish rhetoric in which both sides missed how much they had in common. Both accepted the democratic discourse of small groups and the freedom to inquire. Both groups also feared the direction of capitalism, which would trivialize inquiry, scientific experimentation, and the use of technology. Their disagreement about the role of tradition and its study, as well as the role of fixed principles regarding natural rights, should not have resulted in the intellectual and political split that occurred among the various advocates for each position. The irony is that both the originators of the Great Books program and the pragmatist John Dewey were radical democrats. Nevertheless, the schism between the sides politically showed itself over Henry Wallace's candidacy. Indeed, Scott Buchanan and Stringfellow Barr favored Wallace, while Dewey had strong doubts about Wallace because of his seeming naïveté about the Soviet Union.

The second period in educational ideologies has turned out to be a seemingly irreconcilable split between conservatives and liberals. Conservatives organized themselves around belief in absolutes and essences, which came to mean basics in education, even as they accepted the validity of corporate capitalism and war as tools to defend absolutes. A number of liberals concluded that education had to conform to the practical needs of the market, employment, and skills, while liberals committed to reconstruction sought to incorporate into education the social revolutions of the 1960s. The ongoing struggle remains in American education. What should be known, accepted, and why? What is the history of Americans as a people?

Historians now pick at the scars of the American past to end self-congratulatory hagiography. This forces a new understanding of the past and therefore the character of the future. On the other hand, American conservatives set as their goal the denial of past reality by trying to restore the Humpty Dumpty of myths that had governed American life and the classroom. Proponents of this course, such as Lynne Cheney and the virtue entrepreneur William Bennett, wish to rewrite American history as hagiography. There are two contradictory aspects to the conservative story. One is that universities have become frivolous in what they teach; the other is that too many "unqualified" students have found their way into the university.

Until the First World War, a liberal arts education revolved around Latin, Greek, and the verities. These verities were not even to be found in Shakespeare, which was not considered part of the canon of literature.[23] This parochialism did not fit with the needs of modern production, although attempts were made to give industrialists and the rich a certain amount of liberal education "couth," as in the programs of the University of Chicago at Aspen.

New modes of education were needed to operate a modern industrial state. "Classical " education was to be less heavenly and more profane. Education was to reinforce the economic and social needs of commerce and the state. Industry wanted education to operate as a channeler. Universities were to deprecate rote learning and the humanities, concentrating instead on method and function within specializations. There was not to be a process of critical evaluation and imagination. During the Cold War the national security state organized subventions and grants to universities that would train professors and students in producing the implements of conflict, from missiles and nuclear weapons to propaganda. For both modern production and national security the complexity of modern life and the division of labor in the workplace required specialization and loyalty from the middle class, which would not bother itself with the ends of what it was doing and the general effects its practices had on the democracy itself or on unseen others.[24] This mode of life fits well with a national security science and its definition of instrumental rationality.

SCIENTIFIC OBJECTIVITY AND RATIONALITY

Throughout history scientists have sold their discoveries and advanced themselves through linkage with political, royal, and military elites that comprehended the utility of mechanical success. (It works!) But in the mid-twentieth century this process took on a far more organized and corporatized relationship. For example, scientists sold science to American governments as the endless frontier. Vannevar Bush, President Franklin Roosevelt's science advisor, claimed that the United States had to lead in exploring the unknown if it was to retain its dominant position in the world and be free. Exploring the unknown also created questions about fundamental beliefs even in how the world—and galaxies—worked.

Beyond the presence of Billy Graham at the side of every post–World War II president, blessing and promoting the unity of values of church and state, religion seemed to have lost its premier place in the West to science as the fundamental cultural reality. The sciences were as a new, wondrous language understood for the most part by new priests' elites. More than just talk, the sciences, and their less social class driven and more down to earth cousin, technology, led to wondrous new things that worked and understandings that were of greater value than the informal knowledge, folk wisdom, tinkering, prayer, and endless disputations about the "good" or "beauty" or morality that had occupied the Middle Ages or those in the twentieth-century university who studied the classics and "liberal arts." Supposedly, such scholars did nothing to truly "comprehend" the "real" world or imitate it through mechanical connections.[25] They insisted that values should be understood in qualitative terms rather than reduced to numbers as they are used in market economics.

The political irony in the politics of ideas and the university was that the very place that held on to disputation and essential verities as reflected in a Great Books liberal education, Robert Hutchins's University of Chicago, performed major experiments that showed nuclear fission, and therefore nuclear weapons, could work. It was as if the verities were spliced into a million pieces. Similarly, the University of Chicago's Economics Department, beyond any other, correlated rationality with quantitative efficiency and profit. Of course, the sciences kept elements and rituals of a priesthood, which had its own customs and demands. (The edifice of the National

Academy of Science, in which only the scientific elite were members, was as grand as any religious temple and has the same feeling of awe about it in its public rooms.)

Whether Marxist or capitalist, science was thought to be the key to modernism, wiping away the irrational and traditional modes of belief and coercion. The sciences, it was claimed, were the essence of a liberality of spirit that engulfed the twentieth century. Science and technology were the keys to a universal culture, not bound by any single place or custom. Standards of how to build a bridge, determine excellence, control and categorize people, build prisons, identify and someday remedy genetic defects, build nuclear weapons, plot galaxies through telescopes, and develop toxins or antitoxins transcended any particular parochial community of place or puny ideology. As I have said, standardized measurements, whether in money, nanoseconds, or inches, were meant to define the parameters of reality. Measurements were the coin of the realm that attempted to describe all things objectively, as if doing so was the same as describing objective reality. Natural scientists and technologists were not only the mechanics of the modern age; they were also the modern rhetoricians who were no longer expected to prove certainty. As was their audience, they were content with probability and possibility.

During the Cold War the increase in the operations of the federal government, armed with the blessings of science and religion, brought economic well-being. But there remained the underbelly of profound insecurity caused by nuclearism, war, and war preparations. This was a price people were prepared to pay, for the Cold War was as much fantasy as reality to American society. What was real was material gain through government employment and contracts as well as veterans benefits. For American cold warriors the emergence of the state as the all-important entity, indeed, the world spirit in the Hegelian sense, gave purpose to the nation.

In the world of the hierarchic and corporate organization, influential behavioral psychologists were able to give valuable advice from the point of view of the corporation and government. Thus, psychology and marketing were fused into the manipulation of desire for particular products. Workers were accosted with techniques for accepting corporate authority, often parading under the heading "humanization of work." For government, as in the case of the Defense Department and intelligence agencies, examinations are given to ensure loyalty by using lie detector and stress tests. Behavioral tests are given to junior officers in the armed forces, who are expected to use nuclear weapons only on command. Similar examinations are given in corporations for less grandiose purposes. In the corporate case, the corporate behaviorist is not interested in individuality except, perhaps, as to how the individual consumer's desires can be aroused.

Behaviorist and research director for the J. Walter Thompson advertising agency J. B. Watson encouraged such consumerism on the ground that the product was perfectly fitted to the individual buyer. Scientists such as Watson and Paul Lazarsfeld were concerned with the type of manipulation that, whether or not they so intended, reinforced the idea that the person is accountable to hierarchic power and market capitalism.

Other psychologists sought the "scientific" balance between the "carrot and stick" approach to human and international relations. This was the preferred method of relations developed by American strategists during the Cold War. Within this confluence of ideas, certain powerful notions of will were intended to make social reality bend to the possibilities of one's imagination. Facts were to be created out of will, as was the case with new economic enterprises, from film to computers to biotechnology. Each new activity created a hybrid of social and scientific facts. This hybrid might be referred to as institutional facts that included social and physical reality.[26] The easiest institutional facts to create were often those that were antidemocratic in character, for they followed the idea of commander-commanded. One such case, for example, has been the invention and widespread use of the various standardized tests to obtain entrance to universities. These tests assert four aspects of corporate and bureaucratic life. Unless special permission is given, they are taken against a time clock, much in the way an assembly line is conducted. They imply that the acquisition of knowledge is an individual process rather than one that comes through dialogue. They penalize creativity because they are not predicated on imagination, which must find its own boundaries. Finally, they assert that a person's intelligence can be reduced to a number.

SCIENTIFIC INQUIRY AND MANAGEMENT

The scientific project was ideologically assumed to be beyond politics, although it was meant to fit in and not question its hidden determinants and assumptions since that might result in a scientific analysis of social, economic, and political relationships. From the standpoint of the powerful, such an analysis could guide inquiry in the wrong direction—one that might subvert the status quo.

Scientists who defined their political stance as liberal believed in the mobilization of facts and narrowly defined positivist inquiry intended to come to tentative conclusions that would help reforms go forward. However, the facts gathered were disembodied, without real effort at "problem solving." They often replayed the kind of incrementalism, the national suggestion box, easily absorbed by those who were the managers of power for the status quo.[27]

It is important to note that the technocrats and managers of the system were not the conservatives. Nor were they the liberals of social reconstruction. The administrators who were deemed progressive believed that they had a scientific method for running society beyond ideology, that of understanding and then manipulating reality. Some liberals, who placed great emphasis on technique without concern for ends, often joined up in this form of management. Blinded by the aphrodisiac of power, they asserted a realism that saw no contradiction between techniques of social and scientific control and freedom. Thus, during the Cold War period it was enough to prove one's credentials if he or she was against Soviet totalitarianism and offered management techniques to fight it, just as in the First World War technocrats enlisted in the war against the Hun, conflating liberalism with technique and a method that purported to describe reality or at least operations on reality.[28] And in the Soviet Union its scientists were not able to break out of the social system in which they lived until they led the revolution for human rights with the flawed Andrei Sakharov as their leader.[29] Conservatives invented their own game of power that became the challenge to the technocratic managers and "bureaucracy." The conservative interest was to cut off widespread public participation, directly or indirectly, so that the economy would remain outside of public accountability, which might endanger private aggregates of power. At the end of the century, it was not necessary to look to past conservative thinkers to see how the conservatives intended to "conserve" the land and physical environment. We need merely to state President George W. Bush's program.[30]

There was another strand of conservatism that placed emphasis on abstract ideals, which supposedly were thought to be natural and immutable. Putting itself forward as the guardian against scientism and relativism, this conservative strand contradicted the liberalism of social reconstruction. It was in this realm that liberalism itself could not supply very much of a guide to action. Its commitment to dignity was a given to be effected in practice. But where would this commitment come from? Whereas religious figures in the early Cold War period, such as A. J. Muste, looked for the roots of their purposes in God's teachings and in existential and morally obvious actions that led to humanitarian socialism,[31] Jacques Maritain looked for a religious humanism that would take humanity back to God beyond capitalism and state socialism yet accept hierarchy as a necessary feature in organizing social and political life.[32]

Secularist thinkers, led by Dewey, hoped for help from a radical understanding of empiricism and scientific methods that would find the dignity of the person.[33] The problem for Dewey was that the scientific project was to be analyzed outside its cultural context and according to its own rules of logic and evidence, even though, as he knew, the doing of science, its methods and choice of topics, the evidence thrown away, was never a pristine activity unbesmirched by profane conditions of money, power, and status. Furthermore, it appeared the more that was learned, the more organizations applied scientific findings, the more expensive the scientific project was and the more it required a moral compass that was missing from it and various scientific methods. Because liberals feared moral absolutes, and because they feared disturbing the scientific project even as it fit with much that was questionable, from surveillance systems to nuclear weapons, liberals at first defended conventional science uncritically. Only "peers" could judge each other. The rest were spectators.

Profit-making and profit-attempting corporations also imposed their own definitions of social method on science and technology. The great social movements of the twentieth century created a different intellectual space. They sought to open other ways of thinking about the scientific project, deepening any of its diverse experiments with a new dimension to rationality. An expanded rationality to liberals brought up an old concern. People were to see themselves as part of the experiment and the problem, whatever those might be. A dialogue was to be held with the material and with the Other to understand the situation in which the experiment was embedded and, where necessary, to change the context of concern. New studies emerged as a result of recognizing blacks and women as having the power to define what was to be known about them, by them, and with them.

The corporations did not account for externalities and social costs in their business calculations. In other words, the social costs of "market efficiency" were not tallied, so harm was charged to the individual, his or her indulgence, or the inefficiencies of government. The critical purpose for the corporation was a profitable quarterly balance sheet and little, if anything, was to stand in the way of that goal, certainly not public interest groups. By the beginning of the twenty-first century the second Bush administration considered such advocates as Ralph Nader and public interest groups generally as tiresome and contradictory gnats whose complaints were presented as churlish and unconnected to the "real world" of the corporate bottom line, that is, the world as defined by power. Not only was there a wedge between different groups in need, but there also was a wedge between public interest advocates who saw virtually no way to weld a common agenda. Competing interests were presented as competing methods—one emotional and the other "rational." Because of its instrumental purpose, the business corporation made its own facts and social conditions, to the detriment of the unwary, the oppressed, and the gullible.

There is an irony to corporate capitalism as it matured. It needed workers who were, for the most part, docile and malleable. They were to be committed to high levels of productivity that would then be translated into unrequited consumer desires, created through technology and advertising. This was the new capitalist realism, which brooked no tampering. In the 1960s, questioning this way of life was never far from the surface. These questions were the basis of a profound cultural revolution that was interrupted for over a generation but has increased relevance in the twenty-first century.[34]

7

★

Capitalist Economics
Fails Democracy

H istorians will mark 2001 and 2002 as the beginning of renewed doubt
in capitalism as a sturdy and relatively honest political and economic
system. This doubt translates into what is called lack of confidence
and disbelief that there are reasonable expectations. Where these two attributes of capitalism are shaken, spaces are created for policy shifts, either of an
incremental or more far-reaching nature. Ideas once considered marginal become necessary to understand the collapse of various multi-billion-dollar corporations, investor and worker distrust, massive unemployment, and widespread legal and illegal corruption.

DEMYSTIFYING ECONOMICS

Whatever its size, no democratic society can escape the question of collective responsibility that its members have for one another. And if there is this
collective responsibility, from whence does it come? The answer cannot be
ambiguous. Contrary to some who believe that responsibility is a synonym
for punishment, responsibility stems from human affections, which are invariable and undeniable. They precede any individual interests, for the capacity for affections makes the harmonizing of human interests possible.[1]
Affections reflect and affirm interdependency among people and nature.
These affections need nurturing through institutions that themselves must
begin with the principle of affection as dominant over coercion. Where such
natural affections are weak or do not exist as the basis of political, social,
and economic relationships, there will be social pathology, whether in the

system or the institution. This variant of pathology will be reflected in the person. There is a paradox with this social formulation. We know from our own experience that democracy requires the person to see and be seen as herself and himself, that is, as an individual. In other words, the person's subjectivity is recognized. And this may give rise to a type of egoistic individualism that does not reflect the better self but degenerates into tendencies toward domination without social conscience. This was the story of corporate capitalism at the end of the twentieth century. We know that the individual must have rights, which serve as a fence of protection against collective pathology. Democracy is a balancing act between individualism and the group. A social historian of art, Arnold Hauser, has made this point in the following way:

> Democracy is individualistic in that it gives free reign to competition and the different forces in society, rates each person at his own individual value, and spurs him to the utmost exertions; but it is anti-individualistic in that it levels differences of class and abolishes privileges of birth. It inaugurates a type of culture which is so differentiated that individualism and community spirit can no longer be viewed as alternatives but are seen to be indissolubly connected.[2]

This idea is difficult to put into practice, for how far does individual responsibility extend? Does it end at the family, the locality, the place of work, the state or nation, unseen others in different places, or the unborn? These questions are profoundly moral and economic ones. By their nature they are interdependent and can be answered only problematically, that is, using all forms of specialized knowledge to address the problem.

Like all ideas, with the possible exception of "pure" mathematics, economics is socially and historically bounded. It is related to the technology of the time. In the twentieth century many believed that technology could stimulate the natural affections by overcoming scarcity, whether of things, time, severe income or wealth differences, or immiseration. And in part this hope had substance to it. It was why liberals favored experiment and the acquisition of knowledge in an unfettered form. However, more important than science and technology's feats is what a society views as property in its mores, customs, and laws. Until the last quarter of the nineteenth century, property was dominated by concepts of use value. By the end of the twentieth century property had come to include land, air, water, things, thoughts, images, transactions, exchanges, future promises, and contractual benefits and rights such as Social Security. These conceptions of property are legitimated into law by judges and legislatures that develop the rationalizations and frameworks for the unknowable and mysterious modern economy.[3]

The economy as a concept is a reduction of interactions and needs, although some economists have sought methods that would bring together reality and their understanding of it in a less crude way.[4] Obviously, the more power a particular actor has in markets the more likely it is that that person, institution, or government will be able to affect the reality of other people's lives. Yet, this basic consideration seems to be lost in studies that present an idealized understanding of the economy.

In other words, to understand everyday life, the problematic of power must be kept in mind when discussing an economy. Property, politics, power flows, and the shape of the economy are utterly intertwined. Therefore, modern liberals concerned with social reconstruction are charged with the need to organize a discipline of the political economy that acknowledges the inextricable link among property, politics, power, the economy, meanings of collective and individual responsibility, basic human affections beyond crude notions of interest, and the oppressed partner of humanity, nature. Thinkers in the twenty-first century should not be expected to do less than what Adam Smith did in his period.

"WE ARE THE WORLD" OF MARKET DESIRES

When we consider what we expect from an economics that includes social justice, it is necessary to be aware of new conditions that were somewhat hidden during the Cold War but were present throughout the twentieth century. These conditions revolve around new interdependencies and relationships that strongly suggest that no political economy can stand as an autarchic unit. The state socialist nations tried, and in part their attempt caused their own stagnation. However, the global economy, based on corporate capitalist principles, also proves problematic. The assumptions about human behavior that undergird post–Cold War capitalism are what we may describe as universal market desires in which everyone wants jeans, cellular telephones, and McDonalds hamburgers. Global capitalism is meant to replace or absorb traditional cultures into the global market economy. In reality, the world is far more complex and uncertain, whatever the economic or political system devised by corporate planners.

National leaders neither know the future nor are certain of what constitutes their nation's best interests. There are differing cultures within any one nation whose valuation systems are orthogonal to capitalism. National leaders outside the well-developed nations also recognize that the imperative of communications and technology to standardize remains a profoundly powerful engine that overtakes local cultures without concern for its effects. When we look more closely we see a global economy that is a perverse form of material connectedness guided economically, and therefore to some extent socially and morally, by the world's largest corporations, one hundred of which control close to 15 percent of the world's trade.[5]

Global market proponents share the assumption that concentration in international corporations will result in greater efficiencies and therefore a general increase in prosperity. But this meaning must be decoded. In fact, greater efficiencies mean greater production of commodities through fewer workers or low-paid, unorganized, and poorly skilled workers. It does not follow that greater world prosperity will result. If anything, we are getting shopping-window prosperity in which standards of living will not improve in terms of health, mortality rates, education, etc., despite an increased desire and greater demand for material possessions.[6] Humane conditions and what is produced will remain secondary concerns, if considered at all, by those who conflate the globalization of markets and global corporations with "free markets."

Whether by the magic of the Invisible Hand (which had a strict code of contract observance and debt repayment) or by accident, according to modern economists, the millions of individual choices made by buyers, sellers, and producers result in an uncoordinated, unplanned coordination that no particular governmental plan is able to match in bringing about liberty and progress. The liberty that is talked about has a very specific and constricted meaning. Liberty is a license or corporate charter given by the state to one or a few that, once granted, cannot easily be taken back from the private party or its successors. Proponents of this form of liberty claim that global markets create increased individual choice and encourage innovation, which in turn creates and matches individual desires. There are no "clerks of the international market" to monitor and set boundaries for these activities, in which everything is permitted to be sold and bought. Quite the contrary, the clerks of the international market in such arrangements are cheerleaders for the principle that anything goes for the most powerful, who set the rules of the game.[7]

According to its advocates, past and present, the market operates as the perfect computer even though it is unplanned and uncoordinated and even though it tells us nothing about the quality of the life created through the Invisible Hand. It is easier to believe that the Invisible Hand guides the selfishness of all of us into satisfying each other rather than to look at what is happening. In the economic realm, we, "polite" society, expect the plight of, say, migrant workers, to be overlooked, for they are merely labor commodities who represent blips on the screens of immigration officials and finance speculators. As a group, the latter are thought of as the modern catalysts for prosperity who have mastered the magical features of international financial markets, which are based on shared information and currencies that are *meant* to be manipulated by private speculators.

BEHIND THE MYSTIFICATION OF FREE
MARKETS AND DEGRADED FIRST-STAGE LIBERALISM

At the end of the twentieth century, free-booting capitalism reemerged as the dominant economic ideology, overtaking state socialism and the Keynesian idea of state interventions into the market and civil society for a common good. Whether the free market ever described reality or depicted little more than a set of normative purposes and preferences of the very few who needed an ideology of freedom and liberty to cover their tracks no longer seems important to consider. Of significance, however, is that the free market religious belief system has created a powerful deterrent-shadow to rethinking alternatives outside the eighteenth-century capitalist paradigm. The modern case creates a new set of illusions about equality of bargaining between management and labor, illusions that have little to do with everyday life.

Corporate businesspeople know a different economic reality beyond the illusions to which many now pray. They know that the state as an instrument of taxation, with law and coercion as its big stick, served as the major catalyst for economic development. As in the case of nuclear energy and railroads, the state is the single most important support system for corporate enterprise.[8] But private capital, once it uses the state for its own purpose, is reluctant to pay back, except perhaps in contribution to those politicians who favor the continuous buildup of personal fortunes that leads to the socialization of risk and privatization of gain for a few selves and their respective families—in other words, wolfish capitalism in the godfather's clothes.

The new folklore of capitalism now masks the reality of the dominated, which includes billions in the world economic system, whether they are the Chinese worker lacing together a computer board or track shoe for export, a woman living in desperation in Bangkok servicing the well-off as a sex worker, or an American worker who has just been downsized. Individually they are living anxiety-driven lives in the labor and consumer markets, where they are reduced to being commodities for sale. They are living lived lives. The working poor and marginalized become labor commodities—useful and understandable only in relation to an accounting bottom line—unless they are fortunate enough to find another identity economically. Then they can become debtors in consumer markets, which operate on credit, debt, and desire—that is to say, having and wanting.

People are mystified by the competing worlds they live within, those of production and desire. As atomistic individuals they conclude that no other choices to protect themselves exist. They personify individual salmon battling upstream to lay eggs that they will never see. And within the academy, political party, or religious institutions in the post–Cold War world, especially in the West, little effort to challenge and create an alternative exists. Many in the working and middle classes assume that there will be no Social Security left for them. Government is understood to be dysfunctional, lacking in the capacity to protect the society economically against the markets. Employment of American military force, then, masks economic weakness and manufactured need.[9]

By stating the obvious, that economics is a normative tool in democracy, we have freed ourselves from a rhetoric of economics that claims neutrality about "facts" and processes supposedly found in nature and all human interactions. Laws that surround economic and commercial arrangements take on reconstructive meanings. The rule of law is shifted from property rights per se to a legal conception that includes human rights, viz., social and economic justice. That is to say, the institutional arrangements in the economic sphere give precedence to human rights.

By shifting the underlying ideological premises of economics as a discipline, we would view economic behavior from a different perspective, and behavior itself could change as a result of shifts in emphasis among knowledge workers and academics. Suppose a new valuation system is found that also has a basis in empirical reality, one that remains present with those who take pride in a craft and skill. It must redefine the role and meaning of competition and profit in economics.

Elements of caring and cooperation are part of the primary motivating force of all productive activity. How are these to be valued and rewarded? Fair shares and profits would be bottomed on the importance of trust, caring, mutual benefit, and cooperation in defining economic activities, whether on the productive or even the use side. Future expectations would have meaning as a cooperative social purpose, which in practical terms would mean sharing in the creation of a future common good. This would come about through changes in the laws as they relate to the economic structure, education, and investment markets. Even to place such matters on the table of discourse would shift a number of attitudes that have come to dominate political and economic ideas.

MARKETS AND ECONOMICS AS MORAL INQUIRY

Milton Friedman supplied a useful definition of the market economy: "The ideal type of market economy is one in which individuals act as principals in pursuit of their own interests. If any person serves as an agent for someone else, he does so on a voluntary, mutually agreed upon basis."[10] But this definition does not comport with the real world for at least half of the American workforce. In capitalist economies where megacorporations set the terms of political and economic power as well as choice, there is an economic culture of command disciplined by a competitive, albeit oligopolistic, market. In other words, there are strong elements of a command economy within the market system. The worker fired from her job at a major corporation who then finds minimum wage work at McDonalds is part of a command economy. The woman who cleans chickens in factories that are locked from the outside lives her life in a command economy. And in terms of personal need she is driven to accept the job out of coercion. To describe her condition as voluntary, or to describe the situation of the working poor who trade horrendous environmental conditions, as in the case of North Carolinians, for jobs as "voluntary," burlesques the relationship of social equality to the English language. There is no equality of bargaining power between increasingly weak unions and owners/managers in labor markets.[11] This point is even more obvious in most of those nations in the world where there are no protections for workers and there is high unemployment as well.

Inequality and inequity between capital and labor necessitate the introduction of a moral epistemology in economics. In other words, an economics of reconstruction would reassert normative purposes in methodology and program as they relate to decency, dignity, fairness, just wages in relation to just prices, and human justice. These are aspirations, and in some cases, achievable ones within American life.

They were once the signal purpose of twentieth-century political and economic thinkers and activists. Whether Jacques Maritain, John Dewey, or Joan Robinson, whether it was the Keynesian or institutional economists such as John R. Commons,[12] who entered the profession of economics because it linked freedom to economic and social justice, they believed that this linkage was the worthy goal, indeed the necessity of modern civilization.

These thinkers recognized that there is a moral deficit to a set of economic procedures and methods that assert that economics is "value neutral" and is merely the distribution of scarcity among the poorer members of society while those who are richer and more powerful share in abundance. There is no reason to accept Friedrich Hayek's view that there is an enduring truth to capitalism that is moral, to be found wandering around somewhere between the instinctive and the rational, perhaps like the hundreds of millions of migrant laborers caught crossing borders to earn a pittance. These claims hold to the belief in equilibrium economics. This "neutral" way of considering economic questions creates a profoundly immoral and unstable national, local, and world situation.

If economics at its core is to be understood as a set of moral purposes for our time, not those of the eighteenth century, it must be approached as a form of moral inquiry that seeks to devise structures and institutions of distribution that reflect fairness consistent with the wealth and potential wealth of a particular society that in turn has clear obligations to an emerging world civilization and the natural environment. Unfortunately, conventional economic policy marginalizes those who do not have the capital, or the requisite social character, skills, or gender identification, to survive in a competitive, oligopolistic economy. The result is the reinforcement of misallocation of resources, social stratification, and increasingly limited access to resources for the bulk of the world's population. In the United States these classes know no excess but no personal internal peace.[13] Stress and debt are inextricably intertwined for the anxiety-ridden economic middle and poorer classes.

The logic of global corporations is to cut costs through a low wage base for workers who may be skilled but not unionized. Managers set up production firms or contract out activities to low wage countries. This trend lowers wages in richer nations, giving somewhat higher wages to a certain portion of the wage earners in poor countries but increasing competition among poor countries to attract capital and the roaming corporations. The roaming corporation over a short period of time abandons one nation and moves to another, leaving behind even more chaotic conditions as the poor nation attempts to adjust to a changed economy now dependent on modern equipment and patents from the West or Japan and inundated with unemployed agricultural workers who have swarmed to resource-poor cities. This condition is trumpeted as progress, development, and modernization. Instead of progress, what is set in motion is its reverse, with profound political effects. In its present guise, the "free market" principle increases poverty and disorder. It adds to that attribute of religious faith that assumes that generosity need not be based on political and social equality. Religion of the next world becomes society's safety valve.

ENTITLEMENTS

In Western nations, including the United States, struggles about economic well-being (dignity and decency) continue to revolve around whether that condition is an entitlement, a benefice from benefactors such as the rich or churches, a political goal to attain which groups should organize, as in the struggles of labor unions, or a call to entrepreneurs and workers to work harder. Enlightened conservatives and the Left have claimed that some form of entitlement was necessary if societies were to avoid falling into the abyss of social disorganization. Modern life made it clear that emphasis on individualism required an institutional outlet for the caring function based on shared notions of property.

The social democratic manifestation of this view required that property could not remain only a private consideration for the few. There had to be redistributive aspects to wealth creation not predicated on largesse but on the engagement of unseen or unknown others who should benefit, who in turn would pass on their knowledge and work to future generations. Since wealth was to be thought of as socially created, it was to be socially disposed of, within the context of capitalism. This would then allow for the caring function to be performed at least in part by publicly subsidized social institutions, that is, limited forms of welfarism that would be made possible because of high levels of production; which was thought to be synonymous with the creation of wealth. Perhaps this notion of redistribution stems from the "household" economy in which distribution of product and wealth is based on need and desire.

Instead of redistributing unequal wealth, the U.S. government, as in the Cold War, remains primarily tied to war preparation, rationalizing transportation and education appropriations as necessary for defense and security. The Pentagon is used as a stabilizing mechanism in the American economy. Its system of contracting, allocation, and mobilization of resources is operated on the basis of hierarchy and command through a central office, the Secretary of Defense. It has been termed state capitalism by Seymour Melman, who did seminal work on the relationship among disarmament, social needs, and defense: "By 1994, the Pentagon made prime contracts for more than 138 billion dollars. It controlled 3.6 million of its own uniformed and civilian personnel. These do not include the employees of 'defense-related' industry. They peaked at 3.3 million persons from 1986 through 1988, and thereafter were reduced by 1.4 million."[14] The second Bush administration has increased defense costs as an internal economic stabilizer, although it was presented to the public as a national security measure necessary for war. Administrative reformers and modern liberals wanted government subsidies for industry as well as an insurance and welfare program for that fraction of the working and middle class that in turn attached itself to military activities through pensions and long-term defense employment. This system of government intervention in 1997 facilitated an economic growth rate of over 3.5 percent. However, the rate did not account for negative growth, that is, mistakes made and questionable activities, such as refuse dumping in streams, which had to be rectified but which counted on the tables of statisticians and economists as "growth." In other words, market economics was prepared to count social pathology as part of "growth."

CHIPPING AWAY AT THE WELFARE STATE

During the Reagan era an ideological shift that had been building among social scientists against the poor since the early 1970s unsurprisingly resonated with business. Purveyors of the conservative social reality "discovered new truths." Transfer payments through welfare, Social Security, and medical insurance, which had been made to the populace at large, were deemed to be too high.[15] The Social Security Trust Funds, it was claimed, were on the brink of bankruptcy, and the stock market was much more secure. The purpose of such claims soon unfolded, and they did not have much to do with protecting Social Security pension funds from "bankruptcy" or concerns for the poor, widows, orphans, or African Americans. Mutual, corporate, and investment funds had another purpose.

As private markets collapsed and poor investment choices made Republicans seek more investment capital, the one major pot that was thought to be sacrosanct, outside of the market, was Social Security funds. Social Security was based on principles of economic justice that did not comport with the purists' ideas of the free market. Private investors, through mutual funds and banking houses, sought public Social Security funds as a means of making up for relatively low savings (compared to most European nations) among Americans.

Investment markets and corporations claimed that there was a "capital shortage" and not enough savings for investment purposes. However, savings in the nation were more protected by the government than in volatile stock markets. For example, the ideas of the Boskin commission (Boskin having been a former chair of the Council of Economic Advisors under the first President Bush) put into jeopardy the social security of women and African Americans even as it penalized the white working class. Women worked fewer years than men, and African Americans have a shorter life span than whites, meaning that they would not receive retirement benefits to the extent whites would. The onslaught on the weakest members of society in economic terms occurred because the power of the working class as an organized body had decreased. This was made patently clear to organized labor by Ronald Reagan, who ironically was the only president to ever hold a union card.

Ronald Reagan broke the air traffic controllers' strike, thereby serving notice that corporations should follow the lead of the government and not fear directly confronting employees, using whatever set of arguments and pretexts management cared to adopt. New innovations in technology, increased competition in world markets, and low productivity were used as the pretext to discipline the workforce and remake the social character of the nation into budding individual entrepreneurs. There was no counterweight either in government or in the nation at large that would question the sanctity of competition and claims of low "productivity," which had become the standard to determine whether higher wages could be paid by firms. The standard of productivity meant that workers could expect to receive higher wages only if they worked harder. The contradiction for the firm and the worker was that higher productivity might be achieved through machines, controlled by the corporation, which made the employee's job unnecessary or redundant. But the U.S. production worker was not in a position to share in the gains made because he or she did not have a property share in the machines or the corporation.[16]

In the bipartisan movement for deregulation during the Carter–Reagan period, the managers of capital and corporations concluded that (1) the labor movement was poorly organized, offering no countervailing power to management; (2) skilled workers could be found abroad less expensively; (3) a favorable political climate existed for international corporate expansion without controls over it nationally or internationally; (4) technology controlled from the corporate top through patents is able to create markets and control information and finance flows, thereby changing the very nature of production and distribution; (5) socialism by 1989 in its statist form had turned out to be a shadow of capitalism; it was no match for American capital and a freewheeling culture that emphasized the entrepreneurial spirit, personal liberty, and pent-up desires; and (6) capitalism itself could be reorganized through ridding itself of "inefficiencies" by increasing private debt and merging or selling off "nonprofitable enterprises."

There was also a widespread assumption that governments, as they withered away, would protect the sanctity of the market. In the face of these changed international circumstances and the Republican Party's intense desire (prior to September 11, 2001) to hobble the federal government in economic affairs, it was believed that an unfettered entrepreneurial class could again be created around technology. It was assumed that democratic choice would meld into consumer choice. Elected governments would revert to the 1920s and be little more than appendages of finance and industrial groups, which would organize "rational" markets. Governments, meaning public bodies accountable to the citizenry, would wither, and civil servants would slide even further into demoralization, thus leaving entrepreneurs such as Kenneth Lay in charge.

The average citizen would be reduced to an associate of a state without capacity to exercise control over the direction of the economy or the character of national and international politics. Governments in the welfare state sense would no longer act as balancers against the great corporations. They would forever be subsidizers, enablers, and cheerleaders for corporations and the "new man" entrepreneur, whom Joseph Schumpeter had said was the linchpin of capitalism.

NEW MAN ENTREPRENEUR

Some attention should be paid to the new man entrepreneur, for on the surface there would appear to be validity to Schumpeter's claim. Indeed, it is an important aspect of conservative economic ideology. According to

Schumpeter, capitalist development is spontaneous, and societies are transformed by the entrepreneur who has the ability to combine two types of technical capacity.[17] One is the organization of things and people together and the other awareness, if not mastery, of a new technology. These entrepreneurs are the new men of capitalism. Presently they are found inventing computers and computer programs, circuitry, filmic images, etc. In the 1970s and 1980s they were people who had little or no business experience and therefore were not afraid to take risks. Their task was to coax investors, banks, and large corporations into taking risks in exchange for a "position" in their fledgling corporations and ideas, many of which had been originally funded through the Department of Defense and NASA.

Capitalist entrepreneurs are promoters with a strong belief in their own capacities and a focused interest in their work, which they claim should be richly rewarded. (They are the obverse of Left political organizers, who are usually self-effacing.) They have the capacity to create markets and get consumers to want things. In other words, they create desire, whether it is for a new brand of lipstick, a prizefighter, energy, insurance, or a computer. They do not create equilibrium; they upset it. And according to Schumpeter, such people are found in all societies. They are comfortable with weak governments, powerless labor unions, and limited accountability. They do not like to be questioned.

Ralph Estes, on the other hand, has made the argument for access to internal corporate information as a first step to understand that the stakeholders and entrepreneurs are more than those who hold stock at any one moment in time.[18] Stakeholders include the locality and local population, the workers, consumers, etc., who must be counted as part of the corporate decision-making process. Various proposals to constitutionalize the corporation have been made since the 1930s, most notably by Scott Buchanan.[19] These have fallen on deaf ears. The reason is that among conservatives the corporation is conflated with private property. It has become a metaphysical entity with the godlike power of perpetuity. In this regard it is far more important to understand that megacorporations are not "firms" in the usual sense that they are thought about in economics. They are private governments that operate with the appearance (and it is only an appearance) of public accountability monitored by an understaffed public bureaucracy.

What is raised by this unbalanced relationship is the fundamental meaning of property: whose property and how that meaning is to be determined. Such questions have formidable constitutional consequences. To date, neither Congress, an aroused public, nor the Supreme Court has seen fit to find ways of constitutionalizing corporations in the sense of making them democratically controlled, with all the elements of the body politic having control over the investment of capital and the managerial "prerogative" of where it is invested.

Can a state insist that any corporation clearly invested with the public interest include as a member of the board of directors a designee of the state legislature and governor, or could the United States recharter corporations by amending the Wagner Act or other acts dealing with corporations to ensure democratic control by creating stock issues that would be held publicly, that is by cities, communities, and eleemosynary institutions, such as hospitals, and by workers coops? Or can the state or federal government, outside the present taxing process, legislate percentages of reinvestment in local communities to be used to build up worker- and cooperative-controlled enterprises? Finally, would these actions change the character of public responsibility and public responsiveness? If it can be shown that a particular corporation is environmentally destructive, should its charter be revoked because of harm to the public? These questions are answered through the exercise of political power, a redefinition of the Constitution. As President Roosevelt learned in 1934 when he sought to change the composition of the Supreme Court, in periods of anxiety and insecurity, institutional crutches such as the Supreme Court are not easily changed. However, in Roosevelt's case his onslaught resulted in justices becoming more amenable to finding New Deal legislation constitutional. There is the classic catch-22 problem: Those whose voices and power in the society are heard invariably serve a private rather than a public good.[20]

CORPORATE GOVERNANCE

Through the media, advertising, and so on, the great corporations are rhetorically engaged in shaping the meaning of public accountability. Aggregations of capital and production employ hardy bands of lawyers, accountants, and lobbyists acting as ambassadors and mediators to governments within and outside the United States. When their masks are removed it seems clear that the great corporations have all the indicia of private governments, seeking to control the public space, including the means of communication.

It is usually stated by those who seek to draw a distinction between the power of the great corporations and governments that corporations are not sovereign because they do not have coercive or police power. But this can hardly be true in any ordinary sense and does not go to the essence of their similarities. A sovereign state has control over land and property and is able to allocate resources and directly affect and determine the lives of the people who live within its authority through its agents, especially in the national security area. It generates its own rules, has the power of investment, and is, for the most part, able to generate the rules that it is prepared to live within.[21] It is even prepared to accept the government's interest in contracting out prisoners to private enterprise. Corporations have their own security and police forces, which are intended to keep order and spy on fellow workers, whether by watching them on the plant floor or by surveilling e-mail messages.

The sovereign state can employ its own security, surveillance, and police forces to protect its holdings. If they or their citizens are so inclined, governments can organize their own profit and taxing policies. And they can organize their own foreign economic policies. Except for sending troops elsewhere, the national government's daily activities are also the activities of the largest American corporations. Of course there is nothing to stop a corporation from employing foreign military-type forces to do the bidding of "private" enterprise. Each of these indicia can be ascribed, for example, to Exxon, IBM, or General Motors, including special taxing policies, which may be described as insistence on greater productivity from employees. This opens the question of public accountability and the constitutionalizing of major corporations. Are states helpless in the face of private control over resources ostensibly on private property?[22] Given the linkage of the corporation with the state through politics, to distinguish them without reference to their symbiotic relationship is to miss the point of authoritarianism, a type of Italian fascism.

Under present Supreme Court rulings it is unclear whether a free flow of interstate commerce means that the state is unable to impose any restrictions to protect its own natural resources. It seems to depend on the ideological thrust of the court as it relates to what is being protected by the state. Thus, the Supreme Court in *Reeves Inc. v. Stake* concluded that an individual state could participate in the market directly or regulate that market.[23] If this is so and the state can either regulate or participate in the market directly, then within the framework of even conservative interpretations of the Constitution, enormous changes can occur to protect and engender a mixed economy that recognizes the importance of governments and their role in promoting economic justice and protecting citizen engagement in the public space.

The *Reeves* case is suggestive because it allows cities and states to compete with privately owned firms if they are prepared to do so as part of a market system where no advantage is taken because of their privileged position as state entities. The reality of course is that governments of cities and states will take advantage of their position because they are accountable to the body politic as a whole. So what is the argument for promoting certain activities by governments that could be undertaken by private enterprise? This question is answered in terms of what is most likely in the long run to result in the common good, and which choice is most likely to engage deliberations to ascertain the general will. It is through public discourse that the line between the private and the public is to be drawn. This is a question that is never closed. The framework of the dialogue in a liberal democracy is deepening political equality and economic justice through the society and its institutions.

THE PUBLIC SPACE

Democratic government is the guardian of the public space. It is through the public space that we create a general will dialogue and accountability about economic, social, and environmental policy.[24] In other words, the public space yields more than a clash of personal interests. The public space is not an economic market, although both include important elements of trust. In market capitalism, cooperation operates inside of competition. In a democracy, conflict and competition are subservient to the end point, which is cooperation through reason and deliberation. We civilize ourselves, socialize, and distinguish our own wants from needs. Through this process of dialogue, understanding, social coordination, law, and custom, a framework is constructed in which all of us accept responsibility for one another. In the public space our individuality is fused with our social selves. We recognize our egalitarian interdependence on one another and we define our civic duties. We make real the common good through the general will, which is best defined as reasoned participation in the solution of immediate and long-range public problems. It is through the individual's exercise and then extension of the empathetic sensibility to the self beyond the selfish self that the individual realizes joint benefit.

This issue of "balancing interests" is an old one in the dialectics surrounding the American political economy. In the New Deal there was an important struggle between the Brandeis court and Benjamin V. Cohen wing and the Rex Tugwell group about the shape of the American economy. Was it to be predicated on democratic planning (Tugwell) or on market competition guaranteed through antitrust? This issue was finessed by the Second World War and the Cold War, during which governmental planning, through the Department of Defense and the oligopoly system, dominated markets according to weak consent decrees that supposedly guaranteed competition and the allegiance of the corporations in the "hot" and cold war. The deep fissures in the present system suggest the need for liberals to surrender their reluctance to rethink capitalism and a modern economy that will serve all the people in terms of participation, economic justice, and human rights as articulated in the UN covenant on economic rights.

Twenty-first century liberal democracy in its most general sense must include the following five elements that are the tableaux for political economy. Commitments by governments require escape from the war system and wolfish capitalism.

1. The right of dignity and decency is the sine qua non for all of humanity, and therefore political and economic justice is central to these purposes. It is the task of government to always seek these ends.
2. Properly distributed and with a view to reinvestment needs, resources are to be arranged and redistributed to ensure dignity and decency for the person and the community in their most inclusive sense.
3. Control and direction of technology requires shared knowledge beyond the scientific community and must include long- and short-term implications for society as a whole.
4. Noneconomic elements such as ecological protection are to be factored into dignity and decency.
5. The economy is to be conceptualized so that it will yield greater public and worker participation in the productive and distributive processes.

The liberal objective of the twenty-first-century economy is to ensure the widest possible participation of the citizenry in analyzing environmental, investment, productive, distribution, and allocation decisions for the general welfare nationally and internationally. As I have discussed at some length in *The Common Good,* the present and future of the American economy can be described in terms of (1) a public sector which includes mammoth global firms that operate as private governments; (2) the public service sector which includes jobs in government and the private sector; (3) the small business sector which includes market-oriented competitive small and microbusiness; and (4) the nonprofit, small-scale worker, community, and cooperative sector. Although there are differences in size and style between the different sectors, the economy's overarching purpose is to be measured against the total well-being of the society, especially among those who are thought of as hidden, socially excluded, or without account.

THE ECONOMIC SECTORS OF DEMOCRACY[25]

Given the failure of state socialism in the twentieth century and the conditions of economic and social dislocation, depression, and insecurity, which haunt models of Gingrich-Friedman capitalism, can democratic reconstruction be more successful than other attempts? It would be foolish to think that the lessons of history are determinative.

It would be foolish to think that these lessons of history are determinative. They are, however, important, because they may tell us in a moral and political sense what to avoid. Production and distribution do not come automatically. They require actions and choices in modern economies by power-holding and rule-setting institutions. This means that there is nothing historically or naturally determined about the way economies are organized. This is not to deny that there is an interlocking relationship between social character, the political economy, and the nature of the state, whether it is oriented to war or measures to improve the well-being of its inhabitants.

As William Appleman Williams has pointed out, organized labor at the beginning of the twentieth century had choices as to how to respond to the rise of the modern corporation: "It could have deployed its power to destroy the corporation and substitute a system of cooperative enterprises, to socialize the corporation and thereby the system, to break it up and re-establish the world of the individual entrepreneur, to regulate it through the government, or to organize labor itself within the new framework established by the corporation."[26] The road that was taken instead led to legislation and enforcement (albeit weak enforcement) of fair labor standards, antitrust laws, the forty-hour work week, and child labor laws, among other welfare laws and regulations. Economic relations were meant to bend to these political decisions, just as they can in the future result in shorter work weeks for the same pay, sabbaticals for workers rather than economic purges, minimum and maximum payment for work calibrated on a democratically acceptable range, and public subsidies to those activities deemed necessary to a decent society, breaking the linkage between jobs and income. It is important to note that the rich have for themselves broken the nexus between work and income through prudent investment, of which they are the passive beneficiaries. If the fruits of production are shared more equitably, the poorer classes would also be in a position to save and invest. Indeed, the several directions mentioned by Williams could still be taken in the twenty-first century if they are seen as linked to one another and if they build on the hard-won changes that did occur in the twentieth-century welfare capitalist framework.

The importance of politics in establishing a truly pluralist framework of economic relations cannot be overemphasized. This is a subversive thought that runs counter to laissez-faire and Marxist analysis, which both assume that economic relations dictate politics. A pluralist reconstructive economic framework redefines the meaning of public and private in terms of the economy.

When I refer to politics in this context I do not mean getting ahead in a corporation or even the politics of bargaining between labor and management. Rather, I am referring to a type of politics that operates on three levels. On all of these levels there is to be a continuous dialogue about the value of what is made and the ends that production is to serve in relation to other ends, such as the environment. The purpose of such a continuous discussion is to introduce conditions that begin to help an advanced industrial society

distinguish between common needs and personal desires, which may be catalyzed by the advertising of illusion or that type of acquisitiveness that is antithetical to a decent society. Such a continuing national discourse, which can
be organized through congressional juries at the very least, allows people to
judge more carefully between private and public expenditure, introducing
into the process a set of moral value preferences that might not otherwise become part of the decision-making process.[27] It encourages new forms of economic and political organizations that protect rather than despoil the environment.[28] In the *Affluent Society*, John Kenneth Galbraith pointed out the
skewing of values and preferences that occurred through stimulating consumer desire at the expense of public necessities such as education, health,
and (we would add) the environment.[29] The result of this skewing is that
more is spent on dog food and cosmetics than on primary school education.
What is rational in terms of the common good in public and private expenditures has little meaning.

The first level in the national dialogue on economic preferences outside
of the market is analyzing how and what human needs are being fulfilled
because they are necessary for a free, independent, and deliberating society.
The second is the organizing of the economy in such a manner that the person is able to affect, with others, the decisions of production and distribution, decisions about fair shares. This debate necessarily means analysis of
the character and purpose of private governments (those of oligopoly firms,
including the Fortune 1000 and banks where the public interest is affected)
beyond the performance of a particular service or creation of a product, as
well as the effects of foreign investment in the United States and vice versa.

The third level is the recognition that there are various economies within
a society, various modes of production, and various personal and group objectives. The free market of first-stage liberalism in some sectors of the
economy exists alongside monopoly or oligopoly capital, just as a use conception of economy also may be found in certain sectors of society. This
recognition cannot overwhelm another reality. There are basic needs of a
society that the various economies are called upon to fulfill within a democracy, and where they don't they are operating counter to democracy.
Obviously, one such need is personal and participatory freedom linked to
the fulfillment of common material needs, dignity, and decency.

Whatever the size of the productive enterprise, whether it is privately or
publicly controlled, to no little extent the ethos and mores of the society in
a nation whose aspirations are democratic are called upon to reflect a democratic purpose in that nation's day-to-day operations. Congress is the natural public instrument to lay out the basis of authority for a democratic
planning framework that would keep in place a continuing jury and town
hall investigation into the needs of communities, as well as a framework
that catalyzes individual responsibility for the public purpose.

Presently, the public purpose is a series of private purposes in which the government is manipulated for private ends. One way a government's purpose may be aided is if there is sufficient interest in the civil society among groups of people who make clear that there is a common good that can be determined through public hearings about the productive system in corporations with a national or international purpose. As in a federal jury system, citizens would be deputized through jury rolls to sit on boards and commissions overseeing private corporations. One task would be to help Congress prepare new corporate charters that would include provisions for the protection of the environment and laws guaranteeing fair shares and participatory rights to workers and communities. These rights would be publicly enforced by government and through class suits brought by citizens.

As determined by Congress, the common stock of certain industries would be owned solely by cities, states, communities, labor unions, and eleemosynary institutions. Owners of stock in these firms would receive just compensation for their stock based on a historic rate of return. This approach, which seemed farfetched in the 1990s, is a necessity in the twenty-first century.

With the victory of conservatism in Great Britain, modulated by the Blair government, and then in the United States since the 1970s, there has been a decline in the capacity of public power to deal with the private elements of the economy. Indeed, the private sector, in terms of profit and the provision of services, has been encouraged to lop off public responsibilities even if it usurps the role of governments.

The linkages among geographic place, the meaning of sovereignty, profits, workers, and market stability have become intertwined in the daily lives of transnational corporations. But their concerns and their activities decrease public accountability as these corporations take on more activities contracted out or privatized by the government. Public bodies have been stymied regarding the exercise of control or guidance from a public interest point of view over the corporate behemoths. One does not have to look too far to understand what causes the arrest and tentativeness of public bodies:

1. Corporate business is invited to rewrite regulatory laws in banking, finance, airlines, shipping, etc., in such a manner as to relieve corporations of external obligations.
2. Local communities and states beg and bribe to attract corporations.
3. The shared assumption of the inefficiency of government as against the efficiency of the private corporation has risen to the level of a self-fulfilling truth that virtually all accept without question, even though this is an illusion.
4. The media have become the means to denigrate government action unless it is linked to war making.

An economy is able to destroy political democracy, since on a daily basis people are affected by market exchanges more than by the political voting process. The question is how to arrange the political economy so that it is part of a democratic process.

No particular economic system within or between nations can erase all others. Because there will be continuing and enormous changes in technology, and because of the reality of vastly different cultures in the same historical period (compare Yemen to the United States, or Native Americans of Arizona and American Jews of New Jersey), the struggle for definition of democratic social character, and the needs of different groups, the type of economic system that will emerge is a hybrid system. In practical terms this means that within any particular political and geographical boundary there will be multiple economies, or more precisely, subsystems, that have their own features. And depending on one's employment, social role, class, and consciousness, economic realities will be experienced differently. Nevertheless, certain basic considerations must govern society as a whole—with deference paid to international rules on economic, social, and political rights.

The first of the four economic zones mentioned previously comprises those corporations that, as a result of their power in one or more markets, are able to determine the life of a nation, and of other nations, for that matter.[30] Such corporations require a wholly different shareholder and participation structure in their decision making, allocation of investment, and managerial accountability. They require more than transparency, for not many will care to go behind budgetary and accounting numbers unless they are directly part of the participative and decision-making process. However, there are systemic problems with "private government" firms that operate with impunity nationally and internationally. Five determinants are useful in assessing the mode of public accountability for the largest corporations:

1. Is there worker participation on the board?
2. Are substantial resources of the corporation owned by the public or given to it through research and privatization?
3. Is the corporation one that should be reorganized to ensure human rights over property rights?
4. Will the international corporation be owned by workers of different cultures and nations or subject to international rules?
5. If so, what is the human rights standard to be enforced, and by whom?

The second zone concerns all workers who are employed either directly or indirectly by public entities, namely, the federal government, states, communities, cities, and other public-financed entities. The number of workers includes publicly financed educational institutions, from kindergarten to universities. The second zone includes the emerging independent sector of museums, art galleries, and libraries, which are heavily dependent on government support either through direct subventions or the more passive system of tax exemptions. However, it does not include corporations that may be wholly dependent on government contracts for their business, nor does it include subcontractor providers of public services.[31]

Governments at all levels are critical actors in the economy, and discussions of withering away of the state seem utopian at best and conceivably economically disastrous for millions of people. It is not utopian, however, to investigate to which purposes and objectives governments have set their compasses. To put this question in the most general sense, are the activities in the arena of production life affirming, or are they pathological? The increase in security and defense forces and the decrease of activities that, say, would result in environmental cleanup, are examples of mistaken priorities.

Through the formation of congressional juries by congressional districts, investigations would be initiated under the law-making powers of Congress. The public jury system is an important social invention of the past because it shifts individuals from privacy or docility to becoming active citizens. Such juries, under the auspices of Congress, would undertake a needs assessment program to ascertain the level of need of repair and reconstruction of the American infrastructure. On a regional and local basis, they would make recommendations to Congress, which would then debate their value. The recommendations themselves would include whether repair, maintenance, and functioning of such public functions as subways, roads, waterways, railroad beds, etc., should be undertaken by public or private enterprise. The standard must be that "where a particular industry affects the general welfare, government whether on the local, state, federal or even neighborhood level cannot be stopped from undertaking public enterprise," especially where it is demonstrably clear that no private initiative is possible or forthcoming, as in the case of low-cost housing and nuclear cleanup.[32]

In the 98th Congress, the Committee on Public Works estimated that to repair the American infrastructure through the year 2001 would cost about $700 billion. Unfortunately, if one were to include nuclear and toxic cleanup from the Cold War, the costs in the first decade of the twenty-first century would be double that amount.[33] It is an irony, or perhaps a paradox, that conservatives in their rhetoric claim that they do not want to saddle future generations with debt, but are oblivious to the need for public expenditures and laws that will protect the environment so that it will be humanly livable for future generations. (The natural environment will survive. It is problematic whether human beings will in an environment that will take generations to repair itself.)

Two other aspects of the economy should be addressed through government activities. One is the keeping and dissemination of information on a wide basis. The second is undertaking yardstick industries where private enterprise in any other sector does not fulfill the requirements of public need.

In the first case, corporate advertising is not primarily a means to disseminate information to consumers. Rather it is predicated on the illusion of a dream future. This mode of advertising falls less in the category of trade puffing to be protected by the First Amendment than in illusion and deception, a form of fraud that is best corrected by other types of information, which Congress can fund. For example, the Federal Trade Commission should develop a television consumer protection network that would review products and their effects not only on the individual consumer but on the society, other societies, and nature as well. One of the more outrageous reforms of the Reagan administration ended easy access to government pamphlets, analyses, reports, and comprehensive budgets at minimum cost. The result is that only institutions and lobbies have real access to documents. This formulation is carried over in the national security arena, but attended to with criminal penalties for those who obtain confidential material.

The yardstick industry would operate to show how a particular firm should and could perform, whether in the production of wind and solar energy or new types of social organization within particular industries. The concept of yardstick industries dates back to the stage two liberalism of Roosevelt's New Deal, with the premier case being the Tennessee Valley Authority (TVA). The TVA went through several lives. The first was a grassroots, democratic, participatory project that guided its original development. The second stage was top-down organization, and its third stage included being a supplier for building nuclear weapons. That is, it passed from public participation to secrecy. The underpinning for any yardstick industry must be democratic participation and decision making involving the locales most directly affected.

The third zone of a national economy is predicated on a modified laissez-faire definition of small businesses and enterprises, albeit regulated and licensed by the government in matters of health and public interest. No impediments to labor organization would be imposed by the government. In this zone no individual firm controls a market. By and large, those firms in the third sector ought to be free of onerous governmental regulation, maintain their own method of decision making, and set prices based on market considerations without political interference, but they also have easy access to capital. However, their size would be strictly limited. It is taken for granted that the ordinary employee might not participate in decision making unless the person had specialized knowledge, hierarchic authority, or ownership or negotiated decision-making power through labor negotiations.

In the United States the small and microbusiness sector of the economy is playing a decreasing role. It is important to reiterate that 97 percent of the business establishments in the United States account for far less than one-third of the gross national product (GNP). The "gobbling up" problem of the small by the big—what might be referred to as the business world's Pacman tendency, with the "bigs'" having greater access to capital and wider geographic markets than the small—the merger and absorption problem by transnational corporations, decreases rather than increases the power of small business. Without access to national markets, or without a large distribution system, the small businessperson, even though there are twelve million of them, leads a precarious and insecure existence, judging from bankruptcy rates. As they have been throughout the twentieth century, micro- and small business owners are highly exposed financially and vulnerable politically.

In a democracy of social reconstruction, quite different attitudes toward small business could be held and put into practice. Small and microbusinesses employing substantially fewer than two hundred employees would have two constraints. Workers would continue to be free to organize or join labor unions and bargain for wages, hours, and conditions of employment. A third-party "shadow" or common good interest would frame negotiations. If the small or microbusiness finds that it is unable to support a decent wage for its workers, the public would absorb the difference between wages paid and a decent wage scale. To this end Congress would encourage local government to establish boards intended to determine the public interest value of a particular enterprise. Where the small or microbusiness claims that it is unable to pay decent wages through no business fault of its own, the firm or shop could apply for a matched subsidy from all levels of government equal to the added amount paid to the employee. The subsidy would be determined at the local level in the context of a comprehensive small and microbusiness program whose contours would be set by congressional legislation.

Small and microbusinesses would be required to fulfill health and safety standards for workers, consumers, and the locality. These costs would be borne by local communities as well as the individual business firm with aid from the federal government. Decisions of public boards would be appealable to a court of public maintenance appeals as a separate branch of the federal courts.

The fourth zone of economic activity concerns cooperatives, nonprofits, and small-scale, worker-owned enterprises. To a very great extent the workers' activities in the three other economic zones retain a measure of alienation of the kind that was central to the Industrial Revolution, and against which men with such different points of view as Samuel Coleridge, Williams Morris, and John Ruskin rebelled. The system of work that emerged often assumed a separation within the human being between the work to be performed and belief in what the person did at his or her work. Workers might be understood in objective terms as a category or class, but such categories do not adequately describe alienation, both in terms of property ownership and in feelings about the work being performed. This condition might not apply to the fourth zone of economic activity.

We will find people who retain both entrepreneurial skills and a democratic social character leading a life different from the one linked to the corporate business world. It may be that the most creative inventions and projects will emerge from the fourth zone, whether in worker-controlled technology, the university laboratory, or the regional playhouse. Without romanticizing the fourth zone, it may be the economic sector most likely to stave off oligopoly control because the value system of those in the fourth zone is predicated on attitudes that are less enamored of false claims of efficiency and productivity as defined by unrestrained capitalism.

The social character necessary for the fourth zone is substantially different from that required in the market and oligopoly system. There is greater likelihood of teaching several skills to each member of the enterprise through the work process, since specialization and division of labor take on different meanings in worker cooperatives than they do in a large corporate unit where roles and functions are more rigidly defined.

As a matter of public policy, the fourth zone should be favored through publicly controlled banks, which would lend start-up and shortfall capital. The charters of these banks would be limited to the fourth zone. Attempts in this regard have been made by the Cooperative Bank, which unfortunately was soon absorbed, both in its loans and consciousness in making loans that were little different from those made by commercial banks. Conclusions about the Cooperative Bank's socialization into dominant banking practices should not be drawn too quickly. I merely suggest that there is a problem with the type of political incrementalism that cannot change the underlying framework, in this case the banking process. Credit unions should be examined in depth to see how they could shape the fourth zone of enterprise. Their task would include the specific one of catalyzing the rebuilding of towns and cities while aiding forms of cooperative farming based on sound ecological principles.

The purpose of these four zones of the political economy is to ensure economic justice. If this purpose is not achieved because it is faulty in conception or execution, then other means to achieve economic justice should be found.

According to Fernand Braudel, in the history of capitalism consciousness of the Other was supplied by world trade, which proceeded in an unplanned, almost unconscious way. (Note the shadow of Hayek.) Trading highlighted differences and similarities between insular nations, which reinforced the idea of "unfetteredness" and cosmopolitan ideologies. And Western religion as well saw that it needed to spread and proselytize, to evangelize in the religious markets.

But trading among unequals does not economic justice bring, nor does forcing people off their land and from their villages through globalization; just as risk, speculation, and cheating are an integral part of capitalism, so now economic justice must find its own aspects inherent in individuals and their social interaction. If economic justice is accepted as an overarching category upon which to judge our actions, we will be able to take account in new ways of American society as well as billions of people who live on the world's economic margins. More than the others, the fourth zone reinforces sentiments of caring and empathy, leading as they do to cooperation and liberation, decency and dignity. In a liberal democracy these sentiments are already present if not dominant in some cultural, educational, and religious institutions. But they need to be extended to economic affairs.

That economic justice has been unable to find a central place in capitalism merely means that more thought and energy, more understanding of human nature and human interactions with institutions that begin and end with principles and ideals of economic justice, must be constructed and evaluated. In other words, an expansion of the public space is needed. This will be the major task of the liberal project in twenty-first-century democracy. But liberalism will mean another cover story for American imperialism unless liberals are prepared to confront it directly and with clarity.

GLOBALIZATION: IMPERIALISM REDUX

Several surprising features of the present international political economy should be noted. Once the Soviet Union fell apart, international financial agencies, namely, the International Monetary Fund and the World Bank, pressed even harder for internal economic reforms in various Third World nations and then in Eastern Europe and the former Soviet republics. Wasteful and inefficient use of capital as well as high social welfare costs were to be eliminated. These reforms were ostensibly to open the host nations to greater development and investment. Investors would "trust" the new system, which was supposedly more stable than the prior system. What seemed to be missing from this analysis was the pesky question of who would share the profits, how much would be pulled out of the host nation, and what would happen to social benefits, especially among older populations. Obviously, this question becomes of greater importance when the businesses in the host nation prove to be unprofitable and when the investing group pulls out of one nation looking for greater and more stable profits. This sensible rule of business was one that firms of whatever size understood, but this was not part of the growing mystique of American capitalism that could be found in universities, on Wall Street, and in the boardrooms of the media.

With the fall of the Soviet Union the assumption of the political scientists and economists of the West and elsewhere was that the analysis of Marx had proved either foolish or unrealistic. But capitalism has a way of saving the Marxist analysis just when it should have expired. There are four features to ponder:

1. With the collapse of the Soviet Union, the United States and Western nations had little stomach for keeping the welfare state. Throughout the twentieth century social democracy and liberalism served as the policy alternative to communism. But with communism's failures and death there was no need to surrender belief in free market principles and practices, which are associated with the reality of American capitalism rather than its self-advertisement.
2. There was sufficient evidence to suggest that Marxism failed on a nation-state level because there were countervailing forces to withstand the reach of untrammeled capital. Corporations seemed willing to accept the rules of the game of regulation and government intervention where markets did not seem to work well. But the success of the Western nation-state was stable only to the extent that it accepted regulatory standards and control over capital. When the "let 'er rip" mentality took over, capitalism no longer had the tangy lemon meringue taste for commentators and unsuspecting investors that it had in the 1980s and early 1990s.
3. Instead, the question of profits for corporations began again to raise its head. And here affections and responsibilities gave way to profit, defined in narrow terms and on a quarterly basis. Corporations that started in the American Northeast, when they could, moved their plants down South, listening to the blandishments of its cities and states, which offered privileges and tax breaks. These firms often left behind ghost towns.
4. The odyssey of these corporations was just beginning. If profit margins were not high enough in the South, even though there was no unionized labor and little state governmental interference, the corporation took off for northern Mexico, where it now encountered even cheaper labor costs. And in the next stage this archetypal corporation moved on to Asia, whether China or Indonesia, to lower labor and unit costs even further. Workers in all of these cases find it very difficult indeed to earn sufficient monies to have lives of dignity. The result is a class struggle worldwide. Keynes must be spinning in his grave at the foolish errors and greed evidenced by the owners and managers of capital. Marx must be laughing and saying, "I told you

so." But it is not only the question of world economies that is at stake. The question is whether there can be a world civilization based on human dignity and economic and social justice. Marx would assert iron laws of capitalism and its international structure, which keeps in place the West's romance with world imperialism. He would certainly point to the niggardly amounts given for economic and social development by the richer nations as less an example of personal greed than of profound systemic flaws.

Thus, there are differences between the new and old imperialism. In the early stage of twentieth-century imperialism was unvarnished racism. It was God's will. Racist nations of the West and their leaders claimed superiority over hundreds of millions whom their leaders saw as an uncultured, undifferentiated mass of colored people.[34] That the wretched could and should be exploited was taken for granted. And it did not matter which nation in the West one might visit, the same assumptions about race and the importance of imperialism prevailed. Senator Albert Beveridge in the United States was a proponent of imperialism and America's God-given right to act as teacher and trustee for the rest of the world.[35] But it was such senators as Richard Russell Jr. who brought together apartheid, imperialism, and military power as the unholy trinity of American power in the middle of the twentieth century.[36] American leaders concerned themselves with ensuring that the United States had primacy over Western nations (where it cared to) for obtaining raw materials from poor nations.[37] The poor nations in the American sphere of influence, for example, the Philippines or the Latin American nations, had to seek permission from the United States in social, economic, and political affairs. Nation building and national development were linked as children are to parents and paternalism.

Imperialism in international affairs had different styles and fashions during the twentieth century. Thus, in certain details colonialism, neocolonialism, and development look different. But each has its assumptions in Western domination. Sometimes they have been unbelievably brutal, as in the case of the Belgian suzerain colonial efforts in the Congo, in which millions of Congolese died in the diamond mines for the greater glory of King Leopold.[38] Plunder by the French took on different forms. Whereas the Belgians had no interest in integrating the Congolese as part of a commonwealth, in their colonial activities the French sought to integrate local elites who would accept France's civilizing mission, mouth the ideals of the French Revolution, and allow the French colonial "right" of exploitation. In strict mercantile fashion the French integrated Indochina and Algeria into their exclusive trading and colonial zone. The United States adopted a more subtle formulation of neocolonialism depending on the area of the world in which it held interests. Thus, American economic and security considerations were different in their application for Liberia, Latin America, and Asia.

Because of the U.S. entrance into the First World War, a new formulation was presented once the League of Nations was established. It was the mandate wherein, under the watchful eye of the League of Nations, a colonized people could advance to a new stage, that of being neocolonial with a promise of independent status. There were also advantages to this system for the colonial power. League legitimation of the colonized nation's status meant that there could be no poaching by nations of the West on each other's "property." This system of mandates morphed into the UN trustee system, which ostensibly gave reporting oversight to a UN Trusteeship Committee. In reality, nations had a free hand in how they would use their territories under a UN trusteeship. Thus, Pacific islands entrusted to the United States were used as nuclear test areas.

There is no doubt that the Second World War caused the West to recalibrate its style and purpose related to self-determination. Liberation movements had been unsuccessful in gaining independence before the Second World War (including the movement for self-determination in India) even though they had some support from leftist intellectuals and some trade unions in the mother country. But the Second World War brought the question of domination and oppression onto a new plane. The rhetoric of the Second World War revolved around freedom, self-determination, democracy, and liberation as against totalitarianism and colonialism. And these movements had a new force, seemingly supported by the Soviet Union. The language of liberation was an old story in the West.

Colonialism needed a new face, especially in light of two other events. One was the Bandung conference in 1955, which served notice on the West that Asia and poor nations would no longer be the sherpas for world capitalism. The other was development and neocolonialism. The "developing" nations borrowed but could never borrow enough to pay back interest on their loans. It did not matter what the ideological rubric was for the poor. The ideologies of neocolonialism, development, and globalization retained their exploitative character. For example, in agriculture, products were harnessed to a global market guided by the most affluent nations, especially the United States. This problem touched on virtually all new nations in Africa as well as nations in Latin America, the Caribbean, and Indonesia. These nations were victims of international markets and oligopoly corporations, which kept for themselves the patents of technically advanced goods while forcing the countries to change their agricultural patterns, resulting in economic deprivation and sometimes starvation, as for example in the case of Malawi. As international financier George Soros pointed out in the 1990s, the global capitalist system operated according to the ideology of the new imperialism, which took no prisoners.[39] What that meant was that finance capital balanced its books every day, allowing speculators to move their money from one financial market to another with little or no concern for the effects this had on the "host" nation. Thirty years earlier the policies that planners and Agency for International Development (AID) officials followed in the Cold War period were called development. Aid was thought to be the alternative to trade, the latter being the stance of neoliberals, whose proponents had as yet not gotten the upper hand in the mandarin pyramid. But in both cases the implicit objective of these ideologies was Western "guidance." Development was meant as an answer to the Marxist conception of reallocation, public planning, and public control over capital. Except in the case of military assistance, development was to be a matter for private enterprise. Development was a subset of realpolitik. Where loans were given to former colonies and poor nations, it was understood that they were legal or illegal bribes to elites intended to keep the former colonies friendly to global corporations. Business enterprises friendly to or representative of Western firms stood in a preferred position to receive private loans and contracts, loans that the state, that is, the poor, had to repay if businesses defaulted just because of the hold the business had on the national political structure. Where a particular leader represented a nationalist class without paying proper obeisance either to the United States or the international economic system, he or she faced disruption, with the likelihood of being deposed.[40]

Throughout much of the Cold War bureaucratic economic developers favored two types of projects. One was large-scale activities that did not begin from the grass roots but rather from international technocrats and elites, who used the same economic measuring sticks learned in Western economic and accounting departments without reference to local cultures. The second type of project was linked to infrastructure loans, which could benefit the international corporation in its profitability, as in the reshaping of the environment around the Amazon River.

Alternative ideas of reallocation and control of resources did emerge as a counterpoise to the new imperial method. Small groups on the Left favored grass-roots grants and loans. Usually these groups sparked a new consciousness to inhibit the sacking of the environment. And they have multiplied in numbers and activism. They are transnational in nature. They are not instruments of globalization, nor does it appear that they will be easily co-opted.[41]

The transnational vectoring of groups that reflect the world's left of political parties and also autonomous groups without affiliation to political power as it is usually defined has shown remarkable and growing political strength, especially among younger activists. These groups usually start from a particular issue and soon learn that within each issue are embedded other issues that require answers if there is to be any resolution to what began as a particular concern. Nascent as they are, these groups have formed themselves as a global justice movement with democratic roots.

8

★

Democracy and the
Culture of Technohype

STAGE THREE LIBERAL DEMOCRACY
IN A TECHNOLOGICAL AGE

Marxists and capitalists started from a shared premise; namely, that inhibiting technological change is a stupid, "reactionary" enterprise because it is counterproductive to the modernist spirit of progress. Technological invention, no matter the cost, had gripped the modernist idea that to conquer nature and straighten out the malign quirks of humanity was within grasp.[1] Pragmatists who championed modernism shared these ideas. Even those who expressed doubts, such as Brooks Adams and Henry Adams, believed that the chances of stopping technological modernism were virtually nil, although failure might lead to the death of civilization. Doubts were raised among those who invented ecology to conserve nature. Such doubts transferred the concerns of nineteenth-century writers and theologians about the character of science and technology into scientific categories that could be empirically analyzed.[2] But the fundamental political reality of modern life is that highly organized hierarchic society needed technologies as instruments of control, which, because they were "needed," increased their power. Indeed, in practice technology meant the organizing of things, people, resources, and inventions for particular ends.

Attempts to inhibit technological change have brought issue-specific environmental groups into the public arena. These groups hold conflicting social, ethical, and technical views on any particular innovation, such as nuclear power and genetic engineering. In many situations there will be

cross-cutting divisiveness between those in need, prepared to try any po-
tion, and those who fear quackery when new drugs are not withheld from
the market. In other venues, the antagonists are those who have invested
in a particular technology and those who fear being the object of the technology. Local communities fight toxic and nuclear dumping against those
who control production in the marketplace and those in the national state,
on the basis of expected harm done. But some Native American tribe communities will accept nuclear waste as a means of obtaining revenue sufficient for their local needs in the short term.

Together, modern capitalism, with the aid of science and technology, set
the terms of dreams, consumption patterns, and social control mechanisms
for the present and future. Technocorporations now intend to own and
present the images of the past through copyright, trademark, and patents.
Together, corporatism and technology can call up, retain, or destroy the
past at a flick of the wrist, through the electronic impulse. Beneath this
techno/cultural reality, which is helping to construct a world Potemkin village, there remains the economic reality of profound deprivation. Within
the United States, the gap between the haves and have-nots continues to
grow, with the result that American society is faced with an overfed and
overprivileged class that endangers democracy. While such technology as
automobiles, dishwashers, the telephone, and other "appliances" may appear to have a democratic "leveling" effect, it actually masks the increasing
gap between the rich and poor. The stubborn fact is that technology, in and
of itself, is not a substitute for political and social equality, economic justice, or the struggle for them. There are strategies and policies intended to
reassert the primacy of democracy in the social and political spheres, as well
as an economic pluralism that serves a common good and common bonds
of affection. (See chapter 7.)

The twentieth-century tug of war on questions of control over capital and
the direction of technology was articulated first in radical groups, such as
the People's Party of late nineteenth-century America. Progressives and
muckrakers raised doubts regarding safety in mines and the quality of meat
and drugs.[3] However, for modern liberals the issue has blossomed from that
of oversight to that of control in all aspects of technology, whether patent-
ing of cows, cancer drugs, airplanes, or nuclear reactors. Capitalism, committed to innovation and invention as a pure good, continues to shuck off
controls from the public or government, claiming that self-awareness and
self-policing is the answer.[4]

ASSESSING TECHNOLOGY RISKS AND SOCIETAL RISKS

Are there rules that apply to both democracy and innovative technology?
The first question to consider is where the burden should lie. Should it be

with those who want to bring about change with a new product, or with those who want to stop its introduction? Here it is important to note that modern liberalism, through the emergence of government regulation, began to demand a far higher standard for introducing a new product in the marketplace than did conservatism. Conservatism took to itself conceptions of progress that stem from eighteenth-century laissez-faire liberalism. As I have noted, in practice regulatory agencies often became the champions of the regulated industry, thereby undercutting citizen or consumer concern. Weak regulatory agencies were unable to impose a standard that transcended profit and loss definitions of utility.[5] They were caught in the web of ideas of progress, unfettered capitalism, industrial lobbying, and a hard-to-define common good or public interest. There was no agreed-upon moral compass to guide judgments in particular cases. Furthermore, since industrialists hated intrusion and feared the fettering of capitalism, they sought legal impediments against regulation and intrusion in what was thought to be management prerogatives. For the regulated drug industry, pharmaceutical companies have tolerated the appearance of regulation only because it bestowed governmental legitimacy, for them, against a concerned public that needed protection. (It should also be noted that pharmaceutical companies receive tax breaks and enjoy the fruits of government research while continuing to make high profit margins on drugs, knowing that they have a captive consumer market.)

There are standards that engage a different type of public analysis of innovation. The measurement to be adopted for concrete products is not the same as the risk assessment principle, which asserts a numerical or statistical notion of harm. Nor is it the standard of benefit–cost ratios, which never make clear which group or class receives the benefit or cost, either in the short or long run. Rather, the reconstructive standard emerges from three interlinked considerations, whether

1. the introduction of the "product" is likely to increase the measure of individual dignity and awareness, overall health, and participation in the society;
2. the effects of the product will tend to increase the likelihood of war and its accompanying devastation; or
3. the introduction of the product will damage the environment and increase class, race, and gender conflict without a just resolution.

These considerations give rise to a discourse that can be conducted in the society as a whole on specific and "meta" questions. The democratic discourse goes beyond any specific group discussion, because the implications of any specific product introduction may have far-reaching ramifications. The problem is not intellectual incapacity, which inhibits the citizenry from grasping or discussing abstruse questions. Rather, the citizenry is not attuned to this sort of discussion. It is nothing short of amazing how conversant and knowledgeable the body politic is about sports, fashion designs and trends, and their meanings over a generation. It is by no means clear that various aspects of science could not be well known and "critiqued" by the lay public with the same critical acuity.

Where authority is shared and shifted, democratic discourse usually takes place around concrete problems and questions. In a democracy, which places a high premium on discourse, individuals and groups will seek a cumulative and rolling consensus around general principles, about which preferred solutions to particular problems are found. The organizing question becomes that of devising a proper participatory forum for discussion and decision. Using the three criteria as a means of protecting the common good, examples of defense against particular types of technological innovation by communities abound. The nuclear reactor industry was greatly inhibited in its expansionist plans during the 1970s through citizens' movements, hearings, advocacy science, and whistleblowing. The hearings were carried out at virtually every level of government.[6] Often the regulatory commissions of the state and local governments sided with industry despite the flaws of particular reactors, their placement, and their stunning costs.

These interlinked considerations are based on an idea that both Marxists and free marketers understand: A technological economy is not a neutral enterprise. In a democracy, it can be fashioned to fit a society whose overarching project is to promote dignity and decency. Such an economy cannot escape having a clearly articulated "ought" purpose. Without an "ought" purpose, which reflects the spirit of freedom within the democratic nation, democracy will not escape being a system of overlapping oligarchies reinforced by technology hidden by the corporate form. The fruits of technology will be controlled through the market and private capitalist institutions that are protected by laws serving the very few. The corporation as a legal instrument will continue to take on human characteristics, but with limited obligations assigned legally to the actual human participant managers and owners.

If democracy's spirit, manifested through its cultural, theological, and educational institutions, does not include technological and scientific innovation, the political system will have no moral or political center. Its citizens open themselves to unremitting class war, a stunting of creativity, and corrosive unhappiness, which come from knowing that they, as a desirous people, are marginalized by institutions they neither made nor know how to control.

Given the central role of modern technology, which is seen as absolutely necessary for survival and well-being for the West, the remaking of technology's relationship to humanity becomes an overriding task. Technology, being a human and social construction, does not have to be the Golem of modern life. Properly understood it is an integral part of the future of freedom and democracy.[7]

DO MASS COMMUNICATIONS CREATE ANARCRACY?

The fundamental character of modern democracy has bent to the will of communications technology. And in the process one might see on the horizon an offshoot of democracy, anarcracy. Its features are not the usual attributes of states and operate as a counter to state power.

Great powers and those that strive to be great powers expand until they exhaust themselves in wars and foolish enterprises.[8] Further, there is evidence that centralization beyond a certain point increases the likelihood of collapse. In the American system this result was to be guarded against in two ways. One was through federalism, that is, the distribution of power and authority to the states, and the other was the use of a political formula in which geographic areas under the control of the United States could become states accepted as equals as defined by the Constitution with power then ceded to the individual state.[9] Of course, these two prohibitions did not stop the United States from expansion or being a warrior state. Further, the nature of capitalism as it developed in the United States tended toward gigantism, which required greater national authority over the political economy; an authority difficult to obtain in peacetime but relatively easy to receive in times of war and severe depression.

Anarcracy is a syncretic political form that places emphasis on individualist behavior and fear of centralization. Anarcrats are linked to likeminded people in other places in the world through computer communications. They seem unburdened by geographic boundaries and hold loyalty to any state very lightly.[10] In other words, the anarcrat develops his or her own forms of access, participation, deliberation, and modes of implementation beyond physical or geographic boundaries.

The anarcratic form clashes with political entities that are based on physical and political geography and traditional conceptions of power, such as armed forces, land, and buildings. In the anarcratic formulation technology sets the terms of politics. It is not about things. Anacracy is about a reorganizing principle seeking to break free from its parents, namely, the state and corporation. In anarcracy an invisible community of spontaneity forms through the Internet, telephone, Web, etc., wherein the seemingly invisible community will claim greater power and reality than fixed capital, patents, military power, and state secrets—the sovereign state itself. Like life itself, anarcracy keeps reproducing and enlarging itself to the individual's self-defined limit. As quickly as it exists it can disappear and reform itself. The popular formation of global attack of outside states on U.S. policy in Iraq is a stunning example of the growing emergence, even power, of anarcracy.

Anarcracy gives the appearance of fitting well with twenty-first-century capitalism, for both seek to create information and its movement as the fundamental overriding reality. However, their purposes diverge. Capitalism seeks to control and command information, knowledge, and culture as a commodity. Similarly labor, the employed and workers, are merely commodities. They may be highly paid or paid the wages of workers in Haiti. Hiding under the name "globalization," a word Marx would have enjoyed because it is intended to mask old-style capitalist imperialism, capitalism brings in its suitcase what has now come to be obvious to anyone who looks. In poor nations, globalization brings with it the destruction of community ties that did exist, the fetishization of the "market" and the product, and the end of corporate citizenship as a means of self-control and emphasis. Efficiency is defined narrowly as private profit in money terms and the commodification of those aspects of culture deemed to be profitable.[11]

Obviously, this type of capitalism, one predicated on markets at the expense of communities and cultures, has been presented as the necessary price for progress. Those who identify unrestrained international capitalism as progress have tempered their rhetoric, admitting that there may be collateral damage to poor nations and people.

Anarcrats, especially those left and libertarian inclined, are not enamored of the claims of "superior" knowledge and unearned legitimacy made by large-scale institutions such as the state and corporate capitalism. Anarcracy vectors toward those who are ideologically attuned to the idea of decentralization and dissolution of the modern state. Whether the anarcratic form can be amalgamated with liberal democracy is dependent on the anarcrat's relationship to face-to-face human relations, especially with those that are not technologically driven and with those whose views may differ. The anarcrat's relationship to democracy need not be contradictory, since its mode of communication is, by nature, nonhierarchic.

Associative and nonhierarchic relationships have a more traditional meaning in democracy. They are predicated on fairness and face-to-face relationships.[12] But does anarcracy favor or eschew such relationships? It might be said that one of the "benefits" of anarcracy is that the citizenry would be linked through computers and "as if" realities, without having to bother with human relationships in all their messy dimensions. That is to say, proponents of anarcracy would have to be aware that communications systems are not ends in themselves replacing human relationships but instruments for increasing those confrontations that lead to repairing and creating the bonds of social affection.

ANOMIE AND ANARCRACY

One danger of anarcracy is that it gives credence to the notion that there is no escape from social atomism and individual attempts to compensate through selfish interest. In the twenty-first century, this idea of a world of monads is mediated through the computer screen, which has a variety of meanings, from a place that makes it easier through images to see reality to the mask that hides reality. Yet, the anarcrat seems to speak for a next stage in social relationships, a reconstruction that amalgamates itself with communications technology. Whether it will be a direct and continued challenge to the organization of sovereignty is a likely battle that will be played out in the twenty-first century. A democracy of social reconstruction with anarcratic features will struggle to shape this technology as a liberating instrument.

History teaches contradictory lessons. It does not come unalloyed as new shapes come into being. Some may mistakenly believe that because the nation-state is under attack from decentralized terrorist cells, such cells are a form of anarcracy. Gangs or religious zealots that undertake terrorist acts as a means of ensuring a perverse form of theocracy are the very antithesis of anarcracy as a political form. Sending suicide bombers to kill civilians is a moral outrage. But is there much of a distinction when the state asserts that its armed forces must kill or be killed? One must marvel in horror at, for example, the deprogramming of eighteen-year-old Marine recruits as they adapt to the martial spirit. But if this is all the nation-state has to offer in its definition of defense and heroism, the nation-state will not escape the claims of anarcrats that the state is merely an organized form of violence that justifies itself through law and has nothing to offer the poorer classes, which twentieth-century social democrats have long believed is the purpose of the state. On the other hand, anarcracy is not the answer to a world desperately in need of connection, solidarity, and face-to-face empathic relations.

9

★

The Liberal
Democratic Covenant:
Everyone Sits at the Table

THE NEW AMERICAN COVENANT

The fierce debates surrounding multiculturalism suggest that there is another culture struggling to be born in the United States, one that implicitly asserts that all of humanity is a hybrid of different peoples who intermarried or produced irrespective of "race." With this as the overriding assumption, third-stage liberalism seeks to link democratic ideals to changes that will scramble the old cultural, economic, and political pecking order.[1] During and at the end of the Cold War, the United States accepted a relatively large immigrant population from areas of the world where it claimed interest and responsibility, from Hungary, Vietnam, Thailand, Cambodia, Central America, East Europe, and Ethiopia. Its reasons were various, including the need for skilled workers. The American society is now faced with a type of multiculturalism that hits up against the traditional and fundamental struggle between "white and non-white" communities. There is an added concern, namely, struggles among diverse non-white cultures for a place within the nation, recognition of their own traditions, and hopes for a prosperous place in the national and international employment and market system. Difficulties between these groups will increase over the course of the next generation, unless certain basic decisions are made vis-à-vis the economy. These decisions must veer from a market/oligopoly economy to a common good economy, which means guaranteeing full employment or sufficient income while simultaneously forging a system of education that accepts differences and seeks to develop out of those differences a new social covenant. It may very well be that this covenant will lead to constitutional

149

reconstruction. But whatever that constitutional reconstruction is, in the United States it is necessary that African Americans and Native Americans stand in a preferred position with regard to ensuring social and economic reparations because they are the heirs of slavery and genocide. In other words, the United States must make operational the Thirteenth to Fifteenth Amendments to the Constitution in the twenty-first-century context, thus inviting a new democratic covenant that renegotiates broken treaty arrangements with Native American tribes and agreements about rights guaranteed through struggle since the 1790s.

For some, the new American culture continues the process of people being reborn, without care or memory of the past. For many, being uprooted means an escape from the nightmare of war, oppression, and economic desperation. While many immigrants in the early part of the century came to the United States believing that there was a future wholly different from the past, others came because they were impressed into coming, or they came to breathe political freedom. Some came because they were victims of imperial wars in which they supported the United States. Others used the United States as a staging area for remaking their place of origin, while indigenous people and Hispanics lost their homelands in war.[2] Children of immigrant Americans sought to shed the past, escape from it, and become Americans. They would embrace peculiarly American ways. But to whose ways were they to adapt? Were they to accept the political and economic predominance of the Southern white oligarchs? Were they to be entrepreneurs who would accumulate wealth? Was there an "American spirit" blanketing the nation that could be presented through education and that would define the American identity beyond any particular region?

In 1935, during the Great Depression, the problem of identification was flagged by John Dewey, who hoped that the public school and education would provide an answer for the creation of an American identity that would be democratic. To him, the scientific and the reasonable would provide the basis for the new culture and accumulation of immigrants:

> In the olden times, the diversity of groups was largely a geographic matter. There were many societies, but each, within its own territories was comparatively homogeneous. But with the development of commerce, transportation, intercommunication, and emigration, countries like the United States are composed of a combination of different groups with different traditional customs. It is this situation which has, perhaps more than any other one cause, forced the demand for an educational institution which shall provide something like a homogeneous and balanced environment for the young. Only in this way can the centrifugal forces set up by juxtaposition of different groups within one and the same political unit be counteracted. The intermingling in the school of different races, differing religions, and unlike customs creates for all a new and broader environment. Common subject matter accustoms all to a unity of out-

look upon a broader environment than is visible to the members of any group while it is isolated.[3]

Multiculturalism accepts the liberal democratic framework of pluralism by enunciating three goals; one is recognition that comes from making relevant the narratives, the stories of submerged or militarily and politically defeated cultures that still survive and whose young seek a compromise between the dominant culture and their own. In some of these cultures, such as the African American, individuals believe that they are responsible for America's existence, but they have not been recognized or compensated. The second goal is a political affirmation that seeks integration within the politically dominant culture through recognition of other stories, signs, and symbols, as well as elements of economic justice and compensation. The third goal is protection and the need for new immigrants or submerged cultures, such as Native Americans, to present their own narratives in ways that allow them to reach out to each other and then to collaborate with the culture defined by Western science and technology, which should be suffused with recognition of the historical contributions of non-Western cultures. These three goals are to be sought in different public arenas, from schools and universities to museums, media, places of work, and politics.

It is important to note that multiculturalism does not guarantee liberation from patriarchy or various forms of cultural injustice, personal oppression, or group injustice. In other words, respect for other cultures does not mean blind acceptance of them and their own tendencies, which may contain strong doses of domination and oppression, such as crude or refined modes of domination women have faced in virtually every culture and religion. Instead, within each culture it is necessary to find those elements of advocacy and confrontation that championed human liberation but may have been suppressed. It is absurd to think that feelings of liberation are not universally found, just as it is foolish to believe that Western civilization is an immaculate conception that needs no correction.

The challenge within American society is to "accommodate the future" between people whose cultures in another setting were significantly different from one another and where historical conflicts carry over from nations of origin to the United States, as in the case of the Irish and British, the Armenians and Turks, and the Palestinians and Jews. Throughout history, and especially during the modern period, colonialism meant the attempted destruction of other people's cultures and the humanity of the Other, either as individuals or a group. This tragedy continues to haunt American society, which is nevertheless far more honest about the problem than less polyglot nations where attempts at destruction of the Other to ensure separation or superiority are still present.

Within the United States, Native American and African American cultures seek ways to overcome the wretched conditions imposed by colonialism and virtually always white oppression. Although a few filmmakers have thought to run the reel backward on indigenous peoples to assert a different understanding of the reality of colonialism, and although the actor Marlon Brando substituted a Native American to accept his Academy Award to make a speech about Native American rights, the stubborn fact is that Native Americans continue to be treated as an oppressed people. Whites simultaneously honor Native Americans with Native American names for towns, cities, and sports teams that are dominated by the nonindigenous. In the American context, Native Americans are a conquered people bearing the marks of hundreds of years of oppression. In the face of self-justification by whites over the destruction of their cultures and lands, American Indians have struggled to maintain their pride and some of their past culture as a mode of defense against the dominant culture. De Tocqueville made the point that Indians in his time were treated with greater respect than slaves.[4]

Within the cultures of some Native American tribes there were powerful humane attributes worthy of replication, such as reverence for nature and life, caring, and responsibility of the group to the person, and vice versa.[5] But it is important not to romanticize Native American cultures, for some tribes were hardly pacific and lived their daily lives in terms of cruelty, either because of need of food or expansion.[6] In contemporary America, the dominant economy has caused difficult adjustments for indigenous people seeking to have some control over their own livelihoods. As a result, to survive culturally tribes have become market oriented, taking on gambling casinos. Perhaps they have made a Faustian bargain to retain their own cultures. They have also been willing to accept onto their reservations the nuclear waste and dreck of the dominant culture.[7] As some tribes became economically successful, Western senators true to their forebears were eager to breach historical treaties made with the tribes.[8]

THE VESTIGES OF SLAVERY

The Right, for example Dinesh D'Souza, claims that African Americans are economically more successful than those who stayed in Africa. Consequently, there is little if any historical debt that is owed by the United States to the heirs of slavery. This exculpatory argument is similar to that of those who might assert that concentration camp victims were done a favor by the Nazis because as survivors they achieved a certain measure of affluence in the United States.

The saga of Africans, enslaved and then brought to the United States, needs to be told and retold so that American civilization can both understand the roots of its past and overcome the oppressive stereotypes and institutions that are ever present in our consciousness and policies. They frame the lives of African Americans, both their images of themselves and those images laid upon them by whites. They tell us the problems that whites have in understanding their privileges. For example, the African family was historically a strong economic and social unit, and to the extent possible, African American families sought to continue that sort of strength in the extended family structure. The operational result of slavery was to destroy families, create social disorganization among slaves, and create a group of individuals who would be bound only to their masters and, later, to those who contracted them out as corvee labor.[9] What emerged from this form of slavery in attenuated form became the social welfare, prison, and criminal justice systems as they dealt with minority populations.[10]

The cultural question of black–white relations is further complicated within the United States by issues of incest and rape; white overlords may have taken slaves as their mistresses, and their children were also brutalized and sexually molested.[11]

Conservative social scientists, such as Richard Herrnstein and Charles Murray, further assuage dominant attitudes by claiming that IQ is genetically sealed and blacks are at the low end of the self-serving IQ totem poll. Thus, they explicitly and implicitly claim that education programs are wasted on African Americans. This argument had enormous currency in the 1920s. It was championed by the Harvard psychologist William McDougall, who claimed that civilization was dependent on Nordic superiority and that the United States was speeding down the road to oblivion if it pursued race mixing and liberal policies of immigration.[12] Another noted psychologist of the time, Carl Brigham, claimed that "[t]he intellectual superiority of our Nordic group over the Alpine, Mediterranean and Negro groups has been demonstrated."[13] It should be noted that in the first part of the twentieth century there was considerable argument about whether Jews were white and whether they could be anything but inferior as a matter of genetic type. A generation later the conventional wisdom was changed. They became superior in the popular mind.

The question of separatism and integration is now a main artery to the heart of American democracy. The nature of desegregation that occurred, starting in the 1960s, was basically a one-way street. That is to say, blacks were to be integrated into white society, into its assumptions of class and values. On the other hand, black separatists and nationalists felt strongly that what was being destroyed by such integration was their own culture, which had maintained itself through apartheid with its efforts at cohesion and defense. In the twenty-first century there are strong ethnic and cultural claims of separate identity. When such claims come at the cost of a universal bond with humanity, humanity is sidetracked and regresses to the parochialism of communities based primarily on the existence of fantasy about the Other. This is not to argue that multiculturalism is free of problems.[14] In considering the question of multiculturalism, issues immediately arise about the validity of assimilation, where "acceptable" African Americans are more likely to succeed if they adopt ways of speaking, education, ethics, and aesthetic tastes of the dominant culture while tolerating laws of exclusion.

The lesson of multiculturalism is the acceptance and recognition of cultures that are independently strong that are then suffused with liberatory values and customs. This makes separate and polyglot cultures the democratic ideal, which serves as the foundation for American society and world civilization. What cannot be countenanced is a situation in which skin color as a cultural and class divide is used to promote racial superiority and cultural, economic, and political domination.[15] Further, there are painful examples in nations that are thought to be democratic where skin color is meant to and objectively forecloses a decent life. Over 120 million dalits (the untouchables) in India find themselves in servitude from birth. Although nowhere near such conditions apply in American society, race superiority resides in the American consciousness and practical life of American society. Tragically, this fact should not be considered as alien to Western ideals and practices. Anti-Semitism and race domination played a central role in the development of European civilization. In its most virulent form it served to nurture Nazism.[16] The remnants of these ideas remain in such alliances as NATO, which is class and race oriented. For example, NATO supporters flirt with the idea that the United Nations should be supplanted as the dominant international organization in both political power and legitimacy.

Multiculturalism can have more than a rhetorical meaning if it tolerates and considers critically different values, customs, lifestyle struggles, and understandings, as well as different histories of both the United States and the world. Thus, the way literature is used, the way skills are taught, the way customs and manners are passed on, turns out to be central to a redefinition of American culture. To the chagrin of conservatives, the introduction of black studies at white-dominated universities has had the effect of changing the character of concern at universities by pointing the flashlight into areas of inquiry that hitherto have been unknown or ill considered.

The scale of values that both immigrants and colonized cultures grow up with in the United States is that their own language and history are less important than the dominant ones. Of course, in an expedient sense, this is true. We are more likely to praise someone who knows European languages than African languages, and we are more likely to create a hierarchy that downgrades those customs and mores that do not have roots in the European culture, which itself is an agglomeration. Praise and taking care of "one's own" may register as a betrayal of human responsibility and universal identification.[17]

Whether Muslims have a special responsibility for Muslims, Catholics for Catholics, Jews for Jews, blacks for blacks, Armenians for Armenians, or workers for workers misses the point of the paramount concern of human responsibility. Human responsibility precedes the importance of individual culture, and ethnic, class, or race loyalty. A universalistic ethic in a vibrant democracy requires that any nation or subgroup review its class and social structure to assert identification with the human Other and care for the environment. This identification must take practical economic and social form within the contours of an emerging world civilization. There is little possibility of such identification occurring when economic injustice is practiced through laws, regulations, and social custom. The result of such a state of affairs is, as Frantz Fanon pointed out, a struggle for personal and self-identity. But the success of the person finding an identity of dignity can occur only where the value system of society begins to change through struggle and legitimation by laws based on human rights and liberation. That is to say, a personal project for self-worth is the project of humanity, which is to be legitimated through education, law, economic justice, and recognition of the self in another, outside of hierarchic social roles. The interruption and inhibition of such a project is the essence of human betrayal, for it destroys that human identity that integrates self-worth, political freedom, and economic justice. In 1968 the sanitation workers of Memphis, Tennessee, understood this fact when they carried signs for higher pay that said "I am a Man." Their needs and attitudes moved Martin Luther King Jr. to return to march with them, and then to his death. His task, with tens of thousands of others, was to cross the borders of race to end the colonizer–colonized relationships that distorted the human project of progress and liberation. This is an important element in third-stage liberalism. Cultural border crossing was intuitively understood by the voluble Cornel West in his battle with the arrogant president of Harvard, Lawrence Summers, who thought it was his "responsibility" to rein in Professor West because he did not support Summers's technocratic views of scholarship. On a deeper level, Summers attempted to uphold a university of assimilation in which West was expected to accept standards of etiquette, speech, and grading, as well as acceptable political activity. (The skeptic can only wonder whether if Bill Bradley or Ralph Nader had been elected president, the former secretary of treasury would have been so quick to criticize West, who did not support Gore.) The question is who decides cultural boundaries and how are they to be crossed so that moral and political vitality can exist. It is dangerous for liberal democracy when such questions are decided on the basis of power, authority, and dominator–dominated.

CULTURAL BORDER GUARDS

A liberal democracy encourages people to cross back and forth between their own self-selected group and the Other. Those who live between different cultures—to the extent they diverge—are carriers of a double dynamic. They are carriers of values that can be exercised either as complementary or contradictory to one another. "Border brokers" are go-betweens or mediators who arrange their own lives so that one set of values does not contradict another. However, they soon find that they are brought into a political task, namely, finding ways of fusing, explaining, and transforming dominant and minority values. In many cases this is what mixed marriages of race and religion learn to negotiate between couples and in families. The artist, traveler, trader, teacher, and intellectual also have acted as go-betweens and brokers of different cultures, as have African American studies programs at predominantly white universities. The brokerage task was also taken over in the 1960s by corporate-owned film and television, whose culture workers presented and interpreted the "realities" of everyday life as building blocks of a homogenized popular culture. The content may be altogether benign or vicious, as in the way Arabs are presented.

There are three ways that American blacks have been presented on dominant television networks and in the film industry since the civil rights movement established their existence to white audiences:

1. Symbol manipulation is used wherein individual blacks appear alone or as one of several people to advertise products. From time to time, on public television, attempts have been made to explain the civil rights movement, as in Henry Hampton's *Eyes on the Prize.* On commercial television, Alex Haley's biography of his family, *Roots,* had a large following because it created a narrative that had not figured in the popular culture. Before the success of the civil rights movement, white America's understanding of blacks was bent through the racist prism of *Birth of a Nation* and *Gone with the Wind.*
2. A second generation created program niches of black sitcoms, meant primarily for African American audiences. Large numbers of young whites watched, picking up black styles of dress and behavior (the turned around baseball cap as a symbol of solidarity and rebellion, and a handshake that became mainstream). Similarly, jazz, blues, rock, and church choir music from the black community were absorbed into or plagiarized by the national commercial entertainment market.
3. The third generation of "white-oriented" television appears to be transfixed by black and minority violence, handled by police who perform as if the United States were a fascist state. The detectives on

NYPD Blue revel in their violence against sniveling and cunning blacks. Its producer, Steve Bochko, refers to himself as a racist. The eleven o'clock news is given over to black violence, while punishment and crime seem reserved for the poor.

The connection between a society pandering to worldly possessions and the desires created among the young to obtain consumer goods "by any means necessary" is understood to be the underlying purpose of a consumer culture, which masks itself as multiculturalism beyond consumerism and violence. Instead, television and the media are degraded, operating on the margins of everyday struggles around the economy and police control. The corporate media purpose is either "flash" entertainment to last a moment, an imagistic reflection of what goes on in particular communities, especially ghettos, around violence, or most important, to be adjuncts to the market system to get people to buy. In the latter case, renowned figures from various respective "sub" cultures are used as flaks. They are presented as role models for products, as for example, in the case of Michael Jordan, where excellence and the product are fused in the buyer's mind. This fusing is neither antiracist nor democratic. It is based on consumer stimulation, organized by the celebrity, who plays on his race and sells his or her talent to the corporation to appeal to new markets. The system is copied from white celebrities who appeal by class to white audiences. Advertisement, which was once thought of as meaning buyer information, condemns the individual to endless and never fulfilled consumer desire. While this is a form of colonization, it is not the same as actual imprisonment, for its purpose is considered to be relatively benign. The sellers are purveying nothing more than false dreams and consumer debt, which do not usually result in the purveyor or "buyer" ending up in prison. Debtors' prisons are not the modern method of capitalism. Indeed, capitalism is predicated on debt, with interest. As some have said, the greater the debt, the more successful the economy.

THE PRISON COMMUNITY'S BOUNDARIES OF THE LOSER

Prisons have another purpose. They are the tribute the state and society pay to themselves as organizing instruments of legalized oppression and indignity. They are meant to habituate the individual to authoritarianism and repression through totalitarianism. The criminal justice system in political terms is the purest form of divide and conquer, a method that historically characterized the operations of imperialism against subject populations. Imperialists have long counted on the fact of disagreement between groups and cultures to maintain their own authority and control to maintain power. Colonizers relied on intragroup conflict between submerged groups, aimed at playing one group off against another. However, this stratagem does not undercut the fact that such conflicts exist. This is the social reality in some American cities where "ethnic" gangs consider their "natural" enemies to be other ethnic gangs. The argument is over boundaries, property, sex, and slights between the have-nots. The same struggles exist inside the prison, and prison administrators operate much in the manner of the nineteenth-century white imperialist. Their task is to keep the peace between the various groups, causing and exploiting tensions when that is in the interest of the prison authorities.

Criminals are categorized as outsiders who are also thought of as commodities. Insiders in the criminal justice system—judges, wardens, guards, parole officers, "security" manufacturers and salespeople, and investors—depend on criminals for their economic and social status. Although there are exceptions in which emphasis in some prisons is placed on social rehabilitation, the primary purpose of the prison is social control. Criminal behavior and crime are often different from what prosecutors care about. After all, there is much crime in prisons. But that is a matter of much less concern for people outside of prisons.

The consequence of the prison system is to add an overwhelming weight to very fragile family structures. Why a consequence so obvious is not understood suggests that in fact it is implicitly understood as a form of internal colonialism that feeds on the authoritarian aspects of the state as well as social and economic disintegration. The purpose of prison is the further devastation of families and a return to an updated version of internal colonialism.[18] The supposedly neutral sentencing guidelines are anything but neutral and egalitarian, as can be seen in the differences in sentences for crack cocaine pushers and users as against cocaine pushers and users. These problems can only be exacerbated under the antiterrorism act, which places every manner of police and prosecutorial discretion in the hands of the federal government and local government officials.[19] These powers range from loose definition of what a "suspect" is, to police and federal police agencies breaking and entering without specific judicial authorization, to expansion of the power of the government not to share evidence with a defendant before trial, to holding suspects incommunicado first for seven days and then longer under a "material witness" prosecutorial claim, to keeping suspects away from lawyers, to massive wiretapping and, where necessary, secret military tribunals for accused foreigners.[20] It may be that these specific laws will be used only against terrorists.[21] As my research assistant Christi Fanelli pointed out, while concern flags among the public about drug use, the need for mobilization on the part of the government is now to link crime and drugs to terrorism. The commercials that premiered during the 2002 Super Bowl (and continue to air) portray shamed children apologizing for their unwitting contribution to the September 11 terrorist attacks because they used drugs—in deep and sorrowful reflection, claiming to have sponsored a terrorist's actions even though they were only having fun. The likelihood is that such carte blanche authority can be used against anyone and for virtually any purpose, but minorities and outsiders are automatic targets. Thus, police and prosecutorial discretion can adversely affect the speed of multiculturalism becoming the dominant American reality. State oppression under whatever guise and for whatever purpose cannot stop the values of universalism or narrow the boundaries of communications that technology brings to the formation of a multicultural mind-set.

I have suggested that it is only through terrifying oppressive use of the criminal law against minorities, war, or depression that the values of liberal reconstruction can be avoided. If the United States escapes these values it will be at the price of its own decay. The existence of a lily-white society, even one that asserts fealty to affirmative action, in a sea of non-whites domestically and internationally, is not tenable, especially where the economic system does not open itself to access for economic power beyond the few.

MULTICULTURAL VITALITY

Throughout the twentieth century there were many examples of small magazines published, blues and jazz and other forms of music making, folk life, and high art that had spontaneous qualities and were performed without concern for their monetary value. Yet, they played a fundamental role in the life of the society in its variegated aspects. This kind of culture, which one may view as a culture of liberal reconstruction, defiance, and self-definition, is the basis upon which culture can be re-created, sustained, perpetuated, and open to surprise and accident. Its characteristics are necessary components of third-stage liberal democracy.

The organizing of a multicultural society in America, linked to liberation and humaneness internationally, can build on this liberatory tradition. Correctly understood, the culture of the "small" can have a profound effect in creating a world civilization.[22] Each group and culture in the twenty-first century will want to be recognized as an actor of history with its own dynamic. These actors will seek to be "seen" through international communications systems where access is uninhibited. In this communication process, people will be more able to critically examine their own purpose and values. This can have surprising results.

Cultural transmission is by its nature sneaky and subversive. It is through culture that those who are dominated, once they understand their power, can transform the dominator without repeating the characteristics of that dominator. And from time to time some universities and churches can play this liberatory role. Perhaps the technology of communications can help in this regard. And perhaps new formations of group living, such as those in Latin America, or those who live the word and deed of liberation theology, will expand their influence. Finding the projects and generating the democratic society of dignity and decency with a governing structure and communities of caring within a world civilization is an endless project riddled with failure. Hopefully our reason and empathy will help us recognize mistaken detours. There is no magic bullet or proper vaccine that will bring utopia. That is not what humanity needs or should want, for utopia is really nowhere. There is no room for people to be included in Nowhere.

INCLUSIVITY FOR ALL PEOPLE

Like the American Civil War, as well as the major wars and revolutions of the twentieth century, the struggle for inclusivity, not as the commanded or the imperial objects of others but as equals, has been at the center of politics. Whether taking the form of struggles against slavery and racism, imperialism, or exploitation of workers, women, and children, the horrors of war, civil war, and, in some cases, revolution defined the underlying twentieth-century social and political thrust to turn the "ought" into the "is." Those who held to the ideas of fascism and Nazism professing racial domination, exclusivity, and even genocide failed in their attempts at making the "is" of exclusivity, racism, genocide, and slavery, that is, the "is" of the past, into an "is" of the present and future. No doubt what fails in one generation may again appear as something other than the lingering residue and detritus of the past. Indeed, such voices are still present, and they are found in all cultures, whether African or European. The breakup of states, such as in the Balkans, and the incendiary struggles between the Hutus and Tutsis, suggested deep schisms that could not be contained or redirected in the nation-states of the postwar colonial period.

Because fascism did not come to the twentieth century out of thin air, we see certain persistent strands of such ideas that continue to present themselves in attenuated and diluted form. Subtle and blatant attempts are made to reinforce traditional and pyramidal power. The conservative credo, which can tail off into fascism because of its emphasis on "superior–inferior" through exclusivity, is reasserted through housing, gated communities, private clubs with high membership fees, elite universities with high tuition and room and board costs, spectator sports that distinguish the corporate and celebrity few from the many, and private police forces and surveillance to protect property and the powerful. To this end, fear and insecurity are played upon. The reinforcement of superiority through property acquisition is defended by the law and covered with claims of merit. The thrust toward inclusivity and reapportioning of rights and dignity in the twentieth century has caused conservatives to surround themselves with psychological and political protections to restrict or reinterpret democratic inclusivity. Thus, for example, affirmative action, a benign way of spreading privilege, is fought against on the ground that it is reverse discrimination.[23] It is not thought to be discriminatory if economically poor children, who are often black, do not have equal access to resources. Not many care about the discriminatory and oppressive character of the criminal law.

Exploitation and struggle are carried on with the permission of the insiders against those who are outside the perimeter of the bounded area on the frontier.[24] It is taken for granted that very low wages for workers in the Philippines or China are justified on the ground that having entered the international capital economy the workers are expected to adjust to the discipline of the market. Furthermore, corporations claim that workers are now earning more than they earned before computer assembly lines or Gap or Nike factories came to their nations. The issue is not whether some workers earn more than what they did before (an arguable proposition when costs are taken into account); the real question is whether what is offered through the corporate market with the support of the state is the best or preferred practical alternative for the individual or society.

The political answer can be formulated through a range of options and participatory and deliberative decisions, made both by workers and owners in the framework of laws of protection and modes of investment, that hold workers, consumers, and the environment superior to profit. If this answer is not put into practice through global organizations of legal, economic, and social justice, the international corporate, banking, and legal systems will fall back on nineteenth-century imperial ideas of investment and inequitable contracts. They will use compacts that ensure the power of investors and global corporations as their legitimating international legal instruments. Billions of people will suffer the consequences of an unattended or corrupt "free market."

The original purpose of international banking, as developed at the end of World War II by Lord Keynes and Harry Dexter White, was to close the gap between rich and poor, not widen it.[25] One unnoticed reason that this has not happened is that public international institutions' officers and staff had no clear idea where their responsibilities and allegiances lay. There was no Hippocratic oath based on dignity and decency that would make clear that international institutions, even banking institutions, had as their primary purpose the protection and aid of the poor sectors of the world. But in a period of reconstruction, the international civil servant will seek universal values disclaiming the privilege of the insider against the outsider, thereby transforming prior loyalties and affections or reinterpreting them in line with universal values.[26] He or she would reject becoming part of the bureaucracy of the World Trade Organization or any international organization that in its operations or charter and purpose yields greater oppression and disparity.

One may ask whether this is true of institutions of higher learning as presently constituted. What facts and values do they purvey? Indeed, what are the educated taught to believe as organized mystication? This question should be a research program of education faculties.

10

★

Education and the University: Testing Ground for Liberal Democracy

LIBERAL EDUCATION IN ITS THIRD STAGE

In the twenty-first century the educator is caught in a series of complex problems that are both substantive and organizational. There is little doubt that the character of teaching and learning is changing. For many it is now long distance—anarcratic and not dependent on face-to-face relationships. This situation gives rise to the narrowing of judgment and wisdom, substituting an abundance of information, whether true, false, or imaginary. Further, when education leaves the project of skills and specialization, especially in the sciences (but by no means limited to them), our methods are flawed or nonexistent as they relate to the solution of humanity's most pressing problems.

What is education for in the context of a time that is overwhelmed by real problems of the most profound nature? How are these problems to be considered, and in what manner? And can liberal democracy, so dependent on education and learning, be different from past notions of education, so dependent on hierarchy?

The first and obvious consideration is to note that education is to be found wherever there is wonder and the willingness to transcend class, race, tradition, and academic formalism. In other words, folk knowledge (unverified in the usual sense of double blind experiments), books, and schools are but one means to learn and become aware of the world—indeed, the universe. This merely means that while there are traditional ways to learn and support learning, all levels of the educational process must be open to alternative ways of seeing and understanding the world. These ways must withstand two tests. One is dialogue, which requires critical analysis and moves beyond the aporeia. That is to say, its purpose must escape traditional unchanged arguments by being cognizant of the profound movements of change that have occurred. As an analytic tool it must link concepts together to show complementarity between the seemingly unconnected or the opposite, as for example the relationship between justice and caring or individuality and social freedom. This leads to the second consideration: Education is a continuing activity throughout a person's life, a collective enterprise that should be heavily subsidized for all ages by the society as a whole. In this sense education in a democratic society is always open admission.

For many the important question is not lifetime education but what is to be done with children and high school students who carry the burden of class stratification and racism in a society and world where much potential is lost and knowledge of the kind that is necessary for problem solving of fundamental issues is hidden. There are preconditions for education at any level, especially elementary school and high school. Education must not compete with entertainment. It must deal with the most important issues of the day and show how these issues were dealt with in the past (if they were). It must not dehumanize and destroy the young person's chance to ask and make mistakes. It must assure young people of whatever level that they know things others don't, or they can learn things other people know, including their parents and teachers. Education must also assure people that to learn is to love and respect. It is not based on fear. Some will claim that education must be a painful exercise, one that reinforces and demands competition, favoritism, making choices of who is in and who is out, setting standards to exclude and include.

It is not wrong to wonder whether the problem of American society is not too much permissiveness but rather reluctance to encourage the creative, moral, and imaginative capacities that people have. The educational process can redeem itself by moving from a labeling and categorizing enterprise that upholds the authoritarian in all cases against democracy. Reluctance to see the Other in terms of his or her potentiality and not taking social time for cultivating that purpose leads the liberal democracy into stagnation. The how, why, and what of university life are deeply enmeshed in the question of which way the society is developing or should develop. Special attention should be paid to education as an engine of material and spiritual progress.

Because the category "university" is pivotal in the direction of society and now world civilization, it is important that as an institution it become more self-aware of its purposes and how such objectives link to democracy.

SOME BACKGROUND

The transformation of higher education from a predominantly elitist institution in the United States came about through two policies. The first was the GI bill after World War II. The American Legion-backed legislation was meant as a payback to some thirteen to fourteen million servicemen and women who would otherwise have been social troublemakers. This problem emanated from two public policy considerations; one was the bonus march in which ex-soldiers from World War I were denied aid by the Hoover administration, and the other, more fundamental, was severe unemployment. During the Depression unemployment rates for at least four years rose above 20 percent. Without government intervention there was no reason in 1944 to believe that these conditions would not again pertain at the end of World War II. Thus, as a public policy matter the GI bill became important as a means of keeping GIs out of the unemployment lines. But the question remains, why was this an important consideration? And here we must again advert to the idea of what people thought was the basis of American society. For the poor and middle classes education was understood to be the ticket to a life of decencies, even a good life. Obviously, one can talk about the degraded notions that emerged when technology, imperialism, capitalism, and hyped material desire came together. Again one may claim that higher education serviced the market and advertising-induced desires, and there is much truth to this, especially as universities included in themselves schools of business, marketing, and advertising as part of pluralism. But a core truth did remain. Access to college for children of the working class became a real possibility under the GI bill, and millions of returning servicemen and women were the recipients of this benefit. From Nobel laureates to lawyers and businesspeople, the GI bill swelled the ranks of the middle class.

The second policy was a profound shift in higher education that fit with Deweyan notions of civic education through skills and academic training. President Johnson's Great Society Program developed a massive commitment to the two-year colleges. Their numbers grew from 203 in the Eisenhower period to 615 by the end of the Johnson period as a result of Johnson's and Congress's educational aspirations for the nation. They took as their writ access to lifelong learning offering skills training, broadening and affording education to those who need more preparation or are in need of low-cost education. Some may wonder, and rightly so, whether this is a Pollyanna-ish view of the university as its purpose and structure become more bottom-line oriented and its administrators seek to follow the dictates of the marketplace, trumpeting those values inscribed in the old saying, "Where money speaks God keeps His mouth shut."[1] Yet, it would be a mistake if we did not give credit to the reality of those features of technological prowess and ingenuity, catalyzed and reinforced by universities, that have created, at least for the time being, a public sense of economic possibility and well-being (that is, if you don't happen to fall in the bottom two-thirds of the economic scale). Obviously the reality of the economic, political, and social conditions outside the university can be determinative of what goes in the Halls of Ivy, who is there, and who goes there. In this sense the university is a dependency, although there are ways it seeks to lessen this dependency through gifts, patented inventions, and increasing overhead costs to the federal government and foundations. Its most supportive patron is government, especially the federal government.

The national state saw the research-oriented university as an important instrument in the prosecution of war and cold war. Beginning in World War II, many universities served as adjuncts to the national state in their scientific and technological researches into weaponry, social organization, and communication. The state, with full support from the society, took advantage of a very particular type of positivist rationality that was mission oriented and framed around the phrase "It works." A critical analysis that would consider the question "To what end?" beyond the mission dropped out of the calculus. Facts and values were thought to occupy separate categories of concern. This was justified logically on the ground that there was no way to argue that "ought" necessarily followed "is." The pragmatist idea—which earlier in the century had concerned itself with knowledge for what—or inquiries intended to create a humane society of the kind that Dewey, Robert Lynd, Charles Beard, Thorsten Veblen, and James Robinson hoped for, had dropped out of mainstream thought.[2] There was little question that the elite private universities, as well as many of the great public universities, were framed by several issues for reasons of survival and opportunism.

The first such issue was how universities could relate to the Cold War as an *opportunity*. Those who doubted the Cold War or the militarization of universities bit their tongues and took funds from the federal establishment to enlarge the scopes of their respective universities, as was the case at the University of Chicago, MIT, Harvard, and Stanford. Most universities took advantage of the Cold War to expand facilities and graduate programs. Professors who before the Cold War were poorly paid with few chances for research now found (if they were in a "prestige" university) that they were able to obtain large grants from foundations, and especially the government, if the issues and research were massaged to fit within the needs and ideological proclivities of the granting institution. And often in the case of federal grants this was not even necessary. Universities that prided themselves on their "purity" in research lined up to obtain funds for classified studies and classified Ph.D. theses, which were carried out on campuses or in adjacent laboratories. Students benefited from the National Defense Education Act, which emphasized science and technology as the means of answering the Soviets in their *Sputnik* race.

Since World War II these impulses and tensions have rearranged the fabric of the university as an institution. Simultaneously, higher education became increasingly pivotal as a preparation point for the operation of a complex, highly organized, information-based society. New skills were needed, often abstract ones taught best in a university setting. In more personal terms it was also assumed that with such education and training in the kind of social rationality that universities offered, parents would be able to dispense with their own parental obligations except, perhaps, to pay the bill. Parents believed that a university education would offer personally decent and economically rewarding lives for their children in safe, commodious surroundings. It is in this political and cultural setting that the university exists.[3]

The ghost of Proteus appeared in the 1960s around the question of what and who should give the university its character and purpose. In part because of the Vietnam War, which shone a searchlight on the university, on the table of disputation was the very organization of the university, the meaning of specializations and specialties and concern with cultural and political transformation as well as the question of funding. Clark Kerr's definition of a "multiversity" held together by permits for parking spaces seemed to be an important empirical statement but missed the spirit of what a university in a democracy was for.

Students and professors began to link facts and values in new ways as a result of a shift in identity consciousness and the presence of different cultures on campuses. Powerful attempts at closing the gap between democratic ideals and reality for hitherto excluded or deprived groups affected universities in their customs and mores, as well as in subject matter. Paul Goodman saw the underlying religious nature of these movements and the questions being asked. He named this sensibility "the new reformation."[4] Some professors sought new users for their inquiries and therefore a different type of relevance for the university. Whereas agribusiness had long understood the importance of research for its businesses, and other corporations sought the translation of technical inventions at universities into profit-making products, those concerned with a democracy of reconstruction sought a different type of relevance around political and social equality plus anti-imperialism. A new demand was made. Some wanted the university to be relevant to the marginalized in society, and they wanted social sciences that would transform class, race, and gender inequalities.

Another tradition also held sway at a number of universities. It was to be the antidote to those who sought the democratization of American life. Those who followed this tradition believed that knowledge and inquiry did not have to harmonize with the status quo. The university was to be considered outside the struggle for democracy.

Conservatives and traditionalists on faculties identified high standards with elitism and their view of what an unchanging university should be. They declared that there was a "canon to be taught." This group did not adjust easily to the protean nature of the university. This did not mean that all aspects of the canonist ideal were wrong. It was just that the canonist idealist was seriously flawed; it was that he was parochial. As the cultural revolutions catalyzed by women, African Americans, and other minorities took root in the university, some professors scoffed at traditional canons of thought.[5] They wondered whether the entire tradition of what "man" was and what humanism meant had to be rethought in terms of real world problems, other cultures, and scientific possibilities, as well as obligations to the body politic demanded of the sciences.[6] Others claimed that knowledge was merely a function of pyramidal power, thereby raising the question of whether there was any possibility of independent thought and inquiry.

In this minefield of differences the characteristics usually attributed to universities are indeed linked to the character and meaning of rationality and reason, inquiry, teaching, and tolerance for opposing points of view. These features are thought by many to be the means of finding aspects of that continuously moving target, truth. But this general and lightly held agreement does not mean that there is agreement about "truth" or methods to find it or educate about it.

It is hardly surprising that plenty of room has been left for the reconsideration of "truth" as a category, especially at the end of over fifty years of war and cold war; the arrival of a new century on the Christian calendar; greater centralization in the role of government; unabashed cultural and political imperialism; and the increasing lack of clarity of what is to be known and how it is to be taught to service social, political, and economic hierarchies. These issues are old ones, which erupted in acute form before the Second World War but continue to this day in less abstract form. They revolved around the "canon" of what was to be taught. Were there general propositions to be taught with the underpinning of American civilization? This was not a casual inquiry when one notes the history of religious dogma in the establishment of colleges and universities. The concern about dogma and ideology had its roots in the period after the First World War and the apparent success of the Bolshevik Revolution.

Marxism and communism appeared to be coherent social theories that young people could be educated into, and for a time many followed their siren call, not the least being the Marxist turned anti-Marxist, Sidney Hook. As an answer to the communist revolution, Columbia University developed an integrated course on Western civilization intended to highlight Western democratic values through a liberal arts education.[7] Similar attempts were undertaken at the University of Wisconsin, which sought to show Western civilization as the unfolding of freedom.[8] But these notions were decidedly relativist in tone.[9] And while relativism fit with technology and the early John S. Mill's claims (later repudiated) about the importance of the individual, ideas that fit well with the American frontier society, there was another strand. Both modes are still present but challenged by those who understand the university as a feeder instrument for corporate and state power.

In the 1930s the neo-Thomists of the University of Chicago argued that relativism was not an answer to totalitarianism or authoritarianism. They claimed that much truth could be found in the steady state of values and hierarchies reflected in the Middle Ages. Paradoxically, the chief proponent of this view, Robert Hutchins, was a radical liberal whose political ideas in terms of the operations of a free society were only marginally different from his principal adversary, John Dewey. Both, for example, were isolationists, fearing what entrance into the Second World War would do to the American experiment in freedom. Within the university, according to the Thomist point of view, there had to be a hierarchy of knowledge to attain coherence, metaphysics being the highest, philosophy next, with the sciences low on the totem pole because they could not answer or even debate questions about ends and purposes. It was not the province of the sciences to consider what is good or bad. Science was only a methodological tool to find facts and construct theories to explain or get to them. "Calculative thinking," that is, the work of the scientist, was hardly thinking at all.

On the other hand, the neo-Thomist claim was that without intellectual hierarchy the university would descend into chaotic babel, in which the few talked only to the few within departments. According to its proponents, for example, Mortimer Adler, the "babel" of the university merely reflected the crisis in culture as a whole because, in the argot of today, there was not the willingness to hold certain knowledges as "privileged" and certain essentialist values as part of the natural order.[10]

In 1949 a Harvard report on general education sought to continue the search for enduring values of Western civilization that would explain its superior standing in the world, thereby justifying Western civilization to future generations of young people who might have to carry the burden of war. This report concluded that the nineteenth-century idea of Christian values, in which there was agreement on final meanings and immediate standards for conduct, no longer held sway. The purpose of James Conant, the then-president of Harvard, was to create a meritocratic class that would take its strength from public schools and lessen the power of a ruling class. He found exceedingly distasteful a ruling class held together by blood and connections. The Harvard Report held as its ideal "some overall logic, some strong not easily broken frame, within which both school and college may fulfill its at once diversifying and unifying tasks."[11] In epistemological terms this seemed to mean cooperation on particulars, and on means, without agreement about ultimates or ends, which supposedly would never occur. There could be agreement on facts, which could then be taught or presented as facts if certain methods were used to discover them. What a fact was, and what its meaning was in a particular or general context, remained vague. Aridity followed from this view, although it need not have resulted. With bad teaching, undergraduate education often continued to be the shoveling out of dessicated "facts," without context of how a fact became a fact. And by the 1980s facts had come to be stored in a computer, that intellectual coal bin, without anyone knowing why, whether, or how the social system endowed certain particulars and events as facts and a new category, information. Methodologies became rote systems for many and were assumed by publics to be unassailable, as for example the way the scientific method is taught in the lower grades. Within the academy or interest group those who disagreed with any particular inquiry invariably claimed that the methodology was flawed.

Within the university the negotiating tactic of agreeing to disagree became the modus vivendi in which a political laissez-faire attitude kept the peace among warring factions, disciplines, schools, and specialties. There was a new hierarchy. Thanks to the Cold War, outside of the professional schools, with its own hierarchies, it was the sciences whose privileged research and funding position at the university proved the biblical claim that "the last shall be first," the latter position being the place of science in the nineteenth century at colleges and universities. In the present day, when there has come into being an "anthropological" analysis of science, there has been a circling of the wagons and a burlesquing of the supposed intellectual vandals, just as the canonists sought to downplay new inquiries about literature and its relationship to audiences that did not comport with ideas of education that dominated prior to the 1960s. This is nothing new in intellectual history nor in the life of universities or in the project of inquiry. For example, seventeenth- and eighteenth-century natural philosophers saw as their task the overthrow of the schoolmen of the Middle Ages, claiming that there was a second bible, that of Nature, which now had to be read. In other words, natural philosophy and then science were to replace the learning of the schoolmen. Francis Bacon claimed that the schoolmen were interested only in words, a charge that was not true. Nevertheless, the empirical sciences with their methodologies were meant to free man from his enslavement to nature and the god of deduction.[12]

It becomes increasingly clear that words, things, subjective observations, and judgments are mixed together in our views of reality. The framework of higher education and inquiry allows for the continued correction through rationality of our understanding of natural and social reality, including our epistemological construction of both.

In American higher education those who held differing attitudes toward education struggled among themselves, and not always very politely. The calculative and the ostensibly efficient, as defined in particular disciplines, that is, those who invent models of reality, are increasingly dominant in particular disciplines such as economics. They formulate and present a different language of representations, numbers, to create models of reality that, because they are merely models, fall within the realm of modern schoolmen disputation. Yet, they are presented as reality. Thus, the struggles in the social sciences over various statistical models on welfare, the homeless, and school performance are all conducted with competing numbers about realities that are different from that which is postulated. So too is the case in medical science and the natural sciences, where, for example, models of cosmology are mistaken for reality, while hierarchies within social organizations, such as prison, the armed forces, and corporations that have assembly lines, seek to use the models as ways of enforcing particular social realities that benefit the few.

The question the twenty-first-century democratic university must answer is, to whom does it owe allegiance? For theologically oriented universities there is the ready answer of God and Truth. For some the answer will be that it is enough to have "virtual universities" through the Internet without all the bother of students, faculty, and building maintenance in one place where workers may claim a role in the affairs of the university. Allegiance is owed only to oneself through a computer. This notion fits well with latter-day capitalism, where specific and particular functions in the context of profit are the fundamental understanding of society. For others there is another meaning.

The university is necessary as the high ground where dialogue can be conducted in deep but civil ways to foster the type of citizenship that is a chain of creativity toward greater democracy and inclusivity, and to the extent possible, where a philosophy of reconstruction will help other institutions reform themselves toward a democracy of dignity, decency, and participation. It is a place where research can be conducted without fear and where entrepreneurial relevance and advocacy for the social good are esteemed. It is a place that does not eschew those attempts at universalism that encourage researches across cultures that seek to end oppression, seeing in the eyes of the first Enlightenment and in Kant's eyes the similarity of human beings, which allows for the leap to be made toward political and social equality. And it is a place where those who do not care about the immediate or the consequential but believe deeply in the arts, poetry, literature, and scholarship about the past without apparent relevance will also flourish; for it will often be that it is the irrelevant, the artwork, the strange musical sound, even constructing new cosmological myths or new interpretations of words from the past that is the real guide for the future. How does this idea of the university relate to democracy? The university not only has its own ambiguities, but it also must contend with and participate in the protean character of democracy.

The nature of the university is made even more difficult by the nature of democracy's claims against putative authority. Note the concern Yale University had in opening its election for trustees (fellows) beyond the self-perpetuation mechanism. For some it means a measure of individual liberty and choice, absence of external constraint, and participation in a voting process that affects the political direction of the society. For others democracy is a battleground of social change: of both means and ends intended to touch all social relations from family, to university, to church, to the productive/work process. For some democracy is a process of getting to maybe, to the provisional, to the lightly held rebuttable conclusion, whether in science, the social sciences, humanities, or political elections. The theologian Hans Kung has stated in *Does God Exist?* that modern democracy has no authoritarian norms, no supreme values and ultimate values, although it is dependent on values and norms. It is no wonder that in its dialectic democracy walks on seemingly contradictory paths. On the one hand, it accepts the principle of exclusivity and merit in its civil society, and on the other, its underlying emphasis is inclusivity.

Democracy seeks economic and social justice, but it is difficult for the university to shed the skin of social and racial class stratification and privilege hidden in the clothes of "intelligence" tests. It proclaims commitment to peace and prepares for war; it places much emphasis on science and technology but has no way to integrate remarkable discoveries into a public philosophy that comprehends their short- and long-term implications, nor does it emphasize scientific literacy. The danger for any democracy is not free speech; it is the problem of fostering scientific and technological revolutions without much concern for consequences or the effects a particular invention may have on the society as a whole or on other inventions thought to be unconnected in the world of specialization. American democracy holds to traditional notions of social, political, and economic organization in its rhetoric and public style. It is supremely cautious about political change even in the face of virtually unmonitored technological revolution. For some, democracy of necessity must include within itself various hierarchies based on merit or blood, as well as authoritarian institutions, since this is thought to be the character of human nature and social interaction. Others claim that such institutions, be they corporate, religious, educational, or military, undercut the very notions of economic and social justice. They claim that critical evaluation of authority linked to equality distinguishes democracy from other political forms, and education is fundamental in this purpose. Furthermore, they claim that the underlying contract of the university with democracy should be the acquisition of knowledge, ethics, and inquiry, with democracy as a means of ending war, poverty, and injustice, as well as ameliorating suffering. The inquiry of knowledge workers cannot hide behind a fact–value dichotomy, whether in the social or natural sciences, or even indeed in the humanities. There is a corollary: It is not enough to be satisfied with demystifying and unmasking.

It is no wonder that in this maelstrom the university, which is both reflector and challenger of the social order, is also protean in character. It seeks independence and differentiation from the distribution of economic, political, and social power as it exists, while cultivating those very forces and groups, be they public or private, that give the university protection and financial support. Needless to say, in institutional administrative terms to steer in such an atmosphere is a tough act worthy of a university president with the balancing and pirouetting skills of a Nijinsky who must also double as a beggar. He or she must cover the divergences within the university, where there is no agreement on fundamental propositions, in a language of surface coherence spiced with sufficient educational uplift to impress donors, alumni, governments, foundations, parents, and students alike. This is the way of obtaining funds. Those researchers who chase their own funds have little allegiance to the university and see university administrators as engaged in a rip-off activity.

Given the pyramidal and rather stratified nature of the national university system, the research professor or a professor at an "elite" school, or those caught in the system teaching large classes at minimal salaries, feel no loyalty toward community college professors. Class and stratification distinctions are made and reinforced by law and regulation, as for example in California between the universities such as Berkeley and UCLA against state universities and community colleges. But this method is accepted throughout the nation and is hardly challenged anywhere.

In the twenty-first century one may note shifts in the university as a living and changing social organism. Some are profound, others interesting only to the participants in university and academic guild life. To note just a few, there are

- the emergence of graduate schools and the Ph.D. as a sine qua non for most university professors but not necessarily at the community college level outside of professional schools;
- the increasing class stratification between faculty and graduate students, and among faculty;
- the increased emphasis on research among professors so that research and teaching have become linked in the life of a professor;
- the emphasis on specialization and subspecialization;
- the distaste for tenure among some trustees and administrators, with a greater emphasis on part-time faculty, this being a system that may be analogized to outsourcing or migrant labor, the expressed reason for faculty and graduate students to unionize;

- increased tensions around what is to be taught and what is to be known, especially concerning matters of gender, race, class, religion, and ethnicity;
- the flowering of professional schools, which often see themselves at the university but not of the university because they must meet stringent external requirements beyond those of academic guild accrediting agencies and because their professors' salaries may be higher than salaries in their respective professions; and
- the emergence of political and moral questions within universities regarding questions of service and advocacy, that is, who does the university serve and for what purpose in domestic or international activities?[13] This question becomes central when the underlying compact of the university for human decency is raised as the goal and the assumption of all activities within the university. Is the university a national entity in the service of sovereign states, or is it a universal institution beyond national concerns?

Other issues impinge on the functioning of the university. There is the expanded role of business in directly shaping curriculum and values of the university through contract and partnership arrangements. It is no mystery that both the state and business act as not-so-silent partners, along with foundations, in "guiding" research and the ethos of the university through grants. This complaint is an old one and was discussed by Veblen, who referred to university presidents as "captains of industry." On another level there is the "internationalizing" of the university as American universities continue to lead on the international education landscape, becoming more aware of other cultures and ways of culturally mapping the world and scientifically mapping some of the universe. Necessarily this means either the reinforcement of cultural and political domination by the United States or an emphasis on multiculturalism, the trading of ideas, and the enriching of a type of universalistic relativism found in the Universal Declaration of Human Rights. Through what is researched, taught, and discussed, the university becomes the cultural transmitter of courses of action that are reflective of international definitions of dignity and decency. In political and epistemological terms these changes will mean that the double question—by what authority should I do what you command, and why should I believe what you say as being knowledge?—will require far more sophisticated answers than were given in the past and therefore new queries.

Then there is the mundane. Universities also face maintenance problems no different from those an administration might find in the operations of a small city. This means concern with security, trash collection, building maintenance, real estate, and economic fairness between competing groups. In each seemingly mundane activity there are profound ethical and moral questions. For example, as universities expand their police and security

forces against theft and crime, locking up offices, classrooms, and equipment, they of course are protecting property, and often private property. In
addition, they are, we are, making a statement about the incapacity of people within communities to trust one another. After all, this is the message of
locks. So we build in distrust and unconsciously deny the possibility of decency in favor of a Hobbesian view of reality.

More important in the immediate sense is the role of food and cafete-
ria, buildings and grounds, computer and technical, and other nonre-
search, teaching, or administrative staff. Access to the classes of the
university, to its cultural life, and to decent wages would make the university a beacon in what is expected for a modern democratic society. In
the present "contracting-out" system, the university and other corporate
institutions hire out services so that a decent wage does not have to be
paid. University officials can claim that since workers on campus are contract workers from other service establishments, they can't change the
wage scale of the contractors. This is of course absurd, for the university
can set a wage scale with the service corporation for work carried out at
the university.

No doubt this leaves us with attempting to consider whether the university as presently constituted, with the various pulls and stresses on it, is able
to be a catalyst for expanded democracy and freedom while encouraging
new and deepened meanings of rationality that will include moral judgments. Alfred North Whitehead has pointed out that at different stages in
intellectual history new ideas come from outside the university as universities seem fallow.[14] Ideas must be found all over, especially in the university
and college, where material resources may aid in the solution of public
problems.

Certain elements are important to consider in present and future inquiries. The solutions to them will surely lead to more questions:

1. It is entirely compatible with free inquiry to suggest that there should
   be an agenda of concern to create human dignity. The relationship between is, ought, and the necessary for dignity and decency for the individual and the community must be a fundamental concern and com-
   ponent of a university in a democratic society. Perhaps such an agenda
   can be the basis of a national dialogue and research program for human decency and dignity carried on throughout the society, including
   outside the university as presently defined. This becomes more necessary as universities shake off their ivory-tower character.
2. Given that nature, problems, people, and knowledge do not neatly
   fall in any specific disciplines, having within them elements of other
   disciplines as well, new attempts should be made to change university education into problems requiring discipline configuration. That

is to say, inquiry must also be an activity that is not tied to any particular discipline. New modes of inquiry that are nondisciplinary are necessary and can be used to excite the young scholar and student. Obviously, this requires broadening what is considered in each department, looking for "unnatural" connections of data and subject matter.

3. Similarly, professional schools would reorganize themselves, for example, medical schools might become departments of ecology and environment, while law schools would concentrate on dispute resolution. They would work with other departments of the university such as political science, anthropology, economics, psychology, sociology, and history to make inquiries into ending the war system, while defusing and avoiding multiracial wars and ethnic conflicts. Such law schools would examine the linkage between right and contingent behavior through social organization. "Elite" university law faculties would surrender their role as lawyers for American imperial and global economic capitalism in favor of adopting a different program of legal inquiry, one aimed at working out the laws of economic, social, and political rights in everyday life. Empires need laws of property and the enforcement of pyramidal social structures. These are not laws that need occupy the minds of students and professors in law schools concerned with liberal democracy.

4. Universities should not fear to make demands on societies as a whole. These demands would be made in terms of the new responsibilities the universities would undertake when working on questions concerned with the development of a decent, if not a good, society for all people, even nature. Universities and community colleges should organize large endowment grants from the federal government as a means of providing greater flexibility and independence for universities. Such grants would not take the place of mission-oriented research, although such research would be scrutinized carefully in terms of its wider effects. Endowment funds would be invested in socially responsible economic activities that would include the rebuilding of American cities.

5. Mission-oriented research of the kind first championed by Robert LaFollette Sr. in Wisconsin in the early part of the twentieth century had a well-articulated framework for progressivism. The widespread use of research housed at universities begs for a beginning answer to the question regarding its obligations to a local, national, and international community. How are these to be reflected in the everyday life of the university? Or are such matters left to individuals and groups of scholars? Are there obligations to ensure that special researches are encouraged on poverty, the role of the modern international economic corporation,

disease and hunger, an international peace system, and economic and political systems? Are special obligations necessary to expand dialogue and use the calculative (statistical) as a complementary instrument of analysis and face-to-face discourse? It is not likely that the statistical can ever be more than the handmaiden to social change, because lasting social change is an existential matter. The Pythagoreans understood, as did other philosophic movements in the ancient period, that the use of numbers was merely one aspect for the person to come to himself, invariably in a community of then-like-minded.

6. During the Cold War universities served as instruments and catalysts for economic and technological development in underdeveloped regions of the nation. This method was used in California (Stanford), Austin (University of Texas), and Durham (University of North Carolina). Whether this method can be applied to other regions of the world and other cultures raises the question of purpose. American imperialism might expand the university system to other nations, and many American universities have large-scale programs in this regard. The question for educators interested in cultural and intellectual diffusion is whether it can ever be performed outside of the imperialist mode. It is impressive but tragic that the methods and testing systems are thrust on other nations through the marketing and business practices of American "nonprofit" organizations such as the Standardized Testing Service of Princeton. American universities and intellectual life must be borrowers from other cultures in ways Jefferson and others did not fear when they adapted ideas and ways from other nations and cultures. This does not mean that nations should surrender freedom for slavery. This is a struggle that has lasted for hundreds of years and will continue. Forces of reconstruction within traditional cultures that are not enamored of the Western model but seek radical change toward human dignity can feel supported to change and keep their cultural identities if practical problems such as hunger and disease are dealt with.

7. There are many reasons such problems fester and expand. One is that it is difficult for the university educated to confront the hierarchic "attitude" ingrained in virtually every aspect of public life throughout the world. The categories of helper–helped, globalizer–globalized, superior–inferior, commander–commanded, and colonizer–colonized destroy what is obviously necessary, namely, the shifting and transformation of intellectual political and economic boundaries that will yield new inquiries and radically different alternatives and social relationships. For universities to challenge themselves with these purposes is to shrivel the university as the instrument of militarism and imperialism in the guise of stability and high standards.

8. Universities as employers are economic and political entities. Just as interns, hospital workers, and residents in hospitals are not to be exploited by low wages, the ideas first presented at the beginning of the century to protect professors should ensure that professors are not exploited, especially graduate students, interns, and workers and teachers in community colleges. These ideas should be expanded politically to include community and labor representation on university boards. The captains of industry and the rich are not the sole caretakers of the advancement of knowledge and the protection of universities.

9. What criteria can be used for entrance into university life that take advantage of the idea of a student's potential rather than scores on tests? This question is more than an issue of the student's potential. Certainly one criterion is the need for universities to realize what they don't know about. In other words, if a university is to be a genuine university in the sense of fulfilling its obligations to learning and understanding, it has no choice but to open its doors to widely differing cultures and economic classes so that as an entity it too can learn what it does not know or is not aware of. It makes little sense for a university to tie itself to standardized tests for seventeen and eighteen year olds. How much should a university change its curriculum in relation to what is taught in the lower grades or what the student knows? And should there be future obligations to operate public school systems, that is, if university and technical school faculties have anything to contribute to the improvement of primary and secondary education in its day-to-day execution?

10. Given that some universities favor alumni, the rich, and the prominent in assessing student applications, there is a cynical undertone in denying the cause of affirmative action, which is a very modest means of limiting racism albeit protecting class stratification. The acquisition of social knowledge at universities can thrive only in a setting of ethnic, cultural, gender, and racial differences.

11. Some argue that the increased cost of higher education effectively prevents at least half of the population from ever getting into university and graduating. If this is so, the consequences for democracy are severe and devastating. However, it should be noted that except in the elite universities and private colleges, costs of public university education for the middle class remain relatively low. Inequities could be effectively dealt with through an education insurance fund that would attach to each person at birth and be made available for educational purposes.[15] The government could contribute to the democracy education fund in inverse proportion to what parents are likely to earn in their working lives. A means of reinvigoration of univer-

sity life is through an open enrollment system in which over a twenty-five-year period students or fully one-quarter of a class would be chosen by lot, with the proviso that preparatory education be given through universities and colleges in cooperation with high schools. A radical departure is necessary in a society that is pulling itself apart according to class and ethnic categories. Although democratizing education is not the only determinant for democracy, it is a pillar of democracy. And where the pillars do not support democracy replacement is necessary. Open enrollments are an important means to limit economic and social disparity. The reason conservatives stated against open enrollment was the notion that it was "economically inefficient," and by implication class disparity was important to maintain. Otherwise, taxes and education would become a redistributive mechanism.

12. Finally, the compartmentalization of facts and values can be eliminated as we attempt to bring back a linkage between moral choices and scientific objectivity. This question should be debated in every aspect of university life, especially in the various disciplines.

RECONSTRUCTIVE SOCIAL METHOD AS AN INSTRUMENT OF MORAL EPISTEMOLOGY: SOCIAL METHOD AND NONVIOLENCE

Can a democratic society also emerge and renew itself through great leaps of imagination, and can this be an objective of education? Should there not be serious attempts, as the cosmologists have made, to imagine and construct alternative "utopias," which can be theorized and tested without resorting to Jefferson's (and Leon Trotsky's) theories of permanent revolution based on violence?[16]

Since the French Revolution, these questions have been answered in a number of ways. For French thinkers, leaps of imagination regarding social development, as reflected in the work of the Marquis de Condorcet and the Comte de Saint-Simon and his student, Auguste Comte, were meant to link politics, knowledge, and science mediated through the most learned and ethical thinkers, who would form themselves into institutes. To allow humanity a life of peace, progress, and happiness, if not meaning, a scientific method or inquiry would have to be found or entered into. Nature and the natural rights of man, to the French thinkers, were inextricably linked. As a result, their work was to be linked to that of natural scientists.[17] Such ideas carried over into scientific socialism. There were laws of history, which created and then destroyed or replaced capitalism because of its own contradictions.[18]

There was a widely held belief after Darwin, which Marx also held, that the new sciences saw things as they are; and Marxists believed that production defined ideas and beliefs. For those not burdened by academic economics it seemed incontestable that the few controlled the many out of necessary workings demanded by the economic system itself.

What Marx sought was what Americans such as Twain and Dewey sought: ideas and modes of production in which reason would reign, and where conflict would give way to rational understanding of what was needed and what was to be done in a postrevolutionary good society. But was there a single method to use, a "how" to arrive at reason, rationality, and the shadow God, truth?

Marx believed he had discovered the laws of capital, that the basis of a method for social change could be formulated, and that the progressive direction of history was inexorable, albeit sometimes in need of a shove. The twentieth century allowed for very different answers to this issue in practical terms. Georg Lukacs, the leading Hungarian Marxist philosopher, insisted that Marxism and the dialectical method were the method of understanding and getting to the laws of history. Dewey constantly referred to the "scientific method," although it seemed to be more a mantra than a particular method; Karl Popper's idea of disproof of inductive experiment through contrary evidence and observations seemed to be little more than a variant of the dialectical form wherever evidence could be falsified.[19] Recent researches in scientific method suggest that there are many methods. But what are social methods when applied to politics and the wielding of power? Social methods are well known and in place.

The methods of the established "haves" are instruments of hierarchies, whether in science or social organization, intended to replicate the "laws" of nature through mechanical means, to "manage" social change, or to attract and conserve power for that group that seeks legitimation and authority. These two critical ideas are part of the hierarchic corporate structure, which operates on the basis of production for profit (the bottom line and cleptocracy with a fraudulent profit statement) and explicit command (do this or else), and where necessary for political power reasons will arrange social organization so that predictable and controllable outcomes will occur.

Martin Luther King Jr. and Gandhi claimed that nonviolence—acting against the veiled or structural violence of the oppressive social system— was the method of the dispossessed, the have-nots. Through disaffiliation and refusal to follow orders, a different paradigm of social relations would be created. In other words, they would break Hegel's master–slave paradigm of politics. This method would offer clues as to the ultimate outcomes of what societies and nations should be. In practical terms, these changes could occur through, with, or against the major institutions of society. Any strategy of social change by the powerless and dispossessed was to lead to changes in laws and their implementation so that the struggles of the dispossessed for claims of social, disability, gender, and economic justice were to be immediately legitimated and internalized for future generations. For King, the modernist, this form of legitimation was intended to yield changed institutions and new cultural attitudes that would be the reconstructed framework in which future social problems would be considered. However, without awareness of this need the powerless are left essentially where they were before they set in motion the changes. Parenthetically we must note that Gandhi, who believed in independence for the Indian people, was a traditionalist, believing that India must rediscover its own traditions and ward off the West, whether it was capitalism or some other form of modernism.

While twentieth-century struggles teach, like the Oracle of Delphi, that there are ways to break out of tyranny other than armed force, unfortunately those methods are unclear. Violence and nonviolence are like strands in the double helix. The end to apartheid and the change in the power structure in South Africa came from an adroit use of violence and nonviolence.[20] The American war in Indochina was brought to an end by military defeat of the American armed forces there, the soldiers' own rebellion in the field, and an increasingly militant but nonviolent antiwar movement.[21] There is some evidence that even the Nazis did not respond with ferocious brutality to domestic nonviolent resistance, as they did in similar cases in Eastern Europe. But nonviolence did not change the Nazi hold on Germany.[22]

There have been two profound examples of successful nonviolence. One was the American civil rights movement, which brought together the conception of liberation for both the colonizer and the colonized. The colonizer could finally escape asserting customs and laws of injustice, while the colonized could escape a life of oppression. The second cataclysmic nonviolent event was the disappearance of the Soviet Union when the Communist Party, finding that it had lost touch with the Russian people and the other republics in the Soviet Union, was unable to prevent a systemic change in political structure. Russians were exhausted from war, cold war, internal mistakes in "planning," and the loss of purpose. Too much of their capital, human, technological, and natural resources were eaten away by a faux cold war. So it is not surprising that the Russian people for the most part embraced nonviolence as the preferred means of change, which would have the effect of dismantling the Union of Soviet Socialist Republics.[23]

To comprehend the startling meaning of these two historic events, we must remember how throughout history violence has been considered the most efficacious means of securing and perpetuating liberty. One need not be an exponent of terror, as in the case of Robespierre, Nechaiev, Sorel, or Lenin; we can turn to Thomas Jefferson and see the role of violence as a social method.

Jefferson claimed that the bloodshed of the French Revolution was necessary to foster liberty. In his letter to Colonel William Smith, Jefferson claimed that no country could "preserve its liberties, if its rulers are not warned from time to time, that this people preserve the spirit of resistance. . . . The tree of liberty must be refreshed from time to time, with the blood of patriots and tyrants. . . . It is its natural manure."[24] Yet, there are lessons other than the threat of violence that the twentieth century offers.

Acknowledging profound differences, we may take from the mid-twentieth-century civil rights struggle several clues to a political method for nonviolent change. In the case of the civil rights struggle, social linkages across class, race, and to some extent gender lines were forged, and allies inside and outside of government were linked for the purpose of presenting a new form of legitimacy and legitimation. As a result of political struggle on the streets, in the courts, and in legislatures, laws of inclusivity were written for accommodations, buses, restaurants, schools, jobs, housing, and the armed forces to make room for the actuality of those who were called citizens, in terms of their responsibility to others and their obligations. How many floors did blacks sweep for whites; how many dinners were cooked and babies suckled; how much cotton was picked? How many acts of incest and rape, or for that matter, loving relations, were hidden? And how many legal hijackings besides the mob kind had to be endured? The obligated and responsible had lived in the world of oppression, discrimination, and apartheid. The powerless learned not only of their power but of their commitments to empathy and justice.

The critical reconstructive method served as the basis of the nonviolent movements during the civil rights struggles of the 1950s and 1960s.[25] There was the "ought" of what should be (no apartheid); the "ought" of method, which would challenge the entire society with its own ideals; and the "is" of reality. This challenge required personal risk and the questioning of those institutions that reinforced oppression.

As is education, methods of social change are practical exercises, not ordinarily assessed on the basis of some calculation of rational choice or operations research. They come from an existential need. They occur within moments of potential or real conflict when institutional structures and social relations are decaying or under direct attack and prior moral and social connections and explanations do not apply. Change may come when there is no time to debate different courses of action, and where there is turbulence and chaos. As a result, one is to be satisfied with second best, an articulated moral position. This is the type of heroism and courage that causes the individual to be open about his or her beliefs and actions, to take risks in choices that prove existential commitments to others. This is not to be taken as heroism but as a reinforcement of humanity and social obligation reflected in the Universal Declaration of Human Rights, and to those in need.

In our time we have learned that heroism has many faces. And perhaps the most important face for the twenty-first century is the one manifested through nonviolence. Saying this in the shadow of war and endless conflict surely must be seen as the height of idealism over reality. And one may argue with some success that the family is hardly the teacher of nonviolence, for it is often the cradle of violence. Yet, it remains the pillar of cooperation over conflict where social pathology does not dominate. Perhaps that is the major social task of the twenty-first century: to ensure that cooperation dominates over conflict but in the context of egalitarian interdependence and freedom. Is it foolish to think that education has this responsibility as the primary agent for world cooperation and dignity in action and inquiry? Can the education process develop governmental institutions that are not based on "warriorism"? Obviously, universities reflect different segments of society and propose methods, inquiries, and facts that support those segments. Often they lag behind movements of positive social change and lose the chance of enhancing social methods concerned with means and ends that do not begin with domination, whether of nature or the Other. Thus, we are led to the question of peace and how to organize for it in terms of democratic reconstruction without the poison of domination. This is hardly an easy matter, especially given the semantic, cultural, and religious definitions that reflect major differences, or that one nation's leadership grabs for the brass ring of world diktat.

11

★

Peace and Realpolitik

Machiavelli teaches that to have a weak defense is to lose control over national sovereignty and freedom whether by the ruler or by the people. Indeed, to provide for the common defense is one of the critical aspects of governing. In the twenty-first century the meaning of common defense will change, and I will advert to a few of those changes that do not fit easily into a particular political boundary but that touch upon the character and quality of life throughout the planet. In other words, common defense is linked to the mutual sovereignty of humanity beyond boundaries.

The reality humanity faces is that even if its respective governments are humane and farseeing, and even if the proper frameworks are finally chosen by governments and assented to by the United States, life will remain fragile given the damage already done to the environment. Further, even as moral affections become central to public decisions, the transition from the practice of war, economic injustice, and authoritarian control will require great skill in sustaining. This is understandable. For thousands of years the submerged have believed that there is no other way to live in the world except by being dominated. Even in a world where conflict is at a minimum as a result of the adoption and effectuation of general disarmament; even if global corporations would surrender to an international system of monitoring, adopting environmental, economic, and social rights standards; even if there are credible means of dissolving political disputes into legal ones capable of judicial resolution; even if citizen groups would help in the disarmament inspection process; and even if anarcratic groups emerge that scorn the nation-state and attempts at world or regional domination, serious conflicts would continue. Third-stage liberalism is not a rose garden. But it can result in decent conditions for humanity.

What is clear is that the present dominant policies of the United States are dystopian. They require strutting dominance over others and paradoxically a fear of others, continuous war, ever-ballooning defense expenditures, and massive self-deception about our motives and who and what we are. They require managers of superhuman capacities in bureaucracies that are infallible. These capacities do not seem to be present in politicians or bureaucrats, for such features require the coldness of a computer that makes no accidents, mistakes, or miscalculations. And of course computers are also fallible.

On a propaganda level the Bush imperialists must gather sufficient domestic political power to be believed while seducing or coercing other nations into accepting American leadership and good intentions. As part of its self-deception the United States must trumpet a very old philosophy that negates knowledge of peaceful purposes and affections among people. In American-style machtpolitik all citizens must believe that the good flows out of power and violence even as their leaders attempt to convince other nations that the United States is pacific and has The Way, if others would just accept the pyramid of authority the United States fashions. In an Orwellian sense America must argue against weapons of mass destruction while building up its own, adding to its nuclear arsenal with small bombs aimed at the people and land of the wretched. It must use disarmament rhetoric as a war-making instrument. And it must teach in the schools that this is the only way for a free nation to live in the world, especially one whose leaders and global corporations see no immediate counterforce to them but whose way of life is dependent on such ideas. The government must teach the polity the idea of asymmetry and double standards for the same actions. (Freedom fighters are not terrorists.) Its education system in subtle and overt ways must support this way of looking and acting in the world.

A nation that holds such views believes that it has found the key to world power and world empire. But in reality history suggests that no nation can speak for all of humankind, nor can any one economic system. When a nation tries, conflict turns into a series of unmanageable explosions leading to feelings of hatred and revenge that multiply, including the demise of republican institutions. Surely that was the case in the Roman Empire, where a large slave class, an overtaxed middle class who paid for wars, and continuous wars joined to dictate its demise. Of course, we should not forget that the Roman Empire lasted for several hundred years in agony and despised.

History is strewn with failed empires that placed their faith in war and conquest. The result was dystopia. The liberal hope of integrating the wretched and the working class into a world system of manageable decency, as Immanuel Wallerstein put it, will have failed.

History is cruel, for it forces on us the immediate and urgent problem that seems to require immediate action and answers. Old answers are used and are invariably disappointing in results. The American response to the 2001 attack on the United States was a classic case of the wrong response to the zealot gangs that killed three thousand people and destroyed billions of dollars of property. The second Bush administration, with its rhetoric of war without end, had no intention of changing any policy it thought would surrender the United States' invulnerable status and the power to decide disputes and intervene at will for one side or another in international affairs. It wanted the power to make, use, and break other leaders and nations. And it intended to use the laws domestically to ensure that the populace would be either passive or avid participants in war imperialism. But American society is unruly, and certainly democracy is not always enamored of unity, especially where the "better" classes and elites are split. Anger at the zealot attack papered over the class disparity in the United States in favor of class unity and patriotism. In fairness to the second Bush administration, it is not likely that any sovereign state with a military force would have responded by using legal means to resolve differences. But the question was how military force was to be used and to what end. Unfortunately, it is only the weak who seek international legal decisions. And even if the weak win their case on the merits, the powerful state is not likely to listen.

Perhaps in the grand sweep of history venality, corruption, and favoritism are to be taken for granted. They are the cost of politics in all political systems. Perhaps it does not matter what President Bush knew or didn't know, or that the ruling elites had relationships with the bin Laden family, as did Harvard University and the premium defense and intelligence investor, the Carlisle Group, whose early investors were the bin Laden family (until September 12, 2001). And perhaps it does not matter that the first President Bush was a consultant to the Carlisle Group or that after the September 11 crime the eleven bin Laden family members who were in the United States were flown out of the United States without being detained or questioned. Such matters might cause some wonder among the skeptically minded. After all, it is taken for granted that such privileges should be granted to the very rich and powerful. But there is a far more important lesson in September 11 than such connections and machinations. It has to do with the new distribution of power in the world.

The Soviet Union, seemingly invincible from the outside with its nuclear weapons and claims that it held the secret to historical progress, fell to pieces as a result of its own contradictions and decay. The United States learned in a particularly gruesome way that it is not impregnable; that it is not outside of history, and that all of humanity cannot escape peeing and shitting. What is a nation with worldwide responsibilities (pretensions) to do? Be less Machiavellian and more like Machiavelli—be less like General

George Patton and adopt the principles of Martin Luther King Jr. Machiavelli understood that long-term or strategic purposes should never be sacrificed for short-term gain. Machiavellians, on the other hand, believe only in policies for the short term: That is crisis management.

Machiavelli was not a Machiavellian, perhaps because he had suffered prison and exile at the hands of the powerful throughout much of his life. Extrapolating without doing violence to his own views, Machiavelli would have had a great deal to say about the American situation at the beginning of the twenty-first century. He had hoped for the unification of Italy, and he would hope for a world civilization in our epoch. But to get anywhere near that goal is to surrender the hubris of world empire. A nation may claim total power, but the result is that other nations will undertake to form a balance of power against the "superpower," with atrocious weapons if necessary. This is certainly the case at the beginning of the twenty-first century. When one nation announces itself as king of the hill, that nation is a target, a situation that can result in world disaster. So what is called for?

Leaders must look beyond their seeming invincibility and that of their state and the trappings of power. That is to say, they must devise different standards to measure and comprehend in the social, political, and economic space a reconstructive framework of inclusivity. Leaders need to secure the UN just because in its ethos it accounts primarily for population rather than capital or weaponry. For all of its flaws, the most glaring being the makeup of the permanent members of the Security Council, the UN, because of its ideals and universality, opens the door to a different understanding of how freedom is to be extended and how liberation is to be supported. It rejects the unilateral warrior imperialist model. In a world body we can learn that freedom is not a concept limited to those who own Lexuses, nor is it limited to the religious fanatic or the warriors of dominance and genocide. It is for those whose lives are smashed by poverty, disease, starvation, fear, and exploitation, that is, most of the world's population. Without addressing their needs there is no possibility of world civilization. Instead, its degradation, world empire (machtpolitik, American style), would dominate. Machiavelli would be sure to point out that the meaning of common defense and common security requires the transformation and surrender of sole sovereignty by *all* states to a new political body yet to be born. This does not exclude the most powerful nations, which, barring the use of a veto, are charged with the responsibility of *living within* the confines of international law. With the blessings of Franklin Roosevelt, left New Dealers sought the establishment of the United Nations. Attention was to be paid to problems that are mutual among the classes as well as those that emanate from poverty and wealth. This is not, I dare say, world imperialism directed from Washington, D.C. For most classes in America this is a difficult lesson to learn, for the United States, even after September 11, appears to be sitting on top of the world; therefore there is no reason to change, unless one examines the decay of public education (for example, in New York City); the increasing number of poor, victims of modern-day imperialism, globalization, greed, and domestic pauperization; and all the other services of dignity that life needs.

Machiavelli would have said there is no escape from the human condition, yet, there is the possibility of better and worse: if not happiness itself, then at least its promise. This is the importance of social movements, for they force onto stability a radical change or recalibration. This is what rationality linked to empathy must do. This is what King understood in his political action when he sought to bring together antiracism (racial justice), anti-imperialism, and antiwar:

> To crave security through domination as the major purpose of social existence is to misunderstand our present condition. There are not enough guns and atomic weapons in the world to allow any portion of humanity to feel secure when it retains old conceptions of security based on separateness from the Other, military force, and passion for weaponry rather than people. Security defined through force, and being closed, is a retreat into our own ego shells. It is constantly staking out and using physical spaces and property against the Other, denying any other group its self-dignity except a deformed kind that does not exercise the human affections of caring and empathy. Self-interest and egoism enshrined in present concepts of security lead to a world that is brutish to the weak, nasty and frightening for everyone. Corporate self-interest and attendant irresponsibility to others require the destruction of the environment and the organizing of social relationships so that the strong will dominate the weak. It reinforces the mutual unhappiness and dependence of the colonizer over the colonized. Hubris becomes the coin of the realm and patriotism is defined as being a war lover and power imperialist.[1]

PREPARING PEACEFUL MEANS FOR PEACE: THE REALPOLITIK OF THE POSTWAR ERA

Just as modern war is a product of intentional and unintentional acts of groups and individuals that in fact constitute a system of hubris, misplaced idealism, bureaucratization, and violence, so it is true that abolishing the war system will also appear (to the observer) as a system of intentional and unintentional acts that can be brought together and codified to reflect a change of consciousness and then of practice.

The September 11 bombings, which yielded a general consensus of retaliation against the Taliban, brought into question the war system. First, asymmetrical or sublimited war, either by nonstate actors or poor states subsidized by nonstate actors for military purposes, has finally reached the

United States in a devastating way. The result caused the executive and Congress to adopt measures they thought necessary to protect "security." Together they joined in the establishment of a "homeland" defense force, increased surveillance of citizens, increased wiretaps, the authority to rummage through files of citizens, greater control of immigrants, de facto racial profiling, stringent surveillance at airports and ports, and greatly increased defense and intelligence budgets. Congress passed language allowing the executive to detain suspects or people purportedly with information about anything, without the benefit of being charged, having a proper legal defense, or standing trial.

There is an irony about homeland defense as it is construed. Its aim is protection against terror. Concentrating on terror may have the effect of dispensing with concern for ongoing institutional and structural issues whose damage on a yearly basis is very great. Judged in terms of mortality rates, defense would require a far different meaning than that given by the politicians in the 107th Congress and the second Bush administration. For example, ninety-eight thousand Americans die in hospitals because of hospital error each year; thirty-five thousand are killed on the highways every year, often as a result of poor roads or defective cars; and there are five thousand fatal industrial accidents yearly. Disease and starvation have reached pandemic proportions. Compared to the deaths of three thousand people and the astonishing pain that will stay with family and friends, a horror story in and of itself, one must wonder why other tragedies do not qualify as part of "homeland defense" or national security and international security.

The second change elicited by the bombings of the United States was the infelicitous idea that the American people are in a war without end. Antagonists can be other nations, either individually or as a group, that appear to challenge American hegemony. This hegemony, it is thought, protects the standard of living of the American people by ensuring access to the world's resources and guaranteeing markets for American goods on a profitable basis for the United States. In the case of AIDS it is understood by the international drug companies that AIDS is an expanding market. With U.S. pharmaceutical corporations holding the patents to drugs' production, AIDS is an assured market, guaranteed where necessary by U.S. government subsidy. Further, diseases allow for the expansion of Western medicine and Western nongovernmental organizations as exercises in knowledge philanthropy, that is, domination in a different guise. Whether AIDS will become the social force to end economic, social, and political disparity between classes, races, and genders is dubious. Influenza did not have that effect after the First World War.

The third concern is that of antagonists obtaining weapons of mass destruction and employing those nuclear weapons, missiles, and chemical, biological, and radiological weapons. On the other hand, it is assumed that the United States needs these weapons to keep the peace around the world, which also includes the U.S. use of force in low-intensity warfare. It needs weapons of mass destruction to ensure free markets and retain its paramount position. And it is prepared to use low-yield nuclear weapons in a preventive manner against non-nuclear states. But surely it would be obvious to any college student majoring in international relations or psychology that attempts will be made to find ways of becoming secure from the United States. Thus, the world becomes a self-fulfilling prophecy in which the United States is hated and feared. This surely need not be if efforts were made to link ending the war system to human rights.

The fourth change is more ambiguous. It concerns the value of the United Nations in the face of nationalism. NATO, that white man's club, is preferred by the United States and the West generally to th⌐ UN, where "non-whites" outnumber NATO in terms of population. Preferences aside, the great powers, and especially the United States, see the UN as an instrument of their own foreign and national security policies. The UN is not seen as an entity that can move nations in a direction more in keeping with ending the war system and promulgating symmetrical international law. Nevertheless, there was a nagging doubt from the standpoint of unilateral machtpolitik that the UN as a collective enterprise or through the veto could checkmate some policies of individual states. Leading members of the Department of Defense and the Heritage Foundation since the 1980s have held the Right's conventional belief that the UN is an unnecessary appendage that could be sloughed off in favor of unilateral strategies vis-à-vis arms control, the environment, and other issues. This policy laid the basis for imperial law, in which the United States would set the terms of reference for the world because of its high ideals, the good judgment of its leaders, and its commitment to open markets and democracies oriented to elections, whether sham or real. Pax Americana would be protected by the vast preponderance of military, economic, and technological power. Such policies are to be built on the idea of the American state as the collective Superman, running here, going there, and being fueled by patriotic fervor, which reinforces extreme nationalism and conceals better alternatives.[2] The existence of terrorists, whether of the clerical fascist nature or political criminals, is the complement to American hegemony, for neither offered a threat to the United States as the dominant nation, yet, they serve as the rationalization for misguided policies.

Leaders are in a quandary we might describe as social neurosis or tragedy. They want to expand the nation's reach for resources such as oil because they fear taking a chance on shifting individual preferences that have become embedded in social values, as in the case of the wanton use of cars. Few would argue against limiting their production. Similarly, few would argue that television should be turned off at "study hours," promulgating this as a law that television stations would have to abide by if they intended to retain their licenses. Few would argue in the two major political parties that the United States has reached the stage of wolfish capitalism. Yet, there is an even deeper reality that must be faced.

There is evidence of species decline, perhaps even suicide, given the destruction of the environment, starvation, the killing off of whole continents, diseases such as AIDS, and selfishness that detracts from the possibilities of universal, even local responsibility.

So this chapter is burdened with a subtext: There is a world to be protected and nurtured. Rationality is not the enemy of affections, and supermen exist only in comic books, the dreams of madmen such as Hitler, the obscurantist work of Heidegger, the inane chattering of columnists and TV commentators, and the dreams of bellicose civilians eager to be remembered in history as warrior liberators whose definition of democracy is mass manipulation for war. The tragedy is that people pay dearly for the Superman illusion, as they did in World War II and even in events leading up to September 11. What about revolutions? They are not tea parties. And according to conservatives, they are also illusions.

FEARING AND FAVORING REVOLUTION

Since the time of Jefferson, when radicals and what I would term reconstruction liberals favored the French Revolution in its early stages, Americans have been torn about revolutionary and liberation struggles. This sentiment was one of the strands of American history. Even the Monroe Doctrine was more than a balance of power attempt to keep the Holy Alliance out of Latin America. It reflected an attempt to stand with nascent republics at a time when the United States had little power to do so. The same sentiment can be found in Woodrow Wilson's rhetorical emphasis on self-determination (except for blacks, Latin Americans, Mexicans, and Africans). The second Bush administration holds tightly to the Wilsonian and Jacksonian fig leaf as justification for its triumphal policies. Although they may be difficult to assess, rhetorical claims come to be thought of as actual reasons for policies. They also create in the body politic as a whole a consciousness of self-deception, masking naked military and economic imperialism.

After the First World War American liberals favored, in an abstract way, nationalist movements because they believed that colonized people deserved their own place as subject actors in history rather than as objects of others. Americans mediated freedom through one leader who was the symbol of each new nation. In virtually all cases, Americans knew nothing about the colonized people except the name of the leader, who stood in for knowledge and familiarity with the decolonizing or oppressed group. The neoliberal model of step-by-step enfranchisement served as the guide for the Western enlightened position, although not in all cases.[3]

By the mid-twentieth century political colonialism no longer fit with the anti-imperialist sensibility that gripped millions of people. Revolutionary violence presented itself as an ongoing reality to be yoked to liberation and ideas of justice and nationalism. While the West used such language as rhetorical tools, it was out of the ordinary for leaders of colonial nations to think that *justice* and *peace* were linked to one another.

President Franklin Roosevelt used such language during the Second World War, giving every indication that he meant his talk of justice and his unwillingness to restore the British Empire. But for Winston Churchill and Josef Stalin, the issue was not justice; it was to repel and destroy the Nazi war machine. For Churchill the fruits of war would be to keep Germany as a balance against the East, while retaining the British Empire and securing a "special relationship" with the United States in which it would act as tutor and mentor to the "country cousins." For Stalin the war meant a return of a sphere of influence in East Europe (uneasy as it was), which the Russians had before the First World War. It was taken for granted by British Tories that those with state power could use various instruments, from military force to bribery, persuasion, and intimidation, to achieve their ends. Great Britain intended to hold on to India and "guide" the politics of Greece, Turkey, and the Middle East. To the chagrin of Churchill, Roosevelt's brand of liberalism demanded that a new world order be recognized resulting in its reconstitution, thereby ending Western imperialism.

The British took Roosevelt's rhetoric as an exercise in American cynicism in which the United States would inherit the British, French, and Dutch empires for its own purposes. Further, the United States and its oil corporations would wrest dominance from the British in the Middle East. A condominium emerged between the sheiks and shahs, who sold the oil deposits of their respective "nations" at low prices to American banking and oil companies in exchange for guaranteeing their rule against nationalist and radical upstarts. However, before the Cold War began in earnest, Harry Truman stated the liberal position toward colonialism. On the surface it had nothing to do with capitalism or American expansion, nor did it target the Soviet Union or communism as an unalterable enemy even though Western leaders such as Churchill and Truman never wavered in their hostility to the Soviet Union (Africa and the Middle East remained part of the sphere of influence of Western powers.):

> We believe that all people who are prepared for self-government should be permitted to choose their own form of government by their own freely expressed choice, without interference from any foreign source. That is true in Europe,

in Asia, as well as the Western Hemisphere. . . . By the combined and cooperative action of our war time Allies. . . . [W]e shall try to attain a world in which Nazism, Fascism, and military aggression cannot exist.[4]

In practice, how was justice to be achieved in a world that hardly recognized that term, except during revolutionary moments? Third World revolutionaries were by no means comfortable with the presumptuous idea that nations had to be "prepared" for self-government, and certainly not by the colonial powers. It was hardly surprising that for them, as had been true for the revolutionaries of the eighteenth century, national liberation and violence were intimately linked. Furthermore, revolutionaries believed that they should obtain aid for their cause from any quarter. They sought first violent decolonization (proof of manhood), as Frantz Fanon, the psychiatrist revolutionary, claimed in *Wretched of the Earth*, and then reconciliation.[5] Fanon thought violence necessary because the colonial powers would never give up imperialism unless they were confronted by violence, and therefore the colonized would remain trapped in submission.

The international system, which called for peaceful resolution of disputes according to the terms of the UN charter, for all practical purposes exempted the permanent members of the Security Council. The leaders of the great powers paid little attention to the decisions of international institutions unless the decisions that were made followed their own interests and policies. This was especially true of the United States and the Soviet Union during the Cold War, and then of the United States alone after the Soviet demise. Thus, more than forty years after the establishment of the International Court of Justice, its ability to turn political disputes into law that sovereign great powers would accept was negligible. For example, the United States lost before the International Court of Justice in a case in which Nicaragua claimed that the United States was prosecuting a covert war of terror against a sovereign nation. Having lost the case, the United States made clear that it would not recognize the judgment of the court. The second Bush administration rejected the establishment of the International Criminal Court, fearing it would have jurisdiction over American soldiers as they carried out imperial peacemaking missions in different parts of the world. By September 2002 the second Bush national security document had made clear that "preemptive" war should be expected from the United States, and international law did not apply to American actions. The United States was not only sovereign for itself; it would be sovereign for others, deciding when they needed war to protect or uplift them.

Another puzzling legacy of the Second World War was the question of removing limits and restraints on new levels of technology and the technology of organization, as evidenced by the construction of nuclear weapons and the Nazi project of genocide. Violence had become more than a test of manliness. By 1945 all restraints were removed, from bombing civilian targets to killing prisoners, to destroying people in gas ovens and atomic blasts. Planning for future warfare contemplated that wars would be fought with demonic weapons, although tens of millions of people still lost their lives in "small" regional and civil wars.

Yet, warfare did not happen on a worldwide scale after 1945. Some argue that the very ferocity of weapons on both sides acted as a deterrent against general war between the United States and the Soviet Union. War was limited to the Third World and the construction of an expensive and shameless alliance system. The proxies the superpowers chose fell into different categories. The United States had no admission requirements to its worldwide alliances save allegiance to anticommunism. Its members could be tactical allies, including freebooting gangs that served their versions of God, ideological zealots, or the cynics who corrupted themselves and plundered others.[6] But the United States on most important diplomatic and economic matters expected the smaller nations to ask permission. Without "asking" the less-developed nation was in mortal danger of suffering a coup or civil war (Brazil, Venezuela, and Iran, as examples). The Soviets were less creative in their allies, often being stuck with national liberation movements that turned out to be nightmarish in practice (Ethiopia) or economically costly to sustain (Cuba).

There is nothing in the Cold War record to suggest that the Soviets wanted a war with the United States or would have courted such a war even if neither side had nuclear weapons. Soviet diplomatic leadership under Stalin was always cautious, seeking deals with the West at the expense of local communist parties. This attitude did not change with his successors. Conversely, there is nothing in the record to suggest that the Soviet leadership inhibited itself from supporting nations for ideological or geopolitical purposes because of nuclear weapons and possible nuclear war, as in the case of Cuba.

Another question might have been taken seriously, at least since the Second World War. Were there ever moments in the twentieth century that could have been turned into a framework to avoid wars and arms races? In *The Arms Race,* Philip Noel-Baker, the British arms expert, pointed out that, had the British not pulled out of the disarmament conference of 1935, the Germans would have disarmed. Such judgments cannot be proved, although they were used by the peace movement to legitimize those who argued that a basis always exists for ending the war system. Peace must be more than the interval between wars. Wars, to use Gabriel Kolko's apt phrase, are the very meaning of socially accepted blindness. Humanity deserves pity because wars bring about shifts and surprises that cannot be calculated once war begins. Yet, no nation wants to give up its "arms." Sometimes this is out of fear, but often a country's unwillingness stems from those institutions of the state that are caught in ideological and economic blindness.

The Cold War brought a somewhat different meaning to the U.S. state and ideas of internationalism that seemed embedded in the idealistic foundational documents of the UN, UNESCO, and regional economic programs under the aegis of the UN. Limited agreements were reached between the United States and Soviet Union in the Cold War on arms, troop placements, and strategic weaponry. Similar limited arrangements could have been made with the Soviets that would have helped to control the nuclear arms race. It would have been possible for the United States to reject the idea of building the H-bomb in 1952 had the advice of Enrico Fermi and Isidor Rabi (both men were Nobel prize winners who worked on the atomic bomb's development) been followed; they called for a solemn pledge not to go forward with the development and construction of the H-bomb. The implicit notion was that the Soviets would follow suit. It should be noted that by 1953 in the Soviet Union Stalin was replaced by Georgi Malenkov, who pursued a number of initiatives to end the Cold War. The Fermi–Rabi proposal would have inhibited the arms race just as George Kennan's idea of mutual disengagement would have resulted in the independence of Eastern Europe from the Soviet Union. The result would have been cuts in military budgets, policies spelled out in resolutions of the United Nations, and planning papers prepared by Vassily Leontieff, a Nobel Prize winner in economics. Such ideas were hardly farfetched. The United States concluded an agreement with the Soviet Union for both sides to withdraw their forces from Austria, a treaty arrangement that held throughout the Cold War and allowed for the independence of Austria.

ENDING THE WAR SYSTEM:
SOME FORGOTTEN BACKGROUND

In a famous document that UNESCO published in 1949, the authors claimed that war begins in the minds of men.[7] There is no question that there is a psychological aspect to war that must be taken into account when considering alternatives to the war system. There may be an element of boredom that encourages young men to accept the siren calls of older men to fight in aggressive wars. They take advantage of patriotic conflicts to escape the humdrum of family, job, and school. Certainly war is a form of regimented and chaotic play, a violent bacchanal, as William James implied in his famous essay on alternatives to war.[8] And war is a means of avoiding domestic class conflict in times of distress. Hitler understood this point and brought together a nightmarish brew for the world by mixing together the fears of the lower middle class, the starvation of the poor and working class, a national building program, anti-Semitism, and revanchism for the Versailles treaty.

Leaders and nations are inclined to expand their authority and power through war if there are no countervailing rules of behavior. If they are careful, leaders need not risk very much, instead proving themselves by risking the lives of others, although leaders can be targets for assassins.[9] Those who practice nonviolent resistance as an activist strategy are prepared to risk much more than are the leaders of warrior nations.

Unless conscious and continuous efforts are made to control the psychological, biological, and institutional pressures that favor aggression or the idea that force of arms is the only instrument for resolution of conflict and imperial exploitation, the institutional process of war making may never end. Given that war institutions are the "cultural" furniture of nation-states and subnational groups, war appears as a natural and necessary function of the state. Indeed, anarchist thinkers such as Simone Weil (also an axialist) argued that the sole business of the state is war itself, the protection and expansion of territorial holdings through war or warlike means. In the American tradition, the nineteenth-century American anarchist Benjamin Tucker claimed that the state should be delegitimated because it was solely an instrument of aggression. Similarly, liberal statecraft emphasized mediation, conciliation, arbitration, law, and even appeasement and population exchanges. But none of the seemingly rational alternatives to "organized murder" seemed to work, even when the pacifists William Jennings Bryan and Newton Baker became, respectively, Secretary of State and Secretary of War under Woodrow Wilson. Anarcrats might say that states are doomed to making war, especially where transnational relationships are weak, science is an instrument of state power, and patriotism is tied only to a particular place without similar bonds to humanity as a whole.

On the other hand, in the twentieth century the emergence of total war, which erases boundaries between combatants and noncombatants, made it more important than ever that citizens' movements concentrate on and confront war as an institutional system. Whatever war had been in the past, with its emphasis on heroism and the glorification of suffering, in the twentieth century it revealed itself for all to see as an exercise in political pathology and criminality. It created hopeless despair on the part of the oppressed.[10]

The politics of nations and war are invariably foggy. As demonstrated by John Dewey's life, the role of war in human progress—and defense of liberal values—caused consternation and contradiction for those who were anti-imperialist in their understanding of history. Norman Thomas's Socialist Party, which voted against economic and military intervention on the side of the French and British in 1940, was hardly wrong when it claimed that these two nations were colonizers that oppressed Indochina, Africa, and India through their respective forms of imperialism. Furthermore, in

1940 there was sufficient evidence to suggest that it was not only Vichy France that was collaborationist. French and German thought of the time preached and practiced anti-Semitism, a rapprochement with the European upper classes, and a federated Europe under German tutelage as a bulwark against communism.[11] Many in the British upper class also favored Italian fascism and were prepared to collaborate with Hitler.[12] And in the United States anti-Semitism and racism were practiced in business, the universities, and social life.

However, in the United States some on the Left joined with the Right, fearing alliances that would supposedly interrupt the American experiment of freedom. The competing alliance system before the First World War taught American isolationists and most conservatives in 1940 to heed George Washington's plea that the nation should never enter into entangling alliances.[13] Except for the Wilsonians such as James Shotwell and Quincy Wright, whose emphasis was on international organization rather than alliances, the prevailing scholarship of the time was that antagonistic alliances led directly to war just because of the interlocked arrangements within alliances that trigger the military engagement of each party. This domino effect was the reality of the alliance system that led to the First World War. Indeed, the French and British alliance with Poland triggered their direct engagement against the Germans, thereby becoming the diplomatic match that lit the Second World War. The match was an expensive one.

The costs of the Second World War were great in terms of human suffering, and indeed the nation that suffered the most, the Soviet Union, was never able to recover. On the other hand, in material terms that war was a boon to the United States.[14] The major powers, with the United States as the acknowledged leader, integrated military policy, organization, and technology into an ideology of mass murder, clothed as defense. People and democratic governments became obsessed with security and arms as the solution to society's multiple problems, much the way a neurotic might fixate on a real problem with an irrational solution that increases his or her problem. The enemy was thought to be the other modernism, communism, whose proponents claimed that they were the wave of the future because communism was the necessary stage for human freedom and economic progress.

It should be noted that clerical fascism was wrongly understood by modernists as the residue of a time gone by. Where it existed in the Catholic Church it had lost much of its power except among sects such as Opus Dei, which certainly has more political power than liberation theologians. In the Middle East, for example Saudi Arabia, clerical fascism was thought of by the West and the cynical princes as a quaint tool that could be used against leftist troublemakers. Among American leaders, to be imperial requires a full panoply of weaponry, including an Orwellian attitude toward words. Both are required to compensate for the foolishness born of arrogance.

War preparations are not abstract enterprises in which bureaucracies play war games according to international rules of just war. Indeed, except as window dressing, international law and just war theory or other theories of proportionality have little or nothing to do with weapons acquisition or wars themselves. For example, in the United States we have seen the emergence of strategic nuclear war doctrine, intended to destroy urban centers and military installations, through

1. second or preemptive nuclear strikes;
2. tactical nuclear war, which means the first or second use of nuclear weapons on the battlefield;
3. limited non-nuclear war, which means an engagement similar to that of Korea, Vietnam, or even the Second World War;
4. brushfire wars, which were meant to stop wars of national liberation, as in the end of Vietnam, Nicaragua, and Guatemala;
5. police actions, which were thought to be instruments of UN franchise or authority, as in the case of Korea;
6. low-intensity war, such as a continuing antiguerrilla war (Philippines);
7. low-intensity and high-intensity warfare to be waged against former allies, as in the case of fundamentalist Muslims and drug dealers in Afghanistan;
8. covert actions aimed at fomenting insurrection, inhibiting national self-determination, or overthrowing governments (Chile, Australia);
9. the diffident or gratuitous use of force to prove dominance, as in Panama, Granada, or Clinton's bombing of Iraq and the Sudan; and
10. homeland defense organized after September 11, which, as President George W. Bush stated, would mobilize the entire American citizenry. They would become "soldiers" in the war against terrorism (or any war for that matter). Foreigners could be detained and tried before military tribunals. Through executive orders and the Patriot Act a president is authorized to set up internment camps. Who is to be placed in them is to be determined by the executive.

Added to these war categories are new modes of warfare involving biological viruses and viruses to destroy computer programs. Each of these methods begins from the principle of "violent rationality," by which I mean thinking and planning in and for the use of force. This idea gave rise to the attractive antiseptic notion that from the American perspective wars can be limited exercises because they do not include the use of nuclear weapons or American casualties.

What a limited war is to the outsider superpower is a catastrophe for a small nation. Even so, where the small nation perceives that it is fighting for its independence and self-determination (in other words, its ultimate values, irrespective of what outsiders may conceive of as facts), it may conclude that it has no choice but to accept the possibility of total destruction to maintain or achieve independence. The examples of the hapless Melians during the Peloponnesian Wars and the North Vietnamese come to mind. On the other hand, during the Korean War, when at least a million people died, American Cold War analysts thought the American engagement was a successful limited non-nuclear war.[15] The U.S.-led alliance in the Gulf War was deemed an even greater triumph, since there were few American and allied casualties, and the United States was allowed to bomb at will. This conception of success does not count the hundreds of thousands of Iraqis who were killed or starved without much proof of gain.[16] And there were costs to American soldiers. Substantial evidence made the existence of a Gulf War health syndrome undeniable. Over 125,000 soldiers suffered minor and debilitating illness from that "successful" war.

Perhaps as justification for participation in the expansion of twentieth-century wars of ferocity, the rhetoric about war's political purposes also expanded. Wars were fought to end wars or to make the world safe for democracy. Wars were fought against evil, and smoldering religious wars emerged full force in the post–Cold War period. The populace was to be aroused through Christ or Mohammed. Perhaps Man (literally man) was struggling with violent aspects of his own nature to justify what he was doing with the sentiments and needs of another part of his nature that did not respond easily to murderous impulses. (Young Americans might say that governments psyched them up, as if before a football game, or getting "psyched" through religion because it offers God as the absolute. There is little that can "psyche a person up" that equals a sports contest or religion, both of which are dependent on zealotry.) All religions struggle with the absolutism of those who see the Other as the enemy in what is never a game. For the religious zealot nothing could be more rapturous than killing or being killed in His, Allah's, God's name. There are only His laws, which know no boundaries. The zealot does not believe man exists. There is only God. No wonder Machiavelli feared religion, for there was no proportion in a political sense, only rationalization of blood lust for a *beyond* that could not be appeased.

Modernism and progress claimed the linkage between rationality and peace. Kant's argument for perpetual peace found its way into the official documents of the twentieth century. The pacific self was accorded obeisance and public legitimacy through agreements prepared and used in the post–World War I period among the imperial nations. The 1928 Kellogg–Briand Pact was ineffective in outlawing war because it protected preexisting alliance systems against other nations and countenanced force over the colonies of signatory nations by their owners. However, the effort was important as an example of what the leadership of nations is prepared to do, under public pressure from social movements such as the outlawry of war movement, headed by Salmon Levinson and John Dewey.[17] For Dewey the outlawry of war was meant as a fundamental safeguard for the development of humanness among people, as well as the perfecting of democracy. It should be noted that the fundamental gravamen against the Nazis at Nuremberg was that the Nazi government had breached the Kellogg–Briand Pact. They had broken the peace.

More than others, the important English political scientist and Labour Party activist Harold Laski understood that after World War II the United States would have to choose between being the premier imperial military power or a democracy pressuring internal democratic social reconstruction and redistribution of political and economic power. The choice was made by 1947 to the detriment of democracy. Democratic ideas of citizenship clash with citizenship as a form of militarism. Democratic citizenship reaches beyond political boundaries. But its meaning is shaped by local cultures and control over productive processes and previously passive citizenry aroused by social movements. Vastly different meanings emerge.

Martin Luther King Jr.'s project had very little to do with simply scaling back war, as suggested by some members of the Democratic Party; nor did it have anything to do with the project of war as personified in General Curtis LeMay, who called for bombing the North Vietnamese back to the Stone Age. Lyndon Johnson's attempt to find a golden mean between these two opposing views foundered and cost him his presidency. There is no compromise between these two positions. Political attempts to mediate between them and find a "golden mean" subvert the human possibility of an expanding peace based on economic and social justice. The irony of the second Bush administration is that it is attempting to use the nonviolence movements as a cover story for continuous war; one of the great advertising tricks of American commerce is to package back marginality in a form that masks a different intention. Thus, the second Bush administration appears to accept universal values. Just as churchgoers visit God on Sunday morning and go on with their real business during the rest of the week, so American self-deception regarding its real policy purposes about freedom, justice, and even open markets is seldom believed by leaders and people of other nations. Yet, the second Bush administration claimed that he acted on the basis of universal values in his war with Iraq. The question is whether there are universal values, the second Bush administration's or anyone else's. For liberals, even the Left, the answer must be yes. But whose?

APPLICATION OF UNIVERSAL
VALUES AND MINIMAL CITIZENSHIP

Universal values transform boundaries when they are applied in practice. They are third-stage liberal values, meant to strengthen the empathic sentiments for the known and the unknown Other. Boundary lines between the insider and the outsider are crossed, between the individual and the state within and between all aspects of society, from family to school to work. And each boundary crossing is cause for reconsideration of identity and definition for the participants in their relation to linked social activities among cooperation, empathy, and dignity. This is a frightening thought to those eager to hold onto the identity of self and the group against others. As I have suggested, such sentiments exist in all cultures. No idea of universalism can be successful if it does not take into account differences or the reasonable wishes of those who are not the zealots but who can act as brokers between both sides. In this context the "broker" is the emissary who seeks to accept people as they are and shift the language of good versus evil by ascertaining the nature of evil within institutions and developing rules of international law that change existing boundaries and subject matter. Thus, for example, the issue in the Middle East might not be Israeli presence but the disposition of water. It might be that nations and people read current events through historical moments that are traumatic and unforgettable. Thus, to continue with the Middle East problem, it is likely that Israelis are hard put to forget the role of the Grand Mufti during the Second World War, when he favored the Nazis. But surely Jews who had a rapprochement with the Germans can rethink their own position toward the Arab states and the Palestinian people. This is an astonishing psychological border crossing. Similarly, another border crossing could still occur in the Middle East, where nonviolent groups could organize themselves especially where they are least expected to occur, such as in armies or terrorist groups. Such organization is the "cutting edge" of international affairs.

There is one obvious boundary crossing that makes clear the need for universal standards requiring redefinitions of political rights in terms of fundamental empathic sentiments. Here I refer to migrations and refugees: the political or economic stateless, war refugees, and the wanderers who are the victims of power politics. The twentieth century was famous for creating the modern stateless refugee victim caused by the war system, broken empires, and at the end of the century, wolfish capitalism presenting itself as modernism and the quintessence of freedom. This form of capitalism used sophisticated technology and communications for the movement of capital whose mock investors had no interest in investing in any particular nation. The noted Pakistani political scientist Eqbal Ahmad distinguished between corrupt unproductive capitalism and corrupt capitalism, which sought to develop things and projects for use rather than making money through currency speculation. Corrupt but productive capitalism created its own misery. As tourists moved from North to South, migrant laborers moved in the opposite direction.

Unless the world is to descend into an international dystopia, it must find the means of confronting the changed technological condition from the standpoint of the marginal and the suffering. Dystopias for millions of people give rise to moral and legal solutions for the reformulation of citizenship that add to the protection of all people, including the dispossessed. Citizenship would cease to be a tool against the Other. Instead, citizenship would be recognized as an international human right guaranteed to all, irrespective of boundaries, stemming from recognition of the individual's personhood rather than the accident of birth, wealth, or geographic and cultural boundaries.

Thus, we may note two types of citizenship. The first is a "constructive" world citizenship, granted through the United Nations, to be upheld in international and domestic courts in which all people, but especially the most vulnerable, namely, the stateless and migrant labor, are accorded protections under international and domestic law. Protections must be enforceable in local courts, with transnational and international institutions and associations operating to protect the person. Municipal courts would begin applying international and world law standards within "sovereign" nations. International law, such as the Universal Declaration of Human Rights, would no longer be aspirational.

Such ideas do not require a wholesale attack on national sovereignty. However, they do require the recognition of the political, social, and economic human rights covenants informing in fundamental ways decisions of judges and legislatures in the nations. Through this means the human rights covenants, treaties against torture, or treaties against the development of weapons of mass destruction would begin to seep into the consciousness of groups within nations.[18] These ideas would serve as the inherent dignity that all nations should work to ensure and accept as the basis of their national homelands. In this way a world civilization begins to organize itself around rights that are the basis of being human and acting in a humane manner.

Let us admit that such ideas smack of the utopian while crackpot rationality has a powerful hold on humanity. Let us admit that destroying the environment and adding to global warming through unlimited fossil fuel production is practical, or that the threatened use of weapons of mass destruction is the very meaning of human nature, or that zealots must be stamped out without analyzing what they say. Where does this leave political action on the part of various groups within civil societies or governments that are not enamored of the idea that humanity will be defeated by crackpots, be they rational or irrational, believers or disbelievers? To the disengaged, conventional politics seems to be the problem, because its dynamics have no counterweight. On the other hand, politics is the necessary instrument to organize just humane ends on the basis of our best knowledge. Such knowledge is developed in universities or is folk knowledge, believing in those human capacities that yield human dignity for one's self and the Other. The task of politics is to bring love and knowledge together, defeating absolutism and superpower arrogance.

Such ideas, which were thought to be mainstream at the end of the Second World War, dropped off of the radar screen because they did not fit with conservative, liberal, imperial notions of national security, sovereignty, and property. Congressional members who had worked together in groups such as Members of Congress for Peace through Law allowed their groups to wither and die. More important, the Democratic Party also abandoned the ideas of a universal consciousness of the kind reflected in UN covenants. Both political parties replaced this possibility with the newest stage of imperialism, globalization and triumphant nationalism backed up and interlaced with military and covert power. A crack in the bipartisan foreign policy presented itself for a short period during the debates on the second President Bush's efforts to go to war. Democratic liberals, such as Senator Edward Kennedy and Congressman Dennis Kucinich, sought to delay the decision on going to war, even arguing that the United States should abide by the charter and not arrogate to itself unilateral enforcement of the UN Security Council resolutions. Such sentiments are present in the American body politic and are even widely held. However, Democratic liberals are stymied when it comes to presenting their own comprehensive program of progressive change, one that could reflect the powerful cultural changes as a result of the struggles of the 1960s and early 1970s. These cultural shifts need to be complemented and sustained by changes in the purpose, direction, and manner of American foreign and national security policy. In turn, the changed culture has made changes possible in the actions of the state.

Third-stage liberalism articulates a program that seeks the internalization of international covenants in American law and also as an element in the consideration of domestic cases. Imagine the following situation: A nominee to the federal court is asked at his or her hearing about international law, the covenants, and how he or she would apply them. This line of questioning would expand the consciousness of federal judges. At least a struggle would occur about the role of international law in domestic decisions. Now virtually none exists.

The process of learning about and then developing a new world body of law that would integrate local decisions and vice versa would become one important element in securing dignity. The Declaration of Human Rights asserted a bold principle, that respect for the dignity and rights of all was a necessary prerequisite for human survival. It was not a recipe for the destruction of different cultures. It was, and remains, a statement about the possibilities and needs of a nascent world civilization. There are important practical legal aspects that should absorb a good portion of time in our law schools, both in the development of statutes and in comparing decisions on cases in one country as against another.

Such ideas do not have to be seen as outside the range of possibility given the development of international human rights law since the end of the Second World War. The question is how to build on the work of transnational groups such as Amnesty International and Human Rights Watch, which are in the business of uncovering abuses, shaming the abuser, and protecting the violated. As are the covenants, such protections are predicated on the universal rights of personhood.

In a number of ways these purposes were thought to be the very essence of progressive capitalism from 1944 to 1948 in America. It was not unheard of that some businessmen, such as Henry Wallace, supported, even championed, this understanding of international politics. The wars and famines of the twentieth century broadened international human rights for refugees seeking asylum, detainees, and displaced persons. From the United Nations Covenant on Political Rights and decisions of the UN Committee on Human Rights, as well as regional and national decisions, it is accepted international law that, on paper, both refugees and displaced persons must be accorded minimum human rights. The program of that UN committee is accepted as a legal principle, if not an everyday reality. It states that refugees and asylum seekers

> should not be penalized or exposed to any unfavorable treatment solely on the ground that their presence in the country is considered unlawful; they should not be subjected to restrictions on their movements other than those which are necessary in the interest of public health and public order. They should enjoy the fundamental civil rights internationally recognized; in particular those set out in the Universal Declaration of Human Rights; and they should receive all necessary assistance and be provided with the basic necessities of life including food, shelter and basic sanitary and health facilities.[19]

It is true that a person does not have a right to be admitted to a particular nation under international law. But this right will mature as a result of labor migration across countries and the web of international rules that brings the plight of the migrant laborer, the refugee, and the displaced into focus as a fundamental issue. There are too many wailing in the bow of the whaling ship who insist that empathic notice be taken.

Through a heightened consciousness of human rights, people demand their own place, irrespective of their respective sovereign's will and irrespective of their political weakness. Submerged populations are seeking to be heard and counted, either through the recognition of their separate identities as a legitimate nation free from the oppression of the outsider or as part of a national entity saved from the badge of discrimination and oppression. If their claims are not recognized either as just or the basis for negotiation, the problem will fester and expand. That is to say, the submerged want their grievances to be heard, and unless they are heard, and adjustments and resolutions are made, violent forms of communication will be attempted. The dispute may rise to the level of insurrection, civil war, or war. Violence becomes a substitute for law and brings with it its own law. As Richard McKeon, the leading architect of the philosophy of human rights and UNESCO, put it: "The question of power and sovereignty is less meaningful—both in the sense of corresponding to objective reality and in the sense of adapting to the situations and processes of change than the question of discovering and achieving realizable values and effective rights. In a period of social and cultural revolution violent change can be avoided only by institutionalized revolution and the only stable society is a self renewing society."[20]

Beyond unilateral domination by the United States there are four different types of grievance linked to the problems of the twenty-first century:

1. the struggle over resources, as in the case of water and fungible commodities;
2. the search for identity and recognition of that identity by submerged peoples, who seek political and economic development in the context of negotiated equity;
3. an end to reliance on weapons of mass destruction without causing the collapse of states or continued violence with less-powerful weapons; and
4. morality, as in the case of Israel and Palestine, where both nations feel themselves victims, hooked on either historical or biblical claims.

Where one side refuses recognition of the other while the other does not define its boundaries, the role of the international community becomes critical. Its task is to politicize the struggle between competing parties by appealing over the heads of leaders to women, religious groups, and a citizenry that is invariably divided. For example, in the case of the Palestinians, submerged populations are seeking to be counted, through the recognition of their separate identities, as a legitimate nation-state free from the oppressions of the outsider or sometimes their own leadership. At the least the submerged want their problems to be heard and will even adopt a mode of violent communication to that end. If their claims are not recognized either as just or as the basis for negotiation, the problem will fester, and without ongoing modes of resolution, the anger will fester and then flame in future generations. A surprising result occurs as future generations outside of government seek to universalize and politicize their own struggles, changing their deprivation into an international concern. If the camera sees it, many will hear and see. And some will act, seeing in the situation of others either their own predicament or their need to "stand with" the Other, on problems as seemingly disparate as the indigenous population of the Amazon and their concern for their livelihood, place, and the natural environment and the problems of the down winders in the American Southwest who suffer from uranium poisoning.

How such matters related to formidable international corporations that followed their own customs and self-regulated rules of behavior was only partially answered by UN international conferences, which at best operated as legitimation for those who sought environmental protections and human rights.[21] Human rights activists lived in a world of purgatory where they were recognized but not listened to.

Proponents of environmental protection and human rights were not central to the direction of the international system. Nevertheless, as criticism mounted, international corporations recognized the need to organize a public relations touch-up of their image. Depending on the corporation, this included some attempt at environmental, consumer, and worker protection—so long as these purposes did not interfere with the profitability of the firm. Some corporations accepted codes of conduct and international worker standards that occurred as a result of concerted effort and negotiation with workers and consumer advocates.[22]

Transnational movements began to see the value of making their voices heard beyond any one specific issue, using economic and political human rights as the category to attain decency for those outside the circle of decency. This modern activity underscored the linkage among political freedom, responsible economic enterprise, and cultural diversity. Proponents of such activity used as their guide international law; nonviolent confrontation; and the twentieth-century attempts to mirror laws, UN covenants, and aspirational documents such as the Universal Declaration of Human Rights, through empathic sentiments. In other words, they infused into the corporate culture elements of the democratic social character. The fragile empathic trope strengthened through social action and law fills the space of what has come to mean political freedom, common sense, and justice. Such sentiments had been in the air since the eighteenth-century revolutions. But each of these sentiments required confrontation with superpower arrogance and militarism. In other words, it became necessary to confront superpower arrogance while finding and organizing a world system beyond imperialism and war. The agencies for that purpose are weak so long as they are mediated solely through nation-states and classic views of power, violence, and coercion as the coin of relations between states.

THE SECURITY OF THE SECURE

The screams of the wounded, perhaps the dead as well, or novels about war and a humanistic sentiment emboldened those who hoped that an international organization committed to peace and security would replace an arms race and the international war system. These ideas were found not only on the Left. They could be found among conservative businessmen, especially those who believed that trade was the substitute for war. In self-interested terms they believed American business could dominate the trading process. Further, for a time conservatives were concerned that war increased the power of the state, centralizing more authority in the bureaucracy while upsetting stability. President George W. Bush is not part of that tradition. He believes in a strong and bellicose state encased in the language of freedom. (That is to say, weapons of mass destruction are what the Other has. Weapons and military superiority are to be maintained at all costs.) It is no surprise that according to his notions of superpower, bellicosity does not include peace agreements. Ideas about disarmament at one time thought to be critical to post–World War II statecraft are now thought of as quaint. Instead, phasing out "aging" weapons and replacing them with new ones that fit current military doctrine is defined as arms control.

In 1960 there was some discussion about general and complete disarmament; but such ideas were thought by "realists" to be propaganda. Instead, realists offered a palliative, arms control, which did not necessarily mean fewer weapons but in fact meant, in various cases, more weapons. Strategists and diplomats sold themselves the idea that they were able to manage and control arms races, local conflicts, and alliances, much in the manner of thinking that dominated the minds of general staffs and leaders before the First World War.

There was a difference. New experts (the counterpart to economist technicians) came to the fore to show how to "manage" conflict.[23] This new group comprised different ideological strands of scientists and strategists who believed that they were like Bead players keeping the earth on its axis. They advised on how and when to fight wars, and with what weapons, as well as what weapons could be bargained away if new technological replacements were constructed, such as more sophisticated weapons, missiles, or aircraft. As in a potlatch between two warring tribes that really did not want to go to war with the other, as part of bipartisan foreign policy, Cold War liberals and conservatives found one key to Soviet weakness. It was to spend on wasteful high-tech weapons, which the Soviets believed they had to answer in kind with greater defense expenditures. The American strategy caused much despair among Soviet leaders as their own economy fell into bankruptcy. In what was thought to be a brilliant stroke of realpolitik, the CIA trained, funded, and used radical Muslim fundamentalists to bring about the defeat of the Soviet Union's "invited" intervention in Afghanistan. One can only imagine the chagrin of national security managers when they found that radical fundamentalists turned on the United States and used American technology to war with the United States. As Machiavellians, crisis managers took on the task of managing their own blunders.

There was a further cost to the United States as well since its strategy meant spending on weapons systems that could not work, except as a bargaining tool in the fantasy world of the Cold War. Soviet scientists thought the Strategic Defense Initiative (SDI) was silly, but they could not be sure, so they sought ways of countering it. Congress was also fooled. Its members were told that tests for the SDI had proved successful when, in fact, they either were never performed or were failures.[24] So high expenditures continued and greater Soviet insecurity was ensured—until Gorbachev. He believed that the strength of socialism as a system and an ideal, linked to a reevaluation of Western intentions, could lead to accommodations with the West that would end the Cold War and, therefore, the perceived need for unaffordable defense expenditures. By pursuing this course Mikhail Gorbachev believed that a frayed Soviet Union would have a chance to repair itself economically and finally close the book on Stalinism forever.

But reassessments can get out of hand. No one could control the pent-up fury that the Soviet republics and Russians felt against the Soviet system. The historian Crane Brinton's insight, that revolutionary changes occur both when conditions are improving and when greater attention is paid to people's feelings, proved to be correct for Gorbachev as he removed the cork from the political bottle. He could not regulate the complaints, animosity, and thrust for political freedom that had accumulated over almost three generations within what the subjects of the Soviet Union took to be a frightening, and then stifling, enclosed space. Gorbachev could neither balance himself like Nijinski nor act like Reagan. The Communist Party had become calcified, with none of the revolutionary fervor by which early members were unified—even those who were purged, like Nikolai Bukharin. For those concerned with cultural history, it should not be surprising that, in the twentieth century, the age of the image, Reagan provided a world stage for the collapse of the Soviet Union as a major player in the war system. Neither Alfred Hitchcock nor Bertholt Brecht could have improved on Reagan's fake props, such as SDI. A few years later, the moderate liberal governor who became the Democratic Party nominee for president, Michael Dukakis, sought his own military prop to prove his warrior mettle, posing in a tank when he ran against George H. W. Bush. Looking too small for the tank and his helmet, Dukakis merely proved his ineptitude in arranging military props and thereby his incapacity to be president.

Once the Cold War ended, another reality was noted. The American balance of payments deficits could be compensated only through arms sales abroad. The United States had 57 percent of the trade. It also, by its Cold War methods, had increased drug trafficking in Thailand, Afghanistan, Pakistan, and Latin America to epidemic proportions as a result of partnerships it struck with corrupt politicians, the military in other nations, drug dealers, and transporters. But such changes were thought to be the costs of being an engaged superpower, just as the American soldiers absorbed the enormous damage from the sale and use of drugs in Indochina, which resulted in a generation of soldiers who were felled by drug addiction long after they returned home. Indeed, by the beginning of the twenty-first century, one segment of the American elite had accepted, even championed, the proposition that war was the health of the American state and economy.[25] Thus, a war against Iraq came to be understood as integral to nurturing the nation's health and vitality, just as some believe that wars in Colombia are necessary to ensure the unchallenged status of the United States in Latin America.

OLD FEARS AND NEW INSECURITIES

By 1989 it had become clear that there were stunning changes in the big power politics game. For a few years, in the 1980s and immediately after the Berlin Wall came down, it appeared that Germany and Japan were the economic victors in the Cold War. The major antagonists exhausted themselves in the shadow cold war, and in Germany and Japan a new nationalism was championed. Because of increasing burdens on the U.S. budget, American policymakers urged the Germans and Japanese to void that part of their respective constitutions that hampered a more robust role for their armed forces outside of their own territories.

Fifty years after the Second World War, the Germans and Japanese were ready to break out of the residual restraints placed on them by the victorious powers. The once-defeated nations could again become military powers, to come and go as they chose, unless the United States found a means of controlling their appetites once they sat at the table that emphasized the use of military power. On the one hand, the defeated World War II powers were cajoled by the United States into making their forces available for peacekeeping duty in different areas of the world. On the other hand, the question was how to ensure control over their activities and limit any aggrandizing sentiments that lingered from the past. American diplomats were split on methods to accomplish this task.

For some, this policy meant a covert entente with Russia and the People's Republic of China in a skewed replay of World War II power politics against Germany and Japan. For others, it meant holding Germany and Japan tightly to the American military and economic bosom, on the grounds that China and Russia were weak and would remain so for at least a generation.

Russia sought to keep what was left of its pride and nationhood so that it would not end up as a hollow empire destined to fight continuous wars on its periphery, as it did in Chechnya. With the breakup of the Soviet Union, the war system seemed to be uncontainable. The Cold War duopoly had seemed to give the world a certain amount of stability, wherein each superpower controlled its respective clients.

The United Nations counted 150 small wars and skirmishes between and within nations that were breaking apart and attempting to redefine themselves in a new nationalism. But these wars were of little importance to the United States during Clinton's presidency. Economic and cultural globalization had become the mantra of the American elite.[26]

New players and problems appeared on the horizon of international politics that seemed trivial compared to those that engulfed most of the twentieth century. The United States, as the undisputed world leader, was admired for its technological prowess, which seemed to redefine the universe and humankind's place in it. But admiration did not mask underlying conditions. Liberals, whether technocratically oriented or committed to reconstruction, were unable to find the political agency or leadership to deal with these underlying conditions. For example, liberals had not found a way to turn these conditions into problems that were understood and linked to economic issues that might galvanize the American middle and working classes to action against surface solutions that would merely deepen immiseration and waste.

American business and policymakers pursued a three-pronged strategy. The first was to press for open markets and the easy flow of capital to developing nations. This allowed for greater investment and intrusion in the economic affairs of other nations. (In the lexicon of economic public relations, imperial intrusion was replaced with the more sonorous sounding phrases "global interdependence" and "global governance.") A second strategy involved an effort to guarantee the flow of oil at such low cost that it would be economically foolish to investigate alternative sources of energy. The actual market cost for gas is undervalued as a result of the presence of American military power in the Middle East.[27] Further, the United States has access to Russian and Alaskan oil as backups. It would appear that the United States could continue its wasteful ways without harm to itself except that it is captive to oil at the expense of the environment and it protects the sheiks of the Middle East. And where necessary the United States would support coups (even in Saudi Arabia), as it did in Venezuela, organizing fig leaf democratic governments to its liking.

The third seemingly contradictory strategy relates to speculation by Western and American investors, who invested heavily in Asian and Latin American stock markets. However, the prosperity in these nations did not lead to higher wages for workers. Indeed, once Western investors pulled their funds out of Asian markets, stock valuation became depressed. Lending in Asian banks slowed, resulting in a continuing contraction of the economy. Banks called in their loans and, as is invariably the case, firings and lay-offs followed. Wage increases for Asian workers ended. In turn, greater pressures on American industry to reduce the wages of workers in the United States continued under the guise of the need for greater productivity to meet international competition and for an end to job security. Increasing numbers of middle class "consultants" in fact became part of a secondary labor market. The vulnerability of the American economy was understood in new ways, such as no long-term guarantees for workers, increasing costs for health, and heavy indebtedness. This everyday reality for Americans cannot be overemphasized, especially as it relates to problems of unemployment and a heavily indebted middle class, fearful of losing surface gains that it had made through the enjoyment of consumer goods that were financial liabilities. For this grouping, as is the case with the working class, cutting back social services and those activities thought to be part of the national heritage, such as parks, schools, museums, and public spaces, adds greatly to agitation within American society.

In this context one must judge the implications of George W. Bush's conception of a homeland defense. It will prove to be similar to the National Guard of the latter nineteenth century in American history, which was used to keep order against strikers, anarchists, and dissidents. In the case of the second Bush administration it will be used to keep order throughout the society, accompanied as it is by acceptable incursions into civil liberties. And some will rationalize these actions on the ground that constitutional democracy does not fit with the needs of the time. Even the budgetary niceties for education, health, and the environment may not be affordable as domestic needs are unmet and unproductive militarization of the society is reflected in federal war budgets. When a nation is engaged in a war without end, claiming that the Constitution is not a suicide pact, surface rationality would demand that the laws and organization of the government require radical change. Just as the national security state was necessary for the operations of an empire abroad, so it is that a war without end requires a war without end domestically, turning the citizenry into soldiers and informers.

The Department of Homeland Security, like the National Security Council, includes secret directives intended to govern and coordinate the various security agencies. Their governmental consequence is to add to the plethora of information and increase the system of pyramidal, centralized bureaucratic power. In this process a homeland security department will be protected from citizen inquiry by executive order and legislation. However, the establishment of new departments of government brings with it bureaucratic infighting, which can last as long as five years. But where the framework is established of a war without end, organizational structures will become permanent. This will mean that a suprainternal and national security council will coordinate virtually all nonsocial welfare aspects of governing. This has been a long-standing wish of those committed to reshaping the governmental structure of the United States who believed that the governmental machinery was inadequate to run an empire. Vice President Nelson Rockefeller had hoped for a prime minister role for the vice presidency, overseeing the major functions of government under an ornamental president and passive Congress. Just as the United States reorganized its state structure into a national security state at the end of the Second World War, so it appears that the thrust for a Homeland Security Council is "necessary" if the United States is to protect the homeland from within. Its task includes the justification for fighting continuous wars abroad and establishing through war "friendly" regimes that have the color of legitimacy, while ensuring secured levels of military supplies and unquestioning loyalty from a trusting citizenry that has chosen private gain over public and critical deliberation. The question of what and who to trust is to be driven beneath the surface of the national psyche, moved aside by the drumbeat of patriotic war. Love and knowledge, two staples of social existence, are to be surrendered.

ALLIANCE, INTERNATIONAL
ORGANIZATION, AND SOVIET DEMISE

What had been a popular fantasy and the fear of nuclear strategists during the Cold War—that gangs would threaten and blackmail cities and nations with nuclear weapons—cannot in the twenty-first century be dismissed out of hand. In global free markets, everything is for sale, from sex slaves to nuclear weapons parts to biological viruses. Traditional enmities, suppressed by the Cold War and competing power blocs, came to the fore after 1990. Ethnic rivalries became more virulent, and pre-1914 nationalism took hold among competing factions, from Cambodia, Sri Lanka, and China to Tibet, Hungary, Romany, and the Balkans. In the latter case, the explosive situation seemed only to be held in check through international and U.S. engagement, which meant long-term military commitments of NATO forces.

While some argued that the NATO alliance system brought communism to its knees and that goal was quite sufficient, others argued that it was time for a new *cordon sanitaire* with the expansion of NATO to the borders of Russia. Supposedly this strategy would finally neutralize Russian power in

Europe and restore that middle kingdom to nothing more than a buffer against a resurgent China. Others in the second Bush administration had no interest in the niceties of alliance. The United States intended to lead a condominium of nations in establishing a sphere of influence over Kazakhstan and Kyrgyzstan through military bases and domination over oil reserves and pipelines. The American policy was a fait accompli, and those who wanted to share in this largesse needed only accept American dominance. A question may be asked whether this way of conducting foreign and national security affairs was totally different or merely an extension, a teasing out, of what had been integral to American policy since the Second World War.

There were two competing views about the international system among those who did not favor the fortress America view Joseph Kennedy had put forward after the Second World War. One American position was an attempt to rebuild the League of Nations, but now as a United Nations, which over time would become a universal organization superseding all alliances and in which all foreign policies (except those concerned with U.S. relations to Latin America) would be mediated.[28] The other was a return to the alliance system.

The UN conception, predicated on limited sovereignty and the restriction of the traditional right of states to make war, soon found itself having to compete with more traditional notions of politics among nations, to use Hans Morgenthau's phrase. This meant the reinvigoration of the alliance system as understood by historians, such as Henry Steele Commager, to be nothing less than the defense of Western civilization against the new Sparta, the Soviet Union. The stated underlying claim American leaders made was that unless bullying leaders were stopped early and by force if necessary, wars would expand into larger wars. This was the ideological mantra of American policymakers who ran post–World War II foreign and national security affairs. (Note how this idea of international politics remains the rationalization for American military intervention in the twenty-first century.) Once Henry Wallace and left New Dealers found themselves marginalized by the new bipartisanship of the Cold War consensus, there was very little difference between liberals and moderate conservatives such as Dwight Eisenhower on foreign and national security policy. Cold War liberals were more bellicose and expansionist than conservatives, as was the case with Truman, who committed American troops to Korea using the United Nations Participation Act as the rationale, and then organized and committed American military forces to NATO. (The reason that the Korean War was referred to as a "police action" was that police actions were contemplated in the UN Participation Act, and it was not necessary therefore to obtain a declaration of war from Congress.) American policymakers had an unstated reason that went far beyond the scarecrow fear of Soviet invasion of West Europe.

That reason, which was crafted in evasive language for the American people (Americans had fought two wars in Europe during the twentieth century), was to control Germany, which had sought hegemony over Europe in the first half of the twentieth century. Thus, the Western alliance was an alliance against a nation that had been conquered in two wars and that was occupied by allied troops. NATO only *appeared* to be an alliance against the Soviets. Its military planning was an elaborate game, albeit with real consequences in spent material resources.[29] Similarly, the Warsaw Pact alliance of 1955 appeared to be an answer to NATO. However, its fundamental political purpose was to keep Eastern Europe in line, controlled by the Soviet Union.

The Soviet rejection of the Marshall Plan meant that the Soviet bloc nations intended to take themselves out of the world capitalist system. Over time, this turned out to be a mistaken calculation for the Soviet Union, because it had nowhere near the capacity to subsidize other nations and provide the level of military hardware, maintenance, and training its clients needed. Furthermore, the Soviets did not have a system of entrepreneurial innovation, which the United States was able to offer to its younger, technologically educated elites.

The Soviet Union was an economically underdeveloped nation, which throughout the Cold War was placed by the West in the position of heavyweight adversary when its capacities, in reality (except in the case of nuclear weapons), were fundamentally lightweight.[30] Yet, the Cold War became the global enterprise of the Americans and Soviets. It brought confrontations and responses around liberation movements; ideological pretensions; wars in the Third World; and a new form of jousting through propaganda, play acting at diplomatic meetings, and allowing both sides to increase military expenditures, which had a salutary effect on the employment situation, especially in the United States. Jousting kept a lid on domestic problems by ensuring internal loyalty for the higher good of national patriotism in both the United States and the Soviet Union.

In the United States state power expanded as the capacity and interest in solving internal problems outside of the market waned. War may be the health of the state, and certain sectors of government sponsored defense production. This has not led to the improvement of social services and the everyday well-being of American society. The Soviet government found that it could not financially keep up its side of the Cold War. Prior to the breakup of the Soviet Union, the last Soviet leadership looked for ways to scuttle the Warsaw Pact alliance because of its cost. The attempts of an older generation, which relied on military control to shore up allegiances in the Soviet Union and Eastern Europe, also failed for reasons that touch on the struggles of intellectual elites since the French Revolution for negative freedom.

The emphasis in Russia, from the tsars to the Communist Party, in its citizen socialization was the narrowing of negative freedom so that the public space, as defined by the state, preempted any concept of challenge to it or protection against it. Freedom of association, assembly, and press are part of negative freedom. The freedom of the press, of writing and publishing, was a power and right that the Soviets, beginning with Lenin, were not prepared to grant to noncommunists or independent publishing houses, as for example in the case of the anarchist Peter Kropotkin.

Human rights activists such as Andrei Sakharov understood the importance of negative freedom, although his fellow dissident, the religious reactionary Alexander Solzhenitsyn, had no interest in that part of eighteenth-century revolutions meant to be protective of the person in the context of a vibrant secular society. Solzhenitsyn had concluded that secularism was the enemy of man. His Pan-Slav nationalism could deliver God, but what could socialism deliver in the face of the evanescent and resentful? Socialism, which had done so much to catalyze the consciousness of people for economic security, could not find the means, either politically or economically, to champion human rights in the political sphere.

Movements and purposes had changed. State socialism was left behind, with its adherents still claiming that "bourgeois" rights such as free speech, or attempts (which invariably failed) to control all the social spaces of society, had to be top down, where unions did not represent workers' interests but those of the Party, which became increasingly calcified. On the other hand, liberation in the form of a radical liberalism was reflected initially in modern axial leaders such as Martin Luther King Jr., who inspirited the various solidarity and human rights movements of Eastern Europe almost a generation after his death.[31]

As a result of a new consciousness of human rights, people demanded their own place, irrespective of their sovereign's will or who the sovereign claimed it was or represented. Submerged populations throughout the world, including Eastern Europe (and Native Americans in the Southwest United States), sought to be heard and counted, either in terms of separate identities or at least in terms of their problems. Women, long thought to be war trophies, claimed new rights under international criminal law. By 1990 rape was commonly understood to be a war crime rather than a military benefit. These changes were profoundly important and necessitated what was to be included in a liberal foreign policy and the organization of Nuremberg-like tribunals. However, these efforts paled in the face of the modern conditions of war and war preparation, which had bedeviled the entire century. American foreign policy was of little help, for it did not accept an international criminal court. Progress was not a straight line, as believers in progress, modernists, and Marxists believed. The question was whether it could be the dominant spirit of a time.

Not if conservatives could help it. The United States delayed paying its assessments to the UN while stopping any kind of tax-deductible funding from American taxpayers for the UN. The second Bush administration added new targets to its rogue shooting gallery. Prior to September 11 it made clear that the United States would no longer be tethered by entangling alliances. It would now establish military bases in Central Asia never thought possible during the Cold War. The conservatives who supported Bush and his predecessors had claimed that liberals talked of moral equivalence between "them and us." But the issue was not one of moral equivalence. The issue was moral amnesia, in which Americans cannot remember what the morally arrogant national security leaders do in the nation's name.[32] The commitment to political equality as a goal of liberalism is undercut by the cultivation of inequality through excess, as in the case of corporate managers who think nothing of having salaries and benefits hundreds of times greater than those of the average worker.

World capitalism presents itself as a hegemonic system, and since the defeat of state socialism in large part at its own hand, there is no organized, comprehensive challenge to it. In the twenty-first century the challenge must come from the weakness of this hegemony and its incapacity to solve problems of war, the environment, hunger, and disease. Its method, to ameliorate these conditions through the national security state (continuous small wars) and the control of local economies (the work of uncontrolled and unaccountable international corporations), merely adds to the human tragedy, the evisceration of other cultures that are now to become appendages of the aggressive international military and corporate system.

In the 1960s and 1970s Andre Gorz spoke of nonreformist reforms, that is, reforms that would lead to a transformed condition. Under the heading of liberal reconstruction I too was concerned that incrementalism could be easily co-opted. But this is only true when there is insufficient awareness of how each problem carries within itself the seeds and rules of other realities that necessitate opening the door even wider to democratic social change. For example, the Voting Rights Act of 1957, in itself a minor civil rights step, led to the further legitimacy of civil rights protest and more far-reaching laws.

Transnational movements that have human rights, peace, and economic justice at their core cannot be easily co-opted. Indeed, they become a world beacon once groups in different settings undertake projects and actions that are fought for and sustained by local and international actions. This, for example, was the strength of the human rights movement in the Soviet Union, in which Andrei Sakharov's project of human rights was supported by scientists of other nations. He took existential risks for the participants and reflected individual integrity. The project itself reformulated the meaning of world political justice. But because economic and social justice were not linked to peaceful endeavors, in practice Sakharov's purpose was a limited one predicated on conservative ideas of balance of power. He favored an American MIRV, putting multiple nuclear warheads on individual missiles in the 1980s. This direction was hardly the one to move the world beyond deterrence and first strike. In fact, Sakharov's views did nothing to change the possibilities of first strike and war.

Twenty-first-century human rights movements are more than the carrying of signs in demonstrations or individual witness. They are linked to finding the means for every person to develop and to do so where necessary in relation to others. In practice, this means pushing back social and psychological spaces that appear to be closed to the person and especially those who are directly oppressed. By acting to develop projects that show what could become the dominant features of society, by defending them and then linking with others who develop similar projects, whether a peace center, think tanks, a rape crisis center, an environmental study group, funds for reinvestment of union pensions into regions in need, a health policy clinic, a prison reform project, or an arts center, the vitality is present for opening social, political, and economic spaces. Such projects have to be fought for, and in the process participants must reach out to allies that undertake similar activities of thought and practice in other arenas. From these relationships movements are emerging that have a moral claim on what the contours of modern democracy and a world more just could be.

12

★

War Avoidance and
a Peaceful Framework

After tens of millions died prematurely in twentieth-century wars; after hundreds of millions were traumatized, maimed, and wounded through war; after the physical despoliation of millions of acres of land; after the physical destruction of the past, and cultures reduced to ashes; and after trillions of dollars lost in war preparation and war, it makes practical sense for third-stage liberals to highlight the tasks and plans leading to the transformation and replacement of the war system. As I have said, this goal is not new, although its character has changed given social awareness, consciousness of the Other, and technology. Ending the war system was a major project of progressives prior to and after the First World War. Before that war it seemed that reason could conquer all things. But World War I taught a different lesson. War, as a system, appeared to be intractable. While radical liberals saw war as a form of slavery, others saw it as either integral to human nature or a necessary instrument to bring about positive social change in terms of human liberation.

For antiwar liberals such as Bertrand Russell and John Dewey it was common sense that to avoid war it was necessary to delegitimate violence, a process that should begin in childhood and would lead to a democratic social character where individual and collective violence would be transformed. Unfortunately, children often live in fear, with parents and educators conflating authority, power, and violence. If there is a strong sense of rebellion on the part of the child, his or her adult life will be taken up with accepting or threatening punishment. Liberals believed that this cycle might be broken through education or through a series of actions that touched the consciousness and empathic sentiment within people. The actions would be linked to one another beyond category and social role. No doubt Christ had this in mind when he protected a prostitute. Christ delegitimated the established social order by embracing the outsider and teaching the importance of social and intellectual boundary crossing. In the American context, this is the tradition that King and the Berrigan brothers, both priests, represented. Contrary to what might be thought, it is very political. Actions such as theirs, which stemmed from bearing witness at personal risk, can lead to delegitimation of the social order. Through their personal risks and actions, people inside of bureaucracies and the citizenry at large can come to believe that the existing social order is out of phase with universal human needs and aspirations. In desperation several career officials in the State Department resigned in protest of the second Bush administration's foreign policies. For the pragmatist, this means finding actions and statements that transcend interest and social role and build on exemplary actions, opening the door to transformation. These actions will be based on prior rhetorical commitments in international law and the entire international legal structure to resolve twentieth-century disputes. In other words, reconstruction is also the means of reinterpreting and applying prior "ought" statements and actions as markers to transform institutional custom and individual consciousness.

For example, as originally contemplated at the end of the Second World War, all use of coercion was to be legitimated internationally prior to the use of force, through the UN, by meeting the test of the "threat to the peace" in Article 2, section 4 of the UN charter. Further, a military staff committee was charged under the Security Council with the responsibility for organizing plans for peace. In the United States at the beginning of the twenty-first century, such ideas sound abstract and unnecessary, for there would appear to be no reason to change the fundamental military and national security stance held by U.S. military supremacy.

In practice, unless propaganda value could be found, the United States has been reluctant to lead on issues of disarmament, a position it committed itself to in seven treaties on arms control.[1] No other major nuclear power presses forward with disarmament proposals, although detailed outlines for them exist and have existed for over a generation.[2] Apparently a disaster must occur to spark the urgency of disarmament even as a public relations flourish. The bombings of New York and Arlington coincided with the second Bush administration's implementation of plans for the appearance of nuclear cutbacks and withdrawal from the anti-ballistic missile (ABM) treaty. The administration set in motion a direction at least as dangerous as the Truman decision to develop the hydrogen bomb by making clear that the United States will fight both preemptive and preventive wars at its convenience. At first glance, the intention of the second Bush administration is as breathtaking as that of other democrats and dictators who have sought to remake the political map of the world. But this is an old reality, as Third World nations know. It had not been codified, however, until the current administration. Its interest in demanding that Iraq or other designated rogue or unfriendly states disarm—without touching the core of its own arsenal or for that matter even its older weapons—strikes Third World leaders as little more than racism to ensure inequality among nations. The United States continues to place an emphasis on first strike capabilities, with China and Russia remaining in its sights.

Whether the United States can ever give up what it perceives to be its technological advantage is unlikely, especially since there is no agency of sufficient political strength within the United States to make the argument against an augmented national security state, one that does not even have the prudence of careful cold warriors such as George Kennan.

It is said that Americans are the most religious of people and the most advanced technologically. This certainly gives the United States an advantage in ridding the world of Evil. To negotiate with the impure Devil makes one an immoral person or a naïf carrying out a fool's errand. Of course, there are practical, "benign" sides to not negotiating with Evil. The "posture" of the state is that it always needs increased expenditures, especially to withstand Evil. They are usually wasteful expenditures that can count as a "good" in a society given over to wars without end and little if any interest in improving social and economic conditions within the United States and elsewhere. Defense funds operate as a pump-priming instrument for the economy. It would be a mistake with extreme consequences if President Bush's triumphalism were more than rhetoric. His willingness to fight preventive wars is reminiscent of the Axis of the 1930s and 1940s. The United States, restless as it is, finds that its leaders are eager to spread "democracy" to control the unruly and disrespectful in the Third World with few American casualties. That was surely the wish of the Italians in wars against Libya and Ethiopia in the 1930s, when sophisticated methods of terror through air power were perfected.

The heavy reliance Americans place on high-tech weaponry is to further distance the American warrior from the carnage he might otherwise experience or cause in "limited" wars. Thus, it is the hope of American war planners that the American combatant need never wonder about the moral element of any military action, because war is rather like a video game. Nor need he or she contemplate total war and its totalitarian nature, involving whole populations in suffering, at the mercy of their leaders. But the war and strategic planners' hopes are not enough to escape another aspect of the underlying modern condition, namely, the fallibility of military technology; the most modern planes and missiles have a disturbing habit of blowing up and falling apart, just as computers crash. The antiseptic words *surgical strike* and *collateral damage* are hardly enough to save warriors from nightmares and trauma. It is not surprising that some may want to use science and technology to avert as well as fight wars.

Such aspirations take on science fiction attributes. Just as in the twentieth century there were those who insisted that an extra chromosome caused criminal behavior, there will be those computer scientists given over to jamming the signals of other nations, spreading viruses to stop meaningful communication, and hopefully fighting an antiseptic communications war. More pacific-minded bioscientists look for the answer to war in a gene deficiency.

The search for a war criminal gene among leaders is misguided for the same reason the extra chromosome theory is defective. It assumes causal relationships that have nothing to do with the process of nature, outside of what we produce from nature through our social conventions and institutions. In other words, at the level of war making, the institutions and conventions that are produced over time define social character and in turn reinforce the war system. Would American leaders be willing to undergo an examination to ascertain their propensity for war and bellicosity? The probability is that they already do and must exhibit such characteristics. It would be delightful to believe that imaginative thought experiments that generate new ideas and practical scientific activities could be used to wipe away those social habits of the past that embrace the war system. That is not to be.

On the other hand, there are axial attributes of humanity that could be institutionalized throughout the twenty-first century, beginning with the primacy of peaceful resolution of political disputes linked to economic justice and fairness. Can such an idea translate into movements in capitalist nations for Haitian workers who are paid twenty-five cents an hour or millions of other workers who are paid unjust wages and who have been cut off from their own communal roots? The cynical reply is that this amount of money is more than they had before, thereby erasing any responsibility for the past, present, or future, because things are getting "better" for the wretched. How do such ideas resonate in an international currency system in which developing nations have no recourse to stop currency speculation from betting for and against their respective currency, thereby throwing economic plans of nations into turmoil? Or how do the cleptocracies of business and government in Third World nations that have been encouraged by the United States to have exactly those structures leave the scene without civil wars?

These questions are at the heart of an international market system that has no interest in either human consequences for the many or ends beyond the sale of particular commodities, such as weapons, or profit on betting against or for particular currencies. This is why peaceful settlements must include the means of improving economic conditions through employment, work, and benefits for the poorest in a nation, as well as strict controls over currency speculation. For without considering such questions, conditions of animosity will be created between various economic blocs in the world that will lead to a worldwide Hobbesian nightmare, with Hobbes's solution for the person to surrender total sovereignty to an unaccountable world state. This need not occur, for redistribution mechanisms based on income and need predicated on fairness could become the fundamental global reality. Attempts to this end are not unknown in the United States, as exemplified by liberal attempts at global fairness, such as the positions taken by diverse figures from Walter Reuther, the former president of the United Auto Workers, to Henry Wallace, to the followers of the Swedish Nobelist Gunnar Myrdal. From currency stabilization to the leveling of raw material prices, a guided international market with necessary subsidies could be paid for through a minimal travel surtax.[3] Assessing world economic disparities, world economic growth, and political modes of economic redistribution through the UN or an equivalent is not beyond modern social science, nor is there any reason it should be thought of as beyond nations—especially where there are strong transnational citizen movements showing the intellectual and political way to this end. At the beginning of the twenty-first century there are transnational activists working to organize a worldwide peace and justice movement similar in method to the American civil rights movement and other nonviolent struggles.

Vital to an end to the war system is the recognition that every arrangement made in foreign affairs, to the extent it can be known, and every problem solved peacefully, will be used as the scaffolding for a peaceful international structure. This structure must include attention to economic and social justice as part of any settlement of conflict. It begins from fairness, as comprehended by the international community when it suspends vested interests. In other words, there must be an increasing role for an independent body that speaks for the people beyond national "sovereignty." This body would help nations forswear public bodies paying protection rackets and buying off the richest and the most powerful elements in any particular struggling nation to ensure peace and development. Its primary monitoring task would be to hold developed nations to policies that neither directly nor indirectly penalize poor and developing nations. To put this another way, it is rich nations, not poor nations, that need monitoring and radical reform of their policies. Attempts were made during the Cold War to achieve some level of economic development. For example, as an answer to socialist claims for world economic development beyond the economic restoration of Western Europe, President Truman proposed a technical assistance program for poor nations that was expanded into an aid program. A decade later, Charles de Gaulle's expanded views of development were based on the idea that a percentage of the West's gross national income would be given over to Third World economic and social development. Other plans called for putting aside savings accumulated through cutbacks in armaments, which would then be funneled to poor nations. In effect, this meant recognition of economic rights for the poor.[4]

Overall, however, managers of rich states wanted to do good and do well at the same time. Their idea was and remains the integration of the poor into world markets. These markets, it was claimed, yielded a better standard of living as judged in terms of more plentiful commodities, especially if the poor nation tied itself to exporting commodities and raw materials. Although this system resulted in greater disparities between citizens, these disparities could be masked by the social system of capitalism itself, which built a middle class through the increase of commodity desire, consumer credit, and then debt. But this method is merely capitalism gluing people to commodities and desires that mask many problems that come with "development," when development is defined as an unfettered market system in which accumulation of private property overwhelms collective need and productive activity.

When "development" becomes more than a phrase in speeches of leaders and diplomats, experience suggests that a planning process will include local community assessments outside of markets to determine what people need for three linked stages of social development, namely, survival, dignity, and decency. Depending on the cultural setting one may be more important than the other. These three stages of development must be constantly reexamined by reconstruction liberals to ensure that they are standing with the bottom 80 percent of the world's population, even though their class position and education are often mediated through elite experiences and elite education.

Liberals are trained in modern forms of knowledge, science, and technology that encourage them to assume, often mistakenly, that their forms and techniques are automatically better than the cumulative knowledges learned over generations in different cultures and settings. Nevertheless, universities and institutes can organize their purpose to formulate and abet nations and communities in their struggles for decency, dignity, and economic and social justice. Such a program of research and action will revivify the university and its social purposes once its members surrender arrogance about other cultures and realize that science and technology may bring disruption but not necessarily efficiency or happiness, just as religious belief may distort reason and political agreement. Like universities, researchers live in a world where current fashions of economic and political thought dominate, often in the face of reality. The result is the peddling of scientific ideas against local cultures where those who have had the ideas are unaware of their own officious certitude, an example being the role of Harvard economists in Eastern Europe after the collapse of the Soviet Union. Indeed, as Janine Weidel points out, the great universities and their economists were not averse to benefiting from the changeover to wolfish capitalism.[5]

TECHNOLOGY AND THE WEAKENING OF NATION-STATE SOVEREIGNTY

What happens where there is no control and accountability over force fields of political energy and legitimate authority and the inquiry process itself are ceded to large aggregates of power, as in the case of international corporations?[6]

The will of governments to regulate international corporations through international mechanisms is virtually nonexistent. There are three reasons for this political force field that seems not to touch the international corporation's legitimacy or, for that matter, illegitimacy. One is the belief that the primary way to achieve international growth and innovation is through international markets that are unencumbered by regulation and publicly debated and formulated definitions of the common good. Second, developing nations in need of capital investment see international corporations as the central element in their own growth. Third, international corporations take advantage of fears that various sectors of the American citizenry have regarding international institutions.

In the United States there is fear, both in the populace at large and among states' rights advocates, that there will be a loss of control to foreign international bureaucratic entities, which could result in a kind of unaccountable international tyranny. These sentiments are shared not only by militia groups within the United States but also by consumer advocates, such as Ralph Nader, who have concluded that hard-won battles in consumer protection will be undercut by international agreements such as the North American Free Trade Agreement (NAFTA) and the World Trade Organization (WTO), which will overrule consumer and worker protections in the name of "free trade." Government officials in the United States fear that they will be bound to international rules that would be internalized in domestic law. Conservative states' rights advocates fear that international standards will result in the application of human rights resolutions and covenants to American law.

On the one hand, in the present atmosphere of attempted American hegemony, without any concert of nations balancing off the reach of American leaders, there is anxiety among rightists about the United Nations as an institution because it could evade the American grasp. This fear occurs even as the United States guides the actions of the UN. In reality, the UN franchises its name to U.S.-dominated activities. On the other hand, where the United States is not interested in having the UN directly involved, it invites the UN "out" of what it consider its sphere, as in U.S.–Latin American relations or the Indochina war.

Nevertheless, the changes in sovereignty that have occurred because of the existence of the UN have emboldened the American Right to press hard to cripple the UN or render it otherwise irrelevant. The Right's concern began almost immediately after the UN's founding, when it became clear that judges in the United States took the far-reaching language of the UN charter as a treaty that, with other UN documents, could affect property and human rights within the United States. These concerns remain more than two generations later and mark an important fault line between conservatives and liberals.

The United Nations as an organization and ideal is both a symbol and a product of cross-cutting forces and ideologies. On the one hand, it is merely the organization of power in service of the most powerful nations. It can even operate as a protector of brutal, corrupt governments that use the international law of sovereignty against the human rights of their own citizenry. On the other hand, it carries an idealistic load, framed in the phrase "We the Peoples," the first three words of the UN charter, which carries the intention and the threat that ultimately it is "we the peoples" who will decide.

The UN's history is a contradiction between both realpolitik and control of the organization by the great powers, especially the United States, and the UN's idealistic claim that it serves all of humankind. Dag Hammarskjold, perhaps the most influential UN secretary-general, claimed that it was the small nations that needed the protection of the UN, not their powerful counterparts. His argument could have been extended to include the defenseless such as the indigenous peoples of Latin America, Asia, Africa, and the Middle East—the Palestinians—who remain at everyone's mercy, including the nations in which they reside. Ironically, with the events of September 11, 2001, the United States also needs the UN as a defense against its warrior impulses. And if that is the case, then the United States will have to bend its own definition of sovereignty.

It would be mistaken in the extreme if, in the twenty-first century, the crippled United Nations should be understood only as the structural end point of twentieth-century failure. In reality, the UN carries with it the power of a dream of world peace organized through international institutions that cause the individual nations to place more weight on mutual persuasion and dialogue than on the force of arms.

NATIONAL SOVEREIGNTY AND THE PEOPLES

Prior to the twentieth century, attempts at international organization as a means of controlling war failed because proponents did not know how to get beyond the problem of individual state sovereignty. However, embedded in the "We the Peoples" clause of the UN charter is a powerful statement, that in international law and organization, sovereignty is passing from nation-states to peoples. Ultimately, it is they who have the legitimacy. Obviously this change in the narrative of international relations does not mean that the idea of popular sovereignty is accepted in practice. States hold sovereignty for themselves against other states and often their own people. On the other hand, if "we the peoples" become the building blocks of international affairs, it would mean that people, not states, would finally become the subject actors of international law, thereby requiring an entirely different international and transnational legal and economic governance structure.

It should be noted that there are cracks in the meaning of sovereignty, as state leaders and individuals may be brought to the bar of justice in an international tribunal.[7] Official American doubts notwithstanding, one task of the twenty-first century is to expand the jurisdiction of the International Court of Justice, establish regional courts, and hear cases of disfranchised minorities. The depoliticization of disputes and war crimes by turning them into legal cases will have the effect of dampening the flames of passion that define religious struggles, historical injury, perceived slight, and incomplete, useless wars. The paradox of this form of depoliticization is that it can be brought to fruition only by a militant transnational movement that is highly politicized and attuned to the ideals of the UN charter and other such documents.

In the economic sphere the UN has done virtually nothing to regulate international economic corporations. This may be attributed to the American government's intervention on behalf of U.S.-based international corporations that are protected from regulatory interference. This policy complements market economy rhetoric, which has dominated the World Bank and International Monetary Fund (IMF) for over forty years. Neither institution coordinates its activities with the UN or reports to the General Assembly and Security Council. Instead, their responsibility appears to be to the international banking community, which holds tightly to a series of abstract economic dogmas, favoring balanced budgets through cuts in social spending while using the treasuries of nation-states as collateral for loans. These institutions did nothing during the period of the Cold War to dissuade national spending on defense materials or the military of debtor nations. Indeed, World Bank officers were specifically proscribed from touching military budgets of nations because they were invariably used as repressive agents internally and the means for the United States and other European powers to sell their military wares in the Third World, thereby increasing further their debts. The crushing international debt and military budgets have been an important source of economic and social deterioration in the Third World.[8]

A RIGHT TO PEACE

It is incumbent upon the liberalism of reconstruction to present something more than war-free utopias that have no basis in reality, just as it is incumbent on its adherents to do more than accept a frame of reference they know is mistaken in terms of any sensible definition of pragmatism. The corollary is that liberals must surrender the politics of nationalism because it tails off into arrogance, revanchism, and disdain for rules of international behavior and law. Similarly nationalists may describe their policies in idealistic terms, but their practice is war and continuous preparation for it. Peace becomes the hiatus between wars, and military conflicts are to be fought at all times. But to overcome this reality other purposes and objectives, grand in their own right, need champions.

Reconstruction in the international sphere must sustain emphasis on international laws of liberation and social and economic justice in many different venues that directly engage the citizenry. Just as there are domestic laws and assumed rights protecting individuals against murder, similar rights grow out of already existing international law such as the Nuremberg judgments, which held against the crime of aggressive war and crimes against humanity. The crimes of genocide, rape, and pillage are predicates for the conclusion that people have a right of peace. Obviously, with weapons of mass destruction such a right becomes paramount, for innocent civilians are invariably the ones who bear the burden of warfare. Claims of those who fight just wars to obtain a just peace do not absolve the nation that commits war crimes. In this sense the American reluctance to sign onto an international criminal court is related to the notion that it "subjectively" believes that it fights just wars and so cannot be held responsible for murder through bombings or collateral damage. For the United States it is as if a policeman could not be held accountable for killing in the line of duty, which he defines.

The rethinking of organized killing and its purpose is of paramount importance. This is so particularly given the relative weakness of the UN and its inability to end the war system or deal with superpower military and economic threats and dominance, the character of modern weaponry added to old weaponry, and the little change in attitudes on the part of some who assert that war is an ennobling experience. We may be sure that there is a psychological inversion that causes human beings to take their natural fears and translate them into armaments and then find pretexts for doing so, generating threats from others by one's behavior. But there are also material conditions that give added weight to moral reasons against the arms/war syndrome. Although bellicose leaders from past generations have not been terribly concerned with the financial costs of arming and war, this situation is changing, with drops in most defense budgets since 1990, *exclusive of that of the United States.*

Perhaps once democratically chosen leaders comprehend that the reality they shape through their decisions comprises different interactions, opposing histories and perceptions, and a deepened rationality, a system of shared cooperation and moral judgments may emerge through international and transnational relationships that will result in substantially lower defense budgets. But mere cuts in defense budgets where there is a surfeit of existing weapons only begins the solution to the problem of the war system.

For the United States in the twenty-first century, common security and defense are less matters of military defense and more questions of how to make up for the damage done during the Cold War, including the startling problems generated by nuclear waste; how not to prop up outmoded, anti-democratic organizational structures such as the national security state; how to confront, with other nations, problems of ecology and the environment, economic disparity, and control over unaccounted economic power; how to stop manufacturing threats and fantasies as the basis for new weapons systems; and how to compensate broken societies as a result of judgments and actions taken by American leaders during the Cold War in Third World nations.

Concern about such problems as primary issues of the twenty-first century will require a thoroughgoing shift in the style, character, and agenda of foreign policy. Pursuing this course will leave American foreign policy open to the unfulfilled hopes of the twentieth century, namely, that the object of international relations is no longer limited to nation-states but is concerned with women, men, and children who find that they have and want rights to be proclaimed rhetorically and protected in practice. In other words, they seek a double citizenship, one tied to the nation-state; the other being global and attached to all people irrespective of their geographic place, gender, class, or race. There is a serious problem that is not easily confronted or solved. Perhaps more than at any other time in recorded history, states lie. Propaganda will give the unwary the idea that their government is acting according to truthful statements offered to the public and moral axioms. In other words, governments will play on people's decent moral sentiments as if that is what guides what they do. Schools, churches, and unions—the entire civil society (if civil society is more than a scarecrow)—have an obligation to "call things by their right names," which will improve the human condition.

International relations in the twenty-first century can be war, conflict, or cooperation that emphasizes peace. If the century is dominated by conflict, it will be a terrifying time. Even a benign Pax Americana will not be able to contain threats, ethnic and religious wars stemming from hatred, and partition that may result in the subjugation of minorities within a geographic boundary. The likelihood of regional nuclear wars, perhaps accompanied by the use of chemical and biological weapons, will become more than a fantasy. American military planners and warrior-minded presidents will present preemptive military activity as the way to keep "stability" or pre-empt attacks on the United States. Those who exercise control over the various forms of state violence will be seen as altogether necessary and rational. But what about a citizenry that has other ideas of defense and security? They realize, with the philosopher Alfred North Whitehead, that the "recourse to force, however inevitable, is a disclosure of the failure of civilization, either in the general society, or in a remnant of individuals."[9]

Among international scholars there is support for a right of peace that should be accepted in international and local courts, or the right of exodus, which could be enforced against a warring state by citizens of that state against their respective government or the governments of other states. The right of peace would become part of the ensemble of rights that humanity now expects for itself, through legal, social, and political institutions and ultimately by its own actions. With a right of peace, the burden shifts away from the citizen to blindly follow the call to war, for the nation would be constrained in its activities by those who opt out of the war system. A tragedy of our time is the moral disconnect between the individual's conscience and the activities of government, which are encased in self-serving, moralistic rhetoric and in reality are governed by crude notions of power and domination. Once the right to peace is internationally recognized—with or without American acceptance in the early stages of affirmation by other nations—and such rights are further buttressed by personal accountability for war crimes, which include preparation for war as partially determined by size of defense budgets and the nature of weaponry in an arsenal, there will be far greater weight given by governments to finding alternatives to the system of war as the fundamental way of protecting interests and settling disputes among nations or within nations. With a right to peace, for example, the taxpayer may assign the portion of his or her tax bill that would typically fund defense to local, state, federal, or international activities that have a peaceful and socially useful purpose.

The right to peace challenges the assumptions of national security and defense policy that have burdened the United States since the Second World War. Personal accountability reins in the idea of impunity of government officials who mask their work behind claims of national sovereignty.

The person's protection from war (arming for it by nation-states) has hardly proved successful in the modern period. War and war preparation by nation-states are thought to be continuous, uninterrupted arming with the most modern weapons, missiles, nuclear weapons, and chemical weapons, as well as more standard weapons of mass destruction. For some the arming and war process is to be legitimated through just rule by the powerful in the executive, such as the National Security Council, who decides when to make war outside of constitutional formalities. For others war is to occur only through the populist process of the majority deciding to go to war, which is accomplished through referendum; the American Constitution calls on Congress to declare war.

Americans have believed that they fight only defensive and just wars.[10] Some argue that wars should be fought only by volunteer soldiers so that the populace at large can opt out of the war. For others, war should come about only through an alliance system that would claim practical paramountcy over the UN even as both the UN and the alliance bend to the will of the United States.[11] Others claim that war is outmoded, and assassination or tyrannicide should be the weapon of choice. For example, note the attempts by the United States to assassinate Mu'ammar Khadafy of Libya or Saddam Hussein of Iraq, or the Israeli use of assassination as a method against Palestinian leaders who sanction suicide missions. And note how in all cases, whether Afghanistan, Vietnam, or Panama, nonemotive language, "collateral damage," is used to describe the killing of civilians. (Otherwise, perhaps, collateral damage would be known as state terrorism because it is aimed at terrorizing innocent civilians.) It is not likely that in common law much of a valid defense can be mounted by a defendant who says that although he meant to kill A he killed B. In war, the modern warrior is equipped to kill A or B, and A and B together.

So it is hardly novel to champion a right of peace. Americans would be in a position to argue in the courts that certain weapons by their nature, or certain actions by the government, violate the individual citizen's right to peace even if he or she is an innocent bystander. The bloody wars since the end of the Cold War may not be able to be stopped by a right of peace. But the existence of such a right delegitimates war and legitimates the individual's rights against the state, which over time may be able to be internalized in all societies. Similarly, class actions could be brought in different venues by nonstate actors who would argue that their right to peace and their right of self-defense against war are violated by the state. In the United States, citizens could require defense against war and law to inhibit a runaway executive. In September 2002, President Bush personalized his difference with Saddam Hussein, claiming that Hussein hated us, by which he meant the Bush family and specifically the first President Bush. It would not appear to be a prudent idea to run a "superpower" on the basis of vengeance and a personal vendetta. There is a Mafia quality to such actions, with the difference being that the Mafia seems to be more concerned with "collateral damage." An executive order has been in place since the Nixon–Carter period that forbids the targeting of heads of state for assassination.

MOVEMENTS FROM THE BOTTOM

In the nineteenth and twentieth centuries, international workers' movements appeared that sought the solidarity of workers, much the way royalty had intermarried across national lines to either expand or stabilize, but at least to sustain, its own power. The aim of transnational movements attached to socialism, populism, and democracy, however, was social and economic justice as well as dignity for all of humankind. Solidarity was no longer to be owned by the few or the royal. There was another difference between royal intermarriage and transnational movements from the Left. Life was to be more than chasing after material goods. There was to be a secular spiritual element, a form of humanism, which is present in the writings of the youthful Marx and followers of his earlier work, such as Erich Fromm.

Until the outbreak of World War I, socialists saw war as integral to the operations of the capitalist system. It was a canon among socialists that participation in war was foolhardy, morally corrupt, and disruptive of any attempts to build an international workers' movement. What conceivable benefit was there, thought Eugene Debs, in workers of one nation fighting the workers of another nation? On the other hand, the French socialists favored patriotic nationalism over class solidarity in the First World War, which effectively ended an international socialist movement. Even as class topped the state with the Bolshevik Revolution, the reality was that the revolution merely made the state stronger, and class in its transnational sense was seen as a fifth column for the Soviet state.

Like so many other beliefs and pronouncements of the time, the First World War destroyed the yearning for class solidarity, as nationalism and xenophobia sabotaged nineteenth-century imperialism. But the world of imperial stability and domination had to collapse once having grafted onto itself the eighteenth-century sentiments of the American and French Revolutions. The zone of difference between stated ideals and lived reality was too great. So long as the pre–World War I imperial framework had no way of including economic and social justice or concern for individual dignity except where it was instrumentally necessary to keep power, imperialists lived their lives trying to subdue others in fear of being overthrown. Peasants vulnerable to bad weather and depressed market conditions augmented the fascist alternative as revolutionary movements demanded a new status for the non-white world, and this status had to transcend being the exploited "burden" of the white world. With the breakup of the world economic and political system during the First World War, and with the melding of war, civil war, and revolution, the tsarist, Turkish, and Austro-Hungarian empires collapsed. The collapse of European empires encouraged the formation of liberation movements in colonized countries. Such movements may be committed to modernizing purposes but with brutal governmental methods, as was the case in Turkey, or may be antimodernist, seeking refuge and legitimation in fundamentalist religions whose most important commandment is hatred of the different, who are thought of as "impure" and "unclean." It is easy to forget that Gandhi had elements of these ideas in his antimodernist, anti-British ideology, as did the profascist Indian leader Chandra Bose.

Before the convulsive changes during and after the First World War, the assumption of diplomats and leaders was that relations between states could be frozen in the concrete of alliances and the balance of power. Because of the emergence of Bolshevism, liberation and social movements became more than irritants to status quo nations. For Wilsonians, social movements were to be contained along with Bolshevism in the name of liberal democratic principles. Wilson soon found that concern about the damage inflicted on people through war was secondary to maintaining the status quo. He learned that economic justice and human rights issues were not the concerns of the peacemakers, especially as those terms might apply to the mass of humanity in their day-to-day lives. Because sovereign governments were the only ones who had standing and were "seen" in international law, his hopes for bringing into the field of policy-making the "decent opinion of mankind," to use Jefferson's phrase, had no chance. In any case, his belief in self-determination for new states in practice meant finding and recognizing, for "their" people, the proper course. A single charismatic leader would determine the course of the new nation, with or without the support of public opinion.

The question of public opinion continues to bedevil democracy especially in foreign policy, where those charged with the responsibility of it follow any direction they care to pursue—unless directly inhibited or challenged by authentic mass movements. Transnational movements against the IMF and the World Bank are twenty-first-century attempts to inhibit or stop global capitalism. But they are also movements that are communicating a very powerful message: "We exist and we know as much or more than you do." These movements see globalization as a moving target. That is, they could just as easily confront the nation-state as global corporations. They are also poised to consider social actions around issues of peace. They are a part of a continuous dialogue that will redefine the institutions of the past that have brought humanity to a precarious place. These movements are more sophisticated and likely to be more successful than the socialist movements of the pre–World War I period.

SOCIAL MOVEMENTS AND RESEARCH AGENDAS

During the Cold War it was often stated that the peace movement was bound by its middle class character. This was only partly true, for at various times the labor movement was directly involved in peace activities and in partially funding the peace movement, as in the case of the Brotherhood of Machinists, the Health Workers, and the United Auto Workers.

Successful social movements have certain characteristics that are not necessarily recognized in their initial stages. They are recognized subjectively and objectively when existential pain is turned into political action by those most in need. In the future, movements in developed nations will cross class, gender, and race lines. Understandably, they will have the difficult task of finding common cause with religious groups and differing religions, outlining a democracy of human rights in economics, and ensuring transparency so that those most responsible in the state and corporate structures of the world can be either called to account for or confronted with their acts, or can be negotiated with. Such movements, even within democratically oriented societies when they seek active engagement from different sectors of society, are not free of physical danger. (Perhaps this is why social movements include young people in activist peace projects, for they require heroism, courage, and boldness against war, features usually assigned to the young.)

Although there are honorable exceptions, at present, governments, peace groups, university faculties, and think tanks are stuck with the assumptions and habits of the Cold War, serving power as it still appears to be. Professors and specialists are not rewarded if they pursue rigorous studies and practical activity to revise the assumptions that have brought humanity to its terrifying situation.[12]

American researchers in the last half of the twentieth century concentrated on war and methods of fighting wars. The presence of nuclear weapons and the attraction of national leaders, bureaucracies, scientists, and the military to nuclear weapons set in motion a world where leaders and bureaucracies planned the destruction of hundreds of millions of people in a few hours.[13] During most of the Cold War in the United States, university faculties and think tanks took on the responsibility for analyzing and preparing scenarios for war fighting. The social and physical sciences departments of universities spent their intellectual energies on the project of deterrence and war fighting. The type of international law that was not a mere cover story for state violence fell to the margins of legal concern as those peddling the fables about the utility of different forms of warfare and strategic defense moved to the top of influence in Washington. Understandably, this dynamic created an intellectual and moral exhaustion for those who sought to move the discourse away from the war system as a permanent element in the relations of humankind and nations to the war system as a common problem. Social pathologies, if they were presented in terms of defense and security policy, were not only studied but also praised and given impetus to spread.

To their chagrin, reconstruction liberals who did not believe in the Cold War found themselves unable to present nonviolent modes of resolving conflicts without being consigned to the outer reaches of policy discussion or to university fringes and pacifist organizations. Infinitesimal amounts were spent on peace research and scientific inquiries that would have aided in the establishment of a peaceful world system that citizens could have initiated and enforced in their own nations. Instead of this pragmatist mode of rationality, a far different idea of instrumentalism was created, which has had devastating effects lasting longer than our motivations for the original act. Thus, the orgy of building nuclear weapons and strategic "defenses" on the basis of a false premise of political reality will remain with humanity for countless generations in the form of nuclear military waste and nuclear victims, even if there is no future nuclear war, as other nations actively seek nuclear weapons.

The hesitance of national leaders to break with the institutional habits of the past has meant that rational and comprehensive solutions to the war system and armaments acquisition are not on the table of concern, whether in the Kremlin, Quai D' Orsay, Berlin, Tokyo, Beijing, or the White House. Universities and peace groups have abandoned comprehensive solutions, adopting an incrementalist approach that does not touch the war system. To the extent that there are piecemeal solutions, they are highly technocratic and therefore spark no interest except among a very few scientists and military and civilian strategists. This is a surefire way to ensure that no major changes in the assumptions about the war system will occur, since there is no interest in engaging a democratic public with alternative policy frameworks in international affairs. But what about the torchbearers who carry a different seed of development and reconstruction?

In American thought there has been a continuing current for replacing the war system. Mark Twain and William James, Jane Addams, and Emily Balch, appalled and disgusted at American foreign and military policy; Herbert Hoover, in his many addresses to the nation and to other nations; the flawed Woodrow Wilson; Robert La Follette; capitalists who funded Peace ships; John Dewey; and socialists and communists—all sought an end to the war system. Women initiated Mother's Day as a cry against war; the New Left held to principles against war and imperialism. Libertarians such as A. J. Muste, Martin Luther King Jr., Noam Chomsky, and Paul Goodman, whose concerns were hardly different from various thoughtful liberal Democrats in Congress, serve as the "Other" way to organize America's political purpose. We might inquire whether this sentiment carries over into twenty-first-century America. New forces have come into play that suggest the possibility of moving away from the war system. As in the beginning of the twentieth century, women are again playing an increasingly important role in international relations. The role can be a positive one if they are prepared to change the hierarchic structure and consciousness of nations so that the state apparatus with regard to war making will be lessened and transformed. Because war, the state, and sovereignty are so intertwined and both government and people are to take their cues from those who claim the conch of the state, such as kings and presidents who usurp constitutional authority, the ambitious will see their power tied to sovereign authority, not to the citizenry. This is a perplexing question.

At one point in the history of the women's movement, it was thought that if more women became active in the public space and in male-established institutions, those institutions, their everyday purpose, and their mission would be altered substantially. For example, women are thought of as more cooperative and less concerned about hierarchies in problem solving and as less violent.[14] However, the interest of the woman pilot Lieutenant Kelly Flinn in flying B52 bombers with nuclear weapons on them, and the willingness of a woman to be secretary of the Air Force, a secretary of state, or national security advisor, suggests that if "new players" are socialized into hierarchic state structures, fulfilling social roles from the past without transforming those social roles or insisting that the structure and purpose of the organization change, democratic inclusivity will have only a modest effect on the day-to-day life of people who must then conform to the social structures.[15] There is nothing to suggest that Madeleine Albright, Benezar Bhutto, or Golda Meir were any less warlike than their male counterparts, so long as the institutional structure stayed the same. On the other hand, women in corporate offices may have a greater tendency to tell the truth when there is clear evidence of fakery than their male counterparts. So it appeared during the corporate scandals that were exposed in 2000 and 2001. It is to be noted that in these cases professionalism demanded truth telling. There are important examples of this truth telling in the work of those scientists who play a crucial role in creating a world consciousness that cannot be easily denied.

The two scientific movements that cannot be easily denied concern health and the environment. It is an important event that health workers organized against nuclear war and for economic justice in the United States. It was a signal event that the World Health Organization brought a case in the International Court of Justice concerning the legality of nuclear weapons and nuclear war. Throughout modern history many health workers have sought a connection between the health of the individual and the health of the nation. The reason seems clear. While modern medicine saw as its task dealing with the health of the particular individual, whether through drugs or other forms of intervention, it is also clear that the health of a nation, and of the world, affects the individual, whether it is the starving child in Uganda or those who suffer from the pain of Agent Orange, nuclear poisoning, unclean drinking water, or AIDS. As a result, the health professional increasingly has learned that inquiry and its application are social—never outside of the political and values derived from social and community rela-tionships and experiment. The health professionals are those who from a standpoint of expertise best know the pathologies that can be laid at war's doorstep.

Similarly, an argument can be made about those in movements connected to preserving the environment. Part of any environment is the protection of the living and of future life. If attention is not paid to war and imperial depredation, foolish modernism of the kind that trapped the Soviet Union into environmental degradation will be missed. The connections inhere in the various parts of the problem. And to the extent that these connections are not made, the chance of any one feature of the problem being changed and resolved is not very great. We need look no farther than the problem of nuclear waste and its relation to the war system to see the tragic truth of this observation.

AMERICAN SOCIAL GIFTS

The American gift to the world need not be only Big Macs, Coca-Cola, and the socialization of women and non-whites into hierarchic or violent insti-tutions. The gift can be the rethinking of the character of institutions them-selves, that is, whether they add to or detract from human well-being and liberation. The United States has a chance like no other nation in modern time to help humanity transcend its past by showing how it will live *within* the framework of international law, disarmament, and economic and social justice. No other nation is in the position of providing others with the knowledge and confidence to do likewise. More than any other, American civilization suggests that humankind wants to and possibly can transcend its own past in favor of good ends. Just as individuals make choices (and close doors to other possibilities), so it is obvious that the institutions of so-ciety can foreclose individual choice and social facts (values, in Dewey's terms) of freedom. On the other hand, if the romantics and glorifiers of im-perialism are successful in their quest, American society, as I have said, will suffer the fate of empires that did not know their limits or real strengths. The American state in its pursuit of total dominance, world empire "by any means necessary," will lose the chance of being the peace lover and the hon-est broker that leads by exemplary behavior in international affairs. Just as happened to fifth-century Athens at the end of its golden period, the United States will lose. In our time American society will not be loved for its free-dom and yearning for political equality, economic and social justice, tech-nological innovation, cultural diversity, and caring. It will be known as an arrogant bully, having lost the chance, that is, the choice to open wide the doors of history to decency and dignity. It will have entrapped itself like

Icarus, thinking that the mushroom clouds of nuclear weapons are more real than the sun and nature itself and that destroying or threatening to destroy is the same as preservation and reconstruction. Americans will betray the better part of their collective nature if they do not grasp the possibilities that were there for humanity at the end of the Second World War and that have reappeared again in both a tenuous and strengthened form: strengthened in the sense that the orgies of killing and violence have lost their heroic aura; tenuous in that there is a disconnect between this realization and those who believe that the democracy and attendant values are secondary to maintaining the claim, useless and dangerous as it is, of being the "sole superpower."

CONTINUING THE CHALLENGE
OF AMERICAN CIVILIZATION

Some who live in a religious tradition speak of the human tragedy from which there is no escape. This tradition recognizes bestiality but does not condone it. Some want to understand tragedy and the fragility of the human condition as a means to excuse particular actions or inaction. But the elements of that tragedy are made unspeakable when we avoid the Other, which is always within ourselves in world politics. We neglect to develop and reinforce institutions that can lift some of the burden of war and economic inequity from humankind. And we reinforce hatred, misunderstanding, and envy felt by the Other. In turn such policies inhibit those elements in all cultures that yearn for liberation and an end to oppression. But who is the "we"? It is that which is most rational and humane in the human species. This is not an easy struggle, within ourselves or our institutions.

Prior to the emergence of modern warfare, thinkers, poets, and dramatists, from Homer to Grotius to Kant to James, sought to demystify war and its results. But this literature, and the work of those most concerned, was unable to overcome the martial values that dominated most cultures. With these values, war became the true test of courage, manhood, bravery, and boldness. Liberals from time to time in the United States have glorified war, as did the reluctant liberal Justice Oliver Wendell Holmes, who praised its purgative powers, its camaraderie, and the belief that the sedentary life is not what challenges men to perform noble acts. After the First World War, however, Holmes's views on war as an uplifting tool changed. Those closest to war, who refused to romanticize it in the twentieth century, knew otherwise.[16]

At the close of the nineteenth century, many ideas on disarmament and international organization were floated that sought stability and security without war for tottering empires. Tsarist Russia promoted international disarmament and an international conference on disarmament in 1899. It was also asserted and "proved" by promoters of the idea of progress at the beginning of the twentieth century that war was a thing of the past between "civilized nations." Imperial wars by Western nations in non-white territories were excluded from this logic. It was taken for granted by the white imperial nations that they should police non-white controlled lands; the cost was bloodshed among millions of non-whites and sometimes-successful attempts at crushing their psyches.[17] For imperialist nations, putting down revolts was seen as defense of law to protect imperial power and their civilizing mission.

The Left, including liberals, had a more favorable attitude toward revolution than it did toward war. It saw in revolution democratic stirrings and the rejection of economic and social injustice. Often it focused on ends rather than means, believing that if the end were achieved, over time people would forget the suffering that preceded it. But these distinctions become blurred as revolution leads to civil war, which in turn leads to war beyond the borders of the original warring factions, as it did in the French Revolution, the Napoleonic wars, and the world conflagration of the First World War a hundred years later.

Knowing how twentieth-century revolutions and civil wars fold into each other in violent, frightening, and tragic ways makes the fall of Soviet state socialism in a relatively bloodless manner more remarkable. Perhaps autocratic communism didn't die, but it certainly faded away. So now humanity is left with the struggles that have defined American life virtually from its beginning. It is unspeakable that the gains in democracy and equality made for and by people over two hundred years of struggle should be taken away by those eager to recapture the past glories of imperialism, domination, racism, and sexism. It is frightening that those ideas that promised a universalism of dignity and decency, of economic and social justice, might be discarded as if they were the dreams of fools. It is appalling that the second Bush administration should use the language of citizen responsibility and collective self-sacrifice to hide its authoritarian, antidemocratic purposes.

In the case of the United States, the choice is stark and clear. Either American civilization will build out of its exemplars and the great social movements of the nineteenth and twentieth centuries, or American leaders and future generations will confuse force with morality, military technology with good ends, stability with justice, and hubris with knowledge. American civilization will be determined by militarism and global capitalism, and the bell will toll for the better American dream, the one represented by the great abolitionist movements; the art and poetry of Melville, Twain, and Whitman; the courage of those in the labor movement, who reshaped the very meaning of dignity and decency; and the women's movement, whose words and deeds forced male America to surrender some of its power and privilege.

Whether it was Martin Luther King Jr., whose triple purpose was civil rights, antiwar, and economic justice, or Jane Addams, John Dewey, or Eugene Debs, all had a vision of reconstruction that demands to be put into practice in the twenty-first century as the dominant spirit of the age. Given the reality of new problems and unmet needs, their vision will be deepened by other movements of liberation, aided by future problems, programs, and artistic endeavors. Such work could catalyze the beginning of a world civilization that leaves exploitation, war, and economic injustice on the ash heap of history. It is the work and thought of such exemplars that is best able to withstand absolutism, clerical fascism, and criminal irrationality. It will be the machtpoliticans who are political gravediggers.

The twentieth century was a hard teacher. It showed humanity what to reject—if we are prepared to see and listen. It gave us glimpses of the "ought" and told us what "is." Although moving the "is" to the "ought" involves inquiry and the acquisition of socially agreed-upon knowledge, which is judged against a tableaux similar to or the same as the UN Declaration of Human Rights and other such foundational documents, its meaning can have optimal value only in concrete situations. For some the "is" and the "ought" can come only from saintly and exemplary action—from those axial people who pay no attention to the conventions of the "is" and who point a different way, as Jesus, Socrates, Muhammad, and Buddha did. That is to say, the unique humane leader or saint sets a course of altruism that others link to, simultaneously introducing new language and a changed vision of what to notice.

But the democracy of the future cannot depend on such individuals alone. Instead, democracy depends on building those sentiments into its institutions and honoring them as they manifest themselves in the everyday life of people. The modern axial position links the well-being of democracy's members to the intelligence and collective judgment of its members.[18]

Democracy is never a completion, but like humanity itself it is always in the process of becoming. If we believe otherwise we will suffer the sin of hubris, as if how we live is the final answer of how to live for all time. In a democracy there must be the continuing recognition of human commonality and revision without surrendering the preconditions of a decent life. Some are conditions and principles that must be intertwined like the linkages in protein strands and genetic clusters of life. They must fall in the category of the necessary and natural, such as air, water, and food. Others are in the secondary category of what is necessary for a decent and dignified life, namely, education in or out of school; the freedom of wonderment, speech, and association; and that mode of justice that connotes the importance of human dignity in all social actions at all times for all people. What we note is that these are "is" conditions, and when they are denied or unnoticed it is then that they become the "ought" conditions of human struggle.

Let us conclude this section with another look at the question of "is" and "ought." Philosophers have long known that this question is basic to the modern period, to how we see objectivity and evaluation or normative views of ourselves and the world. We are told by Hume and many less luminous figures that we cannot be sure that A causes B in the sciences, except as our senses decide that that is what we perceive to be the case either by intuition, induction, or statistical logic. In everyday life we know that there is a moral sensibility that tells us immediately that to feel otherwise is the result of a deformation as a result of a social role that we feel bound to carry out in such a way as to obliterate the moral sensibility, as, for example, in the case of the custodian of the gas ovens at Dachau. This is a case where social pathology overwhelms the innate capacity for empathy. The question is, in what form of governing is it likely that the moral sense or empathy for the Other can be best exercised, not in the sense of generosity but in the recognition and prosecution of political equality and economic justice that eschews seeing humanity as either prey or predator? It is in democracy critically evaluated that reasoned arguments and passions find the basis for action and behavior. Argument and passion may be frightening to the suffering who have lost hope and accept their colonized status. Similarly, it is frightening to the instigator and those who despise anyone outside of themselves, viewing altruism as either the coin of some primitive society or something that can never exist. But answers can be found and intuitively felt in "political decision time" by yielding to our moral sentiments. These capacities are there within us, and they are our tropes (with shared experience) that cannot easily be denied, whether by the impersonality of technology or social roles that until the twenty-first century, in the way they were constructed and institutionalized, required humanity to be less than what it is and what it could become. It is in the liberalism of reconstruction that some of the answers may be discovered and these capacities may flourish.

13

✭

Tragic and Hopeful Signs: The Ought and Necessary

S ome may have thought that that harsh teacher, the twentieth century, struck humanity dumb and blind. That is, it has no way but to repeat the mistakes that choked humanity for much of a hundred years. After all, so many ideologies were tried, each found wanting, cruel, sadistic, or foolish. From the Vatican, to Wall Street, to the Kremlin, to war colleges, humanity's collective history is littered with waking nightmares of perfect economic markets, clerical fascism, communism, state socialism, Nazism, capitalism, and militarism. By the end of the century humanity had begun to learn that science and technology did not offer a "free lunch"; their consequences could be disastrous. The twenty-first century finds the American people continuing to struggle with value, results, methods, and purpose. Was it a peaceful democracy or a nation consumed with propaganda ballyhoo, bellicosity, and a Manichean vision of the world caught between our good and their evil? In the United States the second Bush administration, enamored of dreams of glory, sought to play out its nineteenth-century version of taming the Native American tribes, with a virtual monopoly on violence.

But thankfully there were other lessons from the twentieth century as well, paid for through struggle and the realization that political and social freedom with economic justice were within humanity's grasp. The detritus of the past, the commitments to slavery, racism, sexism, and colonialism, had been shaken. No longer were they accepted as the dominant spirit of history and unvarying features of human existence. Modernism did not shrink from the belief that dignity and freedom were the province of all people, that freedom itself was best fulfilled with others and with a healthy understanding and respect of the environment and natural world. It began to dawn even on warriors that all are dependent on each other. Mutual aid was the way both to survive and to find the means to feel identification and responsibility beyond the immediate Other. It was the way to accept the obvious: that universal principles had to have respect for the different and that those we like cannot be judged one way and those we dislike another way for the same action. None of this realization justifies the human quest for purity, a dangerous goal causing terrible pain.

These lessons in their tragic and hopeful guises are the texts for third-stage liberalism, the liberalism of reconstruction. Some would argue that such battles are "beyond politics" because they go to the nature of "Man" himself. And perhaps others would argue that where politics is involved, even "man's" character cannot be helpful, for the good can turn out to be the bad, or as it is said, the bad can turn out to be the good. It is difficult to know what the road not taken would have yielded. Ethics cannot be a political guide. According to this view the human reality is best described in terms of the social Darwinism of Thomas Huxley and Oswald Spengler, in which rationality and vision are the province of the few and humanity is unfree unless it recognizes and accepts the superior over the inferior, embraces the *Übermensch* whether through genetic engineering, money, or the crude use of force. That this is seductive is obvious, for it has been an important element in Western philosophical thought and much of politics for a few thousand years. But this does not make the ideas less foolish, for they neither explain nor take into account what and how humankind survived; how humanity accepted its own individuality of self-love as against selfishness; how it was ashamed when it did not act either justly, with generosity, or in aid of others; how it was understood that progress was in the province of humanity. That some religious, economic, and political gangsters cashed in on the reality of mutual aid among the wretched in no way contradicts this sensibility, which is the fundamental meaning of survival and identification of the Other.

The twenty-first century does not have to flee from an evolving moral and social sensibility. But that sensibility cannot be built on violence. A politics that honors the struggles for freedom must bring forward to public and policy relevance those features of freedom linked to empathy, and those forms of economic, social, and political aspirations that have become the international "ought" tableaux against which the interests of nations and their behavior are to be judged. It is in this stage of liberalism, democratic reconstruction, where democracy must be clear about its underpinnings and its policies, for they carry with them the hopes of humane progress, a progress based on the history of humanity in its struggle to maintain empathy and the affections and secure cooperation among one and the Other. These sentiments must be the foundation of all institutions, whatever their putative function. And where they cannot stand on this foundation they must be transformed and reconfigured. In other words, those who reject the exhaustion of possibilities carry with them democratic reconstruction, for they (we) intuit that human affections, including our reason, mediated through personal relationships and social institutions, are the primary key to the development of world civilization with plural cultures. (This is why ideas that are thought to be the historical underpinnings of cultures, namely, community and family, must be judged critically, without sentimentality, so change for dignity and decency may occur.)

The crucial test for liberal democracies is to prove that they have the proper instruments to effect empathy, caring, and freedom for transforming social, political, and economic institutions. Social movements are charged with the responsibility of bringing about democracy in its fullest meaning through citizen participation and where necessary the type of nonviolence that does not vitiate peaceful democratic ends. The fundamental test for the relevance of higher learning is whether its overarching mission and the questions considered do not shirk the examination of values that inhere in reality, and especially in the social reality we make through our social relations and institutions.

The skeptical reader will wonder whether we have entered into a forest of ambiguity when we consider such matters as either the moral sense or capacities for human affection. But one need look no more deeply than his or her own life to ascertain what these affections are, how they are reflected in the lives of others, how together individuals share mutual affections, which are the sine qua non for a democracy of reconstruction. When these affections are not developed sufficiently we are left with social or personal paranoia and the Machiavellian idea of keeping the peace through the gregarious or authoritarian sovereign ready for war at all times. In that world people do have their role: People are expected to endure until the next war or calamity.

When government becomes no more than the instrument for force and coercion, ensuring a state of war at all times, the words of affection are turned into their opposite and like a cancer are turned against healthy tissue. In the lexicon of power, stability becomes the mailed fist for coercion, order becomes the synonym for authoritarian control, and education and knowledge are reduced to control over people and nature. Economic disparities are hailed as the price of efficiency. Wrongs are to be answered with revenge no matter the cost, even if it means flailing out at the bystanders. Nature is to be abused, conquered, and certainly not respected. As in any authoritarian institution, natural affections are wiped clean or used to enforce control. The social character of a people becomes a mirror of the patterns of oppression.

But as I have argued, history teaches the possibility of another framework, which emerges from liberalism and democracy. This framework is not determined by a set of copybook precepts. Although the features of such a framework are adjustable so long as they advance human dignity and progress, they can be thought of as a guide or certainly the continuation of discourse.

In the development of all cultures, sayings are repeated because they often have truth in them. But probably more often they are repeated as pithy aphorisms to close off dialogue and the search for a measure of happiness and dignity. Certainly religious catechisms can be of this sort, admonishing with punishment for every "infraction." They are complemented by the advertising commercial, which promises happiness through toothpaste and skin softener. I introduce this issue so late in this volume because I am aware that people want complex ideas presented as bottom lines. Businesspeople and scientists want to believe that there are easy, elegant explanations to nature (it works). Many years ago I was a member of a White House panel on education. The chairman, a professor of engineering and physics at MIT, upbraided one of the participants by saying that if you can't fit what you're saying and thinking onto a postage stamp, forget it. And he was serious. We also know, as one great Catholic philosopher said, that disciples always start their assumptions from the conclusions of their masters, so they don't know the reasoning that supports the conclusion. And as a result, over time our thoughts are reduced to unexamined *bobbe mayse,* grandmother's tales that have neither meaning nor explanatory power, not even hortatory value. This is what happens in any form of thought that is frozen and does not value discourse, instead placing one's subjective faith in the Absolute. But this doubt does not mean that there are no limits, boundaries, and even conventions that are useful or even ethical beyond the particular case.

So is there a bottom line to third-stage liberalism? Are there simple, elegant rules that can be reduced to a postage stamp? No. But what there is are some notions to keep in mind, similar to how a medical student learns about the parts of the human body or symptoms of disease and a range of palliatives:

1. Democracy is a means and an end, which includes procedure and content. The ends may change only insofar as they are intended to promote greater human dignity, which will result as we discover more about ourselves, nature, and ourselves in nature. The quest is unending, and so our search for knowledge and understanding is unending. Democratic reconstruction uses as one of its guides, but not the only one, the Universal Declaration of Human Rights. The declaration is linked to the need for social, economic, and political justice, whether for the person or the group. This idea necessitates regarding egalitarian interdependence and freedom as integral to one another.

2. The Universal Declaration of Human Rights should frame the foreign policies of nations. Its relevance grows with the years just because it speaks to individual and group rights. The question is whether there can be transnational and national agencies that hold to these principles in practice as the alternative to the war system. The best answer to these questions is found in the spread and support of peace and justice movements that form projects around basic problems, such as weapons inspection, torture, women's oppression, poverty, disease, and environmental degradation, seeing in each one its relationship to institutional deficits and links to other issues. With changes in education caused by the discovery of a world consciousness, parochial leadership caught in the old ways of imperialism, colonialism, and absolutism may change if people through social movements delegitimate warrior and oppressor states.

3. The plethora of different cultures and different customs adds to the need to redefine and translate common traditions into the reassertion and protection of human dignity.

4. It is the burden of politics, law, and philosophy to assess how inclusivity is organized so that it is accepted as fair by groups that appear to have different interests. Integration is intended to take all people out of the political, economic, and social closet and into a framework that reflects in institutions and everyday life that they are needed and valued.

5. Democratic reconstruction recognizes that individuals and groups are reflected in each other; that separate problems have embedded within them other problems, "rules and solutions" that can be found to apply beyond any particular problem.

6. Without economic justice and egalitarian interdependence, political freedom is a hollow vessel incapable of being filled with dignity and caring.

7. Democracy exhibits within itself rules of moral action that are useful as guides to reconstruction of institutions.

8. Democratic reconstruction fosters and insists on those redistributive mechanisms and institutions that ensure a common bond by sharing material resources, education, social caring, and agricultural, technical, and cultural possibilities as a matter of right for all people.

9. Just laws are the fundamental teachers in a democratic society because they create the changing foundation for a just society and the promotion of social character in which individual action is linked to the common good.

10. Societies need not be overwhelmed by the claims of science, technology, and religion that they have found incontrovertible answers to

problems of life after death, parallel universes, empirical truths, or Hell. But respect for them must be accorded.

11. There is a nowness in the world that forces humanity to judge human actions in terms of human time and therefore human incompleteness. Through continuous public dialogue, the ideal of progress and just laws is to be assessed with a proper dose of skepticism but some belief in human perfectibility.

12. Progress is dependent on openness and change, just as democracy is not a completion. Both are dependent on deepened definitions of rationality in science and logic that will include moral considerations. Without such considerations, politics, even inquiry, becomes an exercise in raw power. Any possibility of a humane world spirit of liberation is turned and degraded into its opposite. It is then that the powerful organize the "contemptible Other" in the consciousness of the unsuspecting so that the powerful may work their will against the Other and the doubter. It is then that struggles over material resources and moral reason are crushed by faux moralists and machtpolitikers.

13. Third-stage liberalism teaches that people are not alone in having needs; so does nature, and living animals are to be protected because of the role humanity has as the trustee of the earth and all that lives. They should be left alone or used only when absolutely necessary.

14. The earth and human beings survive on affections. Where love, trust, mutual aid, equality, and empathy are not linked, the boot, whip, warring, modern inquisitors, and their epigones will supply a rhetoric that accepts humanity's fate as tragic while doing everything to perpetuate that tragedy.

15. There is no magic in any social form, be it family or community, that does not demand radical criticism to ensure its positive benefits.

So, about what we must understand and do, we cannot remain silent and passive.

Appendix A: Universal Declaration of Human Rights

W hen we examine critically the Universal Declaration of Human Rights, we note its need for review even after a cursory glance. Its revision may be necessary. However, if no changes were made and the nations followed its purposes and language, the chances for dignity and economic and social justice would be incomparably better than in our present situation.

The reader will note that my corrections and comments appear in italicized font within brackets.

UNIVERSAL DECLARATION OF HUMAN RIGHTS

Preamble

Whereas recognition of the inherent dignity and of the equal and inalienable rights of all members of the human family is the foundation of freedom, justice and peace in the world, [*Freedom, justice, and peace are difficult concepts, as are equal and inalienable rights. These concepts must be carefully analyzed in terms of different cultures. Similarly, explication demands that we ask whether family is a diverse concept that is culturally bound.*]

Whereas disregard and contempt for human rights have resulted in barbarous acts which have outraged the conscience of mankind, and the advent of a world in which human beings shall enjoy freedom of speech and belief and freedom from fear and want has been proclaimed as the highest aspiration of the common people, [*The issue raised by this clause is appropriate at a time when there are close to two billion people who are at the edge of starvation. The problem with this clause is that it asserts belief as an automatic good. Further, it assumes that there is a universal conscience that all people have, a moral belief that is universally shared rather than a series of arrangements and capacities that human beings have made for choices that recognize the dignity of all people. In this sense it is better to speak of humankind rather than "man."*]

Whereas it is essential, if man is not to be compelled to have recourse, as a last resort, to rebellion against tyranny and oppression, that human rights should be protected by the rule of law, [*The problem in this clause is the meaning of rule of law. Surely it is different from one nation to another, although there will be some similarities. The phrase "rule of law" requires explication so that it becomes something other than a Western concept, which means that it probably must become "rules of justice through the laws."*]

Whereas it is essential to promote the development of friendly relations between nations, [*The beginning of the twenty-first century has taught us that nations are not the only actors worldwide. There are groups, peaceful and otherwise, churches, and corporations that suggest the need for a multilayered set of rules for a just world.*]

Whereas the peoples of the United Nations have in the Charter reaffirmed their faith in fundamental human rights, in the dignity and worth of the human person and in the equal rights of men and women and have determined to promote social progress and better standards of life in larger freedom, [*It is not enough to have faith in the dignity and worth of the human person. What is needed are concrete steps, some of which are understood and others that will become obvious as world civilization develops.*]

Whereas Member States have pledged themselves to achieve, in cooperation with the United Nations, the promotion of universal respect for and observance of human rights and fundamental freedoms, [*The test of this phrase is how nations conduct themselves, how they define these meanings, and whether they are prepared to have a continuous dialogue about them, organizing discourse for the purpose of some common agreement that can be internalized and applied within national laws.*]

Whereas a common understanding of these rights and freedoms is of the greatest importance for the full realization of this pledge, [*The common understanding of these rights can emerge through cross-cultural education in the various institutions of the respective nations and groups. It must extend beyond governments.*]

Now, therefore,

The General Assembly,

Proclaims this Universal Declaration of Human Rights as a common standard of achievement for all peoples and all nations, to the end that every individual and every organ of society, keeping this Declaration constantly in mind, shall strive by teaching and education to promote respect for these rights and freedoms and by progressive measures, national and international, to secure their universal and effective recognition and observance, both among the peoples of Member States themselves and among the peoples of territories under their jurisdiction.

Article 1

All human beings are born free and equal in dignity and rights. They are endowed with reason and conscience and should act towards one another in a spirit of brotherhood. [*The statement is laudable but limited. What is needed is awareness of the need to change the very character of culture and nations of oppression. One need only note the untouchable class in the world's largest democracy to comprehend the need for a human rights covenant that can be enforced through various means short of the violence that would most likely defeat the fundamental purpose of the article. Brotherhood and sisterhood must become part of statements about equality with due recognition of the problem of conflict inside families.*]

Article 2

Everyone is entitled to all the rights and freedoms set forth in this Declaration, without distinction of any kind, such as race, colour, sex, language, religion, political or other opinion, national or social origin, property, birth or other status. [*This article seems to be contradictory. It asserts that rights and freedoms don't have to do with changing the distribution of power in communities in order to have rights and freedoms. As a result its meaning is limited.*]

Furthermore, no distinction shall be made on the basis of the political, jurisdictional or international status of the country or territory to which a person belongs, whether it be independent, trust, non-self-governing or under any other limitation of sovereignty. [*On the other hand, this section of the article appears to call for revolution to attain freedom and rights, which would change the distribution of power.*]

Article 3

Everyone has the right to life, liberty and security of person.

Article 4

No one shall be held in slavery or servitude; slavery and the slave trade shall be prohibited in all their forms. [*The question is how to hold nations to this standard. Usually this population is the most frightened and without options, unless nations are prepared to grant them refugee status and citizenship, including universal citizenship. The key to the success of this article is international women's organizations that, through their activism, can as a group change the entire discourse of international politics.*]

Article 5

No one shall be subjected to torture or to cruel, inhuman or degrading treatment or punishment. [*This article raises difficulties in the United States and throughout the world. One element of the problem is the astonishing violence by police shown on television. Note for example the show* NYPD Blue.]

Article 6

Everyone has the right to recognition everywhere as a person before the law. [*The question in Article 6 is whose law, and how is it made? What is the character of recognition? Is recognition a statement of rights, or merely the right to appear?*]

Article 7

All are equal before the law and are entitled without any discrimination to equal protection of the law. All are entitled to equal protection against any discrimination in violation of this Declaration and against any incitement to such discrimination. [*This article raises the question, which laws? The United States has a plethora of laws, requiring an architectonic of laws for the person to know which takes priority.*]

Article 8

Everyone has the right to an effective remedy by the competent national tribunals for acts violating the fundamental rights granted him by the constitution or by law. [*How is "effective remedy" to be determined, and by whom? And what if no fundamental rights are recognized by a national constitution or its law?*]

Article 9

No one shall be subjected to arbitrary arrest, detention or exile. [*It is necessary to develop international standards to define the meaning of "arbitrary," whether detention can be for an unreasonable time, and whether "exile" refers to population removal for reasons of "national security."*]

Article 10

Everyone is entitled in full equality to a fair and public hearing by an independent and impartial tribunal, in the determination of his rights and obligations and of any criminal charge against him. [*There is some question whether this applies to detention where no criminal charge is brought. If that is the case, this article is incomplete in its purpose. If what is said conveys its purpose, this article is a cynical exercise.*]

Article 11

1. Everyone charged with a penal offence has the right to be presumed innocent until proved guilty according to law in a public trial at which he has had all the guarantees necessary for his defence.
2. No one shall be held guilty of any penal offence on account of any act or omission which did not constitute a penal offence, under national or international law, at the time when it was committed. Nor shall a heavier penalty be imposed than the one that was applicable at the time the penal offence was committed. [*The intriguing issue raised in this article is that of raising international law to the status of national law in its applicability to cases.*]

Article 12

No one shall be subjected to arbitrary interference with his privacy, family, home or correspondence, nor to attacks upon his honour and reputation. Everyone has the right to the protection of the law against such interference or attacks. [*This article denies—and correctly so—the state's power against its own citizens and nationals of other nations, and interference in other nations without international warrant. This article requires reconsideration in light of modern intrusive technologies.*]

Article 13

1. Everyone has the right to freedom of movement and residence within the borders of each State. [*This article has proved troubling because it doesn't take into account overcrowding in the cities as rural people unable to earn livelihoods on farms and in villages move to cities by the tens of millions.*]
2. Everyone has the right to leave any country, including his own, and to return to his country.

Article 14

1. Everyone has the right to seek and to enjoy in other countries asylum from persecution. [*But the question is whether there is an obligation for nations to accept people because of persecution.*]
2. This right may not be invoked in the case of prosecutions genuinely arising from non-political crimes or from acts contrary to the purposes and principles of the United Nations. [*Note the status quo elements of this article, which protects systems of oppression against women, untouchables, and others. It does not take into account cultural institutions.*]

Article 15

1. Everyone has the right to a nationality.
2. No one shall be arbitrarily deprived of his nationality nor denied the right to change his nationality. [*This article has value only as it relates to the disposition and reconfiguration of states as a result of war, collapse of empires, and decolonization.*]

Article 16

1. Men and women of full age, without any limitation due to race, nationality or religion, have the right to marry and to found a family. They are entitled to equal rights as to marriage, during marriage and at its dissolution. [*Same-sex marriages were not contemplated. This is another case where women must take the lead in applying the article's purposes.*]
2. Marriage shall be entered into only with the free and full consent of the intending spouses. [*This is not the way of most marriages in the world. No doubt Article 16.2 will be offensive to patriarchal systems.*]
3. The family is the natural and fundamental group unit of society and is entitled to protection by society and the State. [*If this section were*

to be implemented, for example in the United States, an entirely different mode of punishment and rehabilitation would be necessary, for the present system in the United States, by either design or inattention, has resulted in millions of broken families.]

Article 17

1. Everyone has the right to own property alone as well as in association with others.
2. No one shall be arbitrarily deprived of his property. [*Note that the question here is, how much property? This article may be viewed as the protection of entrepreneurial capitalism and an attack on socialism. However, at the time it was written, corporations and entrepreneurs accepted limits as a result of New Deal requirements and where social democratic attitudes were predominant.*]

Article 18

Everyone has the right to freedom of thought, conscience and religion; this right includes freedom to change his religion or belief, and freedom, either alone or in community with others and in public or private, to manifest his religion or belief in teaching, practice, worship and observance. [*As with the previous articles, the question is whether a "right" is inherent in the person or is exercised at the pleasure of the state, after a harm is done to the individual.*]

Article 19

Everyone has the right to freedom of opinion and expression; this right includes freedom to hold opinions without interference and to seek, receive and impart information and ideas through any media and regardless of frontiers. [*Note that the problem has become a complex one in which the power of Western media is so great that it is effectively able to overwhelm other media sources of poorer nations. This problem turns on what nations consider cultural imperialism.*]

Article 20

1. Everyone has the right to freedom of peaceful assembly and association.
2. No one may be compelled to belong to an association. [*Association and peaceful assembly are by their nature threats to authoritarian nations. The problem is how to ensure that peaceful assembly and the freedom of association are permitted. In nations imbued with the importance of*

family, this section may in fact contradict the idea of the supremacy of the family as the individual looks elsewhere for sustenance.]

Article 21

1. Everyone has the right to take part in the government of his country, directly or through freely chosen representatives. [*"Taking part" is difficult to determine and requires making clear that no punishment will be imposed on those with dissident views.*]
2. Everyone has the right to equal access to public service in his country.
3. The will of the people shall be the basis of the authority of government; this will shall be expressed in periodic and genuine elections which shall be by universal and equal suffrage and shall be held by secret vote or by equivalent free voting procedures. [*This article is silent on whether voting and participation extend to the economic sphere.*]

Article 22

Everyone, as a member of society, has the right to social security and is entitled to realization, through national effort and international co-operation and in accordance with the organization and resources of each State, of the economic, social and cultural rights indispensable for his dignity and the free development of his personality. [*Here is the influence of the New Deal and socialist-social democratic thought and practice. Two questions remain for the twenty-first century. Can guarantees be maintained, and how can lives of dignity be ensured in poor nations? Is aid of the kind carried out in the twentieth century or trade the panacea? The likelihood is that new modes of redistribution will have to be implemented outside the market systems.*]

Article 23

1. Everyone has the right to work, to free choice of employment, to just and favourable conditions of work and to protection against unemployment. [*Note that for this article to become viable will require strong governments, strong labor unions, and corporate structures that understand workers and the public as both visible and invisible stakeholders with participatory rights.*]
2. Everyone, without any discrimination, has the right to equal pay for equal work. [*This was part of the Left New Deal agenda for the United States as articulated by Henry Wallace and socialists and progressives. Its relevance to the Third World is unclear where, for example, 85 percent of the world's agriculture is carried out by women.*]

3. Everyone who works has the right to just and favourable remuneration ensuring for himself and his family an existence worthy of human dignity, and supplemented, if necessary, by other means of social protection. [*Note throughout that the document is male oriented, without adequate understanding of single-parent households and women as workers in labor markets.*]
4. Everyone has the right to form and to join trade unions for the protection of his interests. [*The weakness of labor unions in, for example, the United States adds to national economic disparity. The capacity of capital to move from one place to another undercuts the power of labor unions and the community's ability to control capital. It may be that new forms must be developed to represent communities and workers, resulting in greater controls over and accountability for corporations.*]

Article 24

Everyone has the right to rest and leisure, including reasonable limitation of working hours and periodic holidays with pay. [*The validity of this article becomes obvious when one examines people's working hours, especially those of children and women in poor nations. The problem is integrally related to poverty and to profit by local and international firms. There may be a political consequence to meeting the aspirations of this article. Given more leisure time, workers and their families may organize broader reforms.*]

Article 25

1. Everyone has the right to a standard of living adequate for the health and well-being of himself and of his family, including food, clothing, housing and medical care and necessary social services, and the right to security in the event of unemployment, sickness, disability, widowhood, old age or other lack of livelihood in circumstances beyond his control. [*This article is an essential part of the liberal democracy. Where this is present in a society the chances of human creativity will be great, whether in the arts, sciences, or acquisition of knowledge. Even more, this section lays the predicate for the enjoyment and dissemination of the fruits of collective and individual labor, of culture and ensuring cultural rights. Note that the word "adequate" is used rather than "decent" to describe what people are entitled to.*]
2. Motherhood and childhood are entitled to special care and assistance. All children, whether born in or out of wedlock, shall enjoy the same social protection. [*To take this section seriously would require a radical*

reconfiguration of how child services are implemented in the United States and elsewhere. It should be noted that fathers also have responsibilities and are in need of assistance.]

Article 26

1. Everyone has the right to education. Education shall be free, at least in the elementary and fundamental stages. Elementary education shall be compulsory. Technical and professional education shall be made generally available and higher education shall be equally accessible to all on the basis of merit.
2. Education shall be directed to the full development of the human personality and to the strengthening of respect for human rights and fundamental freedoms. It shall promote understanding, tolerance and friendship among all nations, racial or religious groups, and shall further the activities of the United Nations for the maintenance of peace.
3. Parents have a prior right to choose the kind of education that shall be given to their children. [*The sentiments of this article are laudable. There are two potential defects. First is that parents may not favor the first two sections. Second, poor nations may not have the wherewithal to comply with the terms of this article. The result is that a retrograde education may result that does nothing to educate in terms of knowledge and fundamental freedoms. The article is a direct outgrowth of the modernist revolution, which still fights for its existence.*]

Article 27

1. Everyone has the right freely to participate in the cultural life of the community, to enjoy the arts and to share in scientific advancement and its benefits.
2. Everyone has the right to the protection of the moral and material interests resulting from any scientific, literary or artistic production of which he is the author.

Article 28

Everyone is entitled to a social and international order in which the rights and freedoms set forth in this Declaration can be fully realized. [*This article has meaning in four ways. One is an end to the war system through peaceful means consonant with disarmament. Second is a right to peace under which people can opt out of wars and are protected. Third is concentration on the terms of most of the articles in the human rights declaration, how to bring them into practice in all institutions, especially educational and legal ones. Fourth is the recognition of boundaries that cannot be crossed if humanity is to retain its chances for survival.*]

Article 29

1. Everyone has duties to the community in which alone the free and full development of his personality is possible. [*This section is potentially dangerous. One doesn't know if it is to be read that duties are owed to the community that allow for the full development of the person, or whether responsibilities are owed irrespective of the nature of the community because it is only in the community that a person may develop fully. The latter begs the question of what a community is.*]
2. In the exercise of his rights and freedoms, everyone shall be subject only to such limitations as are determined by law solely for the purpose of securing due recognition and respect for the rights and freedoms of others and of meeting the just requirements of morality, public order and the general welfare in a democratic society. [*The question raised in this section is, what is the meaning of public order? Nonviolent change may in fact upset public order, which might be the power of the dominator over the dominated.*]
3. These rights and freedoms may in no case be exercised contrary to the purposes and principles of the United Nations.

Article 30

Nothing in this Declaration may be interpreted as implying for any State, group or person any right to engage in any activity or to perform any act aimed at the destruction of any of the rights and freedoms set forth herein. [*For the time and what it is, the document serves as an excellent but imperfect guide for third-stage liberalism. Some of it is wrong or not relevant to humanity's future. It is, however, a framework that gives humanity a chance for struggle in the context of the right questions.*]

[*The reader will note that this covenant, although incomplete, reflects an important stage in the development of a world civilization with different cultures. Its purposes and objectives reflect much contained in third-stage liberalism. That modern liberalism and democracy take their cues from the French, American, and Russian Revolutions is obvious. That both contain religious and scientific freedom is their strength. This covenant, with emendations regarding disarmament, conflict resolution, and concrete steps that sustain the environment, can become the basis for twenty-first-century politics.*]

Source: The Office of the High Commissioner for Human Rights, www.unhchr.ch/udhr/lang/eng_print.htm

Appendix B: International Covenant on Economic, Social and Cultural Rights

International Covenant on Economic, Social and Cultural Rights
Adopted and opened for signature, ratification and accession by
General Assembly resolution 2200A (XXI) of 16 December 1966
entry into force 3 January 1976, in accordance with article 27

Preamble
The States Parties to the present Covenant,

Considering that, in accordance with the principles proclaimed in the Charter of the United Nations, recognition of the inherent dignity and of the equal and inalienable rights of all members of the human family is the foundation of freedom, justice and peace in the world,

Recognizing that these rights derive from the inherent dignity of the human person,

Recognizing that, in accordance with the Universal Declaration of Human Rights, the ideal of free human beings enjoying freedom from fear and want can only be achieved if conditions are created whereby everyone may enjoy his economic, social and cultural rights, as well as his civil and political rights,

Considering the obligation of States under the Charter of the United Nations to promote universal respect for, and observance of, human rights and freedoms,

Realizing that the individual, having duties to other individuals and to the community to which he belongs, is under a responsibility to strive for

261

the promotion and observance of the rights recognized in the present Covenant,

Agree upon the following articles:

PART I

Article 1

1. All peoples have the right of self-determination. By virtue of that right they freely determine their political status and freely pursue their economic, social and cultural development.
2. All peoples may, for their own ends, freely dispose of their natural wealth and resources without prejudice to any obligations arising out of international economic co-operation, based upon the principle of mutual benefit, and international law. In no case may a people be deprived of its own means of subsistence.
3. The States Parties to the present Covenant, including those having responsibility for the administration of Non-Self-Governing and Trust Territories, shall promote the realization of the right of self-determination, and shall respect that right, in conformity with the provisions of the Charter of the United Nations.

PART II

Article 2

1. Each State Party to the present Covenant undertakes to take steps, individually and through international assistance and co-operation, especially economic and technical, to the maximum of its available resources, with a view to achieving progressively the full realization of the rights recognized in the present Covenant by all appropriate means, including particularly the adoption of legislative measures.
2. The States Parties to the present Covenant undertake to guarantee that the rights enunciated in the present Covenant will be exercised without discrimination of any kind as to race, colour, sex, language, religion, political or other opinion, national or social origin, property, birth or other status.
3. Developing countries, with due regard to human rights and their national economy, may determine to what extent they would guarantee the economic rights recognized in the present Covenant to non-nationals.

Article 3

The States Parties to the present Covenant undertake to ensure the equal right of men and women to the enjoyment of all economic, social and cultural rights set forth in the present Covenant.

Article 4

The States Parties to the present Covenant recognize that, in the enjoyment of those rights provided by the State in conformity with the present Covenant, the State may subject such rights only to such limitations as are determined by law only in so far as this may be compatible with the nature of these rights and solely for the purpose of promoting the general welfare in a democratic society.

Article 5

1. Nothing in the present Covenant may be interpreted as implying for any State, group or person any right to engage in any activity or to perform any act aimed at the destruction of any of the rights or freedoms recognized herein, or at their limitation to a greater extent than is provided for in the present Covenant.
2. No restriction upon or derogation from any of the fundamental human rights recognized or existing in any country in virtue of law, conventions, regulations or custom shall be admitted on the pretext that the present Covenant does not recognize such rights or that it recognizes them to a lesser extent.

PART III

Article 6

1. The States Parties to the present Covenant recognize the right to work, which includes the right of everyone to the opportunity to gain his living by work which he freely chooses or accepts, and will take appropriate steps to safeguard this right.
2. The steps to be taken by a State Party to the present Covenant to achieve the full realization of this right shall include technical and vocational guidance and training programmes, policies and techniques to achieve steady economic, social and cultural development and full and productive employment under conditions safeguarding fundamental political and economic freedoms to the individual.

Article 7

The States Parties to the present Covenant recognize the right of everyone to the enjoyment of just and favourable conditions of work which ensure, in particular:

(a) Remuneration which provides all workers, as a minimum, with:
   (i) Fair wages and equal remuneration for work of equal value without distinction of any kind, in particular women being guaranteed conditions of work not inferior to those enjoyed by men, with equal pay for equal work;
   (ii) A decent living for themselves and their families in accordance with the provisions of the present Covenant;
(b) Safe and healthy working conditions;
(c) Equal opportunity for everyone to be promoted in his employment to an appropriate higher level, subject to no considerations other than those of seniority and competence;
(d) Rest, leisure and reasonable limitation of working hours and periodic holidays with pay, as well as remuneration for public holidays

Article 8

1. The States Parties to the present Covenant undertake to ensure:
   (a) The right of everyone to form trade unions and join the trade union of his choice, subject only to the rules of the organization concerned, for the promotion and protection of his economic and social interests. No restrictions may be placed on the exercise of this right other than those prescribed by law and which are necessary in a democratic society in the interests of national security or public order or for the protection of the rights and freedoms of others;
   (b) The right of trade unions to establish national federations or confederations and the right of the latter to form or join international trade-union organizations;
   (c) The right of trade unions to function freely subject to no limitations other than those prescribed by law and which are necessary in a democratic society in the interests of national security or public order or for the protection of the rights and freedoms of others;
   (d) The right to strike, provided that it is exercised in conformity with the laws of the particular country.
2. This article shall not prevent the imposition of lawful restrictions on the exercise of these rights by members of the armed forces or of the police or of the administration of the State.
3. Nothing in this article shall authorize States Parties to the International Labour Organisation Convention of 1948 concerning Freedom

of Association and Protection of the Right to Organize to take legislative measures which would prejudice, or apply the law in such a manner as would prejudice, the guarantees provided for in that Convention.

Article 9

The States Parties to the present Covenant recognize the right of everyone to social security, including social insurance.

Article 10

The States Parties to the present Covenant recognize that:

1. The widest possible protection and assistance should be accorded to the family, which is the natural and fundamental group unit of society, particularly for its establishment and while it is responsible for the care and education of dependent children. Marriage must be entered into with the free consent of the intending spouses.
2. Special protection should be accorded to mothers during a reasonable period before and after childbirth. During such period working mothers should be accorded paid leave or leave with adequate social security benefits.
3. Special measures of protection and assistance should be taken on behalf of all children and young persons without any discrimination for reasons of parentage or other conditions. Children and young persons should be protected from economic and social exploitation. Their employment in work harmful to their morals or health or dangerous to life or likely to hamper their normal development should be punishable by law. States should also set age limits below which the paid employment of child labour should be prohibited and punishable by law.

Article 11

1. The States Parties to the present Covenant recognize the right of everyone to an adequate standard of living for himself and his family, including adequate food, clothing and housing, and to the continuous improvement of living conditions. The States Parties will take appropriate steps to ensure the realization of this right, recognizing to this effect the essential importance of international co-operation based on free consent.
2. The States Parties to the present Covenant, recognizing the fundamental right of everyone to be free from hunger, shall take, individually and

through international co-operation, the measures, including specific programmes, which are needed:

(a) To improve methods of production, conservation and distribution of food by making full use of technical and scientific knowledge, by disseminating knowledge of the principles of nutrition and by developing or reforming agrarian systems in such a way as to achieve the most efficient development and utilization of natural resources;

(b) Taking into account the problems of both food-importing and food-exporting countries, to ensure an equitable distribution of world food supplies in relation to need.

Article 12

1. The States Parties to the present Covenant recognize the right of everyone to the enjoyment of the highest attainable standard of physical and mental health.

2. The steps to be taken by the States Parties to the present Covenant to achieve the full realization of this right shall include those necessary for:

(a) The provision for the reduction of the stillbirth-rate and of infant mortality and for the healthy development of the child;

(b) The improvement of all aspects of environmental and industrial hygiene;

(c) The prevention, treatment and control of epidemic, endemic, occupational and other diseases;

(d) The creation of conditions which would assure to all medical service and medical attention in the event of sickness.

Article 13

1. The States Parties to the present Covenant recognize the right of everyone to education. They agree that education shall be directed to the full development of the human personality and the sense of its dignity, and shall strengthen the respect for human rights and fundamental freedoms. They further agree that education shall enable all persons to participate effectively in a free society, promote understanding, tolerance and friendship among all nations and all racial, ethnic or religious groups, and further the activities of the United Nations for the maintenance of peace.

2. The States Parties to the present Covenant recognize that, with a view to achieving the full realization of this right:

(a) Primary education shall be compulsory and available free to all;

(b) Secondary education in its different forms, including technical and vocational secondary education, shall be made generally available and accessible to all by every appropriate means, and in particular by the progressive introduction of free education;

(c) Higher education shall be made equally accessible to all, on the basis of capacity, by every appropriate means, and in particular by the progressive introduction of free education;

(d) Fundamental education shall be encouraged or intensified as far as possible for those persons who have not received or completed the whole period of their primary education;

(e) The development of a system of schools at all levels shall be actively pursued, an adequate fellowship system shall be established, and the material conditions of teaching staff shall be continuously improved.

3. The States Parties to the present Covenant undertake to have respect for the liberty of parents and, when applicable, legal guardians to choose for their children schools, other than those established by the public authorities, which conform to such minimum educational standards as may be laid down or approved by the State and to ensure the religious and moral education of their children in conformity with their own convictions.

4. No part of this article shall be construed so as to interfere with the liberty of individuals and bodies to establish and direct educational institutions, subject always to the observance of the principles set forth in paragraph I of this article and to the requirement that the education given in such institutions shall conform to such minimum standards as may be laid down by the State.

Article 14

Each State Party to the present Covenant which, at the time of becoming a Party, has not been able to secure in its metropolitan territory or other territories under its jurisdiction compulsory primary education, free of charge, undertakes, within two years, to work out and adopt a detailed plan of action for the progressive implementation, within a reasonable number of years, to be fixed in the plan, of the principle of compulsory education free of charge for all.

Article 15

1. The States Parties to the present Covenant recognize the right of everyone:

(a) To take part in cultural life;

(b) To enjoy the benefits of scientific progress and its applications;

(c) To benefit from the protection of the moral and material interests resulting from any scientific, literary or artistic production of which he is the author.

2. The steps to be taken by the States Parties to the present Covenant to achieve the full realization of this right shall include those necessary for the conservation, the development and the diffusion of science and culture.
3. The States Parties to the present Covenant undertake to respect the freedom indispensable for scientific research and creative activity.
4. The States Parties to the present Covenant recognize the benefits to be derived from the encouragement and development of international contacts and co-operation in the scientific and cultural fields.

PART IV

Article 16

1. The States Parties to the present Covenant undertake to submit in conformity with this part of the Covenant reports on the measures which they have adopted and the progress made in achieving the observance of the rights recognized herein.
2. (a) All reports shall be submitted to the Secretary-General of the United Nations, who shall transmit copies to the Economic and Social Council for consideration in accordance with the provisions of the present Covenant;
   (b) The Secretary-General of the United Nations shall also transmit to the specialized agencies copies of the reports, or any relevant parts therefrom, from States Parties to the present Covenant which are also members of these specialized agencies in so far as these reports, or parts therefrom, relate to any matters which fall within the responsibilities of the said agencies in accordance with their constitutional instruments.

Article 17

1. The States Parties to the present Covenant shall furnish their reports in stages, in accordance with a programme to be established by the Economic and Social Council within one year of the entry into force of the present Covenant after consultation with the States Parties and the specialized agencies concerned.
2. Reports may indicate factors and difficulties affecting the degree of fulfilment of obligations under the present Covenant.
3. Where relevant information has previously been furnished to the United Nations or to any specialized agency by any State Party to the present Covenant, it will not be necessary to reproduce that information, but a precise reference to the information so furnished will suffice.

Article 18

Pursuant to its responsibilities under the Charter of the United Nations in the field of human rights and fundamental freedoms, the Economic and Social Council may make arrangements with the specialized agencies in respect of their reporting to it on the progress made in achieving the observance of the provisions of the present Covenant falling within the scope of their activities. These reports may include particulars of decisions and recommendations on such implementation adopted by their competent organs.

Article 19

The Economic and Social Council may transmit to the Commission on Human Rights for study and general recommendation or, as appropriate, for information the reports concerning human rights submitted by States in accordance with articles 16 and 17, and those concerning human rights submitted by the specialized agencies in accordance with article 18.

Article 20

The States Parties to the present Covenant and the specialized agencies concerned may submit comments to the Economic and Social Council on any general recommendation under article 19 or reference to such general recommendation in any report of the Commission on Human Rights or any documentation referred to therein.

Article 21

The Economic and Social Council may submit from time to time to the General Assembly reports with recommendations of a general nature and a summary of the information received from the States Parties to the present Covenant and the specialized agencies on the measures taken and the progress made in achieving general observance of the rights recognized in the present Covenant.

Article 22

The Economic and Social Council may bring to the attention of other organs of the United Nations, their subsidiary organs and specialized agencies concerned with furnishing technical assistance any matters arising out of the reports referred to in this part of the present Covenant which may assist such bodies in deciding, each within its field of competence, on the advisability of international measures likely to contribute to the effective progressive implementation of the present Covenant.

Article 23

The States Parties to the present Covenant agree that international action for the achievement of the rights recognized in the present Covenant includes such methods as the conclusion of conventions, the adoption of recommendations, the furnishing of technical assistance and the holding of regional meetings and technical meetings for the purpose of consultation and study organized in conjunction with the Governments concerned.

Article 24

Nothing in the present Covenant shall be interpreted as impairing the provisions of the Charter of the United Nations and of the constitutions of the specialized agencies which define the respective responsibilities of the various organs of the United Nations and of the specialized agencies in regard to the matters dealt with in the present Covenant.

Article 25

Nothing in the present Covenant shall be interpreted as impairing the inherent right of all peoples to enjoy and utilize fully and freely their natural wealth and resources.

PART V

Article 26

1. The present Covenant is open for signature by any State Member of the United Nations or member of any of its specialized agencies, by any State Party to the Statute of the International Court of Justice, and by any other State which has been invited by the General Assembly of the United Nations to become a party to the present Covenant.
2. The present Covenant is subject to ratification. Instruments of ratification shall be deposited with the Secretary-General of the United Nations.
3. The present Covenant shall be open to accession by any State referred to in paragraph 1 of this article.
4. Accession shall be effected by the deposit of an instrument of accession with the Secretary-General of the United Nations.

5. The Secretary-General of the United Nations shall inform all States which have signed the present Covenant or acceded to it of the deposit of each instrument of ratification or accession.

Article 27

1. The present Covenant shall enter into force three months after the date of the deposit with the Secretary-General of the United Nations of the thirty-fifth instrument of ratification or instrument of accession.
2. For each State ratifying the present Covenant or acceding to it after the deposit of the thirty-fifth instrument of ratification or instrument of accession, the present Covenant shall enter into force three months after the date of the deposit of its own instrument of ratification or instrument of accession.

Article 28

The provisions of the present Covenant shall extend to all parts of federal States without any limitations or exceptions.

Article 29

1. Any State Party to the present Covenant may propose an amendment and file it with the Secretary-General of the United Nations. The Secretary-General shall thereupon communicate any proposed amendments to the States Parties to the present Covenant with a request that they notify him whether they favour a conference of States Parties for the purpose of considering and voting upon the proposals. In the event that at least one third of the States Parties favours such a conference, the Secretary-General shall convene the conference under the auspices of the United Nations. Any amendment adopted by a majority of the States Parties present and voting at the conference shall be submitted to the General Assembly of the United Nations for approval.
2. Amendments shall come into force when they have been approved by the General Assembly of the United Nations and accepted by a two-thirds majority of the States Parties to the present Covenant in accordance with their respective constitutional processes.
3. When amendments come into force they shall be binding on those States Parties which have accepted them, other States Parties still being bound by the provisions of the present Covenant and any earlier amendment which they have accepted.

Article 30

Irrespective of the notifications made under article 26, paragraph 5, the Secretary-General of the United Nations shall inform all States referred to in paragraph I of the same article of the following particulars:

(a) Signatures, ratifications and accessions under article 26;
(b) The date of the entry into force of the present Covenant under article 27 and the date of the entry into force of any amendments under article 29.

Article 31

1. The present Covenant, of which the Chinese, English, French, Russian and Spanish texts are equally authentic, shall be deposited in the archives of the United Nations. [*Obviously the document must be translated into many more languages. As it stands the document is translated into the languages of the permanent members of the Security Council plus Spain, leaving out Arab-speaking nations, African nations, Germany and Japan, and the indigenous languages of Pakistan and India.*]
2. The Secretary-General of the United Nations shall transmit certified copies of the present Covenant to all States referred to in article 26.

Source: www.unhchr.ch/html/menu3/b/a_cescr.htm

Notes

NOTE TO THE READER

1. In one year Americans have learned some bitter lessons. The second Bush administration came to power through the Supreme Court, thereby calling into question the American election process and the legitimacy of the American government. Lecturing other nations about democracy by various administrations has proved hollow and comical in light of our own difficulties. The corporate system and its managers, so arrogant and upstanding, have turned out to be a blight of enormous proportions. Corporate responsibility turns out to be an oxymoron.

2. Marcus Raskin, *The Common Good* (New York: Routledge, 1986).

PREFACE

1. Isaiah Berlin, *Four Essays on Liberty* (Oxford: Oxford University Press, 1969).

INTRODUCTION

1. As in the McCarthy period and other ignoble times in history, word and concept banning was a poisonous intellectual problem. Economists, fearing for their jobs at universities, borrowed from Marx for the purpose of proving capitalism's lasting value. Of course, few of the economists ever gave credit or mention to the very one they were discrediting or mocking. John Cassidy, "The Return of Karl Marx," *The New Yorker* (October 27, 1997): 14.

2. Among the original members were James Roosevelt (California), Robert Kastenmeier (Wisconsin), Byron Johnson (Colorado), and William Meyer (Vermont).

This group was expanded with Don Edwards (California) and John Conyers (Michigan). By 2002 the group had fifty-two members and was known as the Progressive Caucus.

3. Reinhold Niebuhr, *Moral Man and Immoral Society: A Study in Ethics and Politics* (New York: Scribner, 1960).

4. Schlesinger's phrase is not to be confused with former President Clinton's phrase "vital center," which was purged of any liberal leanings.

5. Letter from Eisenhower to Congressman Charlie Halleck, House Republican Leader, *New York Times,* March 30, 1963, 4.

6. Zachary Karabell, *The Last Campaign* (New York: Alfred A. Knopf, 2000), 32.

7. James Roosevelt, ed., *The Liberal Papers* (Garden City, N.Y.: Anchor Books, 1962).

8. The historian Stuart Hughes was the first to point out this connection in discussions with me when I worked at the NSC.

9. The purge of the State Department's Asian advisors (Lattimore Davies, among others) led to misjudgments that resulted in the United States misunderstanding the relationship between Vietnam and China.

10. Norman Birnbaum, *After Progress: American Social Reform and European Socialism in the 20th Century* (Oxford: Oxford University Press, 2001).

11. Arthur Waskow (and Marcus Raskin unlisted), *Limits of Defense* (Garden City, N.Y.: Doubleday, 1962).

12. McGeorge Bundy, *Danger and Survival: Choices about the Bomb in the First Fifty Years* (New York: Random House, 1988).

13. Brookings Institute study report conducted by Stephen Schwartz et al. in the early 1990s.

14. From the first Bikini tests timed to the Moscow foreign ministers conference the United States used this tactic. The Soviets used a similar tactic, testing a fifty-eight-megaton bomb during the 1961 Berlin crisis.

15. Perhaps it should not be surprising, as liberalism believes things change and nature is not fixed, that we cannot expect words and concepts to stay the same when they are made applicable to the problems that impinge on everyday life. Sometimes these problems are generally known. Of course, in problems there are different descriptions and interests. Knowledge can be liberating or stifling, just as the project of obtaining knowledge can be liberating or stifling. Did modern liberals shift their stance? And weren't they supposed to as a result of "reality"? It was certainly true that liberals changed and definitions of liberalism changed as the productive forces changed in the political economy. But there was more. What it meant to be human, a person with feelings and dignity, constantly expanded in both an ideal and practical way, even in the face of numbing cruelty.

CHAPTER 1

1. Can it really be said to be any different for the billions now suffering from that curious euphemism for modern neocolonialism: globalization?

2. The most trenchant analysis of the problem from a liberal perspective was that of John Dewey, who in many of his writings took up this problem. His project was the use of inquiry and education as the means of transforming the modern industrial system into a free and social democratic society. *The Collected Works of John Dewey,* ed. by Jo Ann Boydston (Carbondale: Southern Illinois University Press, 1985).

3. In the interest of full disclosure, Spock and I stood trial together as part of the Boston Five antiwar, antidraft case with Mitchell Goodman, William Sloane Coffin, and Michael Ferber. There were some unindicted coconspirators in the case, namely, Noam Chomsky and Arthur Waskow. It is of note that the Call to Resist Illegitimate Authority, drafted by Waskow and me, was signed by thousands of people. The first signature after our indictment was that of Martin Luther King Jr.

4. Robert Bork, *Slouching towards Gomorrah: Modern Liberalism and American Decline* (New York: Reganbooks, 1996).

5. Bork, *Slouching towards Gomorrah.*

6. Harvey B. Feigenbaum, *Shrinking the State: The Political Underpinnings of Privatization Government* (New York: Cambridge University Press, 1998).

7. But communistic societies, often religious and unforgiving, were established from Indiana to Pennsylvania. Chinese, Japanese, and Hispanic people who were used to build America in the West found that it was well into the twentieth century before the United States made formal attempts to confront structural racism in various institutions of American life. Charles Nordhoff, *The Communistic Societies in the United States* (New York: Dover Publications, 1966).

8. Robert L. Beisner, *Twelve against Empire* (New York: McGraw-Hill, 1968), 12–34.

9. William James, *Essays on Faith and Morals,* sel. Ralph Perry (Magnolia, Mass.: Peter Smith, 1949); Jacques Barzun, *A Stroll with William James* (Chicago: University of Chicago Press, 1984).

CHAPTER 2

1. Reno opinion, *New York Times,* October 4, 1997, 14.

2. Yves Simon, *Philosophy of Democratic Government* (Chicago: University of Chicago Press, 1951).

3. John Dewey, *Quest for Certainty* (New York: Minton Balch, 1929); Dewey, *Reconstruction in Philosophy* (New York: Henry Holt, 1929).

4. In the 1990s generals were given responsibility in Seattle, Washington, D.C., and elsewhere as superintendents of schools to reinforce hierarchy, discipline, and order.

5. J. M. Thompson, *Robespierre and the French Revolution* (New York: Collier Books, 1962).

6. For an important review of the different meanings of democracy and revolution, see *Democracy in a World of Tensions,* ed. by Richard Mc Keon (Chicago: University of Chicago Press, 1950). UNESCO brought together authors around the

question of proletarian democracy and bourgeois democracy. See also Hannah Arendt, *On Revolution* (New York: Viking Press, 1963).

7. Martin Buber, *Paths in Utopia* (New York: Collier Books, 1998, c.1949); Max Otto, "Humanism," in *American Philosophy*, ed. Ralph B. Winn (New York: Philosophical Library, 1955), 172–83; Martin Buber, *I and Thou* (New York: Scribner, 2000, c.1958).

8. James Madison, *The Federalist* No. 10, November 22, 1787. Secrecy was the method used in the Constitutional Convention by its participants, who reflected a republican sense of "noblesse oblige."

9. This complaint can be found in the various works of Noam Chomsky, such as *Necessary Illusions* (Boston: South End Press, 1989); in Paul Goodman, *Compulsory Miseducation* (New York: Random House, 1964); in Herbert Marcuse and Robert Paul Wolff, *Repressive Tolerance* (Boston: Beacon Press, 1970); and in Marcus Raskin, *Being and Doing* (New York: Random House, 1971).

10. The seesaw problem of privacy may be seen in the decisions of Justice Louis Brandeis, Justice William O. Douglas, and the Warren Court, which sought to integrate privacy, that is, "the right to be let alone," into modern daily life in democracy. See Olmstead v. United States, 277 U.S. 438, 478 (1928) (dissenting opinion). Paradoxically, the right to be left alone demands an activist government to protect that right.

11. Lewis Mumford, *Myth of the Machine* (New York: Harcourt Brace Jovanovich, 1964), 354.

12. Frances Fox Piven and Richard A. Cloward, *Regulating the Poor: The Functions of Public Welfare* (New York: Vintage Books, 1972).

13. Paradoxically, the individual finds there are no secrets he or she can keep from being sold by corporations. Ensuring low public accountability in the corporatist and national security state sectors means the virtual exclusion of the public except as surveillanced objects.

14. The Huston Plan is discussed in Marcus Raskin, *Notes on the Old System* (New York: McKay, 1974), 56–57. Note the speeches of Attorney General John Ashcroft in the second Bush administration in support of detaining suspects and material witnesses without benefit of counsel and for an indeterminate time. Federal district courts have found Ashcroft's views lacking in constitutional merit.

15. J. L. Talmon, *The Origins of Totalitarian Democracy* (New York: Norton, 1970).

16. This was a political cancer. However, Jefferson did favor the more moderate elements in the French Revolution. Democratic societies, which were called Jacobin clubs by the Federalists, formed to fight the Jay Treaty. Page Smith, *The Shape of America* (New York: McGraw-Hill, 1980), 222–27.

17. John Dewey, *Collected Works of John Dewey*, vol. 17, ed. by Jo Ann Boydston (Carbondale: Southern Illinois University Press, 1990).

18. Dewey, *Collected Works of John Dewey*.

19. Stephen Cohen, *Bukharin and the Bolshevik Revolution: A Political Biography, 1888–1938* (New York: Vintage Books, 1975, c.1973).

20. Derrick Bell, *And We Are Not Saved: The Elusive Quest for Racial Justice* (New York: Basic Books, 1987).

21. Some work was undertaken by Rex Tugwell at the Center for the Study of Democratic Institutions in the mid-1950s. It remained a think tank exercise.

22. I. F. Stone, *The Trial of Socrates* (Boston: Little, Brown, 1988).

23. Robert Caro, *The Years of Lyndon Johnson: Master of the Senate* (New York: Alfred A. Knopf, 1982–2002).

24. In terms of its foreign policy, the United States was seen by its critics as a "rogue," an extremely nationalist state, attempting to impose on other nations its definition of stability and international law (really imperial law) and nationalistic views of reality and authenticity.

25. Jamin ben Raskin, "The Supreme Court's Racial Double Standard in Redistricting Unequal Protection," University Virginia Law Review 14JPL 591, 1998); Shaw v. Reno, 509 U.S. 63 (1993); *Overruling Democracy* (New York: Routledge, 1993).

26. John Noonan, *Narrowing the Nations of Power: The Supreme Court Sides with the States* (Berkeley: University of California Press, 2002); and Linda Greenhouse, "Narrowing the Nations Power: Deconstructing Recent Supreme Court Decisions," *New York Times,* August 18, 2002.

27. National League of Cities v. Usery, 426 U.S. 833 (1976).

28. Jonathan Elliot, *Elliot's Debates in the Constitutional Convention,* vol. 3 (Salem, N.H.: Ayer, 1987).

29. Friedrich A. von Hayek, *The Constitution of Liberty, "Why I Am Not a Conservative"* (Chicago: University of Chicago Press, 1960), 397–411.

30. Alexis de Tocqueville, *The Present and Probable Future Condition of the Three Races That Inhabit the Territory of the United States* (New York: Alfred A. Knopf, 1991, c.1945).

31. Saul Landau and Paul Jacobs, *To Serve the Devil* (New York: Random House, 1971).

32. Judith Nies, *Native American History* (New York: Ballantine Books, 1996), 265.

33. Isaiah Berlin, *Four Essays on Liberty* (London: Oxford University Press, 1969), 118–72; and Raul Hilberg, *The Destruction of the European Jews* (Chicago: Quadrangle Books, 1961).

34. Schenk v. United States, 249 U.S. 47; and other World War I civil liberties cases.

35. Peter Irons, *Jim Crow's Children, The Broken Promises of the Brown Decision* (New York: Viking, 2002).

36. Fernand Braudel, *Civilization and Capitalism, 15th–18th Century,* vol. 2 of *The Wheels of Commerce* (New York: Harper & Row, 1982), 467.

CHAPTER 3

1. After completing this book and the chapter on "the New Left," I learned about an excellent work, *Intellectuals in Action,* by Kevin Mattson (University Park: Pennsylvania State University Press, 2002). Mattson's book discusses the period 1945 to 1970 in left American history.

2. One prescient professor, Seymour Melman, invented the term "overkill," and in fact that defined nuclear war preparation.

3. Note the dialectic between internal colonization in American life and reconstruction. Marcus Raskin, *Being and Doing* (New York: Random House, 1971). See also lectures in Christian faith and morality, given at Michigan State University in 1967.

4. Christopher Hill, *Liberty against the Law: Some 17th Century Controversies* (London: Allen Lane, Penguin Press, 1996).

5. James Roosevelt, *The Liberal Papers* (Garden City, N.Y.: Anchor Books, 1962).

6. Hannah Arendt, *On Revolution* (New York: Viking Press, 1963).

7. Senate Government Operations Committee Hearing, testimony of George Kemmon before Subcommittee on National Security, Senator Henry Jackson, Chairman, 1960.

8. Walter Isaacson and Evan Thomas, *The Wise Men* (New York: Simon & Schuster, 1986).

9. Franko Venturi, *The History of Populist and Socialist Revolutions in 19th Century Russia* (New York: Alfred A. Knopf, 1960).

10. Ruth Rosen, *The World Split Open* (New York: Viking Press, 2000).

11. There was much resentment about Goodman by former leftists in the Academy, such as the sociologist Lewis Feuer, who claimed that Goodman was nothing more than a seducer of the young.

12. In contradistinction to relativists and postmodernist thinkers, Chomsky, who transformed linguistics and twentieth-century philosophy, believes in an objective scientific reality.

13. Jacques Maritain, *The Person and the Common Good*, trans. by J. J. Fitzgerald (New York: Scribner, 2000).

14. Martin Buber, *Paths in Utopia* (London: Routledge & Kegan Paul, 1949); Gar Alperovitz and Jeff Faux, *Rebuilding America* (New York: Pantheon, 1984); Marcus Raskin, *Common Good* (New York: Routledge & Kegan Paul, (1986).

15. Martin Carnoy, *The Politics of Economics and Race in America* (New York: Cambridge University Press, 1994).

16. Waldemar Nielsen, *The Big Foundations* (New York: Columbia Press, 1972).

17. Robert Paul Wolff, Barrington Moore, and Herbert Marcuse, *Critique of Pure Tolerance* (Boston: Beacon Press, 1969); Walter Truitt Anderson, *Rethinking Liberalism* (New York: Avon Books, 1983); Michael Albert, Leslie Cagan, and Noam Chomsky, *Liberating Theory* (Boston: South End Press, 1986). Much of the work of the Institute for Policy Studies has been and continues to be dedicated to the pragmatism of fundamental alternatives to systemic problems and institutions.

CHAPTER 4

1. Louis B. Sohn, *The Human Rights Movement: From Roosevelt's Four Freedoms to Interdependence of Peace Development and Human Rights* (Cambridge: Harvard Law School Human Rights Program, 1995).

2. A crackpot geopolitical scheme in the twenty-first century would be to attempt monopoly control over oil in the Caspian Sea.

3. Hannah Arendt, *On Revolution* (New York: Viking Press, 1963).

4. Antonio Gramsci, *Letters from Prison*, vol. 2 (New York: Columbia University Press, 1994).

5. Anton Pannekouk, the Dutch physicist who argued with Lenin for workers' councils over the Communist Party.

6. Hannah Arendt, personal conversations with author at IPS, 1970.

7. Paul Feyerabend, *Against Method* (London: New Left Books, 1970).

8. Walter Lippmann, *Public Opinion* (New York: Macmillan, 1960).

9. Christian-Smith Apple, *The Politics of the Textbook* (New York: Routledge, 1991); see also chapter 13. The question in education that tore the heart out of Dewey's pragmatism came from those who argued that ends are not important to know; they are given by the means. This has turned out to be true but disastrous.

10. Joseph Weizenbaum, *Corporate Power and Human Reason* (San Francisco: W. H. Freeman, 1976).

11. Alexis de Tocqueville, *Democracy in America*, ed. by J. P. Mayer; trans. George Lawrence (New York: HarperCollins,1969).

12. Playing on locality and prejudice, it was hardly by accident that Reagan announced the beginning of his first presidential campaign in Philadelphia, Mississippi. Lee Atwater, who served as Reagan's campaign advisor, was the driving force of the Southern strategy.

13. Chief Justice Rehnquist (when he was not on the Court but a political activist) disdained the Civil Rights Act of 1964, claiming that it was unconstitutional. An exponent of states' rights, a term that had fallen out of favor except in the South, he reinforced the idea of uneven economic and social benefits between states, thereby constricting human rights.

14. John Rawls, *Political Liberalism* (New York: Columbia University Press, 1993); John Rawls, *Justice* (Cambridge: Harvard University Press, 1970).

15. In fact, quite the contrary in authoritarian democracies. Jacob L. Talmon, *Totalitarian Democracy and After,* Totalitarian Movements and Political Religions (Portland: Frank Cass, 2002).

16. R. H. S. Crossman, *Plato Today* (New York: Oxford University Press, 1939).

17. George Q. Flynn and Lewis B. Hershey, *Mr. Selective Service* (Chapel Hill: University of North Carolina Press, 1985).

18. This is discussed in an incisive essay by Arran Gare, "The Environmental Record of the Soviet Union," *Capitalism, Nature, Socialism* 13 (September 2002): 52.

19. Richard Falk, *This Endangered Planet* (New York: Random House, 1971).

20. Michael Pertschuk, *Revolt against Regulation, The Rise and Pause of the Consumer Movement* (Berkeley: University of California Press, 1982). The fight has been continuing and exhausting; the Republican Party and members of the business-minded Democratic Party align themselves with limp controls, if any, over basic industries even though these industries through lobbying shape the regulation.

CHAPTER 5

1. Arguably, under certain circumstances suicide was an exception according to the Greeks, but permission was still necessary from the polis.

2. The economics of the white South prior to the Civil War, and for years after, was predicated on the destruction of black families' patriarchy and stable property arrangements between white family members.

3. Carl Mannheim, *Ideology Utopia* (New York: Harvest Books, 1956).

4. Leon Trotsky, *Women in the Family* (New York: Pathfinder Press, 1973).

5. Even the Catholic Church, the bastion for the family, is no match for the liberalism of individual and market choice. While the church seeks to promote an anti-abortion stance, many of its followers weigh having children against the desire for consumer goods, which they learn about in the "desire confessional" of their own homes, where television gives the priestly command to buy and desire.

6. Ruth Rosen, *The World Split Open* (New York: Penguin Group, 2000).

7. For those more statistically minded, an average of 2.7 million cases of child abuse are reported from the family battleground each year. According to the Children's Defense Fund (Washington, D.C.) there are 1 million confirmed cases of child abuse and neglect and 3 million suspected cases annually.

8. Jerome S. Bernstein, "Piercing Our Unconscious," *CG Jung Page*, December 2, 2001, at www.cgjungpage.org/911bernstein.html (accessed June 24, 2002).

9. E. Robert Theobald, *Guaranteed Annual Income* (Garden City, N.Y.: Doubleday, 1966).

10. There is another interesting phenomenon. The Christian fundamentalists, Muslim fundamentalists, and the Catholic Church have joined together to thwart women's rights, namely, abortion rights.

11. Harold Laski, *The American Democracy* (New York: Simon & Schuster, 1948), 436.

12. Note Roosevelt's unsuccessful attempts to put a ceiling on net income at $25,000 a year during World War II. Roosevelt also opened the door to excess profits for defense and other corporations. He then found it impossible to close that door in favor of increased progressivity. Note David M. Kennedy, *Freedom from Fear* (New York: Oxford University Press, 1999).

13. William McNeill, *Plagues and People* (Garden City, N.Y.: Anchor Books, 1976), 236.

14. Part of the struggle of the Catholic Church on economic questions was carried out against left- and communist-led unions as well as Marxism, as has been the case with Opus Dei against liberation movements.

15. Hans Kung, *Does God Exist?* (Garden City, N.Y.: Doubleday, 1980), 229; Walter Rauschenbusch, *Christianity and the Social Crisis* (New York: Macmillan, 1920); and Ernst Bloch, A *Philosophy of the Future* (New York: Herder and Herder, 1970).

16. Phillip Green, *Equality and Democracy* (New York: New Press, 1998).

17. Nineteenth-century American attempts at communitarianism, such as the Oneida community, Brook Farm, and New Harmony, also fell to the exigencies of the market and their own attempts to hold together through a system of authority that wiped out any individual space.

18. Richard J. Herrnstein and Charles Murray, *The Bell Curve: Intelligence for Class Structure in American Life* (New York: Free Press, 1994).

19. Francis Fox Piven and Richard Cloward, *Regulating the Poor: The Functions of Public Welfare* (New York: Pantheon Books, 1971).

20. Talcott Parsons and Edward A. Shils, eds., *Toward a General Theory of Action* (Cambridge: Harvard University Press, 1954).

21. In the latter case the taxpayer paid for the aesthetic. While the Right concerned itself with killing off the National Endowment of the Arts, a liberal invention, because of performance art, it paid no attention to the fact that Lockheed, McDonnell Douglas, and other defense corporations were advertising their products with sleek ads and lobbying Congress and the public with tax-deductible dollars for weapons of war.

22. Quoted in Theodore von Laue, *The World Revolution of Westernization* (New York: Oxford University Press, 1987), 302. Also note, the 2002 UN World Summit on Sustainable Development in South Africa detailed increasing immiseration regarding world poverty, polluted air, and drinking water, as well as the geometric destruction of rain forests. This was referred to at that summit as an international system of global apartheid.

23. Editorial by economist columnist, *New York Times*, October 20, 2002.

CHAPTER 6

1. Fredrick Copleston, *A History of Philosophy,* vol. 5 (New York: Image Books, 1959).

2. Peter Kropotkin, *Mutual Aid* (New York: Alfred A. Knopf, 1916). Among egalitarian impulses the Universal Declaration of Human Rights recognizes that "everyone has a right to recognition everywhere as a person before the law" (Article 6) and that "everyone has duties to the community in which alone the free and full development of his personality possible" (Article 19). For a nineteenth-century perspective on these ideas, note the work of the neo-Kantian philosopher Hermann Cohen.

3. Implications of Lincoln's idea of government can be found in *Democracy in a World of Tensions* (Paris: UNESCO, 1951). The essays by Richard McKeon, G. Borghese, and Paul Sweezy debate the question of "by" and "for" the people.

4. Kropotkin, *Mutual Aid.*

5. Plato's *The Republic*, trans. by Raymond Larson (Arlington Heights, Ill.: AHM Publishing, 1979), Book 8. Aristotle, who felt more comfortable with democracy but nevertheless was an opponent of it, also made the point of the importance of social character reinforcing the nature of the state and vice versa.

6. Erich Fromm, *The Anatomy of Human Aggressiveness* (New York: Holt, Rinehart and Winston, 1971), 226.

7. William J. Bennett, *The Educated Child* (New York: Touchstone Books, 2000).

8. Fromm, *Anatomy of Human Aggressiveness*, 226.

9. Erich Fromm, *The Anatomy of Human Destructiveness* (New York: Holt, Rinehart & Winston, 1973), 349.

10. John R. Commons, *Legal Foundations of Capitalism* (Madison: University of Wisconsin, 1914).

11. Commons, *Legal Foundations of Capitalism*.

12. The right libertarian critique is articulated in Murray N. Rothbard, *For a New Liberty: A Libertarian Manifesto* (New York: Collier, 1978). The ecological attack is presented in Murray Bookchin, *The Ecology of Freedom* (Palo Alto, Calif.: Cheshire, 1982).

13. A valiant effort to break with a romantic, seemingly reactionary past was attempted in Germany between the two world wars. See Peter Gay, *Weimar Culture: The Outsider as Insider* (New York: Harper, 1968); and Maurice Baumont, J. H. E. Fried, and E. Vermeil, *The Third Reich* (New York: Praeger, 1955), 287–315. For a positive discussion of the community of belief as an insight into the cultural transformations of the 1960s, see Paul Goodman, *New Reformation: Notes of a Neolithic Conservative* (New York: Random House, 1970).

14. Notwithstanding its ameliorating conclusions, the Carnegie Corporation refused to follow through with any program grants that would put into practice the implications of the Myrdal study.

15. The traumatized technocrat McNamara stalked the world looking for redemption and posing his redemption as avoiding policy errors of future rulers through a series of technical fixes and "better" quantitative information. Robert S. McNamara, *In Retrospect: The Tragedy and Lessons of Vietnam* (New York: Times Books, 1995).

16. William James, *Varieties of Religious Experience* (New York: Longmans, 1902).

17. Lewis Mumford, *The City in History* (New York: Harcourt Brace, 1960), 232.

18. "Morals and the Political Order by John Dewey," *Ethics* 10 (1932): 343.

19. Ludwig Wittgenstein, *Tractatus Logico-Philosophicus* (London: Routledge, 1922); Ray Monk, *Ludwig Wittgenstein: The Duty of Genius* (New York: Free Press, 1990), 298–301, 484–86.

20. Laura Nader, *Naked Science* (New York: Routledge, 1993).

21. See Buck v. Bell, 274 U.S. 200 (1927).

22. Franklin Delano Roosevelt, address at San Diego Exposition, October 2, 1945.

23. Lawrence Levine, *The Opening of the American Mind* (Boston: Beacon Press, 1996).

24. Clark Kerr, *The Uses of the University*, 5th ed. (Cambridge: Harvard University Press, 1994).

25. Islamic nations and Hindu cultures older than the culture of the West are quick to point out that facts are not truths and that there are many realities, including reality of the spirit, which, they claim, manifests itself in community and tribe.

26. Marcus Raskin and Herbert J. Bernstein, *New Ways of Knowing* (Totowa, N.J.: Rowman & Littlefield, 1987).

27. Edward A. Ross, *Social Control* (New York: Macmillan, 1901).

28. A former acolyte of Dewey, Randolph Bourne was appalled at the way Dewey and his other students supported Wilson's First World War as an attack on German nationalism. Bourne understood the war as a betrayal of pragmatist principles in which

scientists and other technocrats would surrender concern for ends. Of course, this was hardly new, beginning with small pox infestations as "scientific" instruments of war, which came to fruition during the Cold War with special potions concocted by the CIA to support the "national interest." Of course, this is by no means an American problem alone, as we have seen from the work of Soviet scientists in biological warfare or the work of technologists from Iraq and Iran in Iraq using gas against the Kurds there.

29. Sakharov, the inventor of the Soviet H-bomb, was criticized by Dmitri Shostakovich, the great Russian composer, who said that he disliked scientists who handed the Devil (Stalin) the power to destroy the world and at night wrote against it. This style was common among American scientists.

30. 2002–2003 Federal Budget (Washington, D.C.: Government Printing Office, 2002).

31. A. J. Muste was the spiritual leader and editor of *Liberation Magazine,* which throughout the 1950s was an important journal of economics, nonviolence, and critical commentary,

32. Jacques Maritain, *The Person and the Common Good,* trans. John Fitzgerald (London: Geoffrey Bles, 1948); see also Gregory Baum, "An Ethical Critique of Capitalism," *Religion and Economic Justice,* ed. Michael Zweig (Philadelphia: Temple University Press, 1991), 78ff.

33. John Dewey, *The Quest for Certainty* (New York: Minton, Balch, 1929).

34. At a memorial service for McGeorge Bundy in New York I spoke with the late Nobel Prize winner James Tobin, who said that the economics of his generation and that of the New Deal were predicated on human betterment and caring for humanity as a whole: "I don't understand what happened. I don't recognize the profession. It is bloodless with no interest in making things better for humanity!"

CHAPTER 7

1. Francis Hutcheson, *An Essay on the Nature of Passions and Affections* (London: J. Darby and T. Brown, 1728).

2. Arnold Hauser, *The Social History of Art,* vol. 1 (New York: Vintage, 1951), 82.

3. Economists, who as Keynes pointed out, still don't have the skill and knowledge of dentists, act as advisors in the process of justification. What economists and businesspeople do is conjecture about the economy and their own guesses about it (expectations).

4. Vassily Leontieff's work, and from a different perspective, modeling, is an updated mathematicized form of Benjamin Franklin's work on adding as many positive and negative factors as one can think of.

5. Richard J. Barnet and John Cavanagh, *Global Dreams: Imperial Corporations and the New World Order* (New York: Simon & Schuster, 1994).

6. The United Nations Development Program (UNDP) 1998 *Human Development Report* cites striking figures of Western opulence and global misery: Americans spend $8 billion annually on cosmetics, which is $2 billion more than would be required to provide basic primary education for everyone in the world.

7. However, even bankers are showing concern about this freewheeling system. Note the Volker report on the importance of reining in "casino banking."

Testimony of Paul Volker before the Subcommittee on Economic Policy, July 5, 2001.

8. For a review of the Marxist analysis of the conundrum, see James O'Connor, *The Corporations and the State* (New York: Harper Books, 1975), 99–106.

9. As a means of defense, Americans call for simplified living as their corporate structures and modes of communication become more complex while their own lives become more dependent and alienated. The reality of insecurity is reinforced through the amounts of public or foundation funding given over to the creation of futuristic weapons, or advertising as against serious social research for comprehensive alternatives. This is even more true in the post–Cold War period than during the Cold War. Thus, it is important to reconsider the role of different forms of social research, such as economics, to relate its purpose to value considerations that are not adequately considered.

10. On comparative advantage, see David Ricardo, *The Worldly Philosophers* (London: Penguin, 2000).

11. Joseph E. Stiglitz, *Whither Socialism?* (Cambridge: MIT Press, 1994), 158.

12. Oskar Lange and Fred M. Taylor, *On the Economic Theory of Socialism*, ed. Benjamin E. Lippincott (New York: McGraw-Hill, 1964).

13. Juliet B. Schor, *The Overworked American: The Unexpected Decline of Leisure* (New York: Basic Books, 1991).

14. Seymour Melman, From Private to State Capitalism, address to the American Economic Association, New Orleans, December 1997.

15. William Cannon, former vice president of the University of Chicago and director of the Lyndon B. Johnson School of Public Policy, University of Texas, unpublished manuscript, 1980.

16. According to the Bureau of Labor Statistics report "Union Members in 2001," the unionization rate for the U.S. labor force stood at 13.5 percent in both 2000 and 2001, after a decline that brought it down from a high of 20.1 percent in 1983. Available at www.bls.gov.

17. Schumpeter underscored the importance of entrepreneurship as a set of personal qualities—initiative, leadership, etc.—for innovation and capitalist development in *The Theory of Economic Development: An Inquiry into Profits, Capital, Credit, Interest, and the Business Cycle*, trans. Redvers Opie (New Brunswick, N.J.: Transaction Books, 1983). Schumpeter also held that capitalism and rationality were inseparable.

18. Ralph Estes, *Tyranny of the Bottom Line* (San Francisco: Berrett-Koehler, 2000).

19. Scott Buchanan, *So Reason Can Rule: Reflections in Law and Politics* (New York: Farrar, Straus & Giroux, 1982).

20. Ralph Nader, Mark Green, and Joel Seligman, *Taming the Giant Corporation* (New York: Norton, 1976); Marcus G. Raskin, *Being and Doing* (New York: Random House, 1971), 85–93.

21. Nader, Green, and Seligman, *Taming the Giant Corporation*.

22. Although in the wake of corporate scandals Congress voted a substantial increase in the budget of the Securities and Exchange Commission (SEC) for fiscal year 2003–2004, between 1995 and 1998 the SEC budget grew slower than inflation, a period in which corporations continued their unfettered ways, laying the groundwork for future turmoil.

23. Reeves, Inc v. Stake et al., 447 U.S. 429 (1980).

24. Roy Morrison, *Ecological Democracy* (Boston: South End Press, 1995).

25. The words *sector* and *zone* are used here interchangeably.

26. William Appleman Williams, "Large Corporations and American Foreign Policy," in *History as a Way of Learning* (New York: New Viewpoints, 1973), 271.

27. Rigorous public participation requires that Congress extend its authority through the congressional jury system. Marcus Raskin, *Notes on the Old System* (New York: David McKay, 1974), 65–94.

28. Murray Bookchin and Dave Freeman, *Defending the Earth, A Dialogue between Murray Bookchin and Dave Freeman* (Boston: South End Press, 1991), which in stark terms argues for face-to-face communities that are both libertarian and socialist in nature.

29. John Kenneth Galbraith, *Affluent Society* (Boston: Houghton Mifflin, 1958).

30. A consideration of some importance is the investments and holdings of family fortunes where a family, through its collective investments and its managers and retainers, is able to guide decisions in the economic, social, and political spheres in such a manner as to defeat democracy and increase its own standing as part of, or more powerful than, the run-of-the-mill oligarchy. Institute for Policy Studies, Report on Selection of Vice President Nelson Rockefeller, 1974.

31. According to the *Statistical Abstract of the United States: 2001*, 121st ed., in 2000, government employment exceeded manufacturing employment and stood at 20,572,000 people, or roughly 15.7 percent of total nonfarm employment. That does not include the millions of employees at defense companies, which produce primarily for government contracts.

32. *Common Good*, 154.

33. The American Society of Civil Engineers issued a report card on the nation's infrastructure in 2001, giving it a cumulative grade of D+. Its estimate is that $1.3 trillion is needed in the next five years for proper modernization of the infrastructure. See "Statement of the American Society of Civil Engineers on the Federal Role in Meeting Infrastructure Needs before the Subcommittee on Transportation and Infrastructure Committee on Environment and Public Works," U.S. Senate, 108th Cong., 1st sess., July 23, 2001.

34. Adam Hochschild, *King Leopold's Ghost: A Story of Greed, Terror, and Heroism in Colonial Africa* (Boston: Houghton Mifflin, 1998).

35. Claude G. Bowers, *Beveridge and the Progressive Era* (Cambridge, Mass.: Houghton Mifflin, 1932).

36. Robert A. Caro, *Master of the Senate: The Years of Lyndon Johnson* (New York: Alfred A. Knopf, 2002).

37. The issue of America's dependence on foreign raw materials was first explored in the 1950s by the Paley Commission, summoned by President Dwight Eisenhower. See President's Materials Policy Commission, *Resources for Freedom: A Report to the President*, 5 vols. (Washington, D.C.: Government Printing Office, 1952).

38. Hochschild, *King Leopold's Ghost*.

39. George Soros, *Open Society: Reforming Global Capitalism* (New York: Public Affairs, 2000), 171–72.

40. Note the case of Salvador Allende in Chile. The Allende government found that it was not able to borrow on the international markets because of U.S. pressure on the World Bank and International Monetary Fund. This activity of the Nixon government was complemented by covert quasi-military actions, initiated by the CIA.

41. Sarah Anderson, John Cavanagh, et al., *Field Guide to the Global Economy* (New York: New Press, 2000). Note also the Hague Appeal for Peace, organized as a transnational organization by Cora Weiss to study and act on questions having to do with root causes of war, disarmament, and global security.

CHAPTER 8

1. See Oswald Spengler, *Man and Technics: A Contribution to a Philosophy of Life* (New York: Alfred A. Knopf, 1932).

2. J. D. Bernal, *Science in History*, vols. 1 and 2 (Cambridge: MIT Press, 1971).

3. Upton Sinclair, *The Jungle* (New York: Doubleday, 1906). Kefauver hearings on pharmaceutical industry, Senate Anti-trust Committee, 85th Cong., 1957–1959.

4. See Warren Buffet, op-ed., *New York Times*, July 23, 2002.

5. When the American Enterprise Institute launched its bimonthly journal *Regulation* in July 1977, its editor, Anne Brunsdale, wrote in her introduction, "We are committed . . . to the ideal that this regulation should be sensible, cost-efficient, and as unburdensome as the nature of its objectives will allow" ([July/August 1977]: 2). The premier issue included pieces by Irving Kristol and Antonin Scalia.

6. See www.whistleblower.org/www/hanford.htm for the Government Accountability Project's nuclear safety oversight program.

7. Richard E. Sclove, *Democracy and Technology* (New York: Guilford Press, 1995).

8. Beginning with Thucydides, historians such as Edward Gibbon, Arnold Toynbee, Oswald Spengler, and Paul Kennedy have emphasized in their work the decline of empire.

9. Lawrence H. Tribe, *American Constitutional Law*, 2d ed. (Mineola, N.Y.: Foundation Press, 1988).

10. Nicholas Negroponte, *Being Digital* (New York: Vintage Books, 1996).

11. But there is more. Insecurity in jobs became a necessary complement to the bottom line. In the 1990s business managers and their human resources professors in business schools warned that people should forget about having a lifetime job with security. That was not the new wave of a growing society. Instead, a person should expect to have five or six different jobs in his or her life, not for reasons of happiness and security—quite the reverse. The reasons were to be related to the "demands" of the market, and a weird kind of competition in interbusiness struggle, which, like politics itself, is prone to paranoia. Paradoxically, the more a particular firm's management fears its competitors, the more likely oligopoly and then monopoly will result in any particular market.

12. John Dewey, *The Public and Its Problems* (New York: Henry Holt, 1927).

CHAPTER 9

1. These changes can be seen in surprising ways through intermarriage across religion and race. While respect for differences exists, each grouping borrows from

the other in unique ways, whether it is food, music, or sports. Bagels, pizza, mushi beef, tortillas, and pita are becoming food staples. The young golfing prodigy, Tiger Woods, who claims Thai, African American, and European ancestry, and the winner of the Cliburn competition, Jon Nakamatsu, who was born in Hawaii of parents from Okinawa and grandparents from Japan, are both American. The tendency to romanticize about the American dream is great. The reality is explored with insight and depth in Paul Jacobs and Saul Landau, *To Serve the Devil* (New York: Random House, 1971).

2. In some cases political struggles over homelands continued within the United States, as was the case with many Cuban exiles in the Castro era.

3. John Dewey, *Democracy and Education: An Introduction to the Philosophy of Education* (New York: Macmillan, 1916), 21.

4. Alexis de Tocqueville, *Democracy in America,* vol. 1 (New York: Harper-Collins, 1960), 316–39.

5. Benjamin Franklin viewed the Iroquois nations as having set forth a constitution that rivaled eighteenth-century European documents and ancient ones as well.

6. Page Smith points out that one purpose of the Lewis and Clark expeditions was to keep peace between various Native American tribes. Page Smith, *The Shaping of America: A People's History of the Young Republic,* vol. 3 (New York: McGraw-Hill, 1980), 510–29. Also noted in the commission by Thomas Jefferson to Lewis and Clark legitimating their expedition as state policy.

7. Judith Nies, *Native American History* (New York: Ballantine, 1996).

8. For example, the mixed and then dismal record of the Republican senator from Washington, Slade Gordon, from 1981 to 1987 and 1989 to 2001. He sought to narrow the rights of Native Americans and their access and control over resources on Native American-reserved territory, particularly in his second term.

9. W. E. B. DuBois, *Souls of Black Folk* (New York: Penguin Books, 1982); "The Vanishing Black Family: Crisis in Black America," January 25, 1986, CBS television reports.

10. Contrary to dominant stereotypes of the twentieth century, black families were always the first to share, to adopt children, and to answer charitable appeals. According to DuBois this was true in the nineteenth century as well. James Garrett, "Draft for Encyclopedia of Social Reconstruction" (IPS papers, 1972, unpublished).

11. Too many Americans pride themselves on forgetting the past, as they laud the new racism and color blindness, with a canon of beliefs meant to comfort whites. While enjoying the fruits of privilege from an apartheid past, whites claim they have transcended past evils, yet there is no interest in compensating any blacks for slavery and the internal colonial system, which existed at least until 1965. (It should be noted that 1966 was the first free election in the United States in which blacks had the chance to vote across the nation somewhat free of intimidation. But as the presidential election of 2000 showed, structural and mechanical voting inequity remained, with different older voting machines retained in poor neighborhoods.)

12. At the end of the twentieth century Chinese and Japanese students seemed to score better than any other group on standardized tests.

13. Edward A. Purcell, *The Crisis of Democratic Theory* (Lexington: University Press of Kentucky, 1973), 100.

14. One need only point to Sarajevo and other cities in the Balkans where people of different religions lived next to each other, intermarried, and tolerated differences for generations until the collapse of Yugoslavia. The virus of a virulent nationalism was united in its several republics with severe economic underdevelopment and premature diplomatic recognition of the several states, notably Croatia, by Germany. Multiculturalism had little chance just as it has little chance where there are oppressed peoples such as the untouchables in India. It is only possible where there is recognition of political equality and economic justice within a framework of an inclusive democracy.

15. Admittedly the word "countenance" has deep legal ramifications, carrying with it notions of punishment. It can be tolerated so long as it does not reemerge as the dominant feature of American society. In *Rethinking the American Race Problem,* Roy L. Brooks (Berkeley: University of California Press, 1990) presents a succinct analysis of a positive but limited role that the federal government can play in ameliorating economic and social problems of race. He places emphasis on "opportunity," a hope of the Great Society. But opportunity by its very nature does not change underlying systemic problems, which alone cannot be dealt with through social absorption of the few into the middle class. It is important to note that the entire affirmative action debate on all sides assumes limited access on a variety of grounds. See Regents of the University of California v. Bakke, 438 U.S. 265 (1978).

16. It was not only through the popular newspaper, Julius Streicher's *Der Sturmer,* that anti-Semitism was spread. It found its home in the Lutheran and Catholic churches. Philosophy played its role also; see Hans Sluga, *Heidegger's Crisis* (Berkeley: University of California, 1998). One important forerunner of Hitler's racist theories was the racist writer Houston Chamberlain; see "From the Year 1200 to the Year 1800," in *Foundations of the Nineteenth Century,* vol. 2 (New York: John Lane, 1910), 187–232.

17. Because nineteenth-century imperialism was integrally linked to racial superiority, according to Martin Bernal the downgrading of cultural influences from black Africa that found their way into the Middle East was an imperial requirement. These influences were erased from the historical map in favor of an imperial rendition of "Western civilization," which started with Athens and Rome. Martin Bernal, *Black Athena* (Ithaca, N.Y.: Cornell University Press, 1992).

18. Compare this policy to the important work of University of Minnesota researchers at the Center for Restorative Justice and Peacemaking. An African American male living in the United States may expect to be more likely to go to prison than college. There are over two million people in prison. Over half are African Americans. African Americans can expect to go to prison at at least twenty-five times the rate of the population as a whole. These figures are abstracted and updated from Tony Monteiro, "The New Face of Racism," *Peace Review* 6, no. 2 (Summer 1994): 139.

19. USA Patriot Act 2001, Public Law 56, 107th Cong., 1st sess., October 26, 2001.

20. The claims of national and internal security made by Attorney General John Ashcroft for plenary powers to overrule constitutional and criminal law guarantees have even offended a secret federal court that meets without witnesses and in camera. It stated that the Justice Department (the FBI especially) was out of control during the Clinton and second Bush administrations.

21. Ernst Friedrich Schumacher, *Small Is Beautiful: Economics As If People Mattered* (New York: Harper, 1973).

22. Schumacher, *Small Is Beautiful.* But note that any of the types of "civilization" are predicated on ensuring an end to the war system and imperialism. Whether it is anarcracy, a return to village life, or participatory democracy, any political form that begins from the assumption of human liberation and affection cannot escape the detritus of the twentieth century: disease, poverty, war, malnutrition, and environmental devastation.

23. In the Bakke case, universities and colleges were stopped from setting up programs that would ensure that a specific number of black applicants would be accepted if they qualified according to the university and college standards.

24. By which I mean the use of one person by another without recompense, dignity, or human rights.

25. To this end the United States argued that it would have to strip the British Empire of its colonial possessions.

26. There is a legitimation process that axialist civil servants formulate or use as public justification for their acts. They locate "parchment" language for these values in the resolutions and various human rights charters crafted since the Second World War. How the ideals of parchment language are to be translated into practice is the project of the twenty-first century.

CHAPTER 10

1. David F. Noble, *Digital Diploma Mills: The Automation of Higher Education* (New York: New York University Press, 2001); Christopher Simpson, ed., *Universities and Empire* (New York: New Press, 1998).

2. Morton G. White, *Pragmatism and the American Mind: Essays and Reviews in Philosophy and Intellectual History* (New York: Oxford University Press, 1973).

3. According to the website at www.1-teenage-suicide.com/, youth suicide rates have tripled since 1970, and suicide is now the second cause of death among college students after accidents. Every 1.75 hours another young person commits suicide.

4. Paul Goodman, *New Reformation: Notes of a Neolithic Conservative* (New York: Random House, 1970).

5. Lawrence Levine, *The Opening of the American Mind: Canons, Culture, and History* (Boston: Beacon Press, 1996).

6. This problem was of special concern to Dewey, Thomas Nagel, and other American philosophers.

7. What liberal arts and Western civilization meant at Columbia University, which emphasized pluralist values, seemed diametrically opposed to the University of Chicago's Leo Strauss and much of the Great Books program, which sat at the feet of absolutism and transcendent truth. Note also Max Horkheimer, *Eclipse of Reason* (New York: Seabury Press, 1974).

8. Alexander Meiklejohn, *The Experimental College* (New York: Arno Press, 1971).

9. Relativism was to be tethered through science, and notably physics, which was understood to be the very building block of the universe, from the atom to the

galaxy. On the other hand, the twentieth century, as a result of the influence of Heidegger, questioned the very nature of rationality and reason, putting in its place patriotic fervor and belief in the Leader Principle. This pernicious development can be seen in the organizing of national patriotism, where critical or dissenting or alternative views are silenced throughout the society. Although less so at the university, attempts at "silencing" are made, and they are successful. In this sense the shadow of authoritarianism is always present and in different guises.

10. Mortimer J. Adler and Milton Mayer, *Revolution in Education* (Chicago: University of Chicago Press, 1958).

11. Harvard University Report on Undergraduate Education, 1949.

12. Alfred Jospe, *Studies in Jewish Thought* (Detroit: Wayne State University Press, 1981), 135.

13. Christopher Jencks and David Riesman, *The Academic Revolution* (Garden City, N.Y.: Doubleday, 1968). Derek C. Bok, *Beyond the Ivory Tower: Social Responsibilities of the Modern University* (Cambridge: Harvard University Press, 1982).

14. Alfred North Whitehead, *Adventures of Ideas,* ed. Alfred W. J. Harper (New York: Mekler & Deahl, 1934, 1985).

15. Marcus Raskin, *Being and Doing* (New York: Random House, 1971).

16. After all, this was Plato's method and purpose in *The Republic.* Apparently he meant his "Utopia" to be based on education and stability for the return of the aristocracy. However, in modern democracy education is of course also central. Democracy of the kind reflected in American thought and practice assumed that education was the alternative to violence. Surely democratic education means the use of inquiry and commonly shared knowledge (comprehending the ought in the is) as alternatives to propaganda and advertising manipulation. With the skills and the development of organizational structures, and with demands made on existing institutions such as schools, adult education programs, colleges, and universities, democracy can be more than a rhetorical flag.

17. The National Institute of Science and Art was formed in 1794 with this purpose. Sanford Lakoff, *Knowledge and Power* (New York: The Free Press, 1966), 1–65.

18. Karl Marx and Friedrich Engels, *The Communist Manifesto* (New York: Penguin Papers, 1848).

19. Hilary Putnam points out that Charles Peirce preceded Popper with the idea that the researcher's task was to seek falsifying experiences. Hilary Putnam, *Words and Life,* ed. James Conant (Cambridge: Harvard University Press, 1995).

20. Nelson Mandela, *Long Walk to Freedom: The Autobiography of Nelson Mandela* (New York: Little, Brown, 1995).

21. David Cortright, *Soldiers in Revolt* (Garden City, N.Y.: Anchor, 1975).

22. David Childs, *Germany in the Twentieth Century* (New York: Harper-Collins, 1991).

23. Marcus Raskin, *Visions and Revisions: Reflections on Culture and Democracy at the End of the Century* (New York: Olive Branch Press, 1995).

24. Jefferson's chilling words continue to vibrate in the residue of American fantasy and social reality. Films such as *The Rock* reflect Jefferson's feelings; a marine hero general with his cohort seeks to right the wrongs done to dead soldiers and

their families by threatening the civilian population with nuclear weapons unless their demands are met. The hero manqué introduces Jefferson's words as a defense of nuclear destruction, just as was done by the "responsible" leaders of the Soviet Union and the United States during the Cold War.

25. Mary King, *Gandhi and King* (Geneva: United Nations University, 2002); Raskin, *Being and Doing*. Beyond the historical role of the Quakers in nonviolence and pacifism in general, dozens of courses emerged in conflict resolution and peace studies centers at universities, albeit underfunded and usually having marginal status. The assumption of most university courses in international affairs is that there is no way to escape the war system and acting as the dominating nation through force of arms.

CHAPTER 11

1. Marcus Raskin, *Visions and Revisions: Reflections on Culture and Democracy at the End of the Century* (New York: Olive Branch Press, 1996), 314. For a perceptive account of Machiavelli's hatred of the corrupt and the need to favor a universal humanity, see *Niccolo's Smile*, by Maurizio Vivilo (New York: Hill and Wang, 1998).

2. William Bennett, *Why We Fight* (New York: Doubleday, 2002).

3. Throughout the twentieth century liberation movements were opportunistic, turning for aid to any nation that would give it with the fewest strings attached.

4. Truman Statement on Fundamentals of American Foreign Policy, *Department of State Bulletin* 13, October 27, 1945, 653.

5. Jean-Paul Sartre, preface to *The Wretched of the Earth*, by Frantz Fanon, trans. Constance Farrington (New York: Grove Press, 1963), 7–34; and Frantz Fanon, "Concerning Violence," in *The Wretched of the Earth*, 35–106.

6. Who could forget, for example, the signal contributions of Marcos in the Philippines, Diem of South Vietnam, Suharto of Indonesia, Mobutu of Zaire, and many others.

7. Richard McKeon, ed., *Democracy in a World of Tensions: A Symposium Prepared by UNESCO* (Chicago: University of Chicago Press, 1951).

8. William James, "The Moral Equivalent of War," in *The Moral Equivalence of War and Other Essays and Selections from Some Problems on Philosophy*, ed. John K. Roth (New York: Harper Torchbooks, 1971), 3–16; Mary King, *Mahatma Gandhi and Martin Luther King* (Paris: UNESCO Publishing, 1999); Gene Sharp, *The Politics of Nonviolent Action* (Boston: Porter Sargent, 1973).

9. Elias Canetti, *Crowds and Power*, trans. Carol Stewart (New York: Viking Press, 1962).

10. Raul Hilberg, *The Destruction of the European Jews*, 3 vols. (New York: Holmes & Meier, 1985).

11. Ernst Nolte, *Three Faces of Fascism* (New York: Henry Holt, 1966). The story of the rather willing, albeit fraught with complexity, acceptance of the Nazi regime and its murderous ideology by the esteemed German philosophical community is told in Hans Sluga, *Heidegger's Crisis: Philosophy and Politics in Nazi Germany* (Cambridge: Harvard University Press, 1993).

12. Churchill had very warm words to say about the Italian fascism of Mussolini as an antidote to Leninism when he visited Italy in 1926. He reaffirmed his adoration for Mussolini and his regime in 1935. See Robert R. James, *Churchill: A Study in Failure 1900–1939* (New York: World Publishing Company, 1970), 285.

13. George Washington's farewell address after his second term as president. Marcus Raskin, "Presidential Disrespect," www.ips=dc.org (1996).

14. For a discussion of how World War II precipitated a large-scale capital transfer from public hands to big corporations, see Gabriel Kolko, *Century of War: Politics, Conflict and Society since 1914* (New York: New Press, 1994), 79–82.

15. See Robert E. Osgood, "The Korean War," in *Limited War: The Challenge to American Strategy* (Chicago: University of Chicago Press, 1957), 163–93.

16. Tens of thousands of American soldiers suffered a mysterious unidentified disease syndrome probably as a result of drugs taken as an antisepsis against chemical and biological warfare.

17. One may note that the nuclear freeze movement of the 1980s had great popular support, but once the nuclear freeze passed through the maw of the national security state apparatus and Congress, the popular movement became housebroken and irrelevant.

18. See the UN International Covenant on Economic, Social and Cultural Rights, appendix B.

19. "The Movement of Persons across Borders," in *Studies in International Legal Policy*, ed. Louis Sohn and Thomas Buergenthal (Washington, D.C.: American Society of International Law, 1992), 121–22.

20. Richard McKeon, *Philosophy, Science and Culture*, vol. 1 (Berkeley: University of California Press, 2000), 456.

21. UN Conference on Environment and Development, Rio de Janeiro, June 3–14, 1992 (the "earth summit").

22. Note codes of conduct prepared and negotiated by the nongovernmental organization the International Labor Rights Fund for factories owned by American multinational corporations, including "suppliers." The corporations that negotiated this arrangement for doing business in China include Levi, Liz Claiborne, Phillip Van Huesen, Gear for Sports, Adidas, Reebok, and Nike.

23. Some few were members of the Pugwash group started at the height of the Cold War by pacific-minded scientists from the United States and the Soviet Union under the impetus of Cyrus Eaton, Joseph Rotblat, and Bertrand Russell.

24. For an understanding of the young physicists involved in the SDI project, see William J. Broad, *Star Warriors* (New York: Simon & Schuster, 1985). As of 1999, Frances Fitzgerald completes the journalistic account of policy and scientific failure in *Way Out There in the Blue* (New York: Touchstone Books, 2001).

25. Such ideas are clothed in the rhetoric of triumphal democracy made popular by neoconservatives such as the former Democratic advisor Richard Perle and columnist George Will, who joined with Vice President Dick Cheney. When Cheney was in Congress, he was the leader of the arch-conservative wing of the Republican Party.

26. Noam Chomsky, *World Orders, Old and New* (New York: Columbia University Press, 1994); Central Intelligence Agency, *Global Trends, 2015* (Langley, Va.: CIA, 2000). With the election of Jimmy Carter to the presidency, his first secretary of state, Cyrus Vance, enunciated the fundamental role of corporations in American

foreign and economic policy. He resigned when the United States, under the tutelage of National Security Advisor Zbigneiw Brzezinski, favored force as the primary instrument of American foreign policy. Vance was an interesting man who believed in arms control, viewed war as irrational, and thought the American state's relationship to the Third World, its responsiveness, would reflect or deny the nation's moral purpose. Vance resigned immediately after the failed military attempt to rescue the American hostages at the U.S. embassy in Iran. Vance said the mission would fail. When he was overruled by Carter, Vance said that such an attempted military incursion would fail and continue to damage the national interests of the United States in the Middle East. It is worth noting that the U.S. focus on oil during the Carter administration did not take seriously the Soviet concern about Islam fundamentalism, which the United States sought to use as an ideological instrument against the Soviet Union. Cyrus Vance, *Hard Choices* (New York: Simon & Schuster, 1983).

27. This can be seen when comparing oil and gas prices in other nations using Middle East oil to U.S. bills for oil.

28. There is an exception in which Nelson Rockefeller argued that the UN charter recognized Latin America as within the United States' sphere of influence.

29. Each nation, for example, was to have at least one detachment of troops on the front lines facing Eastern Europe, so that if a war did occur each nation's forces would be in harm's way and therefore committed to fight.

30. Struggles between the various national security and defense agencies continued throughout the Cold War.

31. But these movements carried an unwanted passenger in their bags, that of the unrestrained free market, which brought the picaro to the fore.

32. Not many know the recent history of Afghan–U.S. relations. Committed to anticommunism at all costs, the United States objected to rapprochement between the social reformist King Daoad and the Soviet Union.

CHAPTER 12

1. For example, the nuclear test ban treaty covering the atmosphere and under water; the Antarctica treaty creating a nuclear-free zone, and the nonproliferation treaty. Note especially Article 6 of the Nonproliferation Treaty ratified by the U.S. Senate in 1970. For a complete listing of relevant disarmament treaties, see Marcus Raskin, *Essays of a Citizen* (Armonk, N.Y.: Sharpe, 1991), Article 9, 235–36.

2. Note the Soviet and American proposals of 1962, the Forsberg proposal, and a comprehensive treaty proposal by this author in *Abolishing the War System* (Amherst, Mass.: Alethia Press, 1992).

3. Note proposals made by the late professor James Tobin in 1978. James Tobin, "A Proposal for International Monetary Reform," *Eastern Economic Journal* 4 (1978): 153–59. Former undersecretary-general of the UN, Brian Urquhart, discussion of future responsibilities of the UN, found in *New York Review* 1993, 1994.

4. The 2003 aid and assistance budget given to developing nations by the United States is .07 percent of its annual budget. This is somewhat more than the Clinton administration provided for aid purposes. American aid is conditioned on adopting a "free market" economy. It should be noted that the idea of an

international disarmament program that would result in the savings that would find their way into poor nations never got beyond the so-called talking stages. Peace dividends have not fared well internationally or domestically under the power politics paradigm of international affairs.

5. Janine Weidel, *Collision ND Collusion: The Strange Case of East Europe* (New York: Palgrave, 2001).

6. By authority I mean that power legitimately borrowed by government or its agents, who may call in their "political loans" at will, for short periods of time from the sovereign people.

7. However imperfect the mechanism and the ambivalent attitude of the United States in terms of establishing an international criminal court, virtually all nations accept the Nuremberg standards and the UN authorization to bring cases against alleged war criminals. Note the Nuremberg and Asian war crime trials, and recently the UN-authorized trial of Slobodan Milosevich for war crimes.

8. Note the yearly studies of the Swedish International Peace Research Institute during the Cold War, available at www.sipri.se.

9. Alfred North Whitehead, *The Adventure of Ideas* (New York: Macmillan, 1933).

10. The attacks on Pearl Harbor, New York, and the Pentagon add weight to this statement, but when they are fought it should be done with tenacity and the wholehearted support of the citizenry.

11. This method seems inherently unstable, for no nation has been able to govern or guide all others for very long unless it controls the economic and military system of the alliance members.

12. See chapter 3 for comments on the New Left.

13. Hundreds of books and thousands of articles were written during the Cold War on the question of defense and how to fight a nuclear war. Two important books of that period asserted the possibility of fighting a strategic nuclear war: *On Thermonuclear War*, by Herman Kahn (New York: Praeger, 1965), and *Nuclear Weapons and Foreign Policy*, by Henry Kissinger (Garden City, N.Y.: Doubleday Anchor, 1957). With other such books pretending to rationality becomes a demonic activity. For further study on war, see Barbara Ehrenreich, *Blood Rites: Origins and History of the Passions of War* (New York: Henry Holt, 1998).

14. Carol Gilligam, *In a Different Voice* (Cambridge: Harvard University Press, 1982).

15. One brilliant recent exception is Hazel O'Leary, who as the secretary of energy insisted that the Department of Energy make information publicly available about the massive poisoning of American citizens as a result of U.S. nuclear experiments. She was forced to resign.

16. J. Glenn Gray, *The Warriors: Reflections of Men in Battle* (New York: Harper & Row, 1970).

17. Frantz Fanon, *Studies in a Dying Colonialism* (New York: Monthly Review Press, 1962); Kwame Nkrumah, *Neocolonialism* (New York: International Publishers, 1966). An interesting discussion of how anthropologists viewed the Other before the New Left critique can be found in an essay by Kathleen Gough in *The Dissenting Academy*, ed. Theodore Roszak (New York: Pantheon, 1968), 135. But also note the disarray and chaos that have gripped Africa, South Asia, and the Middle

East, caught between the free market, starvation, and environmental degradation, where cleptocracy, ethnic rivalry, and absolutism are found in abundance. Robert D. Kaplan, *The Ends of the Earth* (New York: Random House, 1997).

18. Perhaps new political forms beyond democracy will evolve as technology expands and transforms both the public and private spaces of people into face-to-face units, anarcracies, which are self-defining, recognizing new communities beyond the nation-state and global corporation. But even such cases will be only a variant of democracy and a democratic spirit.

Bibliography

Allen, Robert L. *The Port Chicago Mutiny*. New York: Warner Books, 1989.

Althusser, Louis. "Ideology and Ideological State Apparatuses." In *Lenin and Philosophy and Other Essays*, trans. Dan Brewster. New York: Monthly Review Press, 1972.

Anderson, Sarah, et al. *Field Guide to the Global Economy*. New York: New Press, 2000.

Archer, Jules. *The Plot to Seize the White House*. New York: Hawthorne Books, 1973.

Arendt, Hannah. *On Revolution*. New York: Viking Press, 1963.

Barnet, Richard J., and John Cavanagh. *Global Dreams: Imperial Corporations and the New World Order*. New York: Simon & Schuster, 1994.

Barzun, Jaques. *A Stroll with William James*. Chicago: University of Chicago Press, 1983.

Baum, Gregory. "An Ethical Critique of Capitalism: Contributions of Modern Catholic Social Teaching." In *Religion and Economic Justice*, ed. Michael Zweig. Philadelphia: Temple University Press, 2002.

Beale, Howard K. *Theodore Roosevelt and the Rise of America to World Power*. Baltimore: Johns Hopkins Press, 1956.

Beard, Charles A., and Mary R. Beard. *The Rise of American Civilization*. New York: Macmillan, 1934.

Bellah, Robert. *The Broken Covenant: American Civil Religion in the Time of Trial*. New York: Sudbury Press, 1975.

Beyer, Landon E., and Michael W. Apple, eds. *The Curriculum: Problems, Politics and Possibilities*. Albany: State University of New York Press, 1988.

Birnbaun, Norman. *After Progress: American Social Reform and European Socialism in the Twentieth Century*. New York: Oxford University Press, 2001.

Bluestone, Barry, and Bennett Harrison. *The Deindustrialization of America*. New York: Basic Books, 1982.

Blum, John Morton. "The Price of a Vision: Henry A. Wallace." In *Liberty, Justice, Order: Essays on Past Politics*. New York: Norton, 1993.

Blumenthal, Sidney, and Thomas B. Edsall, eds. *The Reagan Legacy*. New York: Pantheon Books, 1998.

Bok, Derek C. *Beyond the Ivory Tower: Social Responsibilities of the Modern University*. Cambridge: Harvard University Press, 1982.

Bookchin, Murray. *The Ecology of Freedom*. Palo Alto, Calif.: Cheshire, 1982.

Boot, Matt. *The Savage Wars of Peace: Small Wars and the Rise of American Power*. New York: Basic Books, 2002.

Bork, Robert. *Slouching towards Gomorrah: Modern Liberalism and American Decline*. New York: Reagan Books, 1996.

Bowers, Claude G. *Beveridge and the Progressive Era*. Cambridge, Mass.: Houghton Mifflin, 1932.

Branch, Taylor. *Parting the Waters: America in the King Years: 1954–63*. New York: Simon & Schuster, 1988.

"Brando Has Long Backed Rights of Racial Minorities." *New York Times*, March 29, 1973.

Braudel, Fernand. *The Wheels of Commerce*. New York: Harper & Collins, 1983.

Broad, Robin, ed. *Global Backlash: Citizen Initiatives for a Just World Economy*. *New Millenium Books in International Studies*. Lanham, Md.: Rowman & Littlefield, 2002.

Brown, Dee Alexander. *Bury My Heart at Wounded Knee: An American History of the American West*. New York: Holt, Rinehart & Winston, 1970.

Browning, Frank, and John Gerassi. *The American Way of Crime*. New York: Putnam, 1980.

Bryson, Lyman, Louis Finkelstein, and Robert MacIver, eds. *Approaches to National Unity; Fifth Symposium*. (Conference on Science, Philosophy, and Religion in Their Relation to the Democratic Way of Life [Columbia University, 1944]). New York: Harper, 1945.

Buber, Martin. *I and Thou*. 2d ed. Trans. by R. G. Smith. New York: Charles Scribner's Sons, 1958.

———. *Paths in Utopia*. London: Routledge & Kegan Paul, 1949.

Buchanan, Scott. *So Reason Can Rule: Reflection on Law and Politics*. New York: Farrar, Straus & Giroux, 1982.

Bullock, Adam. *Hitler and Stalin*. New York: Alfred A. Knopf, 1992.

Bundy, McGeorge. *Danger and Survival: Choices about the Bomb in the First Fifty Years*. New York: Random House, 1988.

Cannon, William B. "The Dangerous Abuse of the Lower Class." Unpublished manuscript, Austin, Texas, 1977.

Cassidy, Kevin J., and Gregory A. Bischak. *Real Security: Converting the Defense Economy and Building Peace*. Albany: State University of New York Press, 1993.

Cassirer, Ernst. *Myth of the State*. New Haven, Conn.: Yale University Press, 1946.

Catton, Bruce. *War Lords of Washington*. New York: Harcourt Brace, 1946.

Chamberlain, Houston. "From the Year 1200 to the Year 1800." In *Foundations of the Nineteenth Century*, vol. 2, trans. John Lees. New York: John Lane, 1910.

Childs, David. *History of Germany in the Twentieth Century.* New York: Icon Editions, 1991.

Chomsky, Noam. *American Power and the New Mandarins.* New York: Pantheon Books, 1967.

———. *Necessary Illusions: Thought Control in Democratic Societies.* Boston: South End Press, 1989.

———. *Problems of Knowledge and Freedom.* New York: Pantheon Books, 1971.

Cohen, Joshua, Joel Rogers, and Phillip Green. *Retrieving Democracy.* Totowa, N.J.: Rowman & Allanheld, 1985.

Cohen, Morris Raphael. *The Faith of a Liberal: Selected Essays by Morris Raphael Cohen.* New York: Henry Holt, 1946.

Commons, John R. *The Economics of Collective Action.* New York: Macmillan, 1950.

Cortright, David. *Soldiers in Revolt: The American Military Today.* Garden City, N.Y.: Anchor, 1975.

Craig, Gordon A., and Alexander L. George, " Balance of Power: 1815–1914: Three Experiments." In *Force and Statecraft: Diplomatic Problems of Our Time,* 2d ed. New York: Oxford University Press, 1990.

Davis, David. *The Problem of Slavery in the Age of Revolution, 1770–1823.* Ithaca, N.Y.: Cornell University Press, 1975.

De Felice, Renzo. *Fascism: An Informal Introduction to Its Theory and Practice.* Brunswick, N.J.: Transaction Books, 1976.

DeLong, James V. *Property Matters.* New York: The Free Press, 1997.

Dewey, John. *Democracy and Education: An Introduction to the Problem of Education.* New York: Free Press, 1966.

———. "Moral Problems of Business." In *The Later Works, 1925–1953,* vol. 7 of *The Collective Works of John Dewey,* ed. Jo Ann Boydston. Carbondale: Southern Illinois University Press, 1985.

———. "Public and Its Problems." In *The Later Works, 1925–1953,* vol. 2 of *The Collective Works of John Dewey,* ed. Jo Ann Boydston. Carbondale: Southern Illinois University Press, 1985.

———. *The Public and Its Problems.* Chicago: Swallow Press, 1954.

———. *Quest for Certainty.* New York: Minton, Balch, 1929.

———. *Reconstruction in Philosophy.* New York: Henry Holt, 1920.

———. "Social Control of Business and Industry." In *The Later Works, 1925–1953,* vol. 7 of *The Collective Works of John Dewey,* ed. Jo Ann Boydston. Carbondale: Southern Illinois University Press, 1985.

Doan, Edward N. *The La Follettes and the Wisconsin Idea.* New York: Rinehart, 1947.

Douglas, Paul H. *The Coming of a New Party.* New York: Whitlesey House, 1932.

———. *In the Fullness of Time.* New York: Harcourt Brace Jovanovich, 1971.

DuBois, W. E. B. *W.E.B. Du Bois: A Reader.* Ed. David L. Lewis. New York: Henry Holt, 1995.

Dye, Thomas R. *Who's Running America: The Clinton Years.* Englewood Cliffs, N.J.: Prentice-Hall, 1991

Eccles, Marriner S. *Beckoning Frontiers: Public and Personal Recollections.* New York: Alfred A. Knopf, 1951.

Eisenstadt, S. N. *Decline of Empires.* Englewood Cliffs, N.J.: Prentice-Hall, 1967.

Ellul, Jacques. *The Technological Society.* New York: Alfred A. Knopf, 1964.

Falk, Richard A., Robert C. Johansen, and Samuel S. Kim. *The Constitutional Foundation of World Peace.* Albany: State University of New York Press, 1993.

Fanon, Frantz. *Concerning Violence.* New York: Grove Press, 1963.

Fleming, D. F. *The Cold War and Its Origins.* Garden City, N.Y.: Doubleday, 1961.

Flynn, George Q. *Lewis B. Hershey: Mr. Selective Service.* Chapel Hill: University of North Carolina Press, 1985.

Foner, Philip S. *History of the Labor Movement in the U.S.* New York: International Publishers, 1947.

Forman, Paul. "Weimar Culture, Causation, and Quantum Theory." *Historical Studies in the Physical Sciences* 3 (1971): 1–115.

Fornari, Franco. *The Psychoanalysis of War.* Bloomington: Indiana University Press, 1975.

Foster, William Z. *The Great Steel Strike and Its Lessons.* New York: B. W. Huebsch, 1920.

Fowler, Cary. *Unnatural Selection: Technology, Politics and Plant Evolution.* Yverdon, Switzerland: Gordon and Breach, 1994.

Freidman, Milton. *Capitalism and Freedom.* Chicago: University of Chicago Press, 1965.

French, Marilyn. *The War against Women.* New York: Ballantine, 1992.

Fromm, Erich. *The Anatomy of Human Destructiveness.* New York: Holt, Rinehart & Winston, 1973.

———. *Marx's Concept of Man, Milestone of Thought.* New York: Frederick Ungar, 1966.

Gandhi, Mohadas. *The Penguin Gandhi Reader.* Ed. Rudrangshu Mukherjee. New York: Penguin, 1993.

Gans, Herbert J. *The Levittowners: Way of Life and Politics in a New Suburban Community.* New York: Pantheon Books, 1967.

Garrow, David J. *Bearing the Cross: Martin Luther King, Jr., and the Southern Christian Leadership Conference.* New York: William Morrow, 1986.

George, Susan. *The Debt Boomerang: How Third World Debt Harms Us All.* Boulder, Colo.: Westview Press, 1992.

Georgescu-Roegen, Nicholas. *Analytical Economies: Issues and Problems.* Cambridge: Harvard University Press, 1966.

Gilson, Etienne. *Modern Philosophy: Descartes to Kant.* New York: Random House, 1963.

Gingrich, Newt. *To Renew America.* New York: HarperCollins, 1995.

Glazer, Nathan. *We're All Multicultural Now.* Cambridge: Harvard University Press, 1997.

Goldman, Emma. *Living My Life.* 2 vols. New York: Alfred A. Knopf, 1931.

Goodman. Paul. *New Reformation: Notes of a Neolithic Conservative.* New York: Random House, 1970.

———. *People or Personnel: Decentralizing and the Mixed System.* New York: Random House, 1965.

Goodwin, Doris Kearns. *No Ordinary Time: Franklin and Eleanor Roosevelt.* New York: Simon & Schuster, 1994.

Gorbachev, Mikhail. *Memoirs.* New York: Doubleday, 1996.

Graham, Hancock. *Lords of Plenty.* London: Macmillan, 1987.

Gramsci, Antonio. *Letters from Prison.* Vol. 2. New York: Columbia University Press, 1994.

Green, Phillip. *Equality and Democracy.* New York: New Press, 1998.

Handlin, Oscar. *Immigration as a Factor in American History.* Englewood Cliffs, N.J.: Prentice-Hall, 1959.

Haq, Mahbub ul, Inge Kaul, and Isabelle Grunberg, eds. *The Tobin Tax: Coping with Financial Volatility.* New York: Oxford University Press, 1996.

Hartman, Heidi T. "The Family as the Locus of Gender, Class, and Political Struggle." In *Feminism and Methodology,* ed. Sandra Harding. Bloomington: Indiana University Press, 1987.

Hayek, F. A. *The Constitution of Liberty.* Chicago: University of Chicago Press, 1960.

Herrnstein, Richard J., and Charles A. Murray. *The Bell Curve: Intelligence and Class Structure in American Life.* New York: Free Press, 1994.

Hess, Karl. *Community Technology.* New York: Harper & Row, 1970.

Hilberg, Raul. *The Destruction of the European Jews.* New York: Holmes & Meier, 1985.

Hill, Christopher. *Liberty against the Law: Some Seventeenth Century Controversies.* London: Allen Lane, Penguin Press, 1996.

History of the Communist Party. Moscow: Foreign Language Publishing House, 1951.

Hochschild, Adam. *King Leopold's Ghost: A Story of Greed, Terror, and Heroism in Colonial Africa.* Boston: Houghton Mifflin, 1998.

Horkheimer, Max. *Eclipse of Reason.* New York: Seabury Press, 1974.

Hutcheson, Francis. *An Essay on the Nature of Passions and Affections.* London: J. Darby and T. Brown, 1728.

Interdependence of Peace, Development and Human Rights. Cambridge: Harvard Law School Human Rights Program, 1995.

Jacobs, Paul, and Saul Landau. *To Serve the Devil.* New York: Random House, 1971.

James, Robert R. *Churchill: A Study in Failure 1900–1939.* New York: World Publishing, 1970.

James, William. "The Moral Equivalent of War." In *The Moral Equivalence of War and Other Essays and Selections from Some Problems of Philosophy,* ed. John K. Roth. New York: Harper Torchbooks, 1971.

———. *The Varieties of Religious Experience.* Cambridge: Harvard University Press, 1985.

Jencks, Christopher, and David Riesman. *The Academic Revolution.* Garden City, N.Y.: Doubleday, 1968.

Johns, Sheridan, and R. Hunt Davis Jr., eds. *Mandela, Tambo, and the African National Congress: The Struggles against Apartheid, 1948–1900.* New York: Oxford University Press, 1991.

Kagan, Donald. *Pericles of Athens and the Birth of Democracy.* New York: Free Press, 1991.

Kefauver, Estes. *In a Few Hands: Monopoly Power in America.* New York: Pantheon Books, 1965.

King, Martin Luther, Jr. "Letter from Birmingham City Jail." In *A Testament of Hope: The Essential Writings of Martin Luther King Jr.,* ed. James W. Washington. San Francisco: Harper & Row, 1986.

Klare, Michael T. *War without End: American Planning for the Next Vietnam.* New York: Vintage Books, 1972.

Kolko, Gabriel. *Century of War: Politics, Conflict and Society since 1914.* New York: New Press, 1994.

———. *The Triumph of Conservatism: A Reinterpretation of American History.* Chicago: Quadrangle Books, 1963.

Kristol, Irving. *Two Cheers for Capitalism.* New York: Basic Books, 1978.

Kropotkin, Peter. *Mutual Aid: A Factor of Evolution.* New York: Alfred A. Knopf, 1916.

Kung, Hans. *Does God Exist?* 229. Garden City, N.J.: Doubleday, 1980.

Lange, Oskar, and Fred M. Taylor. *On the Economic Theory of Socialism.* Ed. Benjamin E. Lippincott. New York: McGraw-Hill, 1964.

Laski, Harold. *The American Democracy.* New York: Viking Press, 1948.

Leontief, Wassily, and Faye Duchin. "Reduced Military Spending or Increased Aid Transfers." In *Miltary Spending: Facts and Figures, Worldwide Implications and Future Outlook.* New York: Oxford University Press, 1983.

Leslie, John. *The End of the World: The Science and Ethics of Human Extinction.* New York: Routledge, 1996.

Leslie, Stuart W. *The Cold War and American Science: The Military-Industrial Complex at MIT and Stanford.* New York: Columbia University Press, 1992

Levine, Lawrence W. *The Opening of the American Mind: Canons, Culture and History.* Boston: Beacon Press, 1996.

Lippmann, Walter. *Public Opinion.* New York: Macmillan, 1949.

Lowi, Theodore. *The End of Liberalism.* New York: Norton, 1979.

Luce, Henry R. "The American Century." In *The Ideas of Henry Luce.* New York: Atheneum, 1969.

MacDonald, Dwight. *Memoirs of a Revolutionist.* New York: Farrar Straus & Dudahy, 1957.

MacDougall, Curtis D. *Gideon's Army.* New York: Marzani & Munsell, 1965.

Mandela, Nelson. *Long Walk to Freedom: The Autobiography of Nelson Mandela.* Boston: Little, Brown, 1994.

Marable, Manning, ed. *Dispatches from the Ebony Tower: Intellectuals Confront the African American Experience.* New York: Columbia University Press, 2000.

Martin, James, and James E. Samels. "We Were Wrong: Try Partnership, Not Mergers." *Chronicle of Higher Education* (May 17, 2002): B10.

Marx, Karl, and Friedrich Engels. *The Communist Manifesto.* London. [1848.] Pamphlet reprinted widely.

Mayo, Elton. *The Human Problems of an Industrial Civilization.* New York: Viking Press, 1960.

McKeon, Richard. *Democracy in a World of Tensions: A Symposium Prepared by UNESCO.* Paris: UNESCO, 1951.

———. *Selected Writings of Richard McKeon.* Vol. 1. Ed. Zahava K. McKeon and William G. Swenson. Chicago: University of Chicago Press, 1998.

McPherson, Harry. *A Political Education.* Boston: Little, Brown, 1972.

Meiklejohn, Alexander. *The Experimental College*. New York: Arno Press, 1971.
Melman, Seymour. *The Demilitarized Society*. Eugene, Ore.: Harvest House, 1988.
———. *The Permanent War Economy: American Capitalism in Decline*. New York: Simon & Schuster, 1974.
Monk, Ray. *Ludwig Wittgenstein: The Duty of Genius*. New York: Free Press, 1990.
Montgomery, David. *The Fall of the House of Labor*. New York: Cambridge University Press, 1989.
———. *Workers' Control in America: Studies in the History of Work, Technology, and Labor Struggles*. New York: Cambridge University Press, 1979.
Morrison, Roy. *Ecological Democracy*. Boston: South End Press, 1995.
Mumford, Lewis. *Myth of the Machine*. New York: Vintage Books, 1972.
Myrdal, Alva. *The Game of Disarmament: How the United States and Russia Run the Arms Race*. New York: Pantheon Books, 1976.
Myrdal, Gunmar. *An American Dilemma: The Negro Problem and Modern Democracy*. New York: Harper, 1944.
Nader, Laura, ed. *Naked Science: Anthropological Inquiry into Boundaries, Power and Knowledge*. New York: Routledge, 1996.
Nader, Ralph. *Constitutionalizing the Corporation: The Case for Federal Chartering of Giant Corporations*. Washington, D.C.: Corporate Accountability Research Group, 1976.
Nader, Ralph, Mark Green, and Joseph Seligman. *Taming the Giant Corporation*. New York: Norton, 1976.
Neumann, Franz L. *The Democratic and the Authoritarian State: Essays in Political and Legal Theory*. Glencoe, Ill.: Free Press, 1957.
Niebuhr, Reinhold. *The Children of Light and the Children of Darkness: A Vindication of Democracy and Critique of Its Traditional Defense*. New York: Charles Scribner's Sons, 1944.
———. *Moral Man and Immoral Society, A Study in Ethics and Politics*. New York: Scribner, 1960.
Nielsen, Waldemar A. *The Big Foundations*. New York: Columbia University Press, 1972.
Nixon, Richard M. *Six Crises*. Garden City, N.Y.: Doubleday, 1962.
Noble, David F. *Digital Diploma Mills: The Automation of Higher Education*. New York: New York University Press, 2001.
Noel-Baker, Philip John. *The Arms Race*. London: J. Calder, 1960.
Nordhoff, Charles. *Communistic Societies in the United States*. New York: Hillary House, 1960.
Pastoral Letters on Catholic Social Teaching and the U.S. Economy. Washingon, D.C.: National Conference of Catholic Bishops, 1986.
Pauling, Linus. *No More War!* New York: Dodd, Mead, 1983.
Perls, Frederick S., Ralph F. Hefferline, and Paul Goodman. *Gestalt Therapy: Excitement and Growth in the Human Personality*. New York: Julian, 1951.
Pertshuck, Michael. *The Revolt against Regulation: The Rise and Pause of the Consumer Movement*. Berkeley: University of California Press, 1982.
Piven, Frances Fox, and Richard A. Cloward. *Regulating the Poor: The Functions of Public Welfare*. New York: Pantheon Books, 1971.

Polanyi, Michael. *Personal Knowledge: Towards a Post-critical Philosophy*. New York: Harper & Row, 1964.

Popper, Karl. *The Open Society and Its Enemies*. Vol 2. Princeton, N.J.: Princeton University, 1966.

Potter, David. *People of Plenty: Economic Abundance and the American Character, 1954*. New York: Columbia University Press, 1992.

Presidents' Materials Policy Commission. *Resources for Freedom: A Report to the President*. 5 vols. Washington, D.C.: Government Printing Office, 1952.

Purcell, Edward A. *The Crisis of Democratic Theory*. Lexington: University Press of Kentucky, 1973.

Putnam, Hilary. *Pragmatism: An Open Question*. Oxford: Blackwell, 1995.

Raskin, Marcus. *Being and Doing*. New York: Random House, 1971.

———. *The Common Good: Its Politics, Policies and Philosophy*. New York: Routledge & Kegan Paul, 1986.

———. "Death of the Soviet Union." In *Visions and Revisions: Reflection on Culture and Democracy at the End of the Century*. New York: Olive Branch, 1995.

———. *Visions and Revisions: Reflections on Culture and Democracy at the End of the Century*. New York: Olive Branch Press, 1995.

Raskin, Marcus, and Herbert Bernstein. *New Ways of Knowing*. Totowa, N.J.: Rowman & Littlefield, 1987.

Rauschenbush, Walter. *Christianity and the Social Crisis*. New York: Macmillan, 1920.

Rawls, John. *Political Liberalism*. New York: Columbia University Press, 1993.

Reeves, Inc. v. Stake et al., 447 U.S. 429 (1980).

Regents of the University of California v. Bakke, 438 U.S. 265 (1978).

Romilly, Jacqueline de. *Thucydides and Athenian Imperialism*. Oxford: Blackwell, 1963.

Roosevelt, James, ed. *The Liberal Papers*. Garden City, N.Y.: Anchor Books, 1962.

Rorty, Richard. *Essays on Heidegger and Others*. New York: Cambridge University Press, 1991.

Ross, Steven. *Working Class Hollywood: Silent Films and the Shaping of Class in America*. Princeton, N.J.: Princeton University Press, 1998.

Rostow, W. W. *Politics and the Stages of Growth*. Cambridge, England: Cambridge University Press, 1971.

Roszak, Theodore. *The Making of a Counter Culture: Reflections on the Techno-cratic Society and Its Youthful Opposition*. Garden City, N.Y.: Doubleday, 1969.

Rothbard, Murray N. *For a New Liberty: A Libertarian Manifesto*. New York: Collier, 1978.

Sartre, Jean-Paul. *The Wretched of the Earth*. New York: Grove Press, 1963.

Schor, Juliet B. *The Overworked American: The Unexpected Decline of Leisure*. New York: Basic Books, 1991.

Schumacher, Ernst Friedrich. *Small Is Beautiful; Economics As If People Mattered*. New York: Harper & Row, 1973.

Schumpeter, Joseph. *The Theory of Economic Development: An Inquiry into Profits, Capital, Credit, Interest and the Business Cycle*. Trans. Redvers Opie. New Brunswick, N.J.: Transaction Books, 1983.

Securities and Exchange Commission: www.Sec.Gov/foia.docs.budgetact.htm.

Seldes, George. *Witness to a Century.* New York: Ballantine Books, 1987.

Serge, Victor. *Memoirs of a Revolutionary, 1901–1941.* New York: Oxford University Press, 1963.

Simon, Yves. *Philosophy of Democratic Government.* Chicago: University of Chicago Press, 1951.

Sohn, Louis. *The Human Rights Movement: From Roosevelt's Four Freedoms to the Interdependence of Peace, Development and Human Rights.* Cambridge: Harvard Law School Human Rights Program, 1995.

Sohn, Louis, and Thomas Buergenthal, eds. "The Movement of Persons across Borders." Washington, D.C: The American Society of International Law, 1992.

Sorkin, Michael. *Variations on a Theme Park: Scenes from the New American City and the End of Public Space.* New York: Hill and Wang, 1992.

Soros, George. *Open Society: Reforming Global Capitalism.* New York: Public Affairs, 2000.

Spengler, Oswald. *Man and Technics: A Contribution to a Philosophy of Life.* New York: Alfred A. Knopf, 1932.

Spero, Robert. *The Duping of the American Voter: Dishonesty and Deception in Presidential Television Advertising.* New York: Lippincott & Crowell, 1980.

Stiglitz, Joseph E. *Globalization and Its Discontents.* New York: W. W. Norton, 2002.

———. *Whither Socialism?* Cambridge: MIT Press, 1994.

Strauss, Leo. *History of Political Philosophy.* Chicago: University of Chicago Press, 1987.

Sweezy, Paul. "Review of the Month: Supply Side Economics." *Monthly Review* 31, no. 10 (March 1981): 1–7.

Taft, Phillip. *Organized Labor in American History.* New York: Harper & Row, 1964.

Talmon, J. L. *The Origins of Totalitarian Democracy.* New York: Norton, 1970.

Tawney, R. H. *Religion and the Rise of Capitalism.* New York: Penguin, 1926.

Taylor, Branch. *Pillar of Fire: America in the King Years 1963–65.* New York: Touchstone, 1998.

Teilhard de Chardin, Pierre. *The Divine Milieu.* New York: Harper, 1960.

Thompson, J. M. *Robespierre.* New York: H. Fertig, 1968.

Toqueville, Alexander de. *Democracy in America.* Vol. 1. New York: Vintage, 1990.

Tugwell, Rexford G. *The Enlargement of the Presidency.* Garden City, N.Y.: Doubleday, 1960.

USA Patriot Act. Public Law, 107-56, 107th Cong. 1st sess., October 26, 2001.

Venturi, Franco. *Roots of Revolution: The History of the Populist and Socialist Movements in Nineteenth Century Russia.* New York: Alfred A. Knopf, 1960.

Von Laue, Theodore. *The World Revolution of Westernization: The Twentieth Century in Global Perspective.* New York: Oxford University Press, 1987.

Wallace, Henry A. *Century of the Common Man.* New York: Reynal & Hitchcock, 1943.

Watson, John B. *Behaviorism.* New York: Norton, 1925.

Waskow, Arthur. *Limits of Defense.* Garden City, N.Y.: Doubleday, 1962.

Weinberg, Albert Katz. *Manifest Destiny: A Study of Nationalist Expansionism in American History.* Baltimore: Johns Hopkins University Press, 1976.

Weinstein, James. *The Corporate Ideal in the Liberal State, 1900–1918.* Boston: Beacon Press, 1968.

Weizenbaum, Joseph. *Computer Power and Human Reason: From Judgment to Calculations.* San Francisco: W. H. Freeman, 1976.

Wellstone, Paul. "Wellstone Presses President Bush for Real Investment in Education." Press release from his office, March 5, 2001.

Whitaker, Benjamin. *Slavery: Report.* New York: United Nations, 1984.

White, Morton G. *Pragmatism and the American Mind: Essays and Reviews in Philosophy and Intellectual History.* New York: Oxford University Press, 1973.

Whitehead, Alfred North. *Science and the Modern World.* New York: Macmillan, 1967.

Wilkins, Peter. *Noam Chomsky: On Power, Knowledge and Human Nature.* New York: St. Martin's Press, 1997.

Williams, William Appleman. *History as a Way of Learning: Articles, Excerpts and Essays.* New York: New Viewpoints, 1973.

Wills, Gary. *Lincoln at Gettysburg: The Words That Remade America.* New York: Simon & Schuster, 1992.

Winslow, William. *Politics and the Constitution in the History of the United States.* Chicago: University of Chicago Press, 1953–1980.

Wittgenstein, Ludwig. *Tractatus Logico-Philosophicus.* London: Routledge, 1922.

Wofford, Harris. *Of Kennedys and Kings: Making Sense of the Sixties.* Pittsburgh: University of Pittsburgh Press, 1992.

Wolff, Robert Paul, Barrington Moore Jr., and Herbert Marcuse. *Critique of Pure Tolerance.* Boston: Beacon Press, 1969.

Wright, Quincy. *A Study of War.* Chicago: University of Chicago Press, 1965.

Zachary, G. Pascal. *Endless Frontier: Vannevar Bush, Engineer of the American Century.* New York: Free Press, 1997.

Zinn, Howard. *A People's History of the United States.* New York: Longman, 1980.

Index

318 ★ Index

About the Author

Marcus G. Raskin, the highly acclaimed political theorist and activist, is co-founder of the influential Institute for Policy Studies. He is professor at George Washington University and a member of the editorial board of *The Nation* magazine. He is author of numerous well-reviewed books including *Being and Doing, The Common Good, The Politics of National Security, Visions and Revisions, Essays of a Citizen, New Ways of Knowing* (with Herbert J. Bernstein), and *The Vietnam Reader* with Bernard B. Fall. He is the editor of a ten-volume series on Reconstruction and Paths for the 21st Century with three books slated for publication in 2004.

Raskin's numerous scholarly articles have appeared in major journals concerning philosophy, history, and education. His op-eds and popular articles have appeared in newspapers including the *New York Times, Washington Post, Los Angeles Times,* and *Chicago Tribune.* He has appeared in all major media including CNN, NBC, C-Span, NPR, and other radio and TV outlets.

Raskin was a former member of the National Security Council Staff under President John F. Kennedy and chair of Peace Action, a major peace organization. He was an acquitted member of the Boston Five draft conspiracy case, on Nixon's Enemies List, and a Fulbright Lecturer. Raskin is credited with coining the phrase, "the National Security State," currently enjoying a resurgence of interest and concern in the midst of Bush administration policies.

Marcus G. Raskin is a graduate of the University of Chicago College and Law School. He is married to Lynn Raskin, has four children and eight grandchildren, and is an accomplished pianist. He is a resident of Washington, D.C.